*Memoir of a
Revolutionary*

By Milovan Djilas

THE NEW CLASS

LAND WITHOUT JUSTICE

CONVERSATIONS WITH STALIN

MONTENEGRO

THE LEPER AND OTHER STORIES

NJEGOŠ

THE UNPERFECT SOCIETY: BEYOND THE NEW CLASS

UNDER THE COLORS

THE STONE AND THE VIOLETS

MEMOIR OF A REVOLUTIONARY

Milovan Djilas

MEMOIR OF A REVOLUTIONARY

Translated by Drenka Willen

HARCOURT BRACE JOVANOVICH, INC.

NEW YORK

First edition

ISBN 0-15-158850-3
Library of Congress Catalog Card Number: 72-91835
Printed in the United States of America
B C D E

To Mitra Mitrović

Note on the Spelling and Pronunciation of Serbo-Croat Words and Names

s = s as in sink
š = sh as in shift
c = ts as in mats
č = ch as in charge
ć = similar to, but lighter than, č—as in arch
ž = j as in French *jour*
z = z as in zodiac
j = y as in yell
nj = ni as in minion
g = g as in go
dj = g as in George
lj = li as in million

Book One

THE IDEALIST

1

At home they were getting me ready to go away to school in a strange way: my mother, a simple uneducated woman who knew nothing about city life, made a sack of ticking for me and put my peasant clothing into it—shirts, hand-knitted socks, a sweater of coarse wool, and a tin cup of cheese. My father gave me some money, too much considering his circumstances and my needs as a student. He was probably misled by my brother, who liked to spend freely and who always asked for a lot, not always stating how much he spent on food and lodgings. I was upset because I had no decent suit to wear, to say nothing of a suitcase, and I was sure my mother's sack of ticking would never reach Belgrade. My own ideas about the big city and the journey into the distant world were not very clear. I had never seen a train. My father and a few peasants had warned me to be particularly wary of trains because their speed was so great that you couldn't get out of their way even when they were as far as a mile away. Also, how was I to find lodgings, a place to eat? How would I find my way in the streets? All the same, I was excited at the thought of seeing the world, different people, and new situations.

At my brother's suggestion and with my father's approval, I had decided that eventually I would go to school in Paris or Prague. I wanted to study journalism, and there was a school of journalism in Prague. My father wanted me to study medicine. That was the most reliable occupation: people were always getting sick. Similarly, he considered land to be the most reliable property, because it could not be burned or stolen.

I was beginning an entirely new experience and I was full of apprehension, determined to overcome the world or hate it. I was impatient. I thought of all sorts of reasons why I should leave as soon as possible.

It was a sunny day in the middle of August. My father was to take me as far as Kolašin, and since it was so hot, we didn't leave Bijelo Polje until late afternoon. We stopped often, traveling by night, he on horseback, I on foot. We traveled along turbulent brooks, through dark forests, under the icy white moonlight. It was not the first time I had taken a trip with my father. But it was the first time that I found his advice boring, and I quickly switched the conversation to events and people in Montenegrin history, and the history of our family. His stories were lively and rich and he remembered everything. But the beauty of his storytelling was his ability to describe the same event in many different ways—without changing its substance. I felt I was parting with a heroic reality, a legend which had filled my childhood, and while dreaming of the future I tried to absorb his speech, full of rashness and tenderness, of manliness and wildness.

Finally I boarded the bus. It was my first trip of more than just a few miles. The bus was old and rickety, and since I was young and poorly dressed, the driver sent me all the way to the rear. I looked back. Covered with dust, my father was a sad sight, his mustaches and beard drooping, his cap just above his eyes. He was on the verge of tears: another son was on his way to seek his fortune outside his domain and care.

The bus moved slowly. The earth, the mountains, and the distant peaks resembled those of my own region. But as soon as we crossed Mount Vjeternik, there was a sudden change. From the forests we plunged down past gaping quarries, eaten by heat and ice, into a boiling gray desert of broken rock and weed, without pastures or groves, without moisture or clouds. That was real Montenegro, from stories, from poems, from legend, stretching to the Scutari plain—which was also gray and yellow and baked down to its intestines—to the avalanches at the horizon, naked and grim under the ashen burning skies, and to the gray rocky sea.

My father had warned me that in Podgorica one had to watch out for the *chikotnici*, notorious petty thieves and connivers. That same summer they had played a trick on the peasants at the market. It had been rumored that someone had seen a woman with a horse's head, as a forewarning of some great disaster. One day the *chikotnici* shouted at the market: "Here comes the woman with a horse's head!" People surged forth, women abandoned their baskets of figs and grapes, and everyone ran. The *chikotnici* picked up everything. With this story in mind, I entered Podgorica through its straight streets lined with even one-story houses, interrupted by a couple of two or three-story hotels and office buildings and a spacious market.

It was around noon. The bus wasn't to leave until two in the afternoon. I sat down in front of a café and watched two men repairing a car. I assumed they were the bus driver and his assistant. The assistant walked over and offered to take me to Cetinje in his car—for the price of the bus ticket. Naturally I agreed. It certainly would be more comfortable to go by car. It turned out that these two men were neither the driver nor his assistant, and when the real driver turned up he asked for much more money to take me to Cetinje, which I had to pay, since I could not spend the night in Podgorica.

I arrived in Cetinje in darkness. My brother, Aleksa, was stationed there in the army, and I looked him up immediately. He was having a lot of trouble with his superiors. He had been released from detention only a few days before. Attacked by an officer, he had hurled a dish of soup at him. He weaseled out of this incident without major consequences only because several officers, friends of our father, had taken his side. His unbridled character, combined with a profound love of truth, was now more evident than ever. His shoulders were slightly bent, as if to compress these qualities into a single spasm that would erupt someday with great force and energy. He was nearsighted, his big eyes bright under bushy brows and lashes. In anger his pale face turned almost green, and his tight lips blue. His conflict with the army reflected his intellectual and political discontent. The abuse of rank and the poor food revolted him, and he assumed leadership of the general discontent. None of this was a surprise to me, but I was afraid that in a fit of anger he might not be able to stop himself and would be in real trouble.

We walked the streets of Cetinje until late in the night. The town was sunk into the moonlight which reflected sharply from the steep mountainsides. My brother urged me to stay on another day. I couldn't wait for the morning, to get a better view of the town, a magnificent human nest in stone.

The morning emerged, green from the lovely parks and the enormous crowns of old trees. It wasn't until I left the town and walked to Orlov Krš and Belveder that I realized that the field of Cetinje rested in the heart of an endless rock desert. A history, painful and hard, had been coined there. With its freshness and its simple and attractive buildings and streets, with its incomprehensible cleanliness, the town was a human refuge. I felt then, and many times later, that Cetinje was one of the most beautiful towns in the world. Not because of the beauty of its buildings, or because of its rich antiquity, but because of something implicitly human. Destiny forced man to build his nest in naked stone, out of nothing and with nothing at hand; that was how the history of a nation began. Nothing else in the world speaks with such moving simplicity. We built our nest there—not to repose, but to defend. That's Cetinje, more beautiful than beauty: the destiny of a nation in a few houses and a monastery sprung from a rock. And above it all, as if expelled from a chaos of stone rills, hovers Lovćen, with the Bishop of Montenegro resting at the very top, watching over this savage, cursed land, and her men born in the collision of the worlds.

In this environment, my brother felt close to me—all the more so because of his frankness and savageness. I was inspired by a primeval force that sprang from the bottom of this land of stone and by my brother's will to live and defend himself against brute force and stupidity. A new dimension was added to our affection for each other: we now felt the same way about society and the world. We called it Communism. It was not Communism, but, rather, a deep dissatisfaction with existing conditions and an irrepressible desire to change life, not to accept a hopeless monotony. Our parting was brave rather than sad. There was plenty of darkness and murkiness in our feelings, but there was also a great deal of strength.

I was determined not to arrive in Belgrade in my shabby clothing. I was sure everyone recognized in me a half-peasant on his way into the world to be educated.

I had to change trains at Sarajevo, a wait of two or three hours, so I decided to do some sightseeing and to buy a few things. I bought a suit, of very poor quality, to be sure. But that was my first suit with matching pants, and the first I had not inherited from my brother, and I was excited. I also bought a shirt and a tie and changed right there and then, in the shop. It wasn't until I had taken off my rags that I realized just how badly and ridiculously I had been dressed, particularly in contrast to my lofty ambitions, which were to study in Paris and to become a writer.

I arrived in Belgrade blinded and intoxicated by the morning. I engaged a porter, not because I needed him to carry my bundle—in fact we had an argument as to which one of us should carry it—but to guide me to a street where I could rent a room. He walked me up to Balkanska Street, pointed to a sign on the gate to a long yard, and, having quickly deciphered what I was, overcharged me.

A fat old woman escorted me through the kitchen to a room with two beds, one of which was already occupied. I washed and went straight to bed. I fell asleep immediately, the roar of the train still lingering within me. I woke up in the late afternoon, had a piece of cheese pie at the nearest bakery, and headed up "my" steep street into town. Suddenly I reached a plateau, a plaza fronted by buildings, with a fountain in the middle. I asked the policeman to direct me to Terazije, the main square. He smiled and made a circular gesture. This is it! I was deeply disappointed, a few low buildings, a miserable little fountain. Could this be the main square of the capital city? I got on the first streetcar that came by. It was going to Slavija. That was what the sign said anyway. I passed Slavija—my destination—and rode to the end of Makenzijeva Street, where the conductor asked for another fare. Then I rode back to Kalemegdan, which is to say I rode past Slavija and Terazije all over again. I didn't even recognize them. So I paid still another fare. On the way back I caught sight of the fountain and Hotel Moskva; it finally occurred to me that I had been here before. I asked the conductor to tell me when we reached Slavija. He smiled. "I noticed you were riding back and forth. Young man, you've passed it twice." I decided this wouldn't work. I bought a guide and began roaming the city, familiarizing myself with the streets, squares, and important buildings. Within three days I was able to find my way.

Then I thought I'd find out how to get to Paris. It turned out that I lacked several documents from my home district. Besides, getting francs was an enormously complicated process. I gave up, much too easily; in the final analysis it didn't matter where I went to school. So I enrolled in the Department of Yugoslav Literature at the University of Belgrade. At first I spent a lot of time with school friends from home, who had come to Belgrade to study at the University or at the Military Academy. They were all rooming on Balkanska Street, or around it, eating in unsavory joints. They had had an even worse time than I getting adjusted to a new life. But I quickly grew bored with the same people, wasting time in long discussion and arguments over nothing. I moved to Vračar, where I was to live for many years, and I quickly found new friends at the University.

While I still lived on Balkanska Street I ran across Tin Ujević, a well-known poet of those days. The waiter at the Hotel Moskva Celler, which the poet frequented, pointed him out to me. Ujević liked tripe and a powerful brandy. I watched him with curiosity, I almost shadowed him. I could never reconcile the purity of his verse with his unkempt appearance. He was unshaven, his shoes were untied, his coat shabby. He was heavy, in fact obese, his blue eyes large and bulging. I dared not look into them for fear he would discover my curiosity and astonishment. Ujević was the talk of the town. He was like a museum, or a monument. He cursed the middle classes loudly, but took money from them. He had numerous friends, but seemed always alone.

2

In spite of the grave consequences for this peasant country of the Great Depression of 1929, no period in recent history witnessed as much wild spending and waste. It was the period of the January 6th Dictatorship of King Alexander. Belgrade was a faithful reflection of the mood of the country: cafés were full, and people were drinking as if the world were submerged in prosperity.

No one can say for sure that the January 6th Dictatorship intensified the mood of abandon. But it was responsible for stifling the political life of a vast bulk of the people. The first to be affected were the leaders of the political parties. The masses were simply indifferent. However, there were many, particularly in Serbia, who approved of the King's coup d'état because they had been disappointed by the sterile and pointless parliamentary debates, and by the frequent changes of government. It was understandable that older people drank out of anger and despair. But the young had no choice either—in a country in which opportunities for political activity were so completely thwarted. Political parties had been outlawed, the press silenced, and all public life placed under the control of a police organization that was so crude and brutal that its sole mitigating circumstance was its stupidity.

Youthful rebellion first assumed a moral form: the negation of traditional views and relationships. The common man suffered the dictatorship and the other hardships as elementary evils which had rendered him helpless. His concentration was on his family life. He was petit bourgeois. But he did not have any choice if he was not willing to go to prison. Opposition to this kind of life, resistance to it and the bourgeois existence, was the most frequent form rebellion took among young people, particularly among intellectuals.

9

In the course of my two years as a student (1929 to 1931), young people sought relief in a special form of bohemian existence, in which alcohol was perhaps not the chief solace. For one thing, they spent most of their time in long discussions in smoke-filled rooms, in groups created according to common interests. Some gambled; others chased women and drank. Of course, there were students who took their studies seriously. They were scorned as "grinds," "civil servants," and "bootlickers." But how else could one complete one's education?

Of course, I joined the former group. I can't really say I joined it, because the group itself was in the process of being created when I arrived, and I became one of its founders. With the advent of the dictatorship, political organizations at the University were either broken up or they disintegrated. There wasn't a trace left of the Communist organization. There were a few Communists, older students, but they were either so passive or so secretive that one didn't know who they were. I knew one of them, Miloš Tujo Ćetković, but only because he was a Montenegrin, from my region, and a relative of my Aunt Draguna. However, he never said anything to encourage me in my rebellion, so involved was he in himself and in the mechanics of his conspiracy. In my second year he loaned me a few books, among them Bozhart's popularized version of Marx's political economy. Although I found the text hard to digest, I felt the statements to be true, even if boring. But it made no really strong impression on me. People only absorb things for which they are ready. And I was not ready.

But if Ćetković offered no opening into his illegal political activity, he did give many proofs of that secret, Communist, indestructibility—speaking through the teeth, mysterious looks from behind caps, gloomy, emaciated faces.

Occasionally there were brief accounts in the newspapers of the persecution of Communists, often relating to executions. These reports spread fear among Communist sympathizers. The bourgeois democratic opposition mildly condemned these acts, adding an element of malicious triumph: So the extremists are after one another! Yet it is through these crazy Communists, who deserve no better, that the regime reveals its own tyrannical nature.

Ćetković told me that many members of the Central Committee of the Communist party had been executed, among them Djaković, Samardžić, and Bracan Bracanović. Dr. Nešić had been hurled out of the window of Glavnjača (a popular name for the Belgrade central prison). Later on, in jail, I learned the truth: Dr. Nešić had been cowardly in front of the police, and felt so guilty that he jumped from the window. On the other hand, Bracan Bracanović had actually been murdered. He was taken from the police station to a Belgrade suburb and shot. The story was that the King had personally ordered that the entire Central Committee be executed, which was probably true. I don't know the details to this day, but I do know that this was the policy until 1932.

By that time Bracanović had already become a legend. And this legend was a most prized one. I was always sorry that it was shattered several years later. Bracanović was a teacher, a Montenegrin, who had become a Central Committee member by decision of the Comintern itself, following the 1928 Open Letter opposing the factional struggle in the Yugoslav party. He came directly to the Central Committee from a political school in Moscow. Soon the dictatorship came to power; the police broke up the Belgrade party organization and killed Bracanović. They say that he was dark and young and wild, and that he had enormous physical strength. Several times he broke the chains on his wrists and it took as many as ten agents to subdue him. He shouted big angry words at the policemen, spitting at them in spite of horrible physical tortures. Uncompromising and unyielding, proud and strong, covered with blood and wounds, he died one night of a bullet in the nape of his neck, in a ditch near Belgrade. No grave and no stone. In my own mind Bracanović was identified with the heroes of our legendary past, the struggle against the Turks which I had sucked with my mother's milk. The death of such a hero was a crime a hundred times greater than any other, which inspired hatred and thoughts of revenge in any young fiery spirit.

If the secrecy and heroism of the Communists inspired admiration, the persecution of Svetozar Pribićević, a former government minister and a founder of the Yugoslav state, caused moral disgust. There were rumors that he had died on a hunger strike, that he had been poisoned, that he had been released. He was not a revolutionary, but simply a man who couldn't accept the King's dictatorship, and whom the King had personally taken to task because of his sharp tongue and wild nature.

I knew a few older students from the bourgeois parties, among them Stojan Ivezić from Kolašin, the leader of the student radical organization. They had actually spread the news about the torture of Pribićević and his son Stojan. They also spoke about army plots against the monarchy, which were nonexistent, and the wishful thinking of bourgeois politicians and of the few survivors of the officers' *Putsch* of 1903 in which the last Obrenović, King Alexander, and his queen, Draga Mašin, had been killed. The massacre of the royal pair—cutting off her breasts and limbs—was still savored, as if it were greatly significant in itself. The terror against the Communists, no less than the insulting treatment of founders and guardians of the monarchy, added to the discontent. On the other hand, the planting of time bombs on trains by Hungarian and Italian terrorist groups (including the Croatian leader Ante Pavelić's Ustashi) caused disgust and served to strengthen the Serbian regime in Belgrade, offering some moral justification even in the eyes of its most hostile critics. With all my hatred for the regime, I never approved of such methods, and was horrified by the sight of the innocent victims butchered by an infernal machine. The future fascist organizations were training their ranks and perfecting their methods: the old saying that terror breeds terror proved true.

As I look back now, it seems to me that the dictatorship gave rise to a whole new generation, particularly among the intellectuals at Belgrade University, a generation altogether different from the one that preceded it. Stifled by the dictatorship, it was looking for an outlet. It had to find one, and it was found in the ranks of those who were discontented with existing conditions, spiritual, political, and personal.

I believe that the wild drinking was a sign that society was overcoming its bourgeois prejudices. I myself never took to drinking, and I didn't take part in any loud carousing. These things went against nature. I thought them too common for my own sense of measure and taste. Nevertheless I drank more often, which was in harmony with the intellectual preoccupations of the time. Many of my friends did the same. Others gambled and still others chased after women. I found gambling boring. As for love, my approach was much too innocent. For a young writer of the kind I aspired to become, a politically alert, bohemian life—and alcohol—was the most suitable outlet. If later, in the autumn of 1931, I hadn't encountered organized political activity, my life would probably have developed differently. Perhaps I would not have given up alcohol so quickly, perhaps I would have sunk deeper into it until I found my own "right" dose, and perhaps then leaned more toward literature than toward politics.

My rebellious tendencies thrived in the Belgrade of this time: Belgrade with its wild night life, its crisscross of influences from the whole country and abroad, its restricted social and political life—always the same court photographs, the same official press coverage, the same expressions of loyalty and affection for His Majesty the King, who united us all, always the same favorable quotes about us from the foreign press, always the same old songs about the Salonika Front and the blood spilled for "freedom and unity." There were no strikes, no public meetings or manifestoes, no opposition newspapers or magazines. All the forces that yearned for a breath of fresh air were packed into underground cellars. Belgrade was lively, colorful, and full of contrasts—an ostentatious display of newly acquired wealth on the one hand, and misery, hunger, and unemployment on the other. It was a setting that gave form and encouragement to the conscious organized rebellion of the young.

3

The University was unable to channel the student dissatisfaction toward learning and study. The academic system was routine and old-fashioned, yet it did not favor the regime. On the contrary, its acceptance of the dictatorship was quite superficial—it was forced to send occasional greetings to the King and to invite his representatives to various official functions. On the basis of its earlier experience with the Obrenović dynasty, the professors knew that a clash with the government could only interfere with their position as educators. And no matter how they differed in political matters, they were united in maintaining the autonomy of the University and the independence of their own work.

Indeed, until the war, the regime never really violated the autonomy of the University, in spite of the disorders that erupted sporadically and the subsequent takeover by the Communists. The regime attempted to secure influence through the selection of professors, and on the whole sought to compromise choices rather than risk destroying the existing forms of autonomy or challenge the usually united front of professors.

For us, the rebellious youth, the problem of academic freedom and professorial position had no meaning. In the first place, to us it appeared cowardly, if not downright bourgeois: what's the purpose of autonomy if it can't be wielded against the dictatorship? Hadn't the regime secured its political advantage in an indirect way, by giving autonomy to professors who did not oppose its acts? In the initial stages of the dictatorship the question of autonomy had no practical significance. There was no threat to the regime because there was no organized movement of dissent which would make use of the University's autonomy. We were aware of the autonomy, but we could not use it to our ends because there were too few of us and we were still unorganized. Yet without its existence the subsequent development of a powerful revolutionary movement would be hard to explain.

In summary, we objected not to the official support given the regime by the University and the professors, but to their conservative character. Tradition dominated everything. New ideas were not stifled, but they were not allowed or encouraged.

This was the period of the Popović brothers at the University. Looking back, their "rule" was no more than a legend. The presence of the elder brother, Bogdan Popović, was reflected in the smooth, aristocratic dignity in which the learning process took place. A kind of refinement had been developing in pre-World War I Serbia: students were few and mostly from middle-class families and they became a kind of elite. In contrast, the peasant children who invaded the University after World War I felt that this fine behavior was false, at once "bourgeois" and foreign. Bogdan Popović was well known as an esthete of the French School and his reign in public life was unquestioned. There was something fragile and drained about him. A short man, he moved slowly and gently, as if afraid he might break. But he spoke beautifully, his words strung rhythmically and harmoniously. When he did allow himself to digress, he invariably connected the comment to his basic thesis. One could learn a great deal from him—his knowledge of art and literature was vast and full of fine detail. I was not among his admirers; I thought him ineffectual, locked up in an ivory tower away from a tough life in which the human soul was torn and suffering.

In contrast, the younger brother, Pavle, was a lively, ruddy, jolly old man, a prolific writer, active in public life, the head of the Yugoslav Literature Department. He was an angry adversary of the so-called "social literature," which was gaining ground and popularity, since it was the sole legal form of opposition activity. I remember his saying in 1932 that he was not against a message in literature, particularly if it were skillfully incorporated into the work of art, or, as often happened, merely the artistic vehicle for carrying a political message. Needless to say, we considered his position reactionary. I myself never thought that a social or political message was the backbone of literature, although that was the prevalent opinion in the left-wing circles. I considered it essential that any message be "clothed" in an artistic form in order to be convincing. But I felt that there could be no work of art without a clear, basically political message, for otherwise it didn't reflect reality.

Unlike Bogdan, who was cold and reserved, Pavle assumed an attitude of free gentlemanliness, a common and unattractive quality in those old people who have preserved their physical prowess and feel that they are still young by virtue of their desire to be so. He openly encouraged flattery from his students. He was willing to "forget" insults, to "forgive," if a conflict with a student was resolved with public recognition of his honor.

Djuro Gavela was a proud and alert man, but he couldn't resist flattering Pavle Popović. He was a bohemian type, quick and intelligent. He wrote poetry with skill but no strength. He was straightforward and kind, and had it not been for the divergence of our political views, we would probably have developed a close relationship. He had never written literary criticism, but just before taking his final examinations, he produced a study of Popović's work that, under normal circumstances, would have gone unnoticed. Two or three of us leftists reproached him for this. In response he smiled ironically, a gesture directed more at himself than at us. And why not? Why kill oneself studying the literature of Slovenia or Dubrovnik if one can avoid it?

Needless to say, it would be wrong to conclude that in such an atmosphere learning and study were altogether absent, or that a young man could gain nothing from his university years. Far from it. However, social and political conditions at the University often led young rebels to think that the effort was completely futile. The University was unable to channel the discontent in any intellectual direction. And since, owing to its very conservatism, the University had managed to retain much of its tradition of tolerance and freedom, it was easy for students to express opposition and receive a mild response from the professors, even from those who were the King's supporters.

At that time, the chair in agrarian politics at the Law School was held by Dr. Dragoljub Jovanović, the leader of the agrarian left. The difference between Dr. Jovanović and the Communists was considered negligible at that time, and he actually co-operated with them. Just prior to the dictatorship he had founded an intellectual and political group that included Communists—the Belgrade journalist Otokar Keršovani among others.

Dr. Jovanović's lectures were the first under the dictatorship that students found useful—if not as a scene for open struggle, at least as a meeting place. The students belonging to the bourgeois parties showed no interest in these lectures, believing that Jovanović represented a masked form of Communism. On the other hand, old Communists boycotted Jovanović as a "petit bourgeois"—a clever agent planted by the bourgeoisie to undermine Communist influence. But the old Communists, which is to say the Communists who were active prior to the dictatorship, were few in number, and their influence was not felt. They maliciously accused him of having said in his book, *The Agrarian Politics*, that there were four Baltic countries (instead of three), because he took Litva and Lithuania to be two different countries. Of course, this was an error, and it was often cited to prove Jovanović's academic incompetence.

Dr. Dragoljub Jovanović's lectures, held in a large hall, were attended to capacity by followers of the Peasant party and by us Communists. Jovanović was an excellent speaker, full of feeling and emphasis. He was short, round, and bald, an appearance more suited to a bureaucrat than to a man of his political fire and action. He almost always wore a red tie, perhaps to stress his leftist beliefs and his sympathy to Communism.

Young rebels from all branches of the University were drawn to Jovanović's lectures, even if they were not supporters of his Peasant movement and even if they believed his program to be too mild to liberate the country from misery and ruination. I attended several of his lectures, but found them of no special interest. First of all, there was nothing revolutionary about them. He praised certain things in the Soviet Union, and then some things in France. He leaned on political scientists of the most diverse range. However, the truth is that my own personal interest was not in economics, but in literature. I was vacillating between a commitment to social revolution and a psychological preoccupation with the human soul under the moral chaos of the times. Jovanović's cautiously methodical approach could not excite me. I felt that something great must happen to jolt men from the darkness and suffering imposed by poverty and force. Jovanović was a practical politician and ideologist; he was not a radical. He could not give expression to those complex forces of social discontent.

I soon realized that my case was not an isolated one. Even though Jovanović's lectures were so well attended that students had to stand, many of us were looking for something we never found, and we left.

In fact, his lectures did not last very long. He delivered his best series in the winter of 1931. If I remember correctly, the first step against him was a ban on his lectures. He was allowed to keep his title and salary. He could not be expelled from the University unless he had broken a law or was guilty of plagiarism. But they finally got around to that. He was arrested in 1932 and sentenced to one year in prison—a mild sentence, but enough to justify his expulsion from the University.

My professor of Russian, Radovan Košutić, was an unusual person. His conservatism was reflected in his teaching rather than in his social and political opinions. He was the only professor whom the students feared as if they were still in secondary school. He scolded us, made fun of us, forced us to read aloud and in chorus. This ruthless method eventually produced results. Everyone who passed his exam had a solid knowledge of Russian, the language that all Yugoslavs think they know because it is related to their own. But to learn Russian well requires as much work as any other language.

I didn't learn my Russian from him, but, rather, years later, in prison. In the aimless wanderings and literary preoccupations of my youth, and during my political involvements, I never studied much. That was the case with most Communist students; even those who took exams did so without much interest, simply to get through.

Professor Košutić's one diversion was poetry. Even in his seventies he wrote love poetry. It received no recognition, and for good reason, for there was little of value in it. Almost every year he would publish a collection at his own expense, and give us copies as gifts. Of course, we made fun of him. For example: A nightingale sadly asks a slender branch: Why so pale and sad, Radovan? But we respected him for his strong attention to learning and his honest effort to educate his students.

This strange old man helped me and Borislav Kovačević in 1939–1940 with certain expressions in our translation of Gorky's *The Life of Klim Samkin*. We were no longer his students, and he now treated us with a kindness that was lacking when we sat in his classroom. He was obviously pleased that his former students were translating books. He knew Kovačević well, and he remembered me as a lazy and undisciplined student who had interrupted his class to invite everyone to join in a strike.

He was still living after the war. I found out that he had retired, now old and feeble. He asked for nothing, he offered his services to nobody.

In his classes I got to know Mitra better. It was in the spring of 1931. Mitra was one of the best students in our class, but that was not the reason I spotted her. She was a slender, pale young girl with a small mouth and large black eyes which appeared to be pulling her whole body along with them. Her thin little neck could just barely support the weight of her thick black hair. Her hands were white, her fingers long and slender. There was something sad and poetic about her, yet lucid and thoughtful. Until that time, my second year at the University, I had not been attracted to any one girl. One day, at the end of Košutić's class, Mitra stretched herself, tucking her sweater into her skirt. The tips of her breasts showed under her soft cotton blouse, and it was indeed odd that such a slender girl should be so endowed.

At that time I was having my short stories published, and I was also known for "original" outbursts, which might have aroused her curiosity. But it wasn't that. With a group of students we started up King Peter Street, and then spontaneously separated ourselves from the group. I asked her if she would meet me in the early evening. She began figuring things out: I can't at this hour, and I can't at that hour. She already had a date with someone else, but she would meet me at six anyway, in front of the Student Home for Girls. I wondered why I should meet her, since she already had a date. Why impose myself? On the other hand, I thought, perhaps she had no date, and just wanted to provoke me.

I learned later that she had indeed had a date, but she wanted to meet me. These small accidents, which affect the course of life so profoundly, appear in retrospect like strokes of good or bad fortune, depending on how one looks at it. But I wouldn't change them. I wouldn't have it otherwise.

The day we met was cool, the blue sky streaked with clouds, the city and the distant Danube inlaid with sun and shadows.

4

During my first and second years in Belgrade, from 1929 to 1931, there were no organized political groups at the University. At any rate, there were no Marxist or Communist groups. The bourgeois parties were represented by various casual groups organized around personal contacts made at soirées given at rich Belgrade homes. It was not merely that the heavy hand of the dictatorship had scared everyone. The abolition of the traditional forms of political struggle had squashed those movements and parties that had depended exclusively on such rights, and this resulted in confusion and inactivity. The same was true of the Communists. Although the party was banned and its members persecuted, the situation was not as dangerous as it was to become. Whippings were rare and not nearly as severe as they became later; sentences were infrequent and mild, and there were almost no murders. The illegal Communist organization adopted a style of functioning in accord with this semi-legal condition. It is not surprising that these illegal Communist organizations were broken up and their members arrested during the first months of the dictatorship. The cowardly behavior, with very few exceptions, of many high functionaries under torture hastened dissolution and panic. To add to the problem, the Central Committee, before fleeing the country in response to the dictatorship, had cooked up the senseless slogan of "armed uprising." No one took that too seriously except for a few youths. These unfortunate young men attempted to get hold of some ammunition and lost their lives in an encounter with the police.

My political activity during the first two years at Belgrade University was thus sterile and empty. Yet, in spite of a lack of

organized political life, people were able to live a social life based
on general political principles. We gathered together on the basis of
a spontaneous and dark discontent, directed particularly against the
moral values of the ruling class. We also shared a common enthusiasm for certain kinds of literature and a disapproval of the literary
values which the dictatorship imposed—*i.e.*, patriotic poetry, extreme estheticism—and a common dissatisfaction with certain professors, particularly the conservative ones who openly supported
the regime and pushed their politics in their lectures. What's more,
there was a common enthusiasm for café life, and this also held us
together. But these groups formed spontaneously, and disintegrated
just as spontaneously. People came and went.

Such groupings are natural and happen everywhere. But under
the despotic rule in Yugoslavia such groups turned into centers of
resistance and struggle. First they began by gossiping and spreading
inflated news of insignificant and serious matters alike: the cost of
the Queen's evening dress, gold teeth in the mouth of a government
minister's dog, the pressure exerted by France and the refusal of
such and such a foreign bank to grant a loan, the discontent of two
high army generals, the homosexuality of Petar Živković, the Premier, fictitious plots, the imprisonment of Pribićević. There was no
end to these stories; they incited young people and caused great in-
dignation. Should my country be ruled by such people? Should I
live like a slave all my life? That was but one of the many elements
in the story. Life all around us provided the rest. At every step one
faced misery and luxury, brute force and despair. But above all we
were infuriated by not knowing what was going on. The press exaggerated the success and aspirations of the regime, and concealed
obvious evils and failures. Only from time to time were some scan-
dalous affairs exposed: the theft of state property, or a brutal political conflict.

The dictatorship's major undoing was that it took over in Yugoslavia just prior to the Great Depression of 1929. The man in the
street, who knows nothing about world economic laws, could not
be convinced by elaborate but valid explanations in the press that
the government was not wholly responsible for the economic
downturn. Poverty was spreading every step of the way, exposing
gruesome crimes and perversities.

The circle that was formed at the Philosophical Faculty was
more political than literary in character: Borislav Kovačević,
Stefan Mitrović, myself, Vidak Marković, Venijamin Marinković,
and others. Radovan Vuković joined us later. As our discontent

grew, our common interests gradually changed from literary to political pursuits, particularly after the autumn of 1931, the time of the first student demonstration. Strangely enough, we were all partial to Dostoevski and believed that the revelation of internal impulses and motives should be the basis of all art. We even toyed with the idea of forming a movement called "Internality," and of starting a magazine. Unable to express ourselves in public, we turned inside, into ourselves. When we became politically active we believed the exact opposite to be true: we came to hate Dostoevski's mysticism, and we became dry rationalists, explaining everything in terms of the "objective conditions of the material productive forces at a given degree of development." Thus this complex internal discontent eventually gave birth to a simplified and rational view of life. Life and practice confirmed that resistance to established and traditional authority was impossible on any other basis.

If it were not for the dictatorship, this discontent might have culminated in literary experiments. But the circumstance gave rise to a generation of revolutionaries among the intellectual students. Their role I am unable to evaluate, but I feel it has been underestimated by official Yugoslav ideologists in an attempt to emphasize the role of the working class, and those leaders who had, at one time, long ago, been part of the working class.

Had we not lived under dictatorship and had not rapid change brought about so many surprises, Milica Živković might have been the star of our circle. She was the most extreme example of that particular period of our "internal" literary life. She had all the attributes of that life but for this: one of her legs was shorter than the other (she had had tuberculosis as a child), and this deprived her of the physical charm which is also necessary for such a role.

She was a strange girl in every respect. She was from Topola, the heart of Šumadija, and the birthplace of the Karadjordjević dynasty, and she couldn't free herself from the romantic and false notion that Šumadija and her people were the essence of the Serbian race: heroic, human, reasonable, and determined. She liked to contrast Karadjordje's character with that of his great-grandson Alexander, who was as involved in cutting wages at his Topola vineyards as he was in great affairs of state. But her thoughts never assumed political shape. She compared a historic legend with a reality that her clear eye and her unusually sensitive intelligence had spotted.

Her judgments were moral, and, as such, sharper and more personal than our own, which had already become political. We were critical of the King as a despot who might not have been quite as bad if he had had a more favorable environment. At the beginning of the dictatorship it was rumored that the King was merely the captive of a group of officers, the so-called "White Hand," led by Petar Živković, the Commander of the King's Guard, Premier, and Minister of the Interior.

The world of Milica Živković was a world of psychological and moral preoccupations. In many ways that was our own world too. Her imagination was lively, her inner life intense, her search for the joys of life made all the more acute by her handicap. Into the world of reality she built another world based on the books she had read. She compared her friends with heroes from various novels, particularly from Dostoevski. I was Alyosha from *The Brothers Karamazov*, although I was neither as good-natured nor as religious, and Bora Kovačević, perhaps because he was so withdrawn, was Raskolnikov. Her father, Milivoje, was inevitably Feodor Karamazov, lewd and godless. He was in fact a fat unimpressive shopkeeper who might have betrayed his wife at times. This, however, proved sufficient for his overly sensitive daughter to see him as a monster. In this imaginary world she had worked out a clever, honestly spontaneous scheme: she was the central figure around whom interesting students, particularly writers, gathered. She herself had no literary talent. But she was an exceptionally beautiful woman. Her body was small and frail, subtly put together, as if each limb were sculptured separately. Perhaps it was her illness, her unhappiness, and the sense of inferiority arising from the defective leg that gave her this look, and her large black eyes their greenish reflection. Initially her contacts with men were formed on the basis of an intellectual friendship. Her pronounced innocence set the tone for each relationship, and not even the most compulsive of charlatans would dare encroach on it. But occasionally one could see that this frail sick body was torn by deep passions. It wasn't only mine; I believe it was true of all her friendships. In the end she fell in love with every man and they all left her. By and large she maintained good relations with her girl friends until they crossed her, or became interested in one of her men. Then she was possessed. She shouted and screamed with all that wealth of imagination derived from books mixed with that inborn Serbian female bitchiness which her intelligence rendered all the more cunning.

One day she caught sight of me walking with Mitra and immediately turned against this girl whom she hardly knew. "It's that bitch with long hair and large eyes: debauchery, debauchery, my boy! That's her and her feelings for you! You are not Alyosha. I was wrong. Dmitri, Dmitri Karamazov, that's who you are!"

Thus for no good reason she destroyed her friendship with

Mara Maksimović. She rejected Mara because she mistakenly thought that I was in love with her. Mara was the sister of the writer Desanka Maksimović. Her name plus her slender figure emphasized by a short hair cut made her rather popular. Mara's dark eyes had the surprised look of a deer or a lamb. She was shy and old-fashioned. I once told Milica that I found Mara attractive, and that was sufficient to strain Milica's relationship with Mara, so that she attributed to Mara many unattractive characteristics.

Milica and I became good friends during my first year at the University. We took long walks in the park; we talked late into the night in her little room, Milica lying in bed. During the summer that followed we maintained our sentimental friendship through correspondence. The following year our relationship became more intense, but toward the end of that year, in the spring of 1931, we suddenly reached an impasse. My feelings were perfectly honorable, which is to say I felt only friendship. I can't say that I didn't experience brief moments of something else as well, however unclear, but basically I was resigned to the kind of relationship we had.

I still don't understand what possessed her to tell me openly one night in May, in her little room, that she could no longer tolerate our relationship, even if I were to think her a whore—all blood and flesh. Perhaps the fear of Mitra, whom I was seeing with increasing frequency? Perhaps some inner yearning, unfamiliar to me? This particular episode led to such a conflict between us that we stopped speaking to each other. I thought her sly and evil because she tried to turn an innocent friendship into something narrow and trivial. Almost two years went by and we didn't exchange a word. In those two years I had become a revolutionary, and she remained the same —viewing psychology and human behavior as the basic social problem. Then I was imprisoned for three years. When I came back, in 1936, mutual friends brought about a "reconciliation," which wasn't too hard since the meaning of our conflict was lost. She had herself become a Communist, although not a party member. But we were never as close as before. I still sensed in her that twofold feeling of friendship for men, rendered more unclear by Communist camaraderie.

But a great change had taken place as well. Her intellect and her sensitivity no longer appeared so outstanding among us. By comparison to us she was now "ideologically backward," "burdened by her petit-bourgeois background," "individualist," and "decadent." Her pride and vanity notwithstanding, she was forced to acknowl-

edge a continuing series of errors and weaknesses and to read Marxist literature. She was still not a party member, because she wasn't
"mature enough." But she collected heaps of underwear, socks,
bacon, and salami for comrades in prison. She showed remarkable
courage and skill in "pumping the bourgeoisie" for money, clothes,
and food. Finally, in the factional struggle that followed, she joined
the Sima Marković group, named after a post-World War I Communist party leader. This group was led by Professor Ljuban Radovanović. As a result she was considered an "antiparty and foreign
element."

Two or three years went by and she was lost to us, her onetime
friends, in the darkness of ordinary people. She re-emerged momen-
tarily in 1941, at the beginning of the uprising. Ill and lame, she
again tried to find herself. She was captured by the Chetniks, and
executed, nameless for everyone, including her friends.

5

My first year at the University coincided with the first year of the dictatorship. My interest in human problems was thus heightened. The next year—1930–1931—however brought about certain changes.

During the summer vacation I experienced a reality that undermined all the notions I had about our society. Perhaps I should have felt it sooner. But I hadn't. In the autumn, when we were all back in school again, my friend Borislav Kovačević told me about the miserable and hungry life in the rugged mountains of his region; Stefan Mitrović told me about the poverty of the fishermen on the Dalmatian Coast; Radovan Vuković told me about the oppression and hunger of the Albanians in Metohija. And so it went.

The complex and labored world of youth, with its murky psychological quests, was almost instantaneously rubbed out by reality —for me, in the mountains of Pešter, in the village of Mojstir. There my brother was a teacher, and there I visited him at the end of that school year. Many things there reminded me of my native region. Mountain people everywhere have something in common: telling long, imaginative stories, pride in bearing and attitude. But that was where the similarities ended. Political conditions were so different that it was hard to believe the two regions belonged to the same state. The population was mixed—Serbian and Albanian. The majority was Albanian. The village was therefore divided into a Serbian Mojstir and a Turkish Mojstir. Everything else was also divided: pastures and faith, habits and customs. Indeed, the tiny brook that separated them was the smallest, the tamest of the many barriers.

The Idealist

The local authorities—the President of the Municipality, the manager, the gendarmes—and the peasants warmly greeted my brother upon arrival. Until that time there had been no school in the village, and after all those years of slavery and struggle the Serbian peasants were happy to acquire their own teacher. The President of the Municipality had received my brother with particularly great enthusiasm. Fat as a pig, able, he was a peasant who was now meddling a little in trade. His foremost concern, however, was maintaining his position. He interpreted my brother's arrival as a significant reinforcement in the struggle against the Albanians, who, although in the majority, had no way of acquiring authority. Partly by force and threat, partly through cheating and graft, he had been elected president. He gave the dictatorship his enthusiastic approval, and was allowed to retain his position. His duties were to impose a firm rule on the populace, to suppress those who were dissatisfied with his regime—and to use his not so highly paid position to acquire some independent wealth.

The use of force and plunder was so open that it was hard to believe. In broad daylight, in a clearing near the village, the gendarmes caught an Albanian suspected of working with the rebels. They laid him across a felled tree and beat him with the handle of his own axe until his broken ribs penetrated his skin. The whole village—both Serbian and "Turkish"—listened to the wild screams of this unhappy man, one half rejoicing and the other in gloomy submission. And, after he had revived a little, this man sat in front of his house and sunned himself, huge, unshaven, his hands folded in his lap, motionlessly waiting out his slow death.

At the root of this extreme attitude on the part of the authorities were the Albanian rebels, who came over from Albania in the summertime and returned in the winter. But most of all, this was simply an excuse for plundering and lawlessness.

The authorities intensified Serb-Albanian differences in every way, not so much to glorify the Serbs as to strengthen their own position. These differences were deeply engrained. It was not merely a question of the language and faith: the two races fought over pastures and forests; they competed in jumping and rock throwing, and even in singing. They were different in appearance too: the Serbs were short, stocky, fair, and big-headed; the Albanians, slender and dark, quick of tongue, of light and swift gait like wild animals. And now they fought for state power, because the state determined the amount each community had to give to the state, based on the size and extent of each community.

The Serbian peasants were by no means enthusiastic about this kind of government, but it was "their own" after "five hundred years" of Turkish rule. So why give authority to the "Albanians," to the "Turks"? Which of the Albanians would gain power anyway? The very worst: with eyes that filled with blood at the mere sight of a Serb. It was a vicious cycle: since the struggle with the Albanians was considered inevitable, those who were the most persistent and the most ruthless rose up to represent "Serbian" authority. Such people encouraged lawlessness and violence against the Albanians, and occasionally against the Serbs as well.

The Albanians considered army service a misfortune, almost as bad as changing one's faith. Their children sometimes came back from the army with views which were very different from the traditional ones. It was their hatred of the army and the state that played the most important role in this resistance. They resorted to all kinds of things: they mutilated themselves, they starved, they fled to the forests, they drank water drawn from boiled tobacco. This last treatment was considered foolproof—one turns yellow and loses weight like a consumptive, and some occasionally died from it. Such deaths were attributed to the tyrant's hand, the "Serbian" hand.

There were simpler ways of avoiding the draft. The municipality made up lists of persons to be drafted. It was a fairly simple matter to drop a few names from the list. This sort of thing was practiced in everything: in determining the amount of taxes to be paid, in the seizure of village forests, and pastures, and in accusing persons falsely of associating with the rebels. One had to pay ransom on all sides, secretly. But these secret bribes were in fact quite public, and prices were set, release from military service being the most highly priced item.

It was difficult to be a teacher in an area like this, even though the children grasped everything and remembered everything. First of all, the process of enrollment resulted in a small war, particularly with the Albanians, who had finally agreed to send their boys to school, but would not hear of sending their girls. In the end the gendarmes had to step in. At first the Albanians thought that my brother was there to help with the conversion of their children, and that he was merely an arm of the police. But they quickly learned that he accepted no bribes. One of the peasants tucked a five-hundred-dinar note into his pocket while pleading that he not take his daughter in school. Hot-blooded and impetuous, my brother leaped at the peasant, chased him into the yard, and threw the five-hundred-dinar note after him, in full sight of a mob of peasants. He rebuffed all offers of gifts, cheese, and eggs. Following this incident, the peasants, both Serbian and Albanian, realized that he was an unusual man. Gentle and systematic in his work with children, he visited homes, consulted with parents, in short, he changed the peasants' view of the school.

If relations between the school and the people had improved, relations with the municipality and the police became even more strained. It was not an open conflict, but the police were not pleased that my brother associated so little with the authorities and so much with the peasants. This could only "spoil the people." Or was he secretly a Communist? As an honest and just man, my brother was favorably disposed to Communism, but he was not actually a Communist.

Life for the villagers and outsiders alike was extremely crude. What goods were available in the village were cheap: six eggs for one dinar! But there was no one to cook them. The police chief kindly offered to let my brother take his meals at the police station, but he declined. The school building was an old peasant house with only two rooms: a classroom and a room for the teacher, with a bed and a wooden table.

The Albanian rebels were active in this area, and rumor had them popping up here, there, and everywhere. Nevertheless, every afternoon we took long walks. In the evening, after supper, talk would always turn to the rebels.

No hunger was evident in Mojstir, but, rather, the poverty and destitution common to all mountain country, steady, persistent poverty and destitution which make it impossible to tell whether it ever gets better or worse. Oat bread, hard cheese, heavy wool suiting with no underwear, a straw bed—that was it.

6

Signs of the Great Depression were evident at Bijelo Polje as early as the summer of 1930, and the depression deepened in 1931. There were no jobs for the poor peasants, no money, no grain, at least not in Montenegro and Sandžak. There was terrible poverty in the villages and the towns. Dayworkers often labored from morning till night for ten dinars, or as little as five, and no food. I knew families that ate meat only three times a year. But the poor didn't protest. In Montenegro and Sandžak the local authorities exerted no special pressure. The discontent grew, but it was directed against hunger and unemployment, not against the government.

The poor in small towns didn't even bother to grumble; they accepted the hard times as something inevitable, a natural disaster that comes and goes. But the Montenegrin peasants in Sandžak complained bitterly: "What did we fight for? Those bastards who never lifted a rifle got all the loot! This can't go on!"

In the summer of 1930, I had organized casual gatherings with peasants, particularly the younger ones. They asked all kinds of questions. I had to answer them befitting my reputation: an educated man, writer. In some mysterious way they had learned that the poor in Russia held all power and wielded justice. One peasant told me, I remember it well, that in Russia all the grain is piled up high as a mountain for the whole village to use, and everyone takes as much as he needs. To say nothing of the machine which takes in the grain at one end and turns out bread (spread with butter) at the other. The legend about Russia—about equality and the good life of the working people—had been popular before, but now, in their distress and misery, the people embued it with a new strength and truthfulness. I myself never believed such stories, but I explained everything about Russia as if I had been there. From the general notion about equality I synthesized a world of real events and of relations, which was of interest to peasants. It all seemed logical and well-founded, and I myself believed in it absolutely. Unable to extricate myself from the real world or to explain it, I created a seemingly more real world out of my fancy. That was the world I tried to explain to others.

But the peasants were not alone in their discontent. It was evident, in a different way, in small towns as well, particularly among those who had never completed their schooling, and among tradespeople. In Bijelo Polje it included the Ottoman nobles, the *begs* who were suddenly impoverished following World War I, and had reached an impasse of their own.

Risto Ratković was a writer from Bijelo Polje and an intense man of bohemian tastes. He was not really a Communist, but given his bitterness against society and his recklessness, he knew how to boast about Communism and make use of it. He was plainly a rebel. He had been exiled to Bijelo Polje, and as the only "Communist" in this whole area, he had acquired the reputation of being something of a martyr. His brother Krsto, much less of a bohemian, was thought to be the only true Communist in town.

At one time the Ratkovići had been a rich Serbian merchant family, but the Balkan War of 1912 had reduced their holdings to a house and some land at the edge of town, which they were gradually selling off. By the 1930's they were without money, but they still owned a spacious house in the middle of the town, with stables and storerooms in the enclosed yard, from which they drew some income. The Ratkovići had roots in the gracious old Turkish traditions. Their discontent had nothing to do with Communism, as was established later when a true Communist movement developed. They were not prepared for action; violence horrified them, and they were suspicious of anything that might obstruct their way of life, however impoverished. The old man was known in Turkish times as a solid Serb and a negotiator for the liberation from the Turks. However, the liberation did not bring him what he had expected; it crushed one way of life, but offered no acceptable substitute. In front of the Moslems he gave no indication that his dreams hadn't materialized and that, like them, he had been destroyed. Bitter and disappointed, he waited for death.

Risto came home rarely. He was a well-known poet, somewhat unusual in expression. Krsto, on the other hand, lived with his father, who was lost in a world with which he was in unmitigated disagreement. He transferred his sorrow and despair to his children. Krsto was only twenty-five, but already somewhat faded. He sang beautifully, but his were sad, *"beg"* songs, mourning over dead loves, conquered fortresses, the glow of youth, heroism, and wealth.

I was only two or three years older than the Ratkovići and the sons of the *begs*, but very different from both. They had grown up in the immediate postwar period, when there still was a certain amount of freedom, when there was violence on all sides, and when political parties and fronts were not as yet clearly defined. Until 1929 the Ratkovići had been Communist sympathizers. During the dictatorship, they felt that nothing could be done because the government would not allow anything to be done. It was as if that brief period of freedom, however precarious, had softened them, and they gave themselves up to their secret longing for a quiet life. In contrast, we were shaping ourselves intellectually and spiritually under the dictatorship. We knew of no life outside of the dictatorship—that was the life we had to accept if we were unwilling to fight it. During the first few years of the dictatorship, until 1932, we were united with the Ratkovići in a feeling of general discontent, but it was clear from the very start that our discontent was of a different quality: it was tougher, wilder, riper for protest and action.

It was no accident that the Ratkovići friends were mostly former *begs* in their thirties, whereas my friends were young Moslems. We were both attracted to the naïve bohemian life through which young people express their first opposition to traditional values. We both enjoyed the sad old love songs, but the Ratkovići lived those songs, while we only enjoyed them. The Ratkovići and their class hated peasants almost viscerally, as a dumb, raw, and wild mass, the mass that might someday break loose and squash everybody with a primeval dark force. Like all Montenegrin intellectuals, I was myself from a peasant family. I witnessed in this town the disease which had drained the life out of these villages. Misery and force reigned supreme. True enough, our Moslem friends had a somewhat different view of the villages from us Montenegrins, but they knew, rationally if not instinctively, that one could accomplish nothing without the peasants.

Wealthy families undergo changes which I can never explain. In the course of time, classes, movements, even whole nations go into decline—that's inevitable and clear. But the causes behind the physical and mental decline of the onetime wealthy are not altogether clear. Thus "old families" lose not only their wealth and influence, which is natural, but also become extinct, and very fast, as I have noted in this country. What are "old families" after all? Biologically speaking, there is no such thing—all families are equally old since they have all been in existence since the human beginnings, regardless of where they come from or to what class they belong. But what is old in them is a way of life, a mode of thinking. The few such "old families" that existed in Bijelo Polje quickly disintegrated, both physically and financially. Other families, Moslem and Montenegrin settlers, took their place.

Of particular distinction among the Moslems were the four Dobardžić brothers, all engaged in trade. They were the first generation to settle in town, and they lived together. However, they quickly got used to city life, and they enjoyed the seclusion of the large yard and garden behind their spacious house. One of the brothers still spent a great deal of his time in the village, bargaining with peasants and shepherds over cattle and hay.

I was, of course, particularly curious about the struggle with the bourgeoisie and the expropriation of their property: What should be taken away from the rich, like the Dobardžići, who were hardworking modest people? They were thought to be the richest family in town, which was probably true, yet their shop was constructed of cheap fir, their house loosely put together, the walls of unbaked brick. In order to survive, they had to wrestle with the cattle in the mountains, in filth and sweat. Most of the housework was done by their women. Their wealth included a modest property in the village, a house and yard in town, and a shop that was doing reasonably well. Yet our propaganda against the rich was so effective that it appealed even to those who had never left Bijelo Polje. Perhaps this can be explained in terms of the new life we were promising on the one hand, and the blunders committed by the ruling class, not their wealth and luxury, on the other. The Dobardžići played no role in town; on the contrary, they were as wary of the authorities as the rest of the townspeople.

The youngest Dobardžić, Ilijaš, went to school and wrote poetry, and we quickly became friends. But our friendship was not long-lasting, for he was suspicious of anyone with leftist tendencies. His poems had their origin in Moslem folk songs, but they were not nearly as ingenuous or appealing. He worked in the family shop, although reluctantly, making frequent trips to Sarajevo where he bought goods and sent them back to his brothers. Sarajevo was his city in every respect: the way of life, the surviving Moslem customs.

Although he severed contact with me—I was known for my leftist leanings as early as 1932—he continued to greet me courteously in the street. But upon my return from prison in 1936 even that gesture was made reluctantly. In 1930, when we first met, he had felt that the poor should be helped and treated humanely. But when the time came to convert these humane feelings into a political struggle, risking one's property as well as one's life, he paused and finally withdrew. In the 1935 elections he sided with the regime, although not without some embarrassment. During the Stojadinović years he was openly on the side of the government; he justified his position by pointing out that the Moslems were in power and that their demands had been met. When the country was occupied by the fascist armies during World War II he sent a message to the fascist Ustashi government in Zagreb, urging them to incorporate Sandžak—his Moslems felt they were like Croats, ill-served by the Serbian monarchy. I don't know what became of Ilijaš. His brothers, drawing upon past experience, lived quiet uninvolved lives during the occupation. Ilijaš left for Sarajevo in the early days of the Communist uprising, aware of the revenge that was due him because of his invitation to the Ustashi.

It is interesting to note that the leftist movement took little root among artisans. Their protest seemed to be expressed in alcoholism —to alleviate a temporary stress. In 1931–1932 I knew many artisans with leftist tendencies. But they deserted me one and all when I was imprisoned and the political organization began to function. In Sandžak and Montenegro, and I should say in Bosnia and other backward areas, Communism's following consisted chiefly of young intellectuals and peasants.

In addition, at Bijelo Polje the Montenegrins held complete power, although they were not any more numerous than the Serbs and Moslems. Nevertheless neither the Serbs nor the Moslems tried to change this, as if it were not a question of political authority over them. All three police administrators were Montenegrins, practically illiterate but "deserving" because they had fought in the war. The same was true of the other civil servants, from high officials to school janitors. And anyway, the Montenegrins made themselves heard everywhere: at the market and in the café, at receptions and celebrations, obliterating everyone else.

Interestingly enough, the Serbian peasants, long settled in this area, expressed no discontent, although they lived in greater misery than the newly settled Montenegrins. With the exception of a few Moslem intellectuals, Communism in this area was an almost exclusively Montenegrin affair. But so was its major opponent—the government—and eventually the Chetniks.

Whether one should seek explanation for such social and political groupings in the fact that Sandžak remained under the Turks until 1912 is doubtful. But the population was rendered ineffectual after so many years of oppression, particularly around Bijelo Polje and along the Lim Valley. One thing is definitely true: certain ethnic groups produce from time to time men and parties that draw masses, masses already stirred up in their unconscious depths, and lead them toward a new ideal, which becomes identified with their material well-being. Indeed, that material well-being is invariably achieved, even if by small groups. Driven by a hundred-year ideal of national liberation, the Montenegrins sought to drive the Turks out of this region. Some of them acquired positions in the government civil service; others acquired land. But that was merely the beginning of their tumultuous campaign and they were now to sweep along with them people who were not favorably disposed to their ideas, despite their own misery.

Poverty and illness, ignorance and decay: the population in this area was fearful in appearance. On market days the town was teeming with the goitered and the blind, the crippled and the feeble-minded. In mountain regions, around Pljevlje and Nova Varoš and Sjenica, both Moslems and Serbs were healthier and more alert.

But here in the plain . . . That was Sandžak, the "Yugoslav Siberia," which was called Sandžak because at one time it was erroneously incorporated into a Turkish province of that name and remained so until 1912. Originally this area was the center of the feudal Serbian state and Serbian culture.

There is an anecdote about Sandžak: Saint Sava was walking across Sandžak on a freezing-cold day. A dog ran after him and began nipping at him. Saint Sava reached for a rock but couldn't lift it because it was frozen to the ground. He said: "Cursed be a land in which dogs are on the loose and the rocks are tied to the ground."

Death, lawlessness, violence, and poverty stayed in Montenegro. Misery, ignorance, feeble-mindedness, and degeneration in Sandžak. One wades across the Tara, from Montenegro into Sandžak, from the heart of human blood into the torpor of damnation.

7

King Alexander liked to receive delegations from the newly formed principalities. The delegation from the principality of Zeta (mostly Montenegro) made a cruelly primitive and humiliating impression on those Montenegrins in Belgrade who were intoxicated by all that staged, artificial enthusiasm.

These delegations were received at the New Palace (now the Executive Council of the People's Republic of Serbia). Overjoyed by their audience with the King, enlivened by food and drink, a sizable group of people erupted from the Palace and overflowed onto the street, stopping traffic. The Montenegrin national costume, gold and plain cloth, stood out against the carefully selected background of the city's black and polish and outshone it with its glitter and cheap picturesqueness. In the same way, the Montenegrins outshouted a loud crowd with quick screams and sharp flashes of the old Montenegrin accent. Many Montenegrins living in Belgrade—looking for work and pensions—joined them later. They hailed the delegation with cries such as: "Hey, you gray hawk! Hey, you heroes! Hey, Šćepan! Hey, Mrgud!" to which the delegation responded by handing them cigarettes pinched from the Palace during the feast. This colorful crowd finally reached Terazije. Well-fed drunken Montenegrin leaders, joined by the old Independent Montenegro Movement, and the Unconditional Unification with Serbia Movement, a conglomeration of frauds and buffoons who gathered wherever they could get something for nothing, were having a raucous time. The drunken crowd rolled up and down the streets of Belgrade, having enjoyed their "lord," who had shaken several hands, enquired after the state of health of a few of them, the crops of a few others, or how they came by their medals, and that was all he had to say to them or to promise them, leaving further political talks to lackeys and servants. The leaders, for their part, couldn't wait to sit down at tables loaded with heaps of good food. Long before they left their hungry and desolate Montenegro, their mouths had watered in anticipation of the Palace feast.

At Terazije they danced a reel around the fountain, singing songs about the King, old songs in which King Alexander's name was substituted for Nikola's. The crowd suddenly dispersed, as if on orders, to end the celebration at the National Theatre, even though there couldn't have been more than three men among them who had ever heard anything but the shepherds singing or the *gusle* playing, or the professional mourners wailing. They all piled into the theatre. The guards didn't dare hold back the uninvited "relatives" and "friends," not merely because they were afraid of the ancient weapons tucked into their belts, but because they knew the crowd had arrived straight from the Palace accompanied by detectives and gendarmes. The press tried to smooth things over the next day by glorifying the contrived heroism and directness of the Montenegrins and the calculated cordiality of the King.

This incident greatly intensified the suspicion and humiliation which we young people felt. It was the first time in my life that I felt ashamed that I was a Montenegrin, the first time I became aware of the other, submissive, side of the Montenegrin character. Some of my friends had defined this behavior as a form of heroic artlessness, but I found it disgusting. For me it represented the greed of parasites and flunkies, regardless of the courage these men might have once shown in battle. They had lost their human dignity and courage—not because they supported the King and the monarchy but because of the humiliating and reckless way they expressed it.

The Serbian opposition intellectuals took their usual view of Montenegrins, but not without a trace of bitterness: Montenegrins were good-natured primitives whom one should forgive because they are our brothers. Yet it's true that these men intentionally emphasized this trait of their character in order to demonstrate their loyalty and devotion to the King and his policies. What did these poor people have to offer? Croats and Slovenes appeared before the King in top hats and their national costumes, impressing him with their composure in movement and speech; South Serbs (that is, Macedonians) with their songs about Tsar Dušan; Bosnians with their languor and colorfulness; Serbs with their authority derived from being the ancestral cradle of nationalism and their suffering on the Salonika Front. The Montenegrins could only pledge every head to their ruler, as they had done in the past.

But if we Montenegrins had much to be ashamed of, our Serbian colleagues were little better off. With the help of their followers and students receiving government grants, the government had organized a Serbo-Croat student demonstration. The dictatorship was still new, still shrouded in the "Yugoslav idea," which also had roots in the Croatian struggle against Austria and Hungary. A large group of Belgrade students visited Zagreb, all expenses paid by the government, of course, and was "enthusiastically received" there, to quote the press.

Upon their return to Belgrade, the students walked from the station straight to the heart of the city, demonstrating their enthusiasm for King Alexander. I saw it as a mixture of drunken jubilance and superficial enthusiasm. True enough, several hundred students took the trip, but only a third of that number genuinely demonstrated any enthusiasm for the King. There was of course the lure of a free trip and a good time.

The crowd reached the Moskva Hotel and was turning into King Milan Street (now Marshal Tito Street) when one of its leaders shouted: "Long live the Yugoslav Tsar Alexander!" This new slogan was picked up by the modest-sized crowd around him. By the time they reached the New Palace the crowd had grown to five or six thousand people, accompanied by an army of police. The crowd stopped in front of the Palace and continued to demonstrate for some fifteen minutes, growing until it was so closely packed the people could hardly breathe. Finally, in a brightly lit window on the ground floor, the King appeared. He was lit from behind; thus one could only see an outline of his flat head and his long nose topped with a glistening pince-nez. He waved lethargically at the crowd for a minute or two. The light went out, he disappeared, and high above, under the dome, several children appeared dressed in white, flailing their little arms: it was the heir to the throne, his brothers, and the Queen. The crowd was jubilant. Finally the white figures disappeared too and the crowd gradually dispersed.

The following day the newspapers said that thirty thousand Belgrade citizens had demonstrated their affection for the King. What's more, there was a reprint of a speech he never made.

I was in the street that evening and I joined the crowd, out of curiosity rather than enthusiasm. The popularity of the King, or, more specifically, his power, seemed enormous to me; at the same time I felt hatred and disgust for him and the demonstrators. I found my own impotence in this situation insufferable, my own and that of so many people who opposed this power as personified by the King, the tyrant. I felt that this night marked a final break between me, a citizen, and the King, the representative of state power. As it turned out, I was not alone in this reaction: we finally understood that it was the King who was responsible for all that evil. We were led to this conclusion not merely by the stories of the luxury and dissipation in which the court indulged, but also by the wild demonstration in his honor, obviously organized by the regime.

One's initial reaction to such impotence is to either plot an assassination or concoct a scheme which would bring this violence to an end overnight. We recalled that all of Serbia's leaders had been deposed in one way or the other, and that in 1903 King Alexander Obrenović had actually been murdered. These ideas were mostly generated by such leftist groups as the Pribićevići, but they were not alien to our leftist groups either. Needless to say, the idea was not very real and not very profound. We realized that this was not the heart of the problem, and that the system would not benefit by minor changes. As if it had been any better *before* the dictatorship! But at the beginning such feelings were not unfamiliar. With the growth of the organized opposition, they tapered off and dissipated.

We felt contempt and hatred for our nationalist colleagues, particularly for those who joined the regime to get grants and other material benefits. Actually, the number of such students was not great. At that time the issuance of grants was still not directly linked to one's personal politics, yet the regime tended to exercise some influence over those who were already the recipients of grants. But once sown, the seeds of hatred grew and developed. We discovered noble and wonderful human characteristics in each other, while we were aware of our opponents' political reactions only.

This was the atmosphere at the University of Belgrade as the November 1931 elections approached. There was only one choice —the government list headed by General Petar Živković, a demagogue who, backed by the palace, had founded a new party, the Yugoslav Radical Peasant party, based on the country's three leading parties: the Radical party, the Peasant party (Croatian), and the Democratic party. These predictatorship groupings had unfortunately lent some of their prominent leaders to the newly concocted party, thereby aligning themselves with the dictatorship.

I am quite sure that the students of the bourgeois parties wanted to join with the Communists in their activities—after all, the Communists represented the most aggressive element. But such co-operation would have compromised the bourgeois leadership. They were not against the monarchy and they had to maintain a moderate position. Under no circumstances was a demonstration to be turned into a struggle with the police. Killing people and breaking shop windows were to be avoided at all costs. They wanted to let the King know that the people, that most abstract political category, which everyone evoked, didn't approve of these elections, or of the dictatorship, for that matter, but at the same time it was essential to show the people that the old parties were not dead, that they would go on living even if suppressed. Still thinking in terms of predictatorship conditions, the bourgeois leaders could not believe that there were many Communists in the student body. But their student representatives knew better. They could sense the aggressive leftist spirit that was developing among the students, even if it was still unclear and unformed.

We leftists, on the other hand, understood that the "bourgeoisie" wanted to take advantage of us, that they wanted us to take part in activities that were essentially theirs. At the same time, we knew that we couldn't pass up any organized activity, and that we were not strong enough to undertake something on our own. We were so intimidated that we never understood how many people from other schools were ready to join us. Our most active groups were at the Philosophical Faculty and at the Law School.

These groups had no legal character, and we didn't recognize them as groups. They grew out of friendships and were based on common interests, mostly in literature and politics. We were sure we were not infiltrated by police agents, and we never worried about it. The police and its spies were a dark outside power who maintained torture chambers, some twenty yards underground, filled with monsters who took pleasure in beating and butchering people. Not without reason was that the reputation of the police.

We were not in agreement with the older Communists, who opposed every form of joint action with the bourgeoisie. Yet we were somewhat puzzled by the exaggerated caution and conspiratorial air of the bourgeois parties. Young men from the bourgeois parties, mostly children of well-to-do families, had a more realistic view of the police. After all, their fathers were part of the system. Their fear was not so much of physical torture, but, rather, of an all-knowing power which, accordingly, exerted a tremendous moral pressure on them, accusing them of having joined forces with the enemies of the state and fatherland. They were unable to form a clear picture of the balance of power, or of the regime's true power —obscured by the essentially passive character of the Communist groups and of the bourgeois parties. Subsequent events did much to clarify these relationships.

8

Stojan Ivezić, a law student, was an outstanding and prominent supporter of the bourgeois parties. He was a member of the Radical party, but he was so active that he could easily be taken to have represented all parties.

He was a Montenegrin, from Kolašin, like me. I had known him, and his mother, in Montenegro. She was a poor widow who owned a cottage, a small meadow, a pair of hard-working hands, and a son whom she wanted to have educated. The boy was aware from an early age that he would be able to get ahead only if he combined his intelligence with hard work: the former he was born with, and the latter he practiced unsparingly in spite of his delicate health. A large bald head on a short body, a long foxlike nose on a pimpled face gave him a striking appearance. He spoke little and laughed noiselessly, as befit a cynic. For him politics was an art. He made no bones about it. People sensed that Stojan was manipulating them, and yet he was a successful operator. If the times had been more favorable to parliamentary methods, this man would have become an outstanding politician. But he lacked two essential qualities to survive politically in a dictatorship: one was health—he was physically frail, and imprisonment could have been fatal in his case; the other was courage. His idol was Nikola Pašić; get things moving, then withdraw unobtrusively and rule from behind the scenes. But this was no time for such a performance. There was now Communism to contend with, whose adherents were always ready to sacrifice themselves for the party.

Ivezić had been at the University for some five or six years; like so many students involved in politics, he was in no hurry to pass his exams. He was on the payroll of the Radical party. It was not a large sum of money, yet it enabled him to live somewhat better than most students, and they resented it.

To this day I don't know why Stojan Ivezić selected me to consult regarding a plan then under consideration. Probably because we came from the same town and had known each other. He had worked on this proposal for a very long time. The police knew he was a member of the opposition, so our discussions were conducted in secrecy. He didn't try to pursuade me politically; we simply discussed a given situation. He said the regime was not nearly as powerful as it looked; he also emphasized the duties of "politically aware student youth," and most of all he dwelled on the little intrigues of the court and the gossip about Petar Živković.

I realized that he wanted to engage my services, but I couldn't grasp the reasons for his elaborate preparation. I was against the Radicals; I was determined to accept only what appealed to me. But Stojan wanted to be on the safe side; he wanted to give me enough faith to survive in case I was arrested. The bourgeois politicians also lived in an exaggerated fear of the police. Indeed, Stojan was very persuasive. I still wonder whether I would have gone along with his scheme had it not been for his cunning. I favored action, but not action in which I was a tool of a movement which hadn't been my choice.

One day he took me down to the Sava docks. We entered the long yellow building belonging to the Danube Line, and went up to their offices. He left me standing in a dark waiting room while he whispered his name to the receptionist, who immediately opened the door to an office. I saw a large, dark man with prominent brows getting up from his chair behind a desk. This was Dr. Milan Stojadinović, who from 1935 to 1939 was to be the Premier, and responsible for directing Yugoslav foreign policy toward the Axis Powers.

I had never before, or after, been received by any leader of a bourgeois party. Ivezić had implied that "someday," if all should "go well," he would arrange for me to meet Stojadinović, but I had expressed no interest whatever in this prospect.

Stojadinović was already a well-known politician, with a reputation for financial acumen—he had been Minister of Finance prior to the dictatorship. There were rumors that he had made a great deal of money speculating in war claims, and that he was one of the largest holders in the Danube Line. At that time he was the most active politician in the Radical party, one of the staunchest opponents of the dictatorship and of King Alexander personally. Later, of course, he changed.

After emerging from Stojadinović's office, Ivezić explained to me that the "matter" under discussion was not in his possession, and that it would be best if I visited Stojadinović's wife, who was recuperating in a luxurious clinic, to pick up the matter, because I wasn't compromised with the police. The "matter" was a bundle of leaflets signed by the opposition leaders condemning the dictatorship and making a public appeal for a boycott of the elections.

I never met Mrs. Augusta Stojadinović. A woman who spoke no Serbian, and no French either, greeted me at the door of her suite, and after I gave her my message she retreated silently. She came back with two large neatly wrapped packages. I remember to this day how confused I was as I came out into the sunny street. I felt I shouldn't have done it, not because of the danger involved, but because they were the leaflets of the bourgeois parties. And yet I realized that something had to be done even if it were something like this, if I were not to deceive myself, my convictions, my words, and my feelings.

But I didn't really suffer until I got together with "my" people, who were supposed to distribute the leaflets. Stefan Mitrović objected immediately on the grounds that the police would "knock nails into our heels" for distributing bourgeois leaflets. Bora Kovačević took the whole thing with equanimity: some action is preferable to none. And Radovan Vuković was full of nervous foreboding. The same was true of the students at the Law School. Nevertheless they all agreed to join us in the action.

For many years I was ashamed of having distributed those leaflets and for having urged other people to join me. For a whole year my friends kept reproaching me, and their reproach, coupled with my own feelings of guilt, fortified my opposition to the bourgeois parties and their leaders. We were not yet Communists, but we had begun to compete with each other in degrees of hostility toward the bourgeoisie. Later this game assumed the character of deep "class" hatred.

One bundle of leaflets was to be distributed at the Philosophical Faculty and the Law School, and the other in town—not in the streets, but in letter boxes, through open windows, and into yards. The leaflets were picked up in the early evening. They were distributed by 8:00 A.M., thus surprising the police with simultaneous action. Stojan and I met at ten o'clock, as arranged. The distribution had been carried out smoothly, without a single incident. Stojan was pleased. We agreed to meet again the following evening. And off he ran. I thought to myself: Off he goes to telephone his bosses, taking credit for someone else's work.

The distribution of the leaflets made no impact. Students found leaflets in their desks, but very few actually picked them up. They were afraid to touch them, as if they were live coals. However, there was a great deal of talk about the leaflets, which contributed to a mood of rebellion.

The following evening I joined Stojan in a handsome and spacious apartment not far from the Academy of Sciences. It was a meeting of all the group leaders. I represented no one officially, but it was generally understood that I had the left-wing students behind me. We agreed that demonstrations should be held at the Law School at noon the day before the elections. It was felt that we could draw the largest number of students at that hour, as well as a large number of people from the streets near the University. The meeting went quickly and smoothly. We felt close to one another, and a little sad, as one might feel on the eve of a battle. There were about a hundred students involved in the arrangements for the demonstration. We agreed that students from other faculties should also come to the Law School, to have as impressive a crowd as possible, and that Ivezić and others known to the police should not attend.

We had only twenty-four hours in which to prepare for the demonstration. It was a very long twenty-four hours. No one could anticipate how the police would react: Will they shoot? Will they respect the autonomy of the University? Determined to face it all, with a feeling of secrecy and importance, with sadness and affection, Mitrović, Kovačević, and I spent almost the entire night in walk and conversation.

I had been with Mitra until closing time at the Student Home. I wanted to tell her what was going on, but I stuck to the principle of conspiracy. And I was sorry that I couldn't tell her. There was a lot of sadness that evening, between young men determined to fight and girls they were leaving behind in anticipation of something terrible and great, something that is often paid for in human blood.

That was the first public demonstration against the dictatorship. This is not the time to talk of its impact on the development of the opposition and the Communist movement among the students. But those who joined the demonstration felt that they were initiating something new and dangerous, that they were treading into the unknown. Of that there can be no doubt.

9

The first confrontation took place five or six days before the demonstration, and it marked the beginning of a long chain of events. It occurred at an evening meeting held in a café on Ratarska Street (later Queen Marie Street, and now the 27th of March Street). This proregime meeting was also attended by a small group of students. It was about to end when a dozen of us arrived and began heckling the speakers. The squabble was carried into the street, and the students went after us with the help of two or three gendarmes. We armed ourselves with rocks and bricks and retreated toward a park in front of the Student Home. We stopped at the entrance to the park. They were on one side of the street, we on the other. The gendarmes were no longer with them. One of our men ran off to the Student Home for reinforcements, and we began to taunt the others again. Without the protection of the police, they didn't dare enter the park, enshrouded in twilight. There were bitterness and hatred on both sides: we called them lackeys of the regime, and they called us Communist bandits. The hatred was all the greater because we didn't dare attack each other physically, but expressed it all by hissing and growling. They left before the arrival of our reinforcements.

This was by way of preparation for the demonstration that was to take place on the eve of the elections.

On the agreed-upon day, at noon, we made the rounds of all the classrooms at the Law School and the Philosophical Faculty inviting our colleagues to a meeting at the main hall of the Law School. The speakers were not designated until just before the meeting began, when the political group leaders selected me. After a good deal of nervous decision-making it turned out that I was to be the sole speaker. The gathering was small. As usual some people came out of mere curiosity. Most of the students, having heard that the meeting was to protest the elections, left the building as fast as their legs would carry them. Actually no more than three hundred students attended the meeting, of whom perhaps a little more than a half were ready to demonstrate.

I mounted the podium in the main hall and began to speak. I tried not to be too sharp, but I couldn't control myself. I cannot say that, sensing the presence of police in the audience, I wasn't afraid, or that I was altogether composed. But I was in it, and since I was in it I had to go ahead.

When the speech was over the applause may not have been unanimous, but it was powerful. We walked out in front of the building. A large crowd had gathered. The police had set up barriers. The streetcars were still running, their nervous clanging echoing in the crush and commotion. All this was a surprise. The police had obviously known about the demonstration and had stationed themselves in the right spot. Suddenly we were face to face.

A police officer standing at the corner of Karadžićeva Street was angrily shouting that he would not let us through, threatening us with "use of arms, public order, in the name of the law." Someone suggested we all sing the national anthem, which would force the policemen to stand at attention, and possibly soften them as well. The national anthem was surely proof that the demonstration was not directed against the state. This turned out to be a poor idea. They were incensed and began pushing us back. But suddenly there was an opening in the barrier, and they let us through, and once a passageway was made, it soon widened and the mob advanced with us into Karadžićeva Street. I found myself at the head of the mob; to this day I don't understand how that happened. One hundred and fifty students were shouting slogans. I felt confused, sensing that something unusual was in the making. I knew some of the people near me, but there were many I didn't know. I turned around. The gendarmes had closed off Karadžićeva Street, and in front of us there was a double police barrier at the point where Karadžićeva Street meets Knez Mihailova Street. We were caught between the walls of the street and the police barriers on either side. To reach Knez Mihailova Street we would have to push through the barrier in front of us, with the police behind us and among us. What choice did we have? We advanced, even though sensing defeat.

The police were now all action. When we were about ten yards from the new barrier, two young men suddenly grabbed me by the arms. I had spotted one of them while I was delivering my speech. Although he had shouted with the students, there was something cruel and suspect in those dark eyes, and I instinctively felt that he wanted to get me. The action was unfolding extremely fast: twisting my arms, they dragged me toward the gendarmes, while I resisted so hard that my shoes slid on the pavement. I may have called for help—I don't remember. But at one point I suddenly felt they were no longer dragging me. Mirko Vesović, of the Agricultural group, had grabbed the hand of one of these agents and a whole line of students, one by one, was holding on to Vesović. A bunch of gendarmes were holding on to the other agent. For a moment or so I was being pulled back and forth. I stood still, as if crucified, between hostile groups, and the gendarmes finally gave way. I fell on top of Vesović. Back on my feet, I headed for the crowd, which had now turned. Someone fired two shots from a revolver.

I rushed into a building on my right and climbed up a flight of stairs. The commotion soon subsided. Downstairs, I heard voices. Two or three agents, not many. I continued climbing, all the way up to the top floor, and rang a bell.

An old woman opened the door. I told her that I was a student in trouble with the police and would appreciate it if she would give me refuge. She let me in, and I hid temporarily in the laundry room on the top floor, to which the apartment, which she shared with another woman, had access.

The agents arrived a few moments later, but didn't look around. They asked if anyone was hiding there. Other students had also taken refuge in this building, but the majority slipped through the service entrance into the University premises to wait until the police blockade was broken. None of the leaders was arrested, but a number of innocent people in the street were injured.

The two kind ladies gave me lunch. I stayed with them until four o'clock that afternoon. As far as I could see from the window, the gendarmes were still keeping guard at both entrances to Karadži-ćeva Street. We had agreed to meet at the Student Home following the demonstration to make arrangements for further action. Carefully I left the building and took a taxi to the Student Home on King Alexander Street (now the Boulevard of the Revolution). From some distance away I saw that the Home was surrounded by the gendarmes, and a crowd of people. The windows and balconies of the Home were crowded with students. The police had not stopped traffic, and my taxi sailed through. I glanced at the meter, paid the driver, jumped out, and dashed through the gate. Once inside I was safe. The students had recognized me and opened the door. They were excited to see me; they had assumed I'd been arrested.

The subsequent demonstrations at the Student Home were a spontaneous eruption—started by the students who had been dispersed earlier at the organized demonstration. Their arrival at the Home incited the students, who began to demonstrate from the windows and balconies, protesting the arrest of "innocent colleagues" who had held a meeting on the premises of the University (an "autonomous" institution) and then had "peacefully" come out into the street. The demonstrations at the Student Home would have erupted anyway, but, in the normal course of events, not until the next day—election day.

At the Home I rejoined the leadership that had organized the demonstration, and later that evening we held a meeting in the dining room at which each of the speakers took a turn expressing his views. Many of the leaders, myself included, were not residents of the Home, so there was an instant resistance to us by the relatively passive residents. The Home also enjoyed the "autonomy" of the University. However, we quickly organized the defense of the Home against the police, and gained an undisputed supremacy. The majority of the residents were not against the demonstrations, but they urged us to be more moderate: to direct our anger at Petar Živković, not at the King; to ask the Dean to join us for a discussion.

There was no need to invite the Dean. He came anyway, possibly at the instigation of a regime anxious to minimize demonstrations on election day. The Dean was well received by the majority, but he ran into trouble with the demonstration committee. We tried not to promise that we would keep quiet on election day—the most important day to us—but at the same time we didn't want to alienate ourselves from him and thus isolate ourselves from most of the students. For his part, he couldn't even promise the release of our colleagues, because that was not within his power. However, we agreed to await the outcome of his negotiations with the police the following day. Obviously the Dean wasn't altogether opposed to the demonstrations, but he was afraid they would get out of hand and jeopardize the autonomy of the University. The results of our talks were revealed at a meeting in the dining room. Several people made speeches, including me, critical of our weak showing. It was apparent that an organized minority was taking shape and imposing its will on the group. There were a few moderate speakers, but they were quickly silenced. Our skill in public speech-making—passion, invocation of patriotism, responsibility to the people, the duties of the young generation—had a tremendous impact. Certain speakers were able to do anything they wanted to with the crowd. The negotiations with the Dean had become a dead issue. No one said so openly, but it was clear that the committee could not keep the promises it had made. In fact, we were already making preparations for demonstrations the next day.

The meetings were over around eleven o'clock at night. A few guards were left in the empty corridors to keep watch. The "ammunition," consisting of coals, bricks, and chunks of concrete, was piled up in suitable corners, and the guards walked around with metal rods. I was in charge. Naturally I couldn't sleep: I thought I was doing a very important job in providing the security for my colleagues. The Home was silent.

But the armistice didn't last long. Around two in the morning a couple of agents tried to infiltrate the Home by climbing a ladder onto a balcony. A guard spotted them and shouted, and they quickly withdrew. The Home had become a fortress: no one could leave it, and the telephone was closely guarded. It wasn't clear to me whether or not this incident marked the beginning of a general police attack on us. I rushed outside and started banging a pipe against an iron railing in the yard, the agreed-upon signal.

There was something magnificent and fearful in all this, in the deafening noise of the iron rod, the drowsy, half-naked people running in the corridors and onto balconies, yelling like lunatics. This was only a "drill," but everyone worked very hard. There was a lot of good will. However, I realized that twenty gendarmes would have had no trouble taking over the Home once they entered it. The confusion and panic were great. We had great fear of spies. Many were suspected, often with reason, but not always with proof: the father of this young man was So-and-So, this one, on the other hand, was in the King's Guard, that one was seen in such-and-such a place. One fellow was asked to account for a paper that was seen flying out of his room during the demonstration; he had expressed himself against the demonstration. This was the first case where we dealt out justice based on political consideration. He had to justify his ways, humiliate himself. This time the man was released, but he was severely reprimanded. It was clear that the demonstrations would resume the next day. The Home was filled with posters and caricatures, some of them rather indecent: the bare bottom of Petar Živković with a finger pointed at it and the slogan: "Vote here!" Not a single one was directed against the King. The regime was attacked as the "dictatorship of Petar Živković."

From early morning students crowded onto the balconies, shouting slogans and delivering speeches; a space around the Home had been cleared, except for one side of King Aleksandar Street, which was open to pedestrians. Trams, filled to capacity, just barely crawled, and the public filed past us on the sidewalk in vast numbers. From time to time an old man would wave his hat in greeting. Was he reminded of his youth, or was it proof that the spirit of freedom was still alive in the hearts of the new generation? The demonstrations were highly effective on election day itself. But when the elections were over the *raison d'être* was lost and the enthusiasm began to wane. Following enormous mental and physical exertion, everyone was ready for a rest.

With the waning of the fighting spirit, the more moderate elements in the student movement took over. They advocated a resumption of talks with the Dean. There may have been no reason to listen to him earlier, but now his guarantees were essential. The Dean was angry with us, but he showed up nevertheless and told us the police had promised not to touch anyone, but he could not guarantee that the leaders would not be arrested.

On the day following the elections the police cut off the water. This move had been anticipated: we had filled every bowl and bucket in the Home. The food reserves were also plentiful. The Home might have withstood the siege for a long time were it not for the loss of faith. Further resistance seemed senseless. Something had to be done. The same old committee was to meet with the Dean, except for me. It was decided I should not be present at the negotiations to avoid angering the Dean. On the second day after the elections the students gradually began to leave the Home. Some of them had part-time jobs, others did tutoring. Those who left first were immediately arrested, and released a few hours later. They told horror stories of what they had seen in the underground cellars: human beings reduced to skeletons. These accounts reflected the horrors told about Glavnjača prison, or else the audience would have been greatly disappointed. As a rule the students were not beaten, though there was some slapping. Next, the regime loosened up the blockade. On the third day the agents arrested only those they knew. As a matter of fact, the situation had become quite funny: the agents and the students exchanged threats and jokes as if they were in no real conflict. Mirko Banjević approached an agent from the back, covered his eyes, and said: "Guess who it is!"

Banjević was among the most rebellious, and something of an eccentric. An honest man and an unusual poet, he was nevertheless rejected by the Communist youth organization. It is also true that close as he was to the Communists, he didn't join the party until the war, when he became a good fighter, wounded many times. But at the time of the demonstrations, he was an original, somewhat humorous figure, quite capable of staging amusing scenes. He had retained a peasant way of expressing himself—and enjoyed it. He brightened many a day for us with his folksy jokes. At that time the police often accused us of being in the pay of the Italians, a fashionable thing to do, since terrorist activity based in Italy, Hungary, and Bulgaria was fairly widespread. An agent once accused Banjević of receiving Italian money. The accusation was correct, said Banjević, and his overcoat was the best proof. He unbuttoned it and revealed a lining in shreds.

To avoid the police, I made plans to leave the Home. Stefan Mitrović suggested that I go with him to Kotor and stay with his family. At dusk I left. But this romantic and exciting game of hide and seek would not have been complete without a farewell scene with Mitra. She waited for me on a dark street, and I boldly saw her home before leaving for the station. The moment of departure in the dark corridor was warm and touching, but even more pleasing was my realization that her sympathies were with us. Earlier, she had not seemed interested in politics.

I traveled with a false identity card: in the fold of my own student card I slipped someone else's document. My first false document! In spite of the danger, I felt well. I thought of the bluish stony space of the Adriatic.

None of us leftists understood the full significance of the demonstrations. However, the results were soon in evidence. The bourgeois parties had lost control. In the demonstrations they were moderate, and in action they were nowhere to be seen. Ivezić was instructed to cease activity, and he agreed enthusiastically. The rest followed. The sole exception was the Peasant party, particularly the people close to Dragoljub Jovanović. But the most surprising thing of all was that the bourgeois parties had lost all influence on the masses, the raw and unformed masses, rebellious, politically undecided, strongly leftist in outlook. A new generation was growing up under the dictatorship, ready to pounce. The dictatorship had given birth to its own gravedigger.

Following the demonstrations, the left, which is to say the Communist-oriented elements, emerged better organized, with a stronger influence on the student body. The roles seemed to have changed: now we were the ones who called them to action. With a small difference: we were able to organize without them, whereas they had not been able to organize without us. Ivezić and his type suddenly became small and insignificant.

10

The Mitrović family was a typical national product of the Montenegrin coast. Ivo, the father, was a teacher, and a proponent of nationalist ideas through co-operative organizations. The immediate center of their life was Cetinje, the ancient capital of Montenegro, but their ideal was pan-Serbian. At the outbreak of World War I the Austrians executed Ivo's brother, and Ivo himself was sentenced to a long prison term. Emaciated and small, he came out of prison to pick up where he had left off before the war: to look after his family and, since he was appointed superintendent of schools at Kotor, to spread nationalist ideas through education.

His wife, Ivanica, was a heavy good-natured woman, but hard as rock when she had to be. She was one of those rare women with strong character and a natural instinct so powerful that it seems as if the sole purpose of existence is the continuation of the human race. In spite of her size and determination, she obeyed her husband in everything, clashing with him only when it came to protecting her children, particularly in later years when they had many political arguments.

She was wonderful to her mother-in-law, who was then past ninety and sat in the house like a stump in a young forest. Ivanica looked after her as if she were a child, but without that serious and contrived attention which good daughters-in-law accord their mothers-in-law.

The Mitrovići had four sons and two daughters. The eldest son, Niko, was retarded in a curious way. He had occasional flashes of brilliance, even wit. However, there was no rhyme or reason to him: he was constantly tense, quick to quarrel and take offense, unable to concentrate on anything or do anything. He was convinced that the curse of the family was on him. He had no idea what Communism was all about, although he considered himself a Communist, and no one dared trust him with confidential information. Innocent and tragic, he was picked up and executed at Banjica during the war.

The second son, Stefan, was handsome; he had a fine sharp intelligence, but enormous psychological problems. He wrote poetry, and I felt that his writing was not merely an intellectual exercise, but reflected deeper impulses as well. At the beginning his poetry was gloomy. He was in the process of absorbing rationalism with his Marxist education, and his verse was now permeated with contrived explanations of the misery of fishermen and workers. He was a strange mixture of deep inner turmoil and composed action.

Taken as a whole the family showed signs of decay, as if drawing upon some dark force. It often happened in those days that the older children would turn to Communism, and then the younger ones would follow suit. The same was true of Stefan and his younger brothers and sisters, and later on of his mother and father, although the father never admitted it and allegedly was an uncompromising nationalist.

There was romantic, rebellious excess in everything we did at that time. When we went to the Kotor pubs we drank vast quantities of wine with the fishermen and sailors. But we were always careful not to return drunk to the respectable Mitrović home. Of course, the police kept an eye on us, but they never bothered us. They were careful, unless really provoked, not to interfere with respectable homes. The district chief claimed he knew about our participation in the demonstrations. I felt all along that the little town was observing us with curiosity and sympathy—young men in rebellion, in opposition to the dictatorship, seeking to escape persecution.

One day we went to the cemetery, overgrown with cypress trees and damp shadows, to visit the grave of a girl Stefan had been in love with. His love for her may just have been a momentary teenage passion, but because the girl had been consumptive and died it had turned into something sentimentally romantic. This made us recognize the shallow and sinister nature of this love pilgrimage. We were ashamed to admit it, but we never again went to the cemetery. The demonstrations had obviously changed us. We had become fighters. If there was any poetry in us it had to be buried deep down, sparking the inner revolutionary fire but leaving our minds cold and calculating.

We took frequent walks by the sea toward Dobrota with its old homes and mansions, where every inch of land was cultivated. It was an impressive space reflecting hundreds of years of careful human labor, all the more miraculous because it had been snatched from the rocks, as if the earth itself had rushed down to the sea and its vast tranquility. On the way to Dobrota there is a church on an elevated plateau, with stone steps and walls covered with dark green moss. The story has it that when Lord Byron visited Boka he used to spend his evenings there, leaning against that very wall, admiring the sunset. Sunsets in Boka are extraordinary. The sun suddenly disappears, without any glow, as if never to appear again, and somewhere there, in the distance, in the dead darkness, it engulfs the soul. Byron may not have enjoyed these sunsets, but I do believe that he could easily have lost himself, and seemed quite small and human, in this gigantic rocky grotto, pressed in by the skies and throttled by the sea.

Stefan and I were extremely close at that time, closer perhaps than I have been with anyone since. Our friendship had developed quickly—prior to and during the demonstrations. We were drawn to each other by a similar intellectual approach to Communism, although I felt that I was emotionally healthier, more resilient, more of a peasant.

We were unable to organize the Kotor students. The town may have been favorably disposed to us, but still we represented something of a threat. By their refined standards Montenegrins were barbarians who fight well, scream, enjoy vulgar entertainment; they may have power and authority, but they will never be civilized. Some old families had been reduced to one or two women who hadn't left their homes in some twenty years. It was too painful to accept the fact that their own world of seafarers and local aristocrats had been replaced by peasants and civil servants, conquering their markets and mansions, courts and schools, seas and coasts. They had enclosed themselves in the narrow streets of stone, with still narrower steps and rooms, as if enjoying the green mold and the freezing darkness. In Montenegro everything is rock too, but exposed to the sun and the wind, growing into the people, penetrating their blood and bones, while they absorb freshness and sunlight from the open spaces.

The people of Kotor didn't like the dictatorship, but they accepted it as a temporary evil, as they had a Turkish siege or Venetian dominance. They were unwilling to do anything about it, one way or the other, terrified that a change might dislocate them from their stone nests.

The Idealist

Loud, rebellious, outgoing, we may have appealed to them, but they were not willing to follow us. True enough, we were not yet in a position to organize an illegal group, but we hadn't even attracted a circle of sympathizers. In later years too, the Communist organization in Kotor was chiefly in the hands of newcomers.

We had not been accepted even by Adolf Muk, a former worker and a member of the District Committee of the Communist party for Montenegro and Boka at that time. He lived modestly in town and enjoyed considerable respect. At one point he agreed to see us. We tried to extract more information than he was willing to volunteer. And that was the end. He hinted that it might prove embarrassing for us to continue seeing him. We rightly suspected that there was no Communist organization in Kotor—except possibly for Muk and three or four of his friends meeting over black coffee. If Muk hadn't enjoyed the reputation of being a big Communist, I would have thought him a good merchant who would some day become the town's mayor. There certainly was nothing revolutionary about him. Later he emigrated, and was made an important member of the Central Committee. His political career ended in the summer of 1937, when he betrayed his comrades to the Belgrade police in an act of marked human cowardice. But in Kotor in those days he was a mystical figure whose trust we hadn't yet deserved.

11

While we were still in Kotor, Nikola Lopičić suggested that young Montenegrin writers organize a series of literary evenings in Kotor, Cetinje, and Nikšić. This was in the middle of December. The local educational and cultural authorities were receptive to the idea. As cultural events these literary evenings were not particularly significant, but as political events they were very effective, giving legal form to the groups that were permeated with the spirit of the student demonstrations against the Belgrade dictatorship. These groups were more mature than the Belgrade student crowd. But the "young writers" could take no credit for this significant political manifestation, even if their writing was more "rebellious" than was typical of their environment and the older political people who accepted them and helped them to organize.

Of course at Kotor it all went smoothly: the atmosphere was moderate, unenthusiastic. The reading was attended by the police. The Catholic priest, Niko Luković, greeted us in a kindly fashion. This honorable man was an exceptional person—both to his order and to his town.

At Cetinje, however, the atmosphere was very different, and the reception was more than just polite. Everybody important turned up. The local cultural functionaries, led by Vido Latković, the editor-in-chief of *Zapis* (*Notes*), were a little uneasy—they asked the former governor, Džaković, to introduce us.

Džaković was an old man, big and very handsome. In the despotic days of King Nikola he had been persecuted as a leader of the movement favoring freedom and unification with Serbia. After the war he was appointed District Chief of Cetinje. He was adamant in his struggle against the opponents of unification with Serbia, the

Separatists, but not unjust. He opposed the dictatorship. If it had not been for our youth and our Communist sectarianism, we might even have taken some pleasure in Džaković's introductory remarks: he was happy to see that the new generation was following in their ancestors' footsteps in fighting for justice and freedom in our great united country. Some of our colleagues found his words much too nationalistic. I personally felt rather uncomfortable being introduced by a district leader, even if a former one.

But all this was forgotten as soon as we sat down at the dinner organized in our honor and presided over by Vido Latković. Latković was a genuinely cordial man with that capacity—so rare among Montenegrins—to listen to other people's opinions without flatly denying them, on the assumption that even an erroneous opinion may contain a grain of truth. Latković had republican sympathies, which was more unusual than being a Communist, but also less dangerous. In spite of the difference in years and in views, we developed a very warm relationship. I had already contributed to his magazine. This professional co-operation, as well as our friendship, would have developed still further had not the circumstances forced us to part ways—I chose Communism and he chose to adjust himself to existing political conditions.

The literary evening at Cetinje had definite political undertones. The presence of the District Chief with his elaborate bureaucratic machinery, as well as of a large number of civil servants and army officers, contributed to the recognition of the town's divided authority. The town's leading circles boycotted the evening, but the authorities made no attempt to obstruct it, or to censure the reading material.

At Nikšić the situation was again different. The town was in opposition to the regime, although Communist influence was still minor. The opposition leader and editor-in-chief of *Nova misao* (*Free Thought*), Professor Stojan Cerović, was unperturbed by our leftist sympathies and received us wholeheartedly. He favored a gathering together of all antiregime forces.

Strictly speaking, it was his idea to start *Razvršje*, a leftist-oriented magazine with contributions from both Communists and moderate bourgeois elements. The Regional Committee of the Communist party of Yugoslavia approved this collaboration on the pretext that one should take advantage of the bourgeoisie when possible. The magazine was well received. But later on Communists turned against it and boycotted it. Unwelcomed by the regime and with no support from the left, it soon went out of existence.

Politically, Cerović was a member of the Peasant party, but

a man with decidedly democratic views and receptive to other people's ideas. Highly practical, he understood after a while that the bourgeois parties could do little harm to the dictatorship, but why not take advantage of their cultural and economic potential? He was fond of his native land and did his best to help it grow. He worked on the development of the Nikšić brewery, built a hotel on Mount Durmitor with only a small personal loan, and staffed it with students, mostly Communists. When reproached by right-wingers, he had a quick and convincing answer: Communists don't steal.

Tall, heavy, and handsomely dressed, he looked like a wandering bourgeois in this semirural atmosphere. His promotion of capitalist economic forms actually helped along the ideas of Western culture and democracy. With a good-natured if somewhat mischievous smile he would refer to himself as a "bourgeois." In actual fact he was an intellectual with bourgeois democratic views, quick to "adjust" himself for the sake of small practical results. In the period of dogmatic purity and the sharp delineation of ideological fronts, from 1932 on, Communists severed all ties with him; we suddenly saw him as a two-faced bourgeois reactionary. Local Communists, however, remained on good terms with him, because he often used his influence to help them.

Perhaps the best example of his liberalism and tolerance was his visit to me at Ada Ciganlija Prison in Belgrade. He was obviously sorry to see me there and he took ten of my stories with him for publication. Prior to that, he had helped me publish a brochure, *The Case of Dušan Vasiljev*, which was Marxist—anyway, to the extent to which I understood the Marxist idea at the time.

He was the same way with other Communists—in spite of their attacks on him. For him it was all "youthful" passion, for which one must have understanding and patience.

Following the occupation in 1941, he was interned by the Italians as a notorious nationalist and an enemy of the pro-Italian Montenegrin government, but he was released after a few months. In March 1942 I chanced to pass through his village. The staff of the Nikšić Brigade and the District Committee of the Communist party of Yugoslavia were suspicious of him. He was living in semiretirement while we Communists were fighting our fiercest battles with the Chetniks. He heard that I was in the area and asked to see me. I had dinner with him at his home. After a long talk I came to the conclusion that he was an honest if somewhat unstable man, particularly in his approach to treason. But the doubts which I had brought with me from the Committee had vanished. I must admit, though, that I was a little surprised to see him later in a Partisan column. He might have stayed in Chetnik-occupied territory, at no personal risk to himself. But he didn't want to. In this gentle man there was something tough and unbending, as in us Communists. It was a feeling of national honor and pride in his country.

Advanced in years and run down, dressed in civilian clothing, and carrying an umbrella, he looked somewhat pathetic. He died in the spring of 1943, at the peak of the fourth offensive. What had he gone through? After all, he gave up many things, and eventually everything, in joining the Communists, alone, in opposition to his past and his way of life and to many of his friends. For us Communists it was far easier: we had nothing to lose; we were a world to ourselves, with our own ideals.

At Nikšić our literary evening had assumed the form of a political manifestation. But at Podgorica we held no literary evening at all. The authorities were quite hostile to the idea and no "respectable citizen" was willing to stick his neck out for us.

It was here that we plunged into a very lively and active Communist situation for the first time. We received a message from Podgorica that the "comrades" wished to see us. We dropped in on them; Mitrović and Lopičić were asked to go to Cetinje and Kotor, and I was sent home to Bijelo Polje. It was impossible to determine whether the Podgorica group had active organizations going in these towns. They might have had two or three men in each town whom they considered to be members of the local committee. However, the Podgorica group considered themselves members of the Regional Committee because, after a trip to Vienna, Blažo Raičević had allegedly been authorized by the Central Committee to form the leadership. This Committee never concentrated on the systematic development of the organization. It functioned largely through personal connections, relying on people of influence rather than on the organization itself. It published no material, and rarely received any from abroad.

Even so, the existence of the Regional Committee had an impact on Communists who wished to exert political influence in this limited way, through private conversation. The peasant demonstrations in the summer of 1932 were basically spontaneous. Yet they would not have been nearly as effective had it not been for the active role of the Regional Committee. It was no accident that mobs of screaming peasants met the government delegation every step of the way. In Cetinje the situation got completely out of hand, and the delegation left in a great rush—and not via Njeguši, as originally planned, but along the new road to Budva. The story was that the Minister of Construction reminded his colleagues on this occasion of the usefulness of the new road, which they had at one time evidently doubted.

The Regional Committee's financial affairs were disorganized. It was obvious that party and personal finances were mixed up, and that the former existed only inasmuch as they covered the expenses of the individual Committee members. This was especially true of Raičević, whose party expenses were as often personal as not. Raičević was careless with money anyway, and very irregular in paying back loans. He always lived far more comfortably than his income as a schoolteacher would suggest. His friend Dr. Grujo Petrović made financial contributions to the Committee, as did others, mostly former party members, who had ceased to be active in the movement but had continued to support it through Raičević. As a rule Raičević was tough with them: If you are afraid to work for us, the least you can do is give generously.

Dr. Petrović was a fat, good-natured man who liked to live well. It was rather surprising to find him involved in such a dangerous organization of rebels and ascetics. In 1936 he was arrested. His conduct during the interrogation was not exemplary. He was released and soon afterward left for Spain. While in Spain, he was expelled from the party for factionalism, along with Dr. Milan Cetković, also a Montenegrin and a physician. This often happened to predictatorship Communists who were unwilling or unable to grasp the tempo and the discipline imposed by the new, so-called, Tito leadership.

Blažo Raičević suffered a similar fate. To do him justice, the man was a fighter—not merely because he would stand up for his ideas in a café or the street, but because he engaged in illegal action as much as he urged other people to do so. However, he lacked discipline and determination in following the party line. His attitude to women was not impeccable, by the prevailing party standards. But worst of all, he resisted the methodical build-up of party organizations, one of the principal objectives set in 1937. He was, in fact, an individualist, for whom the party organization was chiefly the product of a few influential individuals rather than a firm apparatus which could function without a single gifted individual, even without its leaders. It wasn't until later that I became aware of the negative aspects of Raičević's character. At that time he was an example of revolutionary strength and prowess, of determination and action. Well built and of dark complexion, he impressed one as a man of powerful impulses, strong will, and, above all, as a conspirator. Like many of the Communists of that vintage—those who didn't cease activity under the dictatorship but watched carefully what they were doing—he was always mysterious, suggesting a man who knew much and controlled everything. He emphasized his connections with the Vienna Central Committee and his party position. But in spite of the mystery with which he had surrounded himself, he could be open, and that characteristic was extraordinarily appealing.

Raičević approached us directly: we were young Communists, not organized yet, but for that very reason most useful. He was not bothered by our ideological immaturity—he was not a very well-formed Marxist himself. He was narrow and sectarian, and termed all kinds of things "bourgeois," but he was not nearly as exclusive as the party directives. He approved of the student demonstrations in spite of their political confusion. The attitude of the Central Committee, on the other hand, was condescending: "A manifestation of the discontented bourgeoisie." In 1932 he made two trips to Belgrade, allegedly for reasons of health. He met with various Communists, sat in cafés discussing politics, read some Central Committee or Comintern literature, and returned to Montenegro to tell his men to wait for possible future action. But even this kind of activity represented a sign of life for a persecuted political organization. During a time of heavy police pressures, he spread faith in the strength of the party, partly by making a lot of noise, but also partly through his directness and courage. He played no immediate role in our decision to form a party organization at the University, but he gave us encouragement. For us Montenegrin leftists, he was the first contact with the party organization, even if we overestimated him as a Communist and the strength of the existing Communist party. The party had as yet to be formed, and he was not capable of performing this service. It was up to the younger generation to do so.

In the post-1937 internal struggles, he was included in the purge as an "unhealthy," "factional," "antiparty" element. He spent the war years in enemy prisons and camps—apparently the enemy had a somewhat broader view regarding the definition of Communism and Communists. After the war Sreten Žujović, the Minister of Finance, gave him a government position, but he made a real mess of things. I heard about his fate again in 1948: like most of the men who had in the past disagreed with Tito's Central Committee, he had joined the Soviet campaign against Yugoslavia. In 1950 Ranković told me that Raičević had been lynched in the concentration camp at Goli Otok by a mob of prisoners who had "repented." I must admit that none of us leaders felt sorry for him. True enough, Ranković issued orders that a detailed report be submitted in order to exonerate the role of his own people. There was a feeling of relief that Raičević had met his end in a way which absolved us of "guilt" and excused us from any further concern for him. I thought that way myself.

12

I was always received warmly when I went home to Montenegro on vacation. I already had a reputation as a young writer, but my role in the demonstrations certainly contributed to my popularity. It was rumored that I was a Communist, which the townspeople didn't find particularly appealing. But they chose to interpret this as a youthful protest against the dictatorship rather than a true expression of the spirit of the new generation.

Borislav Kovačević joined me at Bijelo Polje and was a guest in my parents' home. We spent some three weeks together in continuous conversation. Generally we were in an intellectual turmoil. If one is to participate in the political struggle, abandoning "universal" positions is inevitable. We were confronted with an enemy who had little that could be defined as human, let alone universal. From our brief contact with the Communists, we had gotten a taste of class theory, but we tended to confine this theory to the struggle to improve the lot of the poor. The proletariat was a class we neither knew nor clearly understood. We had a romantic notion that each worker was a ready-made fighter, and we knew nothing at all about Marxism. As a matter of fact, it was through practice that our interest in social theory was stimulated.

Had it not been for Bora's presence, Bijelo Polje would have been dull for me. Sunk in mud and boredom, entire families were crowded in one room, around tin stoves, or in the kitchen by the fireplace.

But it wasn't all dull.

Večeslav Vilder, a leader of the Independent Democratic party and the closest associate of Svetozar Pribićević, had been exiled to Bijelo Polje, which was at that time synonymous with the end of the world. He had been there since 1930. Whenever I saw him I greeted him politely, even though we didn't know each other. On my part it was a gesture of defiance as well as of compassion for a lonely man with whom no one dared associate and whose every step was controlled by the police. His sole contact was the town pharmacist, a Serb. Actually, it was rumored that the police had a hand in arranging this. Vilder spent a great deal of his time taking walks. In fact, a spring was later named after him. Vilder's Water, the townspeople called it, in memory of an exile.

He lived alone, in a small room in one of the better homes belonging to people who were on good terms with the authorities. Compared to the hardships of prison life, Vilder's exile was probably more difficult. A Croat (Czech by origin), who joined the Serbian party (for Serbs in Croatia), he must have felt uprooted in this backward and strange environment. Surrounded by so many people who avoided him like poison, he must have felt the full horror of isolation. His way of life—food, accommodation, movement —was more comfortable than in prison, but not his social life. It's preferable to be in prison—in lively, continuous contact with friends.

In the summer of 1931, Radovan Zogović unexpectedly visited me. I hadn't seen him since our last year in school, when we just barely knew each other. Covered with dust and sweat, dressed lightly, he emerged from the dark displaying sudden friendship and intimacy. It turned out our mothers were cousins, and my mother received him as one would a close relative. To get away from the fleas, I had moved from the main house to the attic in the barn. That's where I took my guest. We spent the night talking, mostly about literature and politics.

The night was clear and dewy. We reached a great understanding of each other, which is not at all unusual among young people who find that they think the same way. Zogović was well ahead of me in his knowledge of Communism and the so-called "socialist" literature, which I never really accepted, although I tolerated it for political and ideological reasons. Zogović's sudden arrival made me think that he was on some secret mission, but his genuine involvement with literature, his modesty and discretion quickly dispelled that feeling. He left the following morning and we didn't see each other until I came back from prison in 1936.

Zogović later told me that the real reason behind his "literary" visit was the organization of Vilder's escape from Bijelo Polje on instructions from the Zagreb opposition circles. Štedimlija Savić Marković, a journalist, who knew Zogović through literary contacts, had engaged him. From Zogović's story it was hard to tell how serious Savić Marković had been about organizing Vilder's escape, or to what extent he was simply fooling the Zagreb politicians and taking their money. He was in contact with the Belgrade police, which did not preclude his involvement on several other sides, including the organization of this escape. Needless to say, the escape amounted to nothing. Savić Marković spread the news that the authorities had gotten word of the plan, and he disappeared.

I talked to Vilder on only one occasion: in a small room in back of the pharmacist's shop; it was in the winter of 1932. Vilder was not a man to listen calmly and unemotionally. He kept nervously asking questions. He probably knew who I was. By that time I was widely known as a leftist. He was very enthusiastic about the student demonstrations. He gave no pretentious advice. He understood that our views were different, but he wasn't hard on me. As a matter of fact, I thought him much too far to the left for a bourgeois. He asked me if I would mail a letter for him from Belgrade. It was addressed to a woman in Prague. The Independent party and Pribićević had good contacts with Czech Socialists and Beneš; in fact Pribićević was free at that point and in Czechoslovakia. But since I was under suspicion, I mailed the letter from Plevlje to Mitra, and Mitra sent it on.

Soon after this, Vilder was freed. Later he was the editor of *Nova riječ* (*New Word*), a Zagreb publication, to which Communists also contributed. He favored the idea of a popular front with Communist participation. But following the Soviet-German Pact in 1939, he parted company with the Communists, attacking them sharply. Just before the war broke out he left for England, and never came back.

When I was in London in 1951 Vilder asked to see me. He was a political exile and I was a minister in Tito's government. I decided, without consulting Belgrade, not to meet with him. Any expression of his "sympathy" or offer of "help" was pointless. Besides, I wanted to avoid any repercussions of a seeming willingness to establish contact with the exiled politicians. Did the former Bijelo Polje exile want simply to talk of old days? I would have been ashamed personally, and before my comrades, if I had indulged myself in reminiscences with "such a man," reminiscences which would have brought me more shame than pleasure. But somehow I don't think he remembered me as a youth. A stranger in his country and in his party, defeated in politics, feuding with political friends in exile, what could he have wanted from me without offering repentance?

13

In the three months that I had been away from Belgrade, the situation at the University had changed. The unstable leftist groups had grown stronger and better organized, and had been formed into Marxist circles. The official Communist party could in no way be credited with this development, even though the party did have its representatives in Belgrade, very respectable people at that.

Rajko Jovanović was one of them. He was the leader of the party's so-called "left wing" until 1928. He was passive as far as illegal work went, as was his friend Dr. Labud Kusovac, yet both men kept in touch with the leftist students. Their contact was Jovan Marinović, a law student. Kusovac was inert, distrustful, and, I suspect, a little scared, although perhaps not as scared as Jovanović. The information Marinović passed on to us was sectarian and shrouded in mystery. He was playing a role rather than establishing the actual "contact" with the party. It was not Marinović's fault. He was young and inexperienced, and behind him stood Kusovac, who was confused and overly cautious. The party contact which we sought was first established with Raičević. He never concealed the fact that he was a "contact," a member of the party forum. The only way of getting in touch with the party in Belgrade was through individuals who were politically active and, as such, pronounced reliable by the Central Committee in exile. The Committee kept in touch with them through correspondence and occasional messengers. There was no organization that worked with the masses.

Kusovac's caution was not the only reason the party representatives showed little interest in the Belgrade student movement, the only organization openly opposed to the dictatorship. It was largely a result of the political leadership's condescending attitude to this movement and to the intelligentsia, particularly the young intelligentsia. While the demonstrations were in progress, Petko Miletić, a member of the Central Committee, was in Belgrade illegally. He stood by on the sidewalk and watched us. Later on, in jail, I asked him what he had thought of the demonstrations and why he hadn't given us a helping hand. "What would we proletarians do with the petit bourgeoisie?" he asked. The demonstrations had no clear "revolutionary" character, their slogans were only "democratic," consequently these acts were a momentary explosion of the "bourgeois intelligentsia." To make matters worse, I accepted this view when I became a Communist. I attached greater significance to the demonstration slogans than to their objective meaning: they were not aimed against the King and the bourgeoisie; they were not for the revolution as the only means of overthrowing the dictatorship. They merely sought to achieve unity in a struggle against that dictatorship.

Be that as it may, the impact of the demonstrations was enormous. They gave birth to the postdictatorship Communist organizations, with new and different people. They served as the basis for a broad student movement which grew up under Communist influence. The leaders of the demonstrations instinctively recognized the student potential and determined the organizational forms and slogans.

The official party leadership failed to recognize the importance of the demonstrations. But Dr. Sima Marković, the leader of the onetime legal party, and later chief of the "rightist" faction of the party, did. A familiar figure from the days when the Communist party of Yugoslavia had over fifty deputies in the Parliament (the 1919 elections), he was the best-known Communist leader in the country. Marković was not burdened by the dogmatism of exile politics; he had already been expelled from the party because of his factionalism, so he was under no obligation to accept orders from the Central Committee. In continuous contact with the political life in the country, he understood the significance of the demonstrations and contacted the students in the hope of exerting an influence on the course of future events. Unlike the party leadership, he didn't pile all other parties and politicians indiscriminately in the same old "bourgeois" heap. Yet he was never a real revolutionary. He was an offshoot of the earlier Serbian socialist democracy, and at best he represented its left wing. He never managed to become a

Communist in the Leninist-Stalinist sense. His continued contact with the citizens' democratic parties was for him not merely a question of tactics, which it always was for the Communists, but, rather, something more profound and meaningful, a recognition of their right to their opinion and the expression of that opinion, of their right to political activity. Sima Marković represented Serbian socialism in Serbia, which had a special character.

I returned to Belgrade in March 1932 and found my colleagues organized in groups, absorbing ideology from Marxist pamphlets. They were now sober, coldly analytical, and unsparing in their criticism of "bourgeois remnants," ready to demolish the demonstrations because they were ideologically "unclear" and politically "inconsistent." I felt ashamed because I had "fled" from the police and stayed away so long. It was a feeling of shame I had often felt in life; I had "slipped away" from a complex situation, which went unnoticed by everyone except me. I made up my mind to join one of the circles at once. But on the third day after my arrival I was arrested. However, due to some fluke, this arrest had no grave consequences.

Radovan Vuković and Vidak Marković had brought to the flat I shared with Kovačević a bunch of Communist leaflets and placed them among our books. Since the demonstrations the police eyed me with suspicion, and I objected to such imprudence on their part. Also, they belonged to the Marković group, and I was reluctant to get involved. In the early hours of the morning the police raided the flat and whisked us away in a little Black Maria. We were arraigned at the headquarters of the General Police and moved to Glavnjača, the old prison, room No. 6.

Room No. 6 was notorious. It had always been used for political prisoners, ranging from radicals during the reign of King Milan Obrenović to Georgi Dimitrov, Secretary of the Comintern. Like the rest of the rooms at Glavnjača, No. 6 was in the cellar; it had a small window overlooking the corridor providing a little direct light, a cement floor, and wooden boards for beds. There was no toilet; a tin bucket was provided. An acrid smell dominated in spite of careful airing and floor washing each morning.

In addition to a couple of criminals, there were three other political prisoners in the room: a Belgrade lawyer, a member of the Davidović party; a civil servant, of the same party; and a Rumanian, an army deserter.

The lawyer was not unpleasant to us, but offended us by his ugly and insulting manner with the civil servant. He had a mattress, sheets, and an eiderdown, and received food from a restaurant. The rest of us used plain wooden boards for beds and received two pounds of bread a day. Two pounds of bread a day plus supplies from the family was the system that prevailed in prisons throughout Serbia. But additional supplies were not allowed until the interrogation period was over.

The civil servant was poor, and he looked it. No one brought him food. The lawyer shared his supplies with him, in exchange for which this wretched creature cleaned the room and emptied his bucket. The relationship between the two men was one of master and slave, in which the master is accorded flattery and attention and the servant generosity and mercy.

Since sunlight never reached this room we quickly grew pale, drained by the stale smells. We went out into the yard twice a day for fifteen minutes, washed up at the fountain, and walked in a circle. The criminals were constantly being beaten, the blows, cries, and curses echoing in empty corridors. Apart from this, the prison wasn't bad.

The differences of opinion between us and the lawyer were immediately evident. Although allegedly against the dictatorship, he was also against "all forms of anarchy," which meant, in our terms, he was against all illegal action. Since no legal action was plausible, how did he propose to overthrow the dictatorship? It was obvious that he accepted it in practice. But why was he in prison? We soon found out. A few days after our own arrest, two other lawyers were brought to room No. 6, Čeda Plećević and a friend of his whose name I don't recall. They had been arrested because they tried to organize meetings among the peasants.

From Plećević's discussions with the lawyer we gathered that the latter was an unmitigated royalist, that he stood in opposition to any mass movement, and that he believed politics to be the privilege of a narrow circle of intellectuals. The dictatorship, however, had to be blackmailed, threatened. He had great hope in England and France, which would cause the dictatorship to fall by refusing all moral and economic support. I found this fat, expressionless man repulsive now. I understood the full ugliness of his relationship with the man who picked up the miserable crumbs from his table and emptied political buckets of filth after him.

Plećević had been a Communist, but had developed major differences with the organization and left: he believed that the party had grown too self-centered, too conspiratorial, and that it was merely "sending men to jail." He was not ideologically opposed to Communism and socialism, but he believed that our duty was to attract peasants, develop into a mass movement, and make a serious attempt to unite all opponents of the dictatorship into a single political front. His concept of a united front was similar to the one put forward by the Communists in the years after 1935. But major differences continued to exist between the Communists and Plećević even after 1935. Basically, he was against any use of force; thus the organization he proposed, and partly set up, did not resemble in any way the centralized and strictly disciplined Communist party we were after. Yet he assessed the evolution of opposition parties correctly. While openly criticizing the political leadership for its passivity and opportunism, he wanted all political activity channeled in the direction of a more democratic and a more active mass movement. His strategy had another drawback as well: it was exclusively Serbian in character. Within this limited framework, however, it expressed something of Serbia's heart and soul. Plećević was from Šumadija, the heart of Serbia, and he believed in the boundless resources of the earth that had given birth to the leaders of great uprisings and rebellions. Dissidents from other parties joined him. But the movement gradually faded away; war was in sight and conditions were ripe for a more decisive battle.

We Communists never really trusted him, even though he joined forces with us in 1941. Had he not, after all, abandoned us once before? His negotiations with the Chetniks at the start of the uprising rendered him particularly vulnerable. This large man, independent and tolerant in his opinions, thus became politically isolated and physically run down. At the end of 1941 he withdrew with the Partisans to Nova Varoš. He could not sit on party committees, and he was not physically fit for the army. He asked me if he could go into the villages and propagandize for the Partisan movement. We agreed to let him go ahead. In 1942 he crossed from Bosnia into Serbia, was caught by the Chetniks, and shot. We wrote about him for a while, but as the Communist need for a wide political front diminished, so did the need for his memory.

The Rumanian was illiterate, but very bright. He had made the rounds of numerous international prisons. He had no passport, so each country would hold him a while and then ship him secretly across the border. In no other country—that goes for Austria, Hungary, and Bulgaria—was he beaten. But he was in Serbia, hard and for a long time, because they believed him to be a Hungarian spy. He took prison routine well, and had they fed him a little better he wouldn't have been too upset about having spent well over a year in these various Balkan prisons. His life in the village wasn't much of an improvement on this. In the Balkan prisons he met men of all political shades and opinions, but anarchists appealed to him most. He carefully listened to our critical commentary on various countries and regimes, and at one point stated that upon his release from prison he would go to Europe—to Bulgaria, because food in their prisons was good.

We had no idea why we had been arrested. Uncertainty is hard to take under any circumstances, but especially in prison. Once a man is in conflict with a regime that allows for no freedom, he has a lot of sins.

After eight days we were taken to the police headquarters, which usually meant extensive interrogation. The elevator stopped on the third floor, and we walked into a spacious room. It was about 10:00 A.M. We waited for a whole hour. Then I was ushered into the adjoining office, a nicely furnished room. Behind the desk a stocky well-dressed man was seated. When he rose he didn't look much taller than when he was sitting. His arms were short, his fingers stubby and soft. In fact there was something soft and damp about his whole personality. It was Milan Aćimović, the Chief of the General Police, and chief administrator of the city of Belgrade and Minister of Interior. At that time the city administration carried more weight than the Ministry of Interior, and could investigate political crimes in the whole country. Aćimović was notorious among Communists, as well as among opposition groups. The beginning of his career was marked by a struggle against Communism, following the ban on the Communist party in 1920. After the dictatorship he resumed his job, except that they introduced new methods and we extended our activities.

Throughout the interview he kept twisting a sharp yellow pencil. He told me that he had heard about my writing and that he knew I had taken part in the demonstrations. Still he couldn't take the accusation against me for granted, which was organizing the assassination of a very high official (I believe he had Petar Živković in mind). I was enormously relieved, perhaps too transparently relieved, because I was altogether innocent on this count. It's true that every young man, myself included, entertained thoughts of assassination as the most "efficient" solution. Now and then we even joked about it. But we all understood that the whole system had to go and not just one person, and that was why we were Communists. So I wasn't in the least disturbed by Aćimović's accusation. I began explaining my position, but he interrupted me to say that my arrest had been made on the basis of a report received from out of town, and that the provincial police were sometimes more alert than the occasion demanded. (I recalled my clandestine meeting with Vilder at Bijelo Polje.) However, Aćimović said he felt differently and had decided to let me go. He advised me not to join any illegal organization or undertake any illegal work, or I would get into serious trouble. I could no longer count on the same civilized treatment accorded me on this occasion. He also said he was aware that Communists were not exactly receiving kid-glove treatment, but that the Communists would probably be worse if ever they were to gain power. He was no phony. One of his assistants asked us for a few more particulars and we were released.

It was a warm sunny day in early spring. The snow was melting. It was good to be with friends again. And with Mitra. My stride was unfamiliar, long, as if I were going to take off any minute.

For the next three weeks we were cautious, and then I considered joining a political circle. But something unpleasant happened.

In the spring of 1932 Blažo Raičević arrived and asked us whether we had any contact with the party. We proudly told him we had. But Kusovac told him that we didn't. So our contact must be a fraud. We arranged for him to meet our contact without disclosing his identity: it was Bora Mihailović, an engineer by profession, a fair-haired young man, intelligent and unassuming. Raičević was crude: he set his eyes on Mihailović and burst into laughter— Mihailović belonged to the Sima Marković group, a fact everyone was familiar with except for us young students. Raičević never insisted that the contact with Sima Marković be severed, at least not until he had secured another one. Which he never did. However, our relationship with Mihailović was considerably damaged by the experience and I never joined the circle.

We knew very little about Sima Marković. Some of us had no idea that he had been expelled from the party. Nor did we have a clear picture of what a faction was. For us he was a well-known Communist, and that was that. But the minute we learned that he was in conflict with the Central Committee we became critical of him. If we were to be Communists we had to go about it the right way, and that meant contact with the Central Committee and with Moscow. All the same, we continued to read the brochures of Sima Marković as well as of his opponent Rajko Jovanović. In a second-hand bookshop we even found the transcript of the Constitutional Assembly of 1919–1920, which included the speeches of the Communist deputies. We still hadn't grasped the essence of the conflict between Sima Marković and the "left wing"; even so, we were unwilling to maintain our contact with him. The circles continued to operate, but the link with the Marković people had been weakened and was finally severed.

Apart from any party influence and independent of the Marković group, we approached groups at the University of Zagreb. The contact was made through legal student bodies, but was nevertheless political in character. The struggle for influence and the restoration of the student union began as early as the spring of 1932, giving the movement a constructive popular character which it might not have had at all had it been reduced to student demonstrations alone. In fact there would have been no movement, but merely sporadic explosions of discontent. Now, the sudden outpouring of anger and discontent was channeled into a systematic and constructive opposition activity. Hundreds of young people were engaged in action. Thousands of nonparty agitators put together a tremendous organization, which the police could no longer control, and still less destroy.

Through his representative at the University, Sima Marković stabilized his groups and introduced a systematic study of the Marxist literature. But the practical activity continued to be in the hands of the group formed during the demonstrations. During the summer our contact with the Marković group ceased altogether. With the beginning of the new school year the question of establishing contact with the official Communist party was seriously considered.

I spent my summer vacation at Bijelo Polje. The young people's group, mostly Moslems attending a religious junior high school, assumed organized character, although it could not have been defined as a Communist youth organization for two reasons: it never engaged in action, and it had no contact with the party forums. But our way of thinking was now different: we no longer drank; in fact, we threatened all those who did drink with expulsion. We held group readings of Marxist books and followed magazines concerned with social issues, which was not far removed from organized activity. Later these people carried the spirit of the thing and the form with them to their Skoplje school, and since many of them entered the University in 1934, they became members of the Communist youth organization, and eventually party members.

The most prominent among them was Rifat Burdžović. In contrast to other students, he was poverty-stricken. He had come to the city to survive. He never referred to his family, as if he were ashamed of their poverty, although he loved his mother and sister.

He was a gentle and honorable young man who looked as if he couldn't hurt a fly. Later on in life, as a party member, he grew aggressive and sharp, both with the enemy and regarding discipline within the party. Had he not been a Communist he might have been mistaken for a hermit, always ready to sacrifice himself on the altar of his faith. But he never lost a certain tenderness with people that almost verged on sentimentality. He loved life, in a limited, or, shall I say, poverty-burdened, way. He was modest to a fault: I recall his surprise when I suggested in 1938 that he take over the duties of secretary of the University organization, and still more so later, in 1940, when Ranković and I brought him into the local Belgrade Committee. Courageous and zealous in the execution of his duties, he was brutally murdered by the Chetniks in Bosnia after putting up a fierce fight. At the time of his death he was Secretary of the party organization in the Sandžak Brigade, too insignificant a position for him, but then, our army was too insignificant in numbers to make proper use of so many able people.

Jusuf Medjedović, another Bijelo Polje Moslem, was not nearly as aggressive or politically talented, but he was equally charming and good-natured. Tall, slender, and dark, he looked more like a Montenegrin than a Moslem. He was desperately in love with a Montenegrin girl, a warm-blooded beauty who felt an urge to promise everything and offer little. Her parents couldn't conceive that their daughter, a Serb, would marry this "Turk." Eventually he did marry her. But the many years of his painful and hopeless love for this girl seemed to have slowed him down ideologically and politically. Also, he wrote poetry and acted. After the war, as a Partisan Major, he had no trouble in becoming a member of the Belgrade National Theatre, but once his rank ceased to carry weight he had to give it up. He felt unhappy and rejected, a victim of intrigue and reactionary hatred, and decided to rejoin the army. In search of his artistic identity, he had lost sight of himself as a politician. But he had been an honest and dedicated revolutionary.

Šukrija Medjedović, also a member of this circle, was a Slavic Moslem with not one drop of Asian blood. His complexion was white and pink, his nose thin and gently bent, his forehead broad, and his eyes shady, not an uncommon physical type among the Moslems in Bosnia, and the cleanest and handsomest in the country. Šukrija was a fighter above all. Rifat gave the leftist youth movement of Bijelo Polje a lot that was sensible, and Šukrija gave a lot that was exciting. He lost his life in July 1941, in a battle with the Moslems of Pešter, as if to erase with his young blood the accusation that we were the tools of the "Turks," and that we were giving them support.

Of course there were many more young men and women in the left-wing movement. But I concentrated on the most prominent among them, those who had made up their minds to change the world to its very foundations.

At the end of the summer I left for Podgorica, where I met with leftist students and the Communist leaders. Suddenly I was aware of certain negative qualities in Raičević and other Communist leaders: empty boasting and showing off in front of the authorities, the typical characteristics of "Montenegrin Communism." But how do I explain my "critical ability" at this time? I believe it was more the realization that all was not ideal in the Communist movement than something new I had learned from Marxist theory.

By this time my older brother had been married for a year, and he lived and worked at Slijepač Most, in the same building from which the Chetniks were to take him away and shoot him nine years later, in the autumn of 1941. His one-year-old marriage was not a happy one. Preoccupied with his personal problems, he was outside of our circle in Bijelo Polje, and to some extent a stranger to me. But when he did pause to reflect on the political situation, his reactions were bitter, sharpened perhaps by his unhappy personal life. Subsequent events, my arrest, the loss of his job, and police persecution intensified this bitterness to such an extent that the personal aspect got lost in it altogether. The pensive glow in his dark eyes, his emaciated look and cynical smile reflected a future fighter who didn't know fear or hesitation, who never asked for mercy and never gave it, the type of person that was essential to help begin a new era.

14

The years 1930 to 1932 were as confusing politically and ideologically for me as they were productive in my career as a writer.

The dictatorship had introduced censorship, which had little impact on literary life except for works with predominantly Communist ideas. As a matter of fact my early works contained no opposition material, but the mere existence of censorship bothered me. The feeling grew clearer as I began to assimilate Communist ideas: a writer in political discord with the regime had to keep censorship in mind at all times, and censor his works in the process of creative thinking. This kind of self-censorship was the most humiliating.

By and large the censors were intelligent and well-read people. Later I discovered that some of them made editorial changes as well, and with good reason. Occasionally one could get away with things, but usually one's good fortune was the result of some political stratagem.

My literary work at that time ranged between the treatment of general human problems and social problems. I was first published in *Venac* (*Wreath*), a stereotyped magazine, whose sole redeeming feature was that it gave young people a chance while maintaining a reasonable level of literacy.

I had met Jeremija Živanović, the editor of *Venac*, several times during my first year at the University. I didn't like him—primarily because our views on literature were different. More specifically, it had never occurred to me that literature should be didactic in character, still less didactically patriotic. He was passionate only when the talk turned to Macedonia—or Southern Serbia, as it was officially known at that time. This was not just a reflection of his views, but, rather, of several generations of Serbian intellectuals who had invested all their energies in the effort to acquire this territory for Serbia. It was as if, outside of this idea, he had no other passion, even though he was an editor and a literary critic of a sort.

He was kind to young writers, but he didn't allow them to express their thoughts freely, so preoccupied was he with his nationalism, and his rational and utilitarian demands on literature. He truly believed in Serbia's mission in the south; Macedonians were Serbs, and the medieval monasteries and folk customs there were foundations of Serbian culture. So fanatical and unequivocal was he in this belief that he was capable of sacrificing many Serbian values simply in order to keep Macedonia under Serbia's domination. Freedom and humanitarianism were merely tools to help promote his Macedonian idea. In principle he was against crude police methods, and believed that Southern Serbia should be approached culturally, but if that failed, sword and fire would be enormously effective. My subsequent intellectual development and political thinking made any co-operation with him impossible. Eventually Živanović gave up literature altogether, and as Governor of the Vardar Banat he was determined to carry out his nationalist ideas; in the process of forcing a nation to think and speak in terms of the Serbian national goal, he forgot all that was human and freedom-loving.

The major break in my literary career occurred when I began to contribute to the literary magazine *Misao* (*Thought*). For a beginner it was most important to make contact with a respectable magazine, and *Misao* enjoyed that reputation, second only to *Srpski književni glasnik* (*The Serbian Literary News*). By and large *Misao* was conservative, but its standards were high and the quality of its published works above average. My first contribution came out in 1931 or 1932, if I remember correctly, a poem entitled *"Mladić zvižduće nalaženje samog sebe"* ("A Young Man Whistles with Joy at Having Found Himself"). Years later, in jail, my comrades teased me about the poem, which reflected my surrealistic tendencies.

The publication of this poem in *Misao* got me off to an excellent start, and I was published in all the literary magazines except *Srpski književni glasnik*, whose editor, Milan Bogdanović, did not fancy my writing. Around this time *Politika* started publishing my stories and paid me very well. They were predominantly folkloristic in character.

It has never been clear to what extent Živojinović, the editor of *Misao*, was responsible for the publication of my works. After my first poem appeared, Živojinović praised me highly, and I don't doubt that he was instrumental in determining what writings were to be published. But Smilja Djaković, the owner of the magazine, did exert some influence on him, and she always liked my writing. Živojinović was not a communicative person and it was not easy to learn what was on his mind. A man of culture and intellectually solid, he was basically uninspired. He came to the office only to receive contributors; the bulk of the "dirty work" was done by the owner.

There are people who give themselves unselfishly to an idea although fully aware that it will bring them no personal gain. Smilja Djaković was one of them.

The first impression one got of this woman was downright unpleasant. She was unattractive, hairy, with bulging eyes behind thick glasses and a greedy nervous smile which was not helped by her clawlike hands and tobacco-stained fingers. However, as one got to know her this impression was quickly erased, and her head, with its short-cropped gray hair, and her pleasant posture struck one as thoughtful, even youthful, and her words reflected an old-fashioned wisdom and humanity.

She had inherited some money and decided to spend it on something cultural. That got *Misao* started. The inheritance couldn't have amounted to much, because she slaved in her little office on Knez Mihailova Street from morning till night taking care of the administrative end of the operation, and some of the editorial duties too. The magazine didn't develop as well as had been hoped, and eventually it folded. That was the end of her inheritance. She was left with a small furnished apartment, where she spent the rest of her days, at peace with herself because she knew she had done her duty as a human being.

After my release from prison I called on her several times. She received me nicely, but she regretted that I had substituted politics for literature. After the war she called on me at the Central Committee to ask for my intervention in some matter relating to her apartment, or something to that effect. I sensed that, in spite of my cordiality, she was uncomfortable because I had risen so high, and still more because she had asked me a favor. But after she had relaxed a little, she reproached us Communists for having entered Belgrade as avengers, killing too much and too ruthlessly, rather than as liberators. Her nationalist feelings were deep and genuine, so I chose to interpret her reaction in terms of super-Serbian chauvinism. There was some of that, of course: she insisted we had been more lenient with Zagreb than with Belgrade. But there was also genuine consternation at the deterioration of the human condition. Obviously I was unable to understand her point. I was carried away with our victory and the hopes that it engendered. When she died I did not hear about it. I learned of it years later. I was never a friend to her, but she certainly was to me.

In the spring of 1932, at the *Misao* offices, I met Desanka Maksimović, the well-known Serbian poetess. She was in the company of Jelena Skerlić-Ćorović, the sister of Jovan Skerlić and the wife of Vladimir Ćorović, a university professor and a well-known historian. It was during his tenure as rector of Belgrade University that the most violent demonstrations in the history of the University took place, as a reaction to the crude methods with which he implemented regime policies. He was the first rector to allow the police to enter the University.

His wife, Jelena, was tall and handsome, her eyes bright, her cheekbones high. Desanka Maksimović was pleasant-looking; there was something charming in her broad smile, in spite of her somewhat masculine movement and speech, which in turn were in complete contrast to her innocent and sentimental lyrics. Her poetry had never appealed to me, but I have always respected her as genuinely inspired, particularly in an environment that produced so few female poets.

The two ladies were on their way to take a walk at Kalemegdan, and they asked me to join them. Mrs. Ćorović seemed just barely aware of my presence, whereas Desanka Maksimović treated me with the kindness and ease of an old friend and equal. It was snowing, a thin vicious spring snow. Mrs. Ćorović took photographs of us.

I never again met Mrs. Ćorović, but her mature hard beauty remained in my memory. I saw Desanka Maksimović a couple of times again in the prewar years, and we became friends. After the war she called on me often, particularly after the conflict with the Russians in 1948. She was greatly disturbed by it, because she was brought up on Russian literature and intoxicated by the sentimentality of the Russian soul. She suspected that the Secret Police were after her; perhaps she was right, although they never admitted it to me. She might have been under suspicion because of her friendship with Radovan Zogović. He, in turn, was in conflict with the Central Committee for opposing the "sharpening" of relations with the Soviet Union. As a matter of fact she did ask me whether it was safe for her to continue visiting Zogović. I told her it was, although I am positive that this courageous woman would have continued visiting him anyway. She also called on me many times after I had been removed from power, although my views were in complete contrast with Zogović's. There was a strange duality there. Indeed, she liked the Russians; she was even able to see a certain depth of soul in Russia's contemporary leaders. But she also loved freedom, and she loved to be helpful to people in trouble. Desanka Maksimović did this at a time when my friends had stopped greeting me in the street. That goes for my old party friends as well as for those intellectuals who had joined the party to enjoy a more comfortable life, all those for whom I did favors, believing that I owed it to them as a friend, not as a man in power. It turned out that this warm, gentle, lyrical woman was the most courageous and the most humane among my friends, and with no political or material gain in mind either. I should like it known that there was one woman at that time, one person, who had not lost civic courage and human dignity.

With my gradual acceptance of Communism I found myself alienated from the magazines for which I had been writing. A pattern had developed at that time (one exception was Zogović): when one accepted Communism one gave up literature. The new ideas, and even more the practical demands of the movement, made a claim on a man's physical and spiritual energies, and thereby erased all poetic passion and any other feeling that might stand in the way of the immediate revolutionary objectives. Yet there is another way of considering this fact: with virtually no exceptions the writers who were attracted to the Communist party were without real talent, quick to lend themselves to the simplified, utilitarian objectives of art, as represented by the post-Lenin Communist ideology, and, before him, by the German Social Democrats.

While seeking out Marxist literature, in the autumn of 1931, we came across Jovan Popović, the editor of *Stožer* (*The Pole*), the most prominent exponent in Belgrade of the so-called "social" literature. Jovan Popović made no significant impression on me. I never contributed to *Stožer*, nor did I identify with the magazine's views. I realized that Jovan Popović had no use for my writing, if indeed he was familiar with it. He had a limited circle of contributors, mostly people who didn't write for "bourgeois" magazines. He felt very strongly about this. By the time I had stopped publishing my stuff in the respectable magazines, *Stožer* had gone out of existence.

At first Popović's intellectual consistency, and more so the significant advancement of his views of literature and society, was impressive. But an exaggerated intellectuality and dryness marked all his thinking. His views and style of writing were borrowed from the German Communist movement and were irrelevant in an environment full of impulse and passion. The magazine's impact on art was nonexistent. Even so, in the formation of the Communist ideology the contribution of magazines such as *Stožer* cannot be exaggerated. I would even go so far as to say that it was incomparably greater than all the illegal party literature put together.

Stožer was, in fact, an extension of the magazine *Nova književnost* (*The New Literature*), started by Pavle Bihalji as far back as 1928 in collaboration with the Communist party, and, it was rumored, with party money. However, immediately following Bihalji's arrest, the dictatorship closed down the magazine. Bihalji was beaten by the police, but he conducted himself well. On his release, in place of the magazine, he started a publishing house by the same name which did very well. Bihalji became completely independent of the party and continued to work on his own. The New Literature books were well designed and executed. Bihalji was a master craftsman if perhaps not altogether original. This meant something new on our market, which had remained unchanged since the beginning of the twentieth century. The public was eager for any kind of opposition material, and the regime appeared willing to leave one vent open. The safest one was in the field of social literature, which, it was felt, had never yet overthrown a government. Little did those in power suspect that hundreds of new fighters throughout the country would be educated by it.

Bihalji was actively engaged in editing *Stožer*, although Jovan Popović was both its nominal and actual editor. The relationship between Popović and Bihalji was an unusual one: Bihalji lived extremely well, luxuriously by our standards, whereas Popović slaved away for the sake of ideology, doing all kinds of miserable jobs for a miserable reward. Bihalji was a gifted businessman, able to size up the market and the mood of his readers. The market had become saturated with classical literature, and was ready for something new. By 1937 Bihalji recognized that "social literature" had exhausted its possibilities and that its contrived and vulgar oversimplifications were outmoded. He immediately switched back to the classics. But he was not merely a businessman; he was also a man of principle, culture, and taste, and he promoted the books he believed in. This mixture of the gifted businessman and ideologist was exactly what we needed at a time when we could no longer count on financial assistance from anyone, including the Central Committee, and when abstract expression was still possible. Although stiff and dogmatic, a product of the German Communist school, and inclined to Jewish exclusiveness, Bihalji was aware that he had to make money in order to live, and that was possible only if books were actually published. He made contacts with the censors and people in power, declared his loyalty to the regime, and adapted himself to the bourgeois way of life. Increasingly the authorities looked on him simply as a skilled businessman, an idea he himself had promoted, although never altogether successfully. In 1937 the Central Committee was up in arms against him: they accused him of having used party funds to start a publishing house, which he then appropriated, rejecting party control and refusing assistance to prisoners, the so-called "Red Aid." There was some truth in both statements. But it wasn't the whole truth: as a businessman, Bihalji had contributed to the spread of ideas through literature. Also, he exploited Popović and paid him little on the pretext that it was everyone's duty to make a sacrifice for the idea. The curious thing was that Popović not only allowed himself to be exploited, but also was very fond of Bihalji, full of admiration for his culture and humanity, delighted to have him for a friend and to be given the opportunity to make his unselfish contribution to the greatest idea mankind had ever produced.

Until the very end Jovan Popović was unable to grasp the nature of his relationship with Bihalji. By 1939 the party had grown stronger and, had a compromise not been worked out, this new power might have proved a threat to Bihalji. The influential party leaders, including myself and Zogović, were critical of his attitude to Popović. Bihalji finally increased his wages as well as the honorariums paid to writers with party connections, and Zogović was able to get the Red Aid money that corresponded in some degree to his income.

A gentle and humane man, Popović was also withdrawn. During the war, as a staff member with the First Proletarian Brigade, he would often go without lunch because no one had taken the trouble to invite him. Anyone who had ever read an illegal leaflet felt competent to lecture him on revolutionary values. Popović was intellectually anemic and dry, but he enjoyed not giving in to sentimental moods because dialectical materialism defines such mental states as remnants of bourgeois intellectualism. We lost respect for Popović as a revolutionary because he didn't join the party until the beginning of the war, but we never questioned his character. He believed that he could be more useful to the party if he remained outside it.

Needless to say, once we became well-organized Communists, we were full of scorn for Popović and all those who refused to follow our thinking. When war broke out, the party's attitude toward him changed for the better, particularly since Popović no longer claimed he was more useful outside the movement.

During the war Popović lost an eye in an accident, and in the two years before his death suffered from a serious heart ailment. His second wife, young and beautiful, had been wild before she married him; she was also a leftist, so we decided to "change her ways." I was asked to talk to her. That was in the autumn of 1938. She was already in a state of high nervous tension. In the course of a four-hour talk I told her what was expected of her as a young Communist. She said her nerves were in poor condition; I tried to convince her that as a good Communist she couldn't possibly have trouble with her nerves. For a while her health seemed to be improving, but eventually she ended up in a mental institution.

Popović was not pleased with the way the opposition was treated in the Soviet Union in the 1936–1937 period. Radovan Zogović and I tried to convince him—because we believed it—that nothing about the trials was fictitious and that they were fully justified. He once told us that as an intellectual, outside the party, he was able to see things more objectively. Zogović and I were shocked by this statement. Direct participation, we said, affords one objectivity of which friends of the party, being outside it, are incapable because they do not participate fully in the historic process carried out by the Communist party. I was too busy to spend time "working on" Popović, but Zogović was persistent in his efforts to "save" him, although there really wasn't much to save him from: he was always ready to carry out party orders anyway.

Čedo Minderović was part of Popović's circle. Minderović's brother was a provocateur, and Minderović felt he was also under suspicion. This was only a partial explanation for his failure to join the party until the war began. Basically he also believed that he could be more useful to the movement as a writer than as an illegal operator. His wife, Keti, who was not young or beautiful, but very able, owned a feather and down shop and made a very good living. Minderović used the money to publish brochures of inferior quality, but ideologically useful. For a long time we were unaware of his wife's enormous energies—that little Hungarian Jewess who showed devotion and courage, ability and discipline of a kind we rarely encountered. She was, I recall, with a group I sent from Bosnia back to Serbia to give moral support to the waning rebellion there. It was a cold December night, the first snow had just fallen, and there was a pale hazy moon. With a rucksack and ski boots she left for Zlatibor, cheerful and confident, as if going mountain-climbing. She was killed by Chetnik gunfire.

Janko Djonović belonged to this circle, although he also operated independently. He first became known as a social poet with his "Negroes and Montenegrins," which Bihalji published in *Nova književnost*. For some time Djonović treated us as petit-bourgeois writers. He was primitive. We were no better. We wore shabby clothes, no ties, and we folded our socks under our toes to conceal the holes—a result of poverty and bohemianism, but above all of genuine primitivism. But Janko Djonović enjoyed being primitive. He told us that he had been chucked out of a very elegant Belgrade restaurant because he was in his shirt sleeves. We interpreted this as a bourgeois power play; he interpreted it as yet another wonderful opportunity to express his "folksy" nature. But the more we accepted Communism organizationally, the more Janko felt alienated from Communism. He remained true to his views and his way of life, friendly with many Communists without ever biting into the hard core of illegal work.

My contacts with non-Communist writers, and my literary contributions to the "bourgeois" newspapers and magazines, became the target of a violent attack from the "left," initiated by Štedimlija Savić Marković, Radovan Zogović, and a few less important people in 1932. That period marked a significant moral transformation in me.

Savić Marković was a little-known Zagreb journalist, but an able and clever man. He quickly understood that one could gain a reputation overnight through the "social" leftist literature and that this kind of literature attracted the revolutionary forces of society. He also understood that certain bourgeois democratic circles favored co-operation with the left. First he got in touch with Miroslav Krleža, about whom he wrote a series of flattering articles. Krleža, they said, couldn't resist flattery. Be that as it may, Savić Marković's association with the best-known writer of the left gained him the reputation of a good "progressive" journalist. He later made a similar contact with Stefan Galogaža and Radovan Zogović. In effect, he had spread his nets from Zagreb all the way to Skoplje, where Zogović was his contact. His position was weak in Belgrade because Bihalji was wary of him, fearing his possible Central Committee connections. Savić Marković pretended they existed, which wasn't particularly difficult since this highest forum had extremely loose links with the mother country, and all sorts of opportunists were able to take advantage of the fragmented nature of the party.

Savić Marković always looked mysterious. He dressed in a way that was simple, elegant, and proletarian, all at the same time. He wore dark suits, a little creased, his tie casually knotted but under a starched collar. His shoes were invariably of excellent quality, but never polished. He wore a pince-nez, which gave him an intellectual look. In fact, within five minutes, he could be turned into an elegant dignified gentleman or a beggar. In conversation he was unobtrusive, a good listener. His reaction was always sudden and lively; his initial approach one of quiet aggression. He had a good sharp memory, which enabled him to cite quotations and facts at the drop of a hat, which was disconcerting, even though he put his own interpretation on everything. For example, he maintained that if Lenin had listened to Gorky in 1917, the revolution would have failed, that Marx considered all co-operation with the bourgeoisie impossible, that we had a ripe Bolshevik leadership in 1918.

He was for ideological clarity in art and against co-operation with the "bourgeoisie" in politics. He was very successful in adapting his style of writing to revolutionary ideas under the dictatorship, of course, along the line set by the Central Committee, and by the party people within the country. That meant, on the one hand, a call for armed uprising, which was opposed by the new opposition bourgeois parties, and, on the other, the destruction of Yugoslavia as a state since it was an "artificial creation of the imperialist Versailles Peace Treaty." But even more important, he was able to size up the mood of leftist intellectuals disappointed by the passivity of the bourgeois parties, whose opportunism and willingness to negotiate had led to the January 6th Dictatorship.

This was the reasoning that led Savić Marković to fight for "ideological purity," and against co-operation with the "bourgeoisie," to object strongly to letting Communists write for "bourgeois" magazines. Zogović was on his side in this debate. We used the party's formal permission as an excuse for our continued contribution to such magazines, but it didn't help us one bit. Undisputed authorities, such as Galogaža, maintained the same position, and they did represent the party. In this dispute, the role of the Central Committee was not felt.

In an effort to show my loyalty to the party, and to avoid criticism for employing ideological reasons to justify my co-operation with the "bourgeois" newspapers and magazines, I stopped writing for them. It meant a financial sacrifice as well. My father was badly off at that time, overwhelmed with debts, and could contribute precious little toward my support. This was in the spring of 1932. To help support myself I joined scores of students in making door-to-door milk deliveries. The consequences were far more serious than that, however. The suspension of my contributions to these publications meant in effect the suspension of writing altogether, because the other magazines were so small and exclusive that one couldn't get anywhere near them. In the summer of 1932 I entered a competition in Galogaža's leftist *Literatura* with a short story and won a prize, but Savić Marković and Zogović managed to obstruct its publication on the basis of my political inconsistency.

In the final analysis the dilemma was not whether I should continue to contribute to "bourgeois" magazines, but whether I should choose politics over literature. I craved the latter, but chose the former, in the hopes of being able to do both. Those among my friends who chose literature (Jovan Popović, Čedo Minderović, Tanasije Mladenović) never did make a significant contribution. In fact, they were all basically politicians, who, in the absence of any true talent, used politics to gain temporary literary success, removing themselves from the illegal revolutionary scene as "secondary" and dangerous. I don't mean to imply by this statement that I was any more talented, but in making a choice, I didn't hesitate, even though I found it hard to leave that complex world of feelings and thoughts and images that a young writer carries within him. But I felt that I would betray myself if I made any other choice.

Co-operation with the bourgeois groups and individuals, which had developed spontaneously, came to an end. This process had many other after-effects: it accelerated the dogmatization of young Communist intellectuals; it filled them with intolerance of other people's ideas, with ideological exclusiveness. Those of us who believed that one and the same magazine could represent different opinions were accused of allowing the "bourgeoisie" to "deceive" the "proletariat."

The debate was conducted by two Montenegrin newspapers, *Slobodna misao* (*Free Thought*) and *Zeta*—Great Serbian agents versus separatists. The incident was proof of the immaturity of the Communist movement and of its ideological and organizational confusion.

However, the most interesting detail in this whole episode was the later discovery that Savić Marković was an agent provocateur, working for the Belgrade police. His position with the police was not clear-cut though. If he cared little for the fate of Communists, he cared still less for the fate of the Belgrade ruling class. By selling himself to both sides, he was consistent in only one thing: his belief in an independent Montenegrin state. He must have treated his co-operation with the Belgrade police as a conditional, temporary agreement: obstructing Montenegrin leftists' collaboration with the liberal supporters of unification with Serbia. In addition, his work strengthened the fighting spirit among Communists, but that was also the result of changing conditions generally, which he had to take into account if he was to continue in his role as a double agent. Once those unsettled conditions no longer existed, he was exposed. Once exposed, he became a close collaborator of Sekula Drljević, the leader of the Montenegrin Separatist Movement. He ended up as a theoretician who maintained that Montenegrins were "Red Croats," and in this capacity he became a close collaborator of the Ustashi regime. With the disintegration of the Pavelić state we lost track of this man, this brief bright spot in the dark days of the January 6th Dictatorship.

The Belgrade Surrealists also played a role in those days, but it was a peripheral one. At no time did they participate actively in political struggles, although some of them later became party members. Mostly the children of rich or bankrupt Belgrade families, they caused minor cultural scandals, denying existing moral values and endlessly discussing their relationship to the Communist movement. Some were for conditional participation, others for preserving their independence within the framework of general cultural co-operation.

In a moment of internal crisis, and in order to maintain unity, they decided to establish contact with the Communist party. That contact was again Sima Marković. Years later I saw a letter he wrote to the Surrealists in 1931 or 1932, signed "Central Committee of the Communist Party" (although he had already been expelled from the party), in which he said that although there were certain differences between their respective approaches the Central Committee was anxious to establish co-operation. For a long time the Surrealists used this letter as a weapon against all those who favored practical political activity.

The Surrealists were not involved with the demonstrations or with any other student project, except for Djordje Jovanović-Jarac, who established contact with the leftist students because he favored practical political struggle. I met him in the spring of 1932. The occasion was the planning of demonstrations at the National Theatre against the play *Volga, Volga*, by Dušan Nikolajević.

Jovanović lived with his mother, who, in spite of her Serbian bulk, must have been very good-looking at one time. Abandoned by her husband, she worked as a bank clerk. Djordje was a tall, well-dressed, pleasant young man. He advertised himself as a "Great Serb," he swore with gusto, and was lackadaisical. He did not take Surrealism, or the political struggle, for that matter, too seriously. He was an aide-de-camp to Prince Djordje, King Alexander's brother, and his uncle had been involved in the murder of King Alexander Obrenović; he was the one who cut off Queen Draga's fingers to get at the rings. But Djordje was very fond of his uncle, and amused by his soldierly eccentricities. Djordje boasted courage, but in fact he was a coward. He did have one indisputable virtue: he was honest, straight, and fresh. Surrealism was superimposed on him partly by his own youthful desire for originality, and partly by the intellectual environment in which he moved. At heart he liked a good joke, good food, attractive women, art as a sport, and sport as an art, and politics on the side.

About a hundred students came to the opening night of *Volga, Volga,* and seated themselves in the third gallery. We had heard that the play was reactionary, although few of us knew anything about it. The Surrealists didn't like Nikolajević because he represented the "national spirit," and Communists didn't care for him because he attacked Communism and talked about the tragedy of "Mother Russia." It was the opening-night performance. In response to a highly theatrical statement Jovanović shouted a curse that rocked the theatre. As a Surrealist and a city child he had a flair for scandal. The rest of us "peasants" joined in with political remarks and paper bombs. Suddenly, the whole theatre was in an uproar. Ladies screamed, but the actors went on as if nothing were happening. The audience turned against us and, in a burst of applause, called for the author. The curtain finally came down, and Nikolajević appeared, calling on the "dark powers" to come and face him. The audience found his ostentatious manner distasteful and their enthusiasm waned. I hurled a few more paper bombs at the stage, screaming at the top of my lungs. This caused general commotion and panic. Nikolajević went on talking, the audience rushed for the exits, and the third gallery was blocked off by the gendarmes. There were several arrests, none of them significant, and the play and Nikolajević vanished forever from the Belgrade scene.

The literary climate had given rise to political fighters against the dictatorship, it helped form several generations of revolutionaries, it helped us to grow and make our choice, which was to join organized revolutionary action, rather than settle for passive resistance. My own decision was based on my determination to remain true to myself and my idea, to eliminate a contradiction between my thoughts and my actions, a condition that demeans a man—and to give up my former way of life, in spite of the comforts and advantages it had offered.

15

No revolutionary movement, and this is particularly true of the Communist movement, is a result of a preconceived notion; rather, it is conceived, developed, and then it reaches maturity. The same is true of the people in the movement: they are flexible, sensitive individuals susceptible to change, constant only in subjecting themselves to their Communist beliefs.

The great majority of us young people became revolutionaries in the hopes of realizing brotherhood and equality, of freeing our working people from exploitation, of giving them a happier life. The life that we proposed to change was tight, dictated by the ruling class, impossible to live. It would have been easy to prove this statistically, economically, and sociologically—and it would have been convincing enough. However, we also felt an inner anguish, a dissatisfaction with everything, including ourselves. We were emerging from a closed circle into space and light—and under the circumstances our emergence had assumed the form of a revolutionary struggle, of Communism.

Of course, personal friendships and competition among us played an enormous role. Vidak Marković, for example, didn't possess a single quality that would have made him a Communist, and yet he became one. A gentle and honorable person, he was aware that he would be unable to survive police torture. Yet he joined the movement. He had no knack for Communist theory or practice. It was impossible for him to feel genuine hatred for anybody; hatred was something he acquired as a "good Communist," rather than generated naturally. But he couldn't give us up; he felt he had to deliver what was asked of him, and destroyed himself in the process.

The Idealist

In my early experience I didn't know a single man who had become a Communist out of ambition or hope of material gain. But once the prospects of power became obvious, there were thousands. Moreover, the quality of ambition was very different at the start; it was mostly the desire to gain the love and approval of one's comrades, to make as many unselfish contributions to the movement as possible. Radovan Vuković, for example, was narrow and adamant when it came to defending even the most insignificant party interests. He joined all kinds of committees, and felt himself to be more determined and courageous than any of us, but he was always ready to give up his functions and to make his contribution as a simple fighter, if that were in the interests of the movement. The desire to play a more visible role by joining committees was never the result of selfish personal calculations. I don't mean to say that such inclinations were unknown to the movement, but they were generally confined to the older comrades, predictatorship party members, who had grown used to the unprincipled factional struggles, and had paying jobs with the trade unions or the party. In fact the dictatorship served as a clearing ground for egotists, cowards, and careerists. The movement had to rid itself of them in order to proceed with the revolutionary struggle.

Once a person became psychologically oriented within the movement, though, the intellectual awareness, the changing of views, and the acceptance of revolutionary Marxism played an enormous role. The theory strengthened him, purified him, and rendered him daring and courageous. Marxist literature made no impression at all on me until I had made up my mind that I was for Communism. Then that literature was for me a world of new ideas which reflected my condition and which helped shape my consciousness. Some people accepted the Marxist theory first and, on that basis, made up their minds that the new Communist society would be better and more just. Vojin Kurtović was one.

He had become a Communist at Užice, as a high-school student, under the influence of Dr. Smiljanić, a Communist theoretician. Kurtović was an excellent student, and very intelligent. There was nothing in his nature that would lend itself naturally to being a hard-core Communist: he was soft, anxious to conceal his feelings, used to a comfortable life. The knowledge of Marxism alone was insufficient to sustain him in difficult situations, and he invariably succumbed, betraying both his ideas and his comrades. If he had lived in normal, nonrevolutionary conditions, his intellectual possibilities would have been unlimited. But having thus exposed himself, he went from bad to worse, until he finally changed sides in order to save his life, which was by then of value only to himself.

Brana Jevremović's case was similar: he also came from a rich family but he was somewhat more sturdy. He was active and made an excellent impression with his reasonable, calm manner, but once in prison he conducted himself poorly. After his release he reverted to the comforts of his family, but continued to feel strongly about theory. Just before war broke out he left the country and later became a Soviet agent in the royal government-in-exile, whose employee he was. In the new Yugoslavia, his career developed within the limits of an able man who had little initiative and who was afraid that his sole real achievement—his work with Soviet Intelligence—would be interpreted as a sign of weakness, which of course it was.

My own feeling is that many people chose Communism as a means of consolidating their own inner resources. That was particularly the case with older families. I think this factor played an important role in Bora Kovačević's decision, his unusual moral qualities notwithstanding. This tall, dark man with sensual lips and prematurely gray hair carried within him all the loneliness and sorrow of an old merchant family from the ancient, green, wild Bosnia that was now dying. Whenever a new task was set before him he would react instantly: I am not up to that, comrades! There was no problem in explaining things to him—he was quick and intelligent—but it was hard to convince him that he was capable of making a contribution. What he did, however, he did well and conscientiously.

All of us, from different backgrounds, had joined the common cause to develop our own personal lives and political careers. Misery, despair, and hopelessness may have driven large masses of people to choose Communism, but not a single Communist had become a Communist because he had personally found himself in that position. On the contrary, each one of us had to give up a lot and abandon not only a former outlook but a former existence as well. Professionally, each Communist was among the best, and neither his existence nor his prosperity had been threatened. They were the best workers, the most intelligent peasants, the best physicians. We stood out among students with our ability, intelligence, and skill, in spite of the fact that the more involved we became with the movement the less time we had to study. Party assignments were more important to us than anything else. The same was true of worker Communists: they neglected their work to dedicate themselves to the party. However, it is true that once people became professional

Communists, their will to do anything else quickly vanished. But the beginning was ideal for each one of us: it meant running into problems rather than away from them. Also, it is interesting to note that it wasn't really the poorest among the poor that chose Communism as their solution. Extreme poverty destroys a man altogether. As a rule, Communists came from passive regions, such as Montenegro and Bosnia, from among workers, peasants, and civil servants, poor but not destitute. The majority of student Communists came from relatively prosperous peasant families, also mostly from Montenegro, Bosnia, and Hercegovina. Relatively few came from Serbia. Montenegrins played a considerable role in the city's local organization before the war. Radoje Dakić was Secretary of the local Committee, and Strugar and Burdžović were members, and in the Regional Committee were Dakić, Vukmanović-Tempo, Vukica Mitrović, and myself.

The poverty and violence of those regions explain only in part the revolutionary dedication of their young people. Actually, the rebellion of the hungry mountains against the rich valley has been going on in this country for several centuries and had given birth to many great leaders. Men from these regions, a select few at any rate, seem to have no other way of getting through life except with rebellions and wars. Students from the passive regions, but especially from prosperous families, were in charge from the very beginning of the revolution, in organization and in action. We quickly distinguished ourselves from our predecessors: we felt that Marxism, as a discipline, could explain everything. Earlier revolutionaries possessed no such "complete" or "all-knowing" ideology, but, rather, a mixture of ideas, such as nationalism, Eastern Orthodoxy, and so on. We had only one idea, one ideology. Any remnant of "old," worn-out ideas was a weakness. Sentimentality, generosity, friendliness were applicable within our closed Communist circle, and not outside of it. And within this circle the feelings of love, devotion, unselfishness, and sincerity were intensified to the point of self-obliteration. This emotional development among Communists played a more important role in the creation of the Communist movement and party than the revolutionary Marxist ideology, with all its pretension of a universal understanding of society, the world, and man. In fact, revolutionary Marxist ideology adjusted itself to the emotional needs of revolutionaries, helping them mature rapidly.

Of course, I am talking about the very first revolutionaries—the students—under the dictatorship. Naturally, there were differences in the approach of workers and peasants, but the substance remained the same: joining the movement to effect a change in existing social conditions. Wife, children, friends, one's personal fortunes, all become secondary to the success of the movement. But this was only an objective in the development of revolutionary Communists. It was never achieved fully: Communists have always had certain "human" weaknesses, and not one has ever managed to achieve the state of absolute devotion to the idea. But a true Communist is a person able to dedicate himself wholly to the movement in spite of these weaknesses.

Yet it would be wrong to assume that we had grown "impersonal" as a result of our blind acceptance of the principles of the movement. On the contrary, personal happiness was synonymous with the success of the movement. We were alive, very much alive, full of fire and passion, intellectual zeal, nervous energy, but it was all channeled in one direction. When we loved and when we hated, when we were awake and when we were asleep, we had one final goal in mind: the destruction of the existing system and the triumph of the party.

We were the first organized Communist generation under the dictatorship. We didn't have the experience of the older comrades, but we were more aggressive. Their experience was useless, besides, and could not be applied to conditions under the dictatorship. First, we had to satisfy certain minimal requirements in order to join the organization. Then, we had to establish ourselves organizationally and emotionally, which was not a simple process. Generally speaking, we were better Communists than those before us.

My own feeling is that as Communists, workers were no more consistent or courageous than intellectuals. By and large, they may have produced a somewhat more stable type of functionary, more consistent in preserving the movement's continuity and authority. On the other hand, intellectuals were quicker in sizing up conditions of change and in formulating new assignments in new situations. But with regard to courage, strength, and devotion there were no fundamental differences between them.

As young revolutionaries, we were not aware of this. We had a romantic notion that every worker who ever grumbled against his master or drunkenly cursed out the bourgeoisie was a highly "class-conscious" model revolutionary. We learned this from Marxist books rather than from experience, since there was little activity among the Communist workers. Even so we thought it quite natural that workers should play a leading role. After all, Communism was identified in our minds with the abolition of capitalist exploitation of the workers, and we intellectuals joined them as people who knew the truth. However, this was poor logic: our Communist movement had not yet reached full revolutionary maturity, and no matter who was in the leading role—workers or intellectuals—it had many weaknesses. Today I would even go so far as to say that the workers' movement is not essential to Communism, nor, strictly speaking, can it be considered its product. The workers' movement and the working class, which wallows in ignorance and poverty, were for Communism only an instrument with which to gain power. Once that goal has been achieved, the working class is of no interest, unless it is essential in the further consolidation of that power.

However, it was impossible for a young Communist, a social democrat, or anybody else, for that matter, to grasp this for many years, and we continued to seek co-operation with the workers. But such co-operation was impossible: there simply was no mass movement among them. The few worker Communists who did exist were caught up in the so-called "street cells," which were quickly uncovered by the police and broken up. This period—1931–1932—was typical of the narrow spirit in party organizations set up in a hurry and without any roots among the masses. The party organization at the University evolved more gradually and more spontaneously, and was never altogether destroyed.

Notwithstanding the enormous differences between those who joined the party during the dictatorship and those who had been Communists before, there was a certain amount of organizational continuity. This continuity was interrupted at the University, whereas in the city it survived. In other respects, the line of continuity was not interrupted: Communism and Communists were being discussed; Communist literature, predominantly in the form of fiction, was being published. The atmosphere was ripe for Communism. Communists favored a revolution, the overthrow of the existing system; they alone were tortured in jails, and murdered. They were the only group that posed a real threat to the dictatorship.

Thus the first student groups moved from discontent and rebellion to the revolutionary struggle and on to full-fledged Communist organizations. The various phases of that growth may not be clear, but the evolution was discernible: in individual ideological development, and in the form the organized struggle was taking.

16

By autumn of 1932 the ground was ready for the creation of a Communist organization at the University. The only missing element was the party contact which Blažo Raičević had promised us the previous spring. Labud Kusovac, who was to have been that contact, had fled to Italy during the summer, along with Rajko Jovanović. The immediate cause for his flight was the arrest of Petko Miletić, a member of the Central Committee.

At the end of September I ran into Dr. Milovan Ćetković, whom I remembered from my boyhood as a Communist. Dr. Ćetković promised me a contact and arranged a rendezvous at the entrance to the park at Kalemegdan. I expected that he himself would be the contact, but instead he gave me the address of Veselin Masleša. We knew of Masleša, a Communist publicist and writer, but we hadn't met him. He was first arrested in a 1929 police raid, which had caused the breakup of the Belgrade organization: Nešić jumped out of the window, Bracunović was killed, and Ivan Milutinović was arrested. Masleša was tried and released. He was arrested again in connection with Petko Miletić's arrest, and released two months later without trial.

By the time we made our contact with Masleša we had already formed a Communist organization at the University. It was divided into groups according to each faculty, the secretaries of individual groups forming the University Committee. I was elected Secretary of the Committee. We called it simply the University Communist Organization, which made possible continued co-operation with the Sima Marković group.

Masleša, however, did not solve the contact problem. He offered little help with the printing and distribution of leaflets and no contact with the workers, whereas Sima Marković did both. Stefan Mitrović, Radovan Vuković, and Djordje Jovanović were critical of Masleša for his passivity and claimed that Sima Marković was more useful. They also accused me unjustly of insisting on the categorical severance of relations with the Marković group because I was passive myself and afraid of the police. They were right with regard to the passivity of the party contact, particularly when it came to the distribution of leaflets, the chief activity of the party organizations. As to the accusation of fear on my part, this was my first lesson in the lack of principles in factional fighting, and from my closest friend, Stefan Mitrović.

When I told Masleša how widespread the University organization was, he couldn't conceal his surprise. He assumed he would be dealing with loose, disorganized leftist groups that could be persuaded to do legal and semilegal work at the University. Instead he was faced with a fully organized group. I asked for two things from him: equipment for duplicating illegal literature, and contact with workers—placing students in their cells to elevate their class consciousness.

He gave me nothing. There was still no illegal literature; we had to wait for leaflets. The city party organizations (of workers) were still in the making. His position was one of caution, which I sensed immediately. He avoided all discussion of illegal activity, and urged students to restrict themselves to legal action.

He was of medium height, handsome, but walleyed (later he became blind). He was a careful listener and reluctant to answer questions he didn't like. That reluctance always seemed unnatural because he wasn't really cunning. He had a healthy optimism which echoed in loud laughter, but he also possessed an almost fatalistic indifference, particularly when the talk turned to possible arrests. He said that in case of arrest student activity should not assume the character of that of an illegal Communist organization, but of something semilegal. I believe this was the party line, rather than his own, although he obviously opposed "leafleteering" as an expensive, inefficient form of activity. His approach was gradual and cautious, and his advice, particularly regarding political activity, very useful. He helped us acquire a clearer political vision.

Masleša had no idea just how excited I was. I told him that some of the comrades continued to maintain contact with Sima Marković. He said unequivocally that they had to sever that contact. He was the first person to explain to me the nature of the conflict between the Central Committee and Sima Marković. But the students, even those opposing co-operation with Sima Marković, were unhappy because no illegal literature was available. So I found myself caught between Masleša, who represented the party but was powerless to give us what we asked for, and a great passion for illegal activity, which in real terms defined the conflict between the party and the Marković group. My own mind was clearly made up: to follow the party. The conflict with friends, particularly with Mitrović and Vuković, had not, as yet, assumed the bitterness of a final break, although it was obviously heading that way.

They were arrested on the eve of the anniversary of the October Revolution, for which occasion Sima Marković had prepared a leaflet. They said they would participate in the distribution of leaflets "along with the workers," and I didn't try to prevent them. How could I? After all, it was a leaflet on the Russian Revolution! As a matter of fact, I distributed a few myself. We met at the appointed hour; everything worked out well and we all went our separate ways.

I had trouble locating Mitra at Kalemegdan because of the fog, and since I had a terrible headache I went home. I lived on Pašićeva Street, in a kitchen I shared with a friend who was not a Communist.

Early the following morning Vukica Mitrović came to see me: her brother, Stefan, had been arrested. We decided to go to see Vuković and Kovačević, who lived on Dušanova Street. Assuming there might be a trap laid for us, I had her go first, while I waited outside. Soon she came out, accompanied by a young agent, who noticed that she was looking in my direction, but he couldn't exactly leave her in order to run after me, so I managed to sneak away. I immediately informed Masleša of the arrests, alerted the comrades who had the most reason to feel threatened, and hid myself at a friend's apartment in Zemun. Sima Marković, Djordje Jovanović, and Koča Popović had been arrested that night, too. That was it. I stayed in Zemun for two weeks, but came into Belgrade from time to time for meetings. It soon became evident that the raid was confined to the Sima Marković group and that it would not spread to the party organization.

This event ended the internal struggle, and the work of the organization continued normally.

The formal status of our Communist youth organization was not clearly defined until many years later, and in 1936 it was still being referred to as a party organization, rather than the League of Young

Communists. In fact, there was no difference between the party and the League of Young Communists except age. The regime, in its persecutions, made no distinction either. Today this differentiation may seem irrelevant, but it wasn't then: if one were a member of the League of Young Communists, one was excluded from performing party functions. One had to work hard and prove oneself a good young Communist before being accepted by the party. Of course, frequent police raids weakened this theory, and in the end it was practice rather than abstract rules that regulated this question at the University.

The contact with the party altered the nature of our activity. Instead of turning outward—by public rebellion against the regime, such as demonstrations—we turned inward, to the student struggle and the consolidation of Communist forces. Narrow illegal methods (riots within the University, leaflets, and so on) were increasingly used against the regime.

While I was in hiding in Zemun, strained relations developed between the students and Professor Milan Bartoš. In one of his lectures on international law he had attacked the leftist rebels for bringing chaos to the University and turning on the most "sacred national values." Someone suggested we beat him up. I approved, but in a modified form: cause chaos at his lecture, but don't hurt him seriously. On the appointed day a large number of Communist students from different faculties came to his lecture. When the lecture was over, they formed a circle around him, cursed him, and spit at him; in the commotion a few blows were dealt, but not on the head. Petar Radović was in charge of this minor riot. Unusually strong physically, he was handsome, tall, and fair, his skin the color of bronze. He dressed stylishly, and was successful with women. He loved riots and commotion, and showed unusual courage and skill in conducting them. Later, in 1937, he was arrested in Subotica and behaved poorly before the police. On his release from prison, he joined Petko Miletić's group, and was expelled from the party as an "enemy." But at the beginning of the war he joined the Partisans and was a great hero, one of the best fighters the First Proletarian Brigade ever had. He became a party member again and was appointed Commissar of the Navy. He killed himself on the island of Vis in the spring of 1944 because of his weakness for women. He couldn't face being expelled from the party again. His death, as I recall, was unpleasant, but we at the top didn't really mourn him: he couldn't rid himself of his weaknesses.

After the war, on the *Queen Elizabeth*, on my way to a United

Nations session in New York, I talked with Bartoš about the incident in his classroom in 1932. Of course I was careful not to hurt his feelings. He told me that the event marked a turning point in his life; he asked himself why young people were against him. And indeed, not long thereafter he began associating with the leftists. But he got involved with Dušan Kusovac, who was part of Petko Miletić's group, so we thought him a semi-Trotskyist. He didn't become a party member until the beginning of the war. As a prisoner of war in Germany, he was with the Communists. When he came home he called on me at the Central Committee to "clarify his position."

On one occasion, at the beginning of 1933, we went to see the University Rector with certain demands. But he would not receive us. The door was closed. If I had said the word, nothing would have happened. But I thought I should not "suppress" the revolutionary spirit. The thin door fell apart, and, as if gone wild, we pulled out drawers, turned over tables, and scattered books and papers around.

We also caused an incident on St. Sava's Day—the University's patron saint—which was celebrated with pomp and ceremony, speeches and prizes. Professors and honored guests gathered for the occasion in the great hall of the New University. The students were in the galleries. The King's deputy and the University Rector were busy cutting the cake. It was a crucial moment—one of those situations in which the slightest move may cause an explosion. There was great tension, which grew to excruciating proportions as some one hundred and fifty of us waited for action. I crumpled a piece of paper into a ball and hurled it down. Several heads turned around, but the ceremony continued unperturbed. The tension among us slackened: the arrow had been released. I whistled; the rest of the students joined in. The celebration came to a halt.

These two incidents put us on very bad terms with the University authorities, and a number of students were expelled. But, interestingly enough, neither I nor any other leader was expelled. We now had new and long-lasting negotiations with the Rector. A section of the student body, mostly bourgeois party members, separated themselves from us. The Communists seemed to have become more compact.

Masleša was not delighted with our activities, but he didn't stop us. He enjoyed one of them in spite of himself. The White Russian émigrés held a celebration at Kolarčev University and for the occasion they presented the opera *Life for the Tsar*. I must admit that most of us thought the opera was written before the Revolution, glorifying Tsar Nicholas II, although it was that same opera by Glinka that is now being performed in Russia under the title *Ivan Susanin*. But the title of the opera and the celebration provoked us, and we were dying to spoil it all for them.

We decided to use tear gas. Students in the chemistry department made up tubes, and I asked Mitra and Brana Djerić, both good-looking and well dressed, to smuggle them in. At the right moment they broke off the tips of the tubes, and the tear gas spread fast. The audience was in tears; the performance was suspended. Mitra told me how funny it was to hear an old Russian crying from the stage: "Gentlemen, they have released gas!" It was such a great scandal that the press had to take note of it.

Around the same time action was taken against a gifted writer, Miloš Crnjanski, an extreme rightist who had denounced New Literature as a publishing house for Communist propaganda. We young writers joined the action conducted by Veselin Masleša and Milan Bogdanović.

Such activities helped maintain fighting spirit at the University and established the Communist image in the public eye. They strengthened us Communists in a world of our own. We felt like a secret power, and, in the eyes of ordinary people, we were indestructible. There couldn't have been more than forty of us acting as organized Communists. But we had a large segment of the dissatisfied student body in open sympathy with us.

In February 1932 it looked as if we might finally have our contact with the workers.

In order to win over mass opinion and suppress bourgeois groups, we obviously used students, Communists, and fellow-travelers, to work within other political groups. There were two ways of conducting this activity: through organized infiltration or spontaneous action of individuals already in those organizations. The peasant-worker group of Dragoljub Jovanović, particularly its left wing, was prominent in the latter activity. They competed with us in our radical approach, but they were without our Communist single-mindedness. Thus some of their most courageous members, like Mirko Tomić and Mirko Vesović, joined our ranks. Radan Grajičić, a notorious policeman, worked for us in 1932–1933, among the peasants. Radan was poor and bright, but quite unmilitant, and greedy for the good life, of which he had his first taste in Belgrade when he got a decent room of his own and good food. Physically weak, pale, with thick dark hair and slightly curled lips, he looked foreign. He talked a lot and boasted. He infiltrated the peasant movement in order to betray it later, and then found a still better situation. As he was already on poor terms with us Communists, nothing stood between him and the police, in which context his law degree was secondary and his knowledge of the new Communist generation primary. He carefully studied all of the Communist literature, and if he hadn't let himself slip intellectually, he might have become one of the leading anti-Communist policemen.

17

A non-Communist friend of mine, a Montenegrin whose name I cannot recall now, made contact with a Communist group in Belgrade and started distributing their literature among us. We were convinced that the group was a workers' party organization with which Masleša would not get in touch. However, it turned out Masleša didn't know anything about it. Obviously it was a "wildcat" group that had nothing to do with the party. I was later told that "wildcat" groups, organized largely by former party members, existed in other parts of the country as well. Anyway, Masleša showed considerable interest in this group, particularly because his own local committee had very few organizations under its own wing. My assignment was to investigate the situation.

My non-Communist friend sent someone to see me one day, a man slightly built, poorly dressed, of uncertain occupation, about thirty. He walked as if his hips were out of joint. He talked a lot, boasted a bit, but in a good-natured way. I told him outright that I wanted contact with this group, which reflected my own poor judgment. This man knew everything about me. I knew nothing about him. He was the first underground worker Communist I had met. In his presence I felt my romantic enthusiasm for workers fading away. Yet I continued to believe that his class consciousness was far greater than mine, in fact so great that he would be capable of resisting all torture. Personally, he didn't impress me, but the lesson about the worker Communist had been well absorbed.

Our first meeting was strange and funny. He insisted that student Communists organize and submit to the local committee. This was, of course, expressed in phrases such as: revolutionary discipline and Communist duty. I carefully explained to him that we had already made the "right connection." Not with Sima Marković of course. At Masleša's insistence I had several more meetings with this stranger, in the hope of clarifying our relations with his group. I got a lot of underground literature from him, for which we were all so eager. Finally, at the beginning of March, he admitted that they had no contact with the party, that they were a group of workers seeking that contact, at which point I became his contact rather than he mine.

Masleša made it official, and asked that I provide assistance in the form of articles for their magazine. The literature they produced in large quantities was reasonably good—it followed the party line, and it contained the recent decisions of the Comintern. The students could no longer complain that they had nothing to "work with." The party was finally supplying them with the right material. I must admit that I was very proud of my role.

This group, as I was to learn later, was far more active than the actual party organization. It had functioned successfully for several months, distributing illegal literature and making contact with the provinces. Around that time, in March or in April 1933, Žarko Zrenjanin, a member of this group, was arrested. But he stood up well before the police, and the group was not uncovered.

Two men, I gathered later, played major roles in this organization: my initial contact, Vasilije Stajkić, who was a carpenter by trade, and Dimitrije Jovanović, a barber's apprentice. Stajkić gave the group political and organizational experience; Jovanović gave it action and skill. There were several workers in the group. Beška Bembas and her sister Pirika, two Jewish girls, did all the typing on a machine borrowed from Berta Papo, also a student. The group was founded on personal relationships: it was compact and properly secretive; it never relied on former party members, who were largely cowards and liquidators. This explained why the group was able to survive as long as it did in spite of its considerable "publishing" activity.

Around the middle of March I received a letter from Mitrović and Vuković, which Mitrović's sister Vukica had smuggled out of prison, stating that Petko Miletić must be freed from prison as soon as possible, at any rate before he was scheduled to stand trial. Miletić was with them in the Circuit Court prison. Later a small penitentiary was made available on Ada Ciganlija, after political trials had become a regular procedure and the special court had had to be in continuous session.

The Circuit Court prison, located behind the building, which was demolished in 1955 to make room for the Marx-Engels Square in Belgrade, was separated from it by a narrow corridor, formed by a prison yard wall and the court building. The entrance was through the courthouse, which during office hours was full of people. And the gate of the prison yard was guarded by a gendarme.

Mitrović and Vuković suggested the following plan: We were to disarm and, if necessary, kill the gendarme guarding the gate, toss over a rope ladder, supply Miletić with a gun, and have a car waiting for him in front of the building. Vuković was a sharp, able man, and I had no doubt that he would do the right thing. However, it turned out later that the operation was relatively simple. The gendarme was a Montenegrin who was impressed by Miletić because he was a Central Committee member and a fellow Montenegrin. Having looked over the court building and prison several times, I knew that the gendarmes along that narrow corridor were not particularly alert. They even allowed us to talk to the prisoners at the windows, only gently motioning us away. After all, it was a criminal prison, and the regime was much more lenient with its criminal than with its political prisoners.

I told Masleša about our plan, and after some hesitation he gave it his approval. I began negotiating with Stajkić. His group had got hold of a taxi driver, who was normally stationed at the courthouse, who would give a lift to the "gentlemen" who would, at a set time, get into his cab. Stajkić was to hand Petko the gun and escort him to the taxi. I asked Petar Radović and another man, equally strong physically, to deal with the gendarme. They were to place a towel soaked in chloroform on his mouth, and I was to stand next to them with a pistol. Getting hold of a pistol had not been a simple matter. I got it from Brana Jevremović, and Brana in turn had gotten it from the Military Institute at Užice through a friend of Mitra's. The excitement was growing from day to day, and we were wild with joy at the thought of walking away from prison in the middle of the day, at the center of Belgrade, with a member of the Central Committee, because it would be a great blow to the police and the regime.

The escape of Petko Miletić would, no doubt, have succeeded had not events taken an altogether different turn.

On the afternoon of April 22 Stajkić didn't show up. It was a bad sign, and I was worried. I didn't want to go into hiding that night—not yet anyway, since I had confidence in Stajkić.

I lived then on Dalmatinska Street, in the back building, and had a view of the Botanical Gardens. That was the most beautiful apartment Mitra and I ever had. The trees hadn't turned green yet, but spring was in the air and in the cool moisture of plants. This turned out to be our last evening together for many years, in the course of which our lives were to undergo a fundamental change.

18

It was early morning. The sun hadn't yet come up. My landlady knocked on the door. She had something important to tell me. I opened the door, and a police agent, a certain Todor, whom I knew well, charged into the room, held me at gunpoint, and ordered me to get dressed. Another agent was with him, and a third was guarding the door. Two "citizens" were there too, as witnesses, but no one paid them any attention. The agents were efficient and tough, and the search was quick and superficial. They took a couple of books, just so as not to walk away empty-handed. This kind of search was typical: many years of experience had taught them that one finds nothing by searching, but, rather, by beating.

The procedure and the atmosphere in no way resembled the previous year's arrest, when they had been careful, measured, even pleasant. They chained my hands right away. The minute we got into the car Todor kicked me in the groin, cursed me, and threatened that this time I would admit everything and remember everything, even when I bit my mother's breast. He was a tall, tough man, of great physical strength, all bones, hair, and a powerful jaw. His eyes were still, cold, and gray, and his hair smooth and shiny, pointing up his cruelty. His companion, Kanački, looked positively bored, limp and tired, and his face and his clothing were creased. The third man was young, fair, and handsome. He was dressed strikingly if cheaply.

The streets were deserted. We took an elevator to the fourth floor. Todor went into an office, but returned quickly. The Chief wasn't there. It was all my fault, he said, because they couldn't find me right away. They searched me superficially and never noticed that in my pocket there was a fine, long penknife. They escorted me to the top floor, knocked on a door, and handed me over to a young gendarme. "One more of those," they said, and left. The gendarme slapped my face a couple of times, and then another one joined him and shoved me in the ribs because of my allegedly improper posture. All this was done calmly, professionally. Eventually I ended up in room No. 6, which was already occupied by a thin, frightened-looking man. Upset and hurt, I sat down on the floor. I closed my eyes, wishing to fall asleep, regretting that I hadn't tried to escape by leaping into the Botanical Gardens. I had expected a raid. Why was I so hesitant? Or was it fate?

I fared better during my first interrogation than most, probably because the Chief of Gendarmes was not around. The customary treatment of prisoners was tough, accompanied by cruel jokes and tricks. The gendarmes called the nightstick "the constitution." Beating may not be constitutional, they said, but since it was done with the constitution, it wouldn't hurt nearly as much. Exceptionally cruel, primitive people, they thought they were actually doing their duty. Their favorite way of humiliating Communists was to make them shout "Long live the King, the Premier, and the Royal Family." Radovan Vuković was practically beaten to death because he refused to do it. The gendarmes quickly learned which ones of us were serious transgressors by how hard we were beaten on the fourth floor, where interrogations were conducted. They would sharpen their methods accordingly, bitter at the prisoner for making things hard for everyone involved. However, if someone proved stubborn, which was rare, they were full of admiration. Relations between the gendarmes and the agents were cool: in their eyes "those civilians" got good salaries for no work to speak of, and they treated gendarmes as stupid "cops" whom Communists could always outsmart.

Contact between rooms on the top floor was strictly forbidden. When prisoners had to go to the toilet or have a drink of water, they had to pound on the door. Cell doors were always closed, obviously to prevent prisoners from communicating, and the gendarmes cursed and beat anyone who coughed in the corridor or asked a question in a loud voice, allegedly because they were sending messages. Of course, there were ways of getting around this. All it took was courage.

When I finally got to the top floor the sun was up. In this cave of curses, blows, screams, and vituperation, early morning was the quietest part of the day. Evenings were terrible. The real office hours began at night. "We must work" meant for the agents working at night, and "we must convert" meant to torture somebody.

It was spring, and we wouldn't have been cold if we had been able to move around. Sleeping on bare floors, dressed in light clothing, eating bread and drinking water, we were always cold, unless, of course, we were being beaten.

It turned out that Stajkić was also in this prison. I recognized his voice, although it sounded very weak. My cellmate was a Slovenian, a dental technician, and an Esperanto expert. He claimed that the Communists had betrayed him, which turned out to be true. A member of the group had borrowed his apartment on the pretext of taking a girl there, but he actually used it to print leaflets.

My window had a view of the river Sava and the distant valley; down below I could see a piece of the street and hear the city noises. I thought how nice it would be if only Mitra came by; I could wave to her through the bars. And, indeed, that was exactly what happened two days later. She walked back and forth until it got dark. In 1945 I visited this same prison, and that same cell, accompanied by Alexander Ranković. But the windows had been boarded up, at an angle toward the sky, to let the air in, but block the view. Some Communist, a former prisoner like me, must have thought of this, fearful that those now in prison might get a glimpse of someone dear to them from those windows.

Djordje Kosmajac turned up just before noon, cursing, door-banging, and slapping away. He was cruel and unbalanced, and liked to demonstrate his "power" and temper. He rarely participated in the more subtle torturing of prisoners late at night; rather, he would beat them at random, for no rhyme or reason, or while they were waiting for systematic torture. Even his superiors feared the cruel blows of this drunkard, who was obsessed by the idea that Communists would kill him, which is indeed what happened, but not until 1943. His own boss, a man by the name of Vujković, said he was an animal—without whom no good police department could function. The story had it that both Kosmajac and Vujković had at one time been Communists. But it wasn't true. In his youth Kosmajac had joined the League of Young Communists, under false pretenses, and intending to betray. Vujković's case was clear-cut: as a young man, at the Salonika Front, he reported malcontents to Intelligence, and after the war he was transferred from the army secret service to the civilian police.

Kosmajac was tall and heavy, his face pockmarked, his lips curled, his nostrils wide and quivering in passionate excitement

when beating someone, his face crimson with blood. By the time he
got to me he was already in this condition. He looked at my Slovenian cellmate contemptuously, but he was of no interest to him. I
was sitting on the floor. That really provoked him. He shouted at
me to stand up "before him," and when I told him who I was he
laughed a grotesque laugh that twisted his whole face. He stank of
cheap wine and brandy, but he was not drunk. Grabbing me by the
shirt, high up, right under my throat, he asked about my role in the
demonstrations. He was waiting for an excuse to begin his routine. I
felt I would not be able to resist him. We stared at each other testing which of us would lower his eyes first. His look was cruel, but
not hateful. They had finally caught up with me, he said; I had been
on their list of dangerous Communists a long time. He wanted the
names of the people in my cell and of my next "contact" right there
and then. He swore loudly. I told him I didn't know anything. He
slapped my face hard. I had fully expected it, and yet I was surprised. I lost balance, and my head hit the wall, which he interpreted
as faking. He was beating me and kicking me all over, except on the
head. The room suddenly grew too small for the two of us. He
threw me into a corner, turned me over on my belly, and pounded
me with his fist. I lifted myself and him, like two feathers, but I
couldn't shake him off. He leaped at my neck, bent me forward,
shoved me in the ribs several times, and pushed me into the corner
again. He swore and threatened: this was "only the beginning,"
he said; he was pleased I wouldn't talk; he would see to it that one
more Communist bandit was eliminated. He was out of breath. I
could hear him barking at the gendarme as he left. The gendarme
didn't say anything. He was used to it. My nose was bleeding pro-
fusely. My whole body burned from the blows, but I felt no severe
pain in any one part. What hurt most was the feeling of humiliation
and helplessness. My Slovenian wept softly, over me, over human
fate.

Around one o'clock that night two agents came in and escorted
me to the fourth floor. They pushed me into a large office, and I
was face to face with a heavy-set, gray-haired man with an elongated nose and glasses. This was Svetozar Vujković, the Chief
of the anti-Communist division of the Belgrade police. We had
hardly looked at each other when he began to laugh, a noiseless
cold laugh. Whereas Kosmajac laughed for his own pleasure, like
an animal lapping up the blood of the enemy, Vujković did it deliberately, carefully following the victim's every move. The agents
leaped on me, screaming and grunting, pushing me from foot to fist,

from fist to foot. I stumbled on a little table holding a typewriter; Vujković swore at me for "wanting" to break his machine, slapped my face twice, straightened my head, looked me in the eyes, and asked me if I knew Stajkić. I said I didn't. He ordered Stajkić brought in. He asked me if I had written articles for the group and given them to Stajkić. I denied that too. He laughed. It was a natural, evil laugh. He pulled out my manuscripts from a pile of papers on his desk, and asked me if I had written them. Faced with my own writing I could not deny the accusation. I said the manuscript was mine. Vujković screamed in anger. Someone hit me on the back of the head, a reminder to tell the truth.

Stajkić was brought in. Vujković asked me if I knew him. I was silent. He repeated the question, and someone again hit me on the back. Stajkić volunteered the answer: he said we knew each other, but I didn't know his name. Perhaps he thought that would help me. His voice was so low that I could just barely recognize it. Someone hit him because he had talked out of turn. Vujković asked me if Stajkić's statement was true. I said it was.

Vujković employed no subtle ways in his interrogations. He never cross-examined his prisoners; he never tried to reason with them. Many years of experience had taught him that Communists were not stupid people, and that his best bet was beating them, which came to him naturally anyway. In his investigation he insisted on one thing: everything had to be explained one way or the other, and put together with sufficient logic to impress his superiors and at the same time be sufficiently factual to stand up in court. Little else interested him. He had one characteristic typical of great policemen: memory. He never took notes. Once the interrogation was over, he would dictate a report to his secretary in the presence of the accused. His memory for faces and names was indeed exceptional.

I looked at Stajkić in the hope of giving him a sign to hold his own, not to talk. But he wasn't looking at me, as if ashamed. He had always been frail physically, but now he looked crushed, his face worn but not swollen.

I was angry: he kept my manuscripts, which was something he should never have done, and now he was about to betray me. My Slovenian had told me that Stajkić had already betrayed everyone else, including him.

The minute Stajkić was taken out of the room, Vujković asked me the question I had expected all along: who put us in touch? But I refused to answer. He repeated his question and added that

Stajkić would answer it anyway. I said we had met accidentally in the street. The agents laughed. So did Vujković. That was such an obvious lie. I decided to say nothing the next time around. Vujković seemed discouraged and ordered me taken to my room.

Waiting is possibly the worst thing that can happen to a man in prison. He has no idea how much the authorities know. And in a situation like mine, I had no way of judging how much Stajkić would tell them. The night passed very slowly. From time to time the agents called out names, breathing heavily, anxious to get at their new victims as soon as possible. Then silence followed for an hour or more. When the victims were brought back, one could hear them sighing and grunting, weeping and sobbing. They had obviously been tortured. But how? Did they drive needles under their fingernails? Did they tie rope around their skulls? Stajkić made several trips back and forth. He must be talking. His demonstration of weakness was hard for me to take: my romantic notion about the strength and endurance of workers was shattered, and there was nothing to fill the vacuum. At one point the door of the room across from us opened a little and a man peeked through. He whispered with bitterness that Stajkić was a "coward." Short and thickset, he held his arms above his head in a gesture of pride. It was Dimitrije Jovanović, now Bojanovski. Next to Stajkić, he was the most important man in the organization. However, when Jovanović was brought back from the fourth floor some of his pride was gone. He could hardly move. He had revealed the names of the girls who had done the typing, saying that he really had no "choice" since Stajkić had already "blabbered." Did that mean that no one could resist confession if he was "accused," and that one could conceal only things known to oneself alone? Some people couldn't even do that.

It became clear during the night that quite a number of our people were in prison, perhaps thirty. And the number was growing.

I was most surprised to hear that Jovan Bubanja was there, a law student with whom I had shared a kitchen on Pašićeva Street until a month before my arrest. Why was he in prison, and what did they want from him? Bubanja never got mixed up in politics. He came from a poor family, but through various connections he had managed to get a job in Belgrade and to study at the same time. He hung on to his job for dear life, he was against Communism, but he never rejected Communists as friends. He was neat, almost compulsively so. He always wore the same spotless, immaculately pressed black suit with a starched collar and pointed well-polished black shoes. He was an honorable man, modest in his personal life as well as in his hopes for a career. Our relations were good, if not exactly cordial. To him I was a "conceited Communist bastard," and for me he was a "typical bourgeois." Both were probably true. I was fed up with his sermons on how hopeless it was to be a Communist, and never tried to get him to join the cause. I was convinced such a "limited" man was a hopeless proposition. Our relationship was reduced to the mutual respect of good roommates.

The night didn't gradually peter out; rather, it was suddenly cut off, around two or three in the morning. Silence set in—only a restless sigh from time to time or the squeaking of floorboards. But I couldn't sleep. I dozed off now and then only to be startled into wakefulness, wondering how much they already knew about me and how much they would learn.

The following evening Bubanja's presence in prison was finally explained. Stajkić had met him in our flat. He knew Bubanja was not a Communist, but he thought it quite "clever" to charge Bubanja with having put the two of us in touch, to protect the student who had actually done it. Poor Bubanja suddenly rose to prominence in the eyes of the police, and they practically beat him to death to get him to reveal the names of other "contacts." And Bubanja confessed! However, he then had to explain how and under what circumstances he had met Stajkić. He gave them the usual naïve story: they had met in the street, or something like that. But Stajkić had apparently said that they had met in a restaurant. The matter remained unresolved. Not knowing what Stajkić had in mind, I also said that Bubanja had introduced us, but insisted that he was not a Communist. There is an unusual amount of resistance in an innocent man, so Bubanja withdrew his "confession" the minute they had stopped beating him. He was an unusual phenomenon for the police: a man who cried sincerely and withdrew his confessions. Two weeks later he was released. The police had become convinced of his innocence, particularly after I had withdrawn my own confession concerning him and stuck by my former statement that I had met Stajkić in the street.

Stajkić never felt there was anything wrong with his "confession" implicating Bubanja. And I always felt ashamed. Although Bubanja didn't blame me at all, he did blame Stajkić. I ran into Bubanja once or twice after the war. He never asked for anything. He lived a modest life. But he was proud of our former "friendship" and mutual "hardships." I passed him on the street following my conflict with the Central Committee in the summer of 1954; he didn't return my greeting. After the war he had become a party member in keeping with his career in the civil service. He felt he should ignore me because now I, in turn, was a "bourgeois."

It was dark in the room for some hours. I was sure I would be tortured that night. Strangely enough, I felt far less anxious than the night before.

Around eight o'clock in the evening they took me to Aćimović's room. I was much changed since the last time I was in that room. I was a conscious organized revolutionary. The political situation, at home and abroad, was also changed. Hitler was in power in Germany, the University had a strong Communist organization, and the opposition was acting throughout the country. But Aćimović had remained the same. He had the same pleasant expression, the same sharp yellow pencil. He reminded me of the advice he had given me the year before. However, he was quite matter-of-fact: that was my choice, and they, the police, had to act accordingly. Torture was not what they had in mind, but I would be tortured unless I told them what they knew I knew. He appeared to be in a hurry; he rose from his chair. As I was being led away, he put on his elegant black coat and issued orders.

I was taken back to my room. My encounter with Aćimović had calmed me down somewhat. At least now I knew what to expect.

Around ten o'clock that evening I was escorted to Vujković's office. Todor and Kanački, his two agents, were present. Vujković appeared calm as he asked me three questions: my next contact, the University organization, and the source of the revolver.

I made up my mind not to say anything, to deny everything. I had already confessed that the manuscripts were mine, and gone along with Stajkić's idiotic idea of Bubanja's involvement. Now I had reached the point where, if I said anything, I would be denouncing other people, causing more arrests, and revealing activities in which they had engaged believing in me, and still more in the ideals for which we were fighting.

And yet I wouldn't be telling the absolute truth if I said that it was my feeling for the movement alone that played the major role in my decision not to betray anyone to the police. Of course it played an important role. However, for me the issue was chiefly a moral one: I couldn't imagine bringing to the police people who had such trust in me, those same people whom I had personally brought to the organization. It meant standing downcast and broken before the police and accusing my comrades to their faces and saying everything the bloodthirsty monsters wanted me to say. I felt it was more honorable, and far more simple, to die.

On the desk in front of Vujković there were chains and locks, dried and braided pizzles, and a few other instruments of torture. Although I knew they would torture me, I faintly hoped they had lined up all the instruments only to intimidate me. I was ordered to sit down; Vujković was brief: higher contact, the organization, the gun. I said I knew nothing. No one shoved me. No one hit me. Silence. Vujković broke the silence by saying that I had obviously chosen to be tortured. I replied that since I knew nothing I couldn't tell them anything.

But they didn't start in right away. Vujković suddenly decided to go out on a raid. They left me sitting there for two hours in front of those instruments of torture. Why did they do it? Because they sensed in me an exceptionally tough person, tougher than most? Or because they wanted to wear me out emotionally before the final attack? In any case, I sat there, and as I sat there my inner strength grew, rather than diminished.

The most common way of torturing people at this prison was by beating the soles of their feet with a pizzle. There were other ways as well, such as driving needles under nails, breaking teeth, hammering nails into heels. However, I actually never knew anyone who had experienced all of these things, not even Krsto Popivoda or Spasenija Babović, two people who were tortured in every conceivable way in 1937, perhaps worse than any other Communists in prewar Yugoslavia.

Beating with the pizzle on the soles of the feet was a method inherited from the Turks. It was widely used in Serbia during the Obrenović period. The night stick didn't prove sufficiently effective: it was round and soft and it didn't give that sharp edge to the pain. It was commonly used for beating people on the back. The pizzles were dried and finished. I personally saw Kosmajac carrying a whole package of raw pizzles and handing them to prisoners who were expert at drying and finishing. Once done, the pizzles were mounted on wooden sticks, shaped to fit the hand, their tips often decorated to resemble snakes, dragons, lions. This craft was a thriving business at Glavnjača, which, they say, was the major supplier of police stations throughout the country. At one time the pizzles were used on horses and oxen, but this had long since stopped. It was perpetuated only on humans.

When Vujković came back he asked for broiled beef and brandy. They were eating, telling crude jokes, laughing at the "respectable" family which was stunned when their apartment was raided because their niece, Berta Papo, had lent a typewriter to the Communists. Vujković boasted that he had carried the raid out in a "civilized" fashion, reducing the whole thing to bare formalities. They continued to eat and drink quickly while I waited to be tortured.

They ordered me to take my shoes off and to kneel down. I hadn't taken my shoes off for several days in prison. The stench was hard to take, even for me. One of the agents said for that reason alone I deserved to be beaten. That was obviously a standard joke around there. I knelt down and stretched my arms in the back, and they tied my hands and feet securely with a chain and brought them together for a moment. Vujković tested the pizzle. Todor pushed me. I fell on my stomach, and as I fell the soles of my feet turned up. I could no longer stretch my legs, because the chain on my hands, tied behind my back, kept them bent. Nor could I wiggle them, because they were fastened around the ankles. He then leaped on my shoulders and stuffed a rag in my mouth.

I could tell Vujković was close to me. I heard the gentle whistle of the pizzle and a sharp pain on the soles of my feet. The pain was sharper than I had expected. But it was now a familiar pain and I knew I would survive. It's the kind of pain that's transmitted directly to the brain: on the feet it feels like a cut with a knife, but even worse is the sharp reaction in the head. The body feels nothing. To each blow the victim ordinarily responds with a scream, but the scream, stifled with a rag, turns into a painful grunt from the depths of one's intestines. I experienced absolute terror at the thought that the fresh blows might land on the same spot. But they never did. Perhaps Vujković knew what he was doing—saving my skin for the next time.

I tried to count the blows, but quickly abandoned the effort. The blows grew sharper and were breaking me up. Vujković whispered into my ear: he ordered me, he asked me gently, he pleaded with me to talk. At one point he shouted: "Talk now; stop torturing us both!" Every time he asked me whether I was going to talk—the interval was two or three blows—I replied that I knew nothing or that I had already told them what I knew. Finally, I got angry and said I didn't want to talk. I clenched my teeth, determined not even to groan any more. They must have thought I had fainted. Vujković hit me a few more times and then stopped. He poured a bucket of water on my feet. I felt them burning, as if the water had come to a boil.

They knew how to work with chains. They released them from my body in a split second. I rose and stumbled. My feet tingled, as if I were standing on hot sand. I don't know why—perhaps because I was angry—but I was crying, and tears kept flowing in spite of me. Vujković was in his shirtsleeves and a waistcoat, drenched in sweat. He had already developed quite a paunch. He combed his smooth, grayish hair, wiped the sweat off his face, and sprinkled some cologne on his hands and forehead. He saw me stumble and commented ironically, his mouth stretched into a smile: "That's nothing. Communists perform well. The real thing is yet to come."

How long did all this last? Not less than half an hour. A lot of talk, shouting, swearing, and threatening. And how many blows? Between thirty and forty. There couldn't have been any more, or the skin would have split. They knew how to distribute blows over the body so as to leave no trace; they could also tell when the torture had become ineffective. In spite of the hatred and bitterness, I had to admit to myself that they had conducted the operation deliberately and professionally.

They dragged me back to my room. Strangely enough, the gendarme helped me into it. My Slovenian was frightened to death. I didn't really trust him but I told him, as if in a state of euphoria, that I had survived the torture without disclosing a thing. He was so thrilled that he kissed me many times. He signaled the Macedonian across the corridor, who was overjoyed to hear that I had betrayed no one. Everyone on the floor knew when a colleague was taken downstairs to be tortured. They waited for him to come back —proud and alone, or broken up, dragging behind him a chain of victims he had betrayed. I was the only one taken downstairs that night. And I came back stronger than before.

I lay down on the floor. My feet hurt. I could no longer put my shoes on. I wrapped myself in my coat, curled my feet up under me, and fell asleep. It was good sound sleep.

My meeting with Stajkić the following evening was painful. I had withdrawn my statement about Bubanja, exposing Stajkić to fresh pressures. He, in turn, was incapable of resisting threats of torture, let alone the actual torture. He talked with unusual clarity about the contact and the student organization. He told them in detail how much material he gave me and when. His memory was simply fabulous. As a rule, men who behave poorly before the police have a fantastic memory for detail. What's more, they are particularly concerned with detail and show great curiosity. It's hard to tell whether they acquire the information spontaneously so as not to run out of material when pressed by the police, but there is no doubt at all that this is a rule without exception. Specific details are the most important proof for the police that the prisoner is not making things up. I was no longer angry with Stajkić for his cowardice, but the way he kept volunteering details sent shivers up and down my spine and filled me with hatred and contempt. Let him tell them what he knew, if he had to, but why all this detail? Petko's escape was the only thing he hadn't touched on yet, but there was no reason to believe he wouldn't get around to it.

The second night of my torture was torturous indeed—not because of the beating, but because of my fear that Stajkić would reveal the details of Petko's planned escape. This would open a series of new questions: who conceived the plan, our contact with the Circuit Court prison, and, worst of all, the planned murder of the gendarme, which might result in a death sentence or, at the very least, the loss of all restraint in the treatment of prisoners. This would have been politically harmful as well, since the party condemned terrorism. It was essential to find some sort of a solution. But what, and how, in chains, between four walls, with Stajkić, who, like a torn sack, was spilling things in his trail?

That night I was tortured in a different way. Kosmajac was present, introducing into the proceedings a tone all his own, as if I had harmed him personally. He placed pencils between my toes and then squeezed them together. He pressed harder and harder, and looked as if he were going to burst. This seemingly innocent game caused extraordinary pain, which spread through my whole body. I suffered, I sweated all over, and then released a howl so long and so loud that I was terrorized by it myself. Someone held my mouth while Kosmajac continued to press. Finally they let me go. Everything was different from the night before: Vujković and the agents were excited, their eyes wild, as if determined to tear me to shreds. At long last they would get through to the Communist "student bandits" and to the local committee. I was sure they would learn nothing from me, but I continued to wonder what Stajkić would do next.

Everything appeared different that night, even objects. For example, a pencil was now an acceptable instrument of torture. A desk drawer: they could put one's hand in it and slam it shut. A pen: they could cut one up with it. At one point Kosmajac grabbed a bottle, put my neck between his legs, and started beating me with it on the shins. Who warned him to stop? Probably Vujković, who didn't lose his head even when he was wild with anger. Why did everything look so different that night? I felt as if stripped stark naked in front of them, no wisecracking, no vying, except with my body which would survive or succumb. Brains were useless.

It all started around nine o'clock in the evening. I was convinced they would not apply the same methods of torture as the night before, although deep down at heart I hoped they would, since it was relatively mild. Again they tied my legs and arms together, but this time in the front, my arms making a circle just below my knees. Then they shoved a round stick under my knees, which reached almost up to my chin. They lifted me up and rested the ends of the stick on two tables. I was suspended head down, all my joints aching to the point of madness; I tried to lift up my head, but actually found it more comfortable with the head lying limply and the blood rushing into it. But they wouldn't let it go at that: someone lifted up my head and stuffed my mouth with a kerchief.

They were beating me on the soles of my feet again. Kosmajac was beating me, and Vujković, leaning across the table, was telling me that I should talk, that I should stop destroying myself and them. The blows were more frequent than the night before, but the pauses in between were longer, and they poured water on my feet.

I was being turned into a shapeless heap of bloody flesh, which was still panting, but would soon cease to feel pain. I wanted to faint, and in fact did for a second or two: I recall having been lifted off the floor twice, although I don't recall having been put on the floor. I was wet through. But I was never really in a dead faint, at least not that I knew of.

I also recall that I was now afraid they would hit me on the testicles rather than on the same spot repeatedly, which was what I had feared the night before. As if sensing this fear, Kosmajac hit me several times close to the testicles. I knew that a blow on the testicles wouldn't kill me, but I was afraid of a new, permanent pain. There was no such blow. Instead, that animal, Kosmajac, rolled up my trouser leg and grabbed me by the testicles, and amid crude jokes and laughter about castrating all Communists he began squeezing and twisting them. It was a concentrated pain but all the more horrible as it then spread like an endless wave through the whole body and blocked out every other feeling, even the feeling of humiliation, which superseded all other feelings when the torture first started. How long did it last? Perhaps only a very short time, perhaps indefinitely.

There were other "small," but very painful tortures that night: fingers pressing under my ears, the separation and squeezing of individual muscles, done fast and in between major things. It was well past midnight when they dragged me back upstairs. I cursed the agents who were trying to get me to walk faster. I was in a state of complete frenzy, anxiety, and humiliation.

The next day I made up my mind to attempt suicide if they continued to beat me. Although I really had no intention of killing myself unless, of course, everything else failed. I felt that a man should die honestly if he couldn't live honestly.

My intention was to stop the interrogation with my attempted suicide. The truth was I could still put up with torture. In fact, I felt I might be able to stick it out for some time. But my human dignity was at stake, and I felt it my duty to lodge a protest against the beating, a public protest if at all possible. I was a well-known figure and I knew that the police and its methods would be compromised if the news of my "suicide" reached the public. But my chief concern was to prevent an interrogation concerning the organization of Petko's escape.

Early in the morning, I plunged my penknife just below my left shoulder, but not deep enough for it to penetrate the chest; I pretended to have fainted, gasping for breath. I must admit that, because of my general exhaustion and excitement, I was at times indeed on the verge of losing consciousness. My Slovenian raised a storm; he alarmed the guards. In less than ten minutes I was carried down several flights of stairs and driven off to a clinic. I kept my eyes closed until I was placed in a bed and a doctor arrived. It was the clinic of the famous surgeon Dr. Koen. Around ten o'clock he personally walked in and asked immediately whether I had been beaten. Around one o'clock his son Milan, a student, came to see me. Milan was dressed as a doctor, and although I was closely guarded, he sat on the edge of my bed and asked me questions: name, cause of "suicide," etc. He was a Communist sympathizer, and very closely involved in intellectual circles.

That same day all Belgrade knew of my case. The intellectual opposition and leftist circles leaped into action. The police issued a communiqué stating that a large Communist organization had been uncovered and that, faced with facts, I had attempted suicide. Two days later Vujković called on me: he was furious—furious at the policeman on duty who was fooled into rushing me off to the hospital and furious at his superiors who had issued the communiqué. But he didn't really count any longer.

A few days later my father and older brother came to Belgrade. My father had activated his old Montenegrin political contacts and the opposition lawyers, and they were even allowed to visit me. My father was worried, my brother bitter. He said: "I hear there is a man here who never stops beating. If anything happens to you, I'll kill him." I calmed him down, of course.

I also gave them a message for Mitra. But she had already done what I asked: we had agreed that if I were arrested she should destroy all my manuscripts as well as all addresses. I had given this same message to my Slovenian, who was due to be released, but he was questioned following my "suicide," and under extreme pressure revealed this information to the police. He was an honest and good man, but frightened. Anyway, a police agent called on Mitra with the password, but he gave himself away. He had no idea what it was all about, so he asked for a "higher contact" and "contact with the organization." Mitra quickly understood that the password meant she should burn the material. They never arrested her, because the matter was unclear and because her brother Živan, a *Politika* correspondent, had excellent connections. And Mitra walked up and down the street once or twice, just so she could wave to me.

The doctors wanted to remove my appendix in order to extend my hospital stay. But I rejected the idea, and ten days later I was returned to prison, this time to Glavnjača. The rest of the group had been transferred when the investigation was over to wait there before appearing at the Court for the Protection of State Interests, that is, the prison on Ada Ciganlija designated that spring as the prison for political prisoners.

Vujković greeted me with curses. I had simply extended my comrades' prison term with my "tricks," he said; by now they would all have appeared before the judge. Surprisingly enough, some of my comrades accepted this theory, even though it was customary to be held by the police four to six weeks. Vujković threatened, but I knew he would not beat me. The hearing went smoothly.

There was an unwritten law at Glavnjača concerning political prisoners: no member of the criminal police had any authority over them, unless it was a question of maintaining discipline. They were not allowed to question them or torture them. When a criminal was elected foreman of the cell, he always showed special courtesy to Communists. This was partly due to the traditional respect that criminal prisoners held for political prisoners, but it was also partly routine.

I ran into Veljko Kovačević in this prison. He was a law student and a Socialist. We had known each other for some time and had participated together in a number of student confrontations. Tall, strong, and dark-eyed, this Hercegovinian spoke with unusual passion about freedom and democracy at student gatherings. We Communists asked him how he could muster so much passion? He replied that he genuinely believed in freedom. We had our doubts on that score: we felt one could believe genuinely only in social justice, and in the revolution as the only means of achieving it. Kovačević had been picked up because he had on him the words and music of a popular opposition song. He hadn't yet been interrogated. I felt that the matter was not important enough to cause the police to beat him—in fact, I convinced him that was so. Also, I made a few suggestions as to what he should say when questioned. We gradually developed a cordial, frank relationship. We shared food and other things, but most important we shared friendly conversation. He spoke deliberately, as if enjoying well-chosen words. He was wise and intelligent, courageous and enthusiastic, and I wondered sadly why such a man was not a Communist. I decided to tell him about our underground activities and to urge him to join the movement. Didn't he realize, I insisted, that he could not have his socialism without a revolution? He said he would never dispute revolution as a means of fighting the dictatorship, but he doubted whether revolution would lead to socialism. And since he didn't agree with the Communists on this point, he couldn't become a Communist. That was an honest position and I accepted it. This difference didn't stand in the way of our friendship. Our ideals were not far apart, in spite of differences on how to make them work. He hated the regime, but not the way I did—especially following my experience with the police.

Kovačević and I shared a cell with a certain Galib-beg, a Bosnian Moslem who had traveled all over the world, and spoke many languages. Of slight build, bald, with a clipped mustache and a ruddy complexion, Galib-beg was light and fast, like a cat. He could jump safely from a third-floor window, and his bones were so pliant he could work his way out of chains. He was a hypnotist, and in this capacity he had a way of treating migraine headaches: he would oil his hands and arms up to his elbows and then slowly rub one side of the neck, pressing his knee against the spine. The momentary stoppage of the flow of blood to the brain would cause the patient to faint briefly, and the headache would go away. If at that moment his skull were rubbed on a special spot, he would behave as if hypnotized. He cured one of my headaches that way. I continued to suffer from migraines, particularly after the war, but I never used this method again. I felt that such treatment must damage the brain and memory in some way. The police had a great deal of trouble with this skillful burglar and thief because they could never find proof. He had an unusually good and exact memory and knew all the tricks of the trade. Another criminal was brought to our room, and Galib-beg extracted a confession from him regarding the murder of Draga Mitrović, a rich old lady from Belgrade. The police and newspapers had worked on this case for many years. Whether the police brought the two of them together by design or whether Galib-beg wanted to do the police a favor and thus help himself is hard to tell, but he did get the poor man to talk in his sleep. Every so often he would bring up the murder in conversation. One night our new cellmate was taken away, and shortly thereafter Galib-beg was released. I was asked to appear before the Criminal Division to tell them what I had overheard. I wondered what a Communist should do in a situation like that? I decided that a Communist should say nothing, not even regarding criminal cases. The police were our enemy under any circumstances.

Kovačević and I spent a lot of time discussing the wasted talent among criminals. We decided that the new society would solve this problem by re-educating such people. After all, the ills of this world had their origins in capitalism. Kovačević believed that the process would take a very long time, whereas I claimed it would not. I pointed to the Soviet Union, which had already successfully "re-educated" people. He had little faith in the success of the Soviet Union in this respect, although he did believe in the new society.

I parted with Kovačević with regret, all the more so because we didn't agree on everything, which he, being more tolerant, didn't seem to mind. We often ran into each other after my release from prison, and then again immediately after the war. But our real re-union took place twenty-two years later when he represented me as my attorney at the trial set up by my comrades—the very same comrades with whom I had fought the great struggle for liberation. Kovačević remained loyal to the ideals of his youth, whereas I had already become disenchanted with mine. He had no way of realizing his goals, whereas mine had turned into something altogether opposite. In his steady longing for freedom, he grew resigned to living the life of an ordinary deprived citizen, whereas mine was stormy and full of change.

Everything was green when they took us to Ada Ciganlija in a Black Maria. It felt as if we were going to some new world. We were, in a way: we knew that no one would beat us there and that we would be able to say what we wanted, that we would be given books and newspapers and the right to have food brought to us by relatives from the city.

In the van, we tried to decide who should say what before the examining magistrate in order to have a few people freed. I didn't have much to say to Stajkić, although he was willing to take a lot of responsibility. I got to know Stajkić very well in jail: he was an unusually good and gentle person, although insecure. We never became real friends, but I no longer felt hatred for him, and he no longer felt guilt on my account.

As far as my record with the police was concerned, several people, including Jovanović, held my "attempted suicide" against me. However, faced with a party commission in prison, they were nowhere to be seen or heard: they had squealed on others, whereas I was picked up alone, and I left alone. Suddenly my reputation grew; even Jovanović was impressed.

At the time of my arrest the party position on confession was as follows: when faced with facts, such as manuscripts and leaflets, confession was considered reasonable, but reporting the names of other people was considered treason. When I was released from prison in 1936, the party line had changed. Any form of confession was considered a sign of weakness—almost treason.

I myself was neither a hero nor a traitor. But there weren't many men in prison who held up as well as I did. The large majority passed the blame on to other people and revealed minor secrets. A few revealed everything they knew. They were real traitors. As a rule they did it unprompted by any beating, as soon as the police got hold of them. We knew all about them, and they were marked for life. However, Stajkić confessed under stress, and the police had to squeeze confession from him word for word. He didn't tell them "everything" he knew, only what the police already knew that he knew. He didn't come off too badly before the party commission: his major problem was that it all started with him. He was arrested with material evidence produced by a provocateur. He could have prevented further arrests only if he had been a hero. And that he was not.

19

Ada Ciganlija was wet and muddy from the spring rains. The Sava River had flooded the yard, and underground wells started up at the mere touch of the foot. Mosquitoes were a great pest throughout the summer.

The prison routine was not very strict. We took walks in the morning and afternoon. We were allowed to help each other out with food, exchange books, and so on. The only real restriction concerned communication between prisoners, to prevent them from "consulting" for purposes of the court investigation. Of course, getting around this was easy.

Our examining magistrate was Judge Job, the brother of a well-known painter. He was a tough, arrogant man, not very scrupulous. However, in later years he did favors for the Communist lawyer Bora Prodanović; he reported to him on how people behaved during police interrogations. A nationalist by conviction, and a Dalmatian, Job joined the Partisan movement at the end of the war.

The court investigation was completed quickly. Job had great faith in police interrogation. As a rule the court freed prisoners for whom they had no evidence. Masleša, for example, was released because of lack of evidence. Testimony given to the examining magistrate was decisive, and, once given, remained valid even if withdrawn.

The guards were well trained, strict, and straight. Their chief was a Slovenian by the name of Diklič, who liked to drink, but was virtuous in his strict interpretation of the rules, which afforded numerous loopholes and helped relax the strict prison regime. He had a great weakness for intellectuals, treated them well, but simply couldn't understand why such enlightened men were Communists. Interestingly enough, many years later his own son became a left-ist, and we used him as a contact with our prisoners at Ada Cigan-lija.

While I was at Ada Ciganlija, several political groups passed through—Communists, nationalists, and spies.

The central figure of the Marković group was, of course, Sima Marković himself, a short stocky man, with a bald head and an up-turned nose, large yellowish eyes, and thin sharp lips. He was a strong-willed man, capable of putting up with the worst insults without batting an eyelash, but also given to sudden outbursts of fury and bitterness. On the whole, though, his manners were smooth and he was well spoken. He addressed his wife formally, which we folksy revolutionaries ridiculed as a bourgeois habit, one more evil in a series attributed to him.

Marković had been a Socialist in Serbia since before World War I. As a young man he belonged to a semianarchist group that sought direct action and was critical of the official leadership of the Serbian Social-Democratic party. A mathematician by profession, he followed contemporary science, and was, in fact, the first and the most consistent believer in Einstein's theory in Yugoslavia. He was in correspondence with Einstein, and the great scientist inter-vened with the Yugoslav government by telegram every time Mar-ković was arrested. He was one of the most knowledgeable men I ever knew. Spirited and quick-witted, he was always ready to jump from one subject to another, including topics that were not his "specialty." Psychoanalysis was in vogue at that time, even among Communists, and he had "firsthand" knowledge of it. He was pro-ficient in four major languages and constantly read books and maga-zines and made notes. And his pursuit of intellectual matters grew as the scope of his political activity diminished.

Marković was the head of the Yugoslav Communist party at the time it was outlawed, causing him to be sentenced to two years in prison. Factional struggle flared up within the party, and he became the leader of the right-wing faction, which had its roots in Serbia, chiefly among intellectuals and older workers. This faction also drew on its association with the Social-Democratic party, on its ideas and methods. Nevertheless, the ruling circles and the intellectuals held Sima Marković to be the ideological leader of the Communists. He was less sharp and implacable than the Bolsheviks and Commu-nists trained in Moscow, easier for them to deal with. But there was no truth in the rumor, promoted by the left wing, that the police

encouraged his activities because that was in their interest. Marković was arrested often, but not beaten, a rare privilege under the
dictatorship. He stood up well, though, and confessed nothing.

While in prison, Petko Miletić managed to win the whole group
imprisoned with Marković over to his side. That was not a particularly difficult job: Marković's moderate attitude was no longer suitable to the aggressive spirit of men who had grown up under the
dictatorship, and who had joined him because his was the only
effective party group. They were now putting pressure on him to
"yield" to the party. Marković must have understood that his battle
with the party was lost: a new generation was gaining prominence
with the Central Committee and Moscow.

Actually, we paid little attention to these conflicts. We made
an honest effort to understand the arguments on both sides, but the
simple fact was that Stalin argued against him and the Central Committee was in disagreement with him. Also, we were irritated by his
"petit bourgeois" mentality, his nonargumentative, "opportunistic"
attitude to the guards and the court, his "intellectualism." In his
leaflets he never referred to King Alexander as that "bloody dog
Alexander the last," which had become a stock phrase among us
Communists and a confirmation of our revolutionary integrity, and
he concentrated his attack on the dictatorship rather than on the
bourgeoisie. Of course, he felt the isolation, but to avoid open conflict, he was tolerant and careful of what he said.

Politically he had no consistent view of the world or of the situation in Yugoslavia. He remained somewhere in the middle, between
the old Serbian Social Democracy and Bolshevism, between revolutionary Marxism and reformism, in useless attempts to explain the
new world with old patterns.

Indeed, Sima Marković was in part responsible for the gossip
about him. As a politician he was without any moral scruples, and
not very selective when it came to employing various means to
achieve his end. He didn't appear to be given to intrigues, but he
changed his opinions so often, agreeing now with one man and
now with another, that intrigues spawned themselves. He thought
nothing of stating totally contrary opinions if that would yield immediate practical results. That was the reason we younger Communists considered him a "bourgeois" politician, a Communist ruined
by "bourgeois parliamentarianism" and "scheming."

We had another proof that Sima Marković was guilty of most of
our accusations. He had cried at his trial because the police arrested
him at his sister's funeral. He tried to "move" a "bourgeois court,"

made up of those hangmen and bloodthirsty monsters. When he was told by the judges that he was free to go, he jovially shook hands with them and thanked them for their "objectivity"—the objectivity of the same court that had sentenced his comrades to many years in prison for the very same activity that he himself had been conducting! Under somewhat different parliamentary procedures he might have become a significant figure, but he didn't have a single quality required of a revolutionary under a dictatorship.

Upon release from prison, Marković was interned at Plevlje. He remained there until 1934, when an escape was organized for him. The Central Committee wanted to remove him from Yugoslavia, and he in turn wanted to reach a compromise with both the Central Committee and the Comintern. He ended up in the Soviet Union. Apparently he stuck to his views to the bitter end, for the 1936–1937 purges did not spare him. He was sentenced to ten years, and died somewhere in Siberia.

In spite of his uncertainty and opportunism, he did not hesitate in proving his loyalty to the revolutionary socialist ideal. But we Stalinist Communists were pleased, as I recall, to know that the Soviet Union had relieved us of Sima Marković and his theories.

20

Among the many people who passed through Ada Ciganlija were a large group of Ustashi from Lika. Their leader was Juraj-Juco Rukavina, a colonel during World War II and organizer of the massacre of Serbs in Lika.

This group was made up mostly of the Lika peasants, who were bright and primitive, honest, and, above all, poor. They learned quickly, reducing everything to their own simplified clear-cut formulas. Their peasant reasons for hating the Belgrade regime were different from those of the intellectuals in the Ustashi movement. They sought jobs and better prospects for life, which the "Serbian government" and the "Serbian gendarmes" would not give them. Austria, where many of their compatriots had jobs, was, for them, a well-organized country where people earned good wages and lived well. And now, in Yugoslavia, they were obsessed by every evil: drought, administrative plunder, high taxation, and, worst of all, the impossibility of earning a living.

The fascist ideology of the Ustashi had not yet been fully developed. The "Führer principle" had not been accepted; Ante Pavelić was recognized as their leader, but no exceptional "divine" properties were attributed to him. He was their boss, a man who could be replaced by someone else when and if it became necessary.

Nor were they at home yet with the term "Ustashi." They preferred to call themselves "Croatian nationalists" and, under Communist influence, "Croatian national revolutionaries."

The gap between us Communists and the Ustashi was not nearly as great as it was to become in the late 1930's and during the war. The Central Committee and the Comintern emphasized the importance of co-operation with "national revolutionaries" in certain areas. At one point negotiations were conducted with them, but no agreement was reached. In an effort to revive "nationalist revolutionary movements," the party leadership tried to set up nationalist organizations in places where conditions were not particularly favorable, as in Slovenia. And I recall that in prison, until 1936, we thought of Macedonian nationalists, who were as a rule Bulgarian agents too, as "Macedonian nationalist revolutionaries." Consequently, we tried to engage them in political co-operation.

Obviously, the prison atmosphere explains in part our relatively good relations with the Ustashi. We had a common enemy: the government and the regime. And we lived under much the same conditions. But there were other, more important, reasons as well.

First of all, both groups believed that Yugoslavia should be broken up into its component parts. The Ustashi wanted a series of independent states, whereas we Communists had a somewhat vaguer concept. We believed that each one of these independent state units would join the Soviet Union, which is to say, the Balkan federation. But we both contended that Yugoslavia, as an "artificial creation of the imperialist Versailles Peace Treaty," should and must disappear. We stuck to this contention until Hitler's first aggression, practically until the Seventh Congress of the Comintern in 1935. Sima Marković was criticized for his inconsistent views on this point. By reducing the national question to a constitutional issue, he favored in effect a joint state of the Yugoslav peoples. Even if the reality of revolution was absent from his thinking, I feel that he anticipated the reality of Yugoslavia. Even though a Socialist, he belonged to the generation for which the creation of a common state was the ultimate aim.

In our conversations with the Ustashi we did find a common language, particularly when it came to our attitude toward the Croatian Peasant party, which was alien to us. They were peasants who rose up against authority because they had not been allowed to organize, because municipal rule and high taxation were imposed on them, or because of frequent military service. They considered the state their own even though they were deprived of their rights. But what put us Communists off the most was their opposition to the revolution. They were morally shocked by the dictatorship's use of force; in their primitive way they thought that no good could come of it. They had suffered through several centuries of landlords, military aggressors, sickness, and all kinds of oppressions, but they survived and remained "rulers of their own hearth." There was something fatalistic in their patience. The Ustashi despised them, and we Communists considered them a heap the dictatorship could shape any way they liked, a job that would take a thousand years to complete, though. The Peasant party membership was large, but they did not come to prison in big groups as the Ustashi did. Betraying a friend under torture was considered shameful. The important thing was to maintain, to the very end, an inner resistance to force, total unacceptance of it. When Maček came to power in 1939, I spent some time in Croatia as an underground party worker. It seemed as if these peasants had again withdrawn into their primitive environment, which moves slowly, every two or three hundred years, usually at crucial times in history.

The intellectuals in Radić's Peasant party differed from the Ustashi in one important respect: the Ustashi did not choose their means carefully, not even when it came to relying on foreign countries, such as Italy and Hungary, whereas the Radić people showed a certain reserve in this respect.

We Communists did not blame the Ustashi for their reliance on Italy and Hungary, although we didn't approve either. We instinctively felt that the Ustashi action could only help further our own aim: the destruction of Yugoslavia. Thus moral and patriotic aspects of this problem were inconsequential.

I never felt that the party's anti-Yugoslav position was based on the needs of the people, or intimately tied in with my own revolutionary feelings. Having grown up and fought during the dictatorship, with people from all parts of the country, we accepted the party's anti-Yugoslav position as a matter of discipline rather than of conviction. It was the position of the Comintern, as well as of older Communists, who were disappointed in the idea of Yugoslav unity expressed in the aggressive reactionary measures of the centralistic government.

Thus our Communist-Ustashi "friendship" was conditional and temporary. Eventually they joined the fascist forces, and we accepted a line of defending the country. Our relations deteriorated, until by 1936 they were reduced to a common struggle exclusively in the field of improvements in prison life.

But in 1933 we were still on good terms. Based on our Communist sociological premise, we concentrated, with a vengeance, I might add, on "re-educating" peasants, at first casually and later in a more organized fashion. The results, we thought, were encouraging.

The Ustashi agreed with all our ranting against the rulers, and even against religion and the church. Yet, in spite of their ideological confusion, they remained true to themselves: fanatic believers in a nationalism that, under the circumstances, could assume no other than fascist and racist forms. We managed to win over only a few, mostly younger intellectuals. Almost without exception, the Ustashi rejected us when we started fighting fascism on a new "patriotic" level.

After the release of the Sima Marković group, I was moved to the upper floor, which was considered a privilege. I shared a room with Juco Rukavina and Koren, an Italian spy. I spent some two or three months with them. Koren was tried and convicted in September, and Rukavina remained until his trial in October, if I recall correctly.

Rukavina and I became real friends, not an exceptional case. Other Communists were making friends with "nationalists" and such friendships often outlasted prison years.

Rukavina came from Gospić. He had been an officer in the Austrian army, and during World War I he had fought on the Italian Front. At the end of the war he joined the Serbian (Yugoslav) army, but not for long: he got into a fight with a Serbian major, was expelled, and returned to his home town. The dictatorship revived memories of the years of hatred and the discontent of a dishonorably discharged officer, to whom the war had offered magnificent prospects.

Tall, slender, and tough, like so many men from that region, he had a disconcerting smile which changed quickly from anger to self-satisfaction. Not forty yet, he was already graying, which made his dark bony face even more striking. He was generous, perhaps not exactly in a discreet way, but generous nevertheless. He was also proud—that pride characteristic of the Austrian aristocrat which our frontier officers had absorbed from contact with them. But above all he was a loyal friend. And like all mountain people, he loved his native region, he longed for its crags, the roast lamb and prshuta, the bitter drinks, and women full of secret passion.

He had courage, but a sudden, unstable courage, inspired by moments of anger and a desire to show off.

Rukavina was brutally tortured by the police in Gospić and in Zagreb. His limbs were stretched to such an extent that one of his hips was dislocated.

In order to squash any attempt at armed rebellion, the government dispatched a special unit to Lika. They ruthlessly arrested peasants, and transported a number of more serious offenders to Zagreb for further interrogation. The "raid" was touched off by a poorly organized night attack on a police station. The authorities had known nothing about the smuggling of arms, although it had assumed considerable proportions. The special unit was composed chiefly of Serbs, and emissaries from Belgrade played a major role in the Zagreb interrogations. The regime didn't have enough sense to handle the whole matter through Croatian policemen, although they were no less cruel than Serbs. It placed trust only in its own people, who, inspired by this trust, acted with all the more venom.

The gendarmes' orgiastic torture of the men of Lika was accompanied by all kinds of brutalities toward their families. They beat their women, they burned paper under their shirts, they broke their ribs and shattered their teeth.

Juco Rukavina didn't hold up too well during his interrogation, which bothered him, particularly in contact with us Communists; we attached so much importance to courageous behavior before the police. Very few of the Ustashi held up well under beating: they felt that once they were caught they could no longer fight, whereas for us Communists imprisonment meant the beginning of the fiercest kind of struggle with the "class enemy." The Lika peasants, intimidated by beating, would keep quiet, bearing up patiently under torture until their leaders began to talk. Then suddenly they would come out with it all.

The Ustashi group in prison was relatively small. Only those directly involved in the preparation of the armed attack were detained. The organization of an armed uprising and the smuggling of arms from Italy had given the regime an easy justification for the brutality. At the same time they acknowledged that the movement had assumed large proportions—because of the difficult sociopolitical conditions, particularly in the Croatian regions. Several influential Zagreb lawyers volunteered their services at the trial of the Lika Ustashi, and sympathetic Croatian opinion exerted a great pressure on Belgrade. It had become clear that Croatian political life was awakening following the first blows of the dictatorship and several years of darkness. Rukavina was the only one sentenced to death. Earlier, for a similar offense, there would have been many death sentences.

Rukavina's group left to hear the reading of their sentence. At lunchtime I heard singing from the river Sava, recognized Rukavina's voice, and leaped to the window. A rowboat was approaching shore. With his hands tied, Rukavina was sitting upright, singing into the sunny day. He had been sentenced to death—I knew it instantly. He entered our room, his head still up, and to my questioning glance he made a gesture of tying a noose round his neck and hanging it above his head.

He had not expected the death sentence, because of the numerous interventions in his behalf rather than because of his defense, which Sima Marković had helped him plan. We younger Communists were angry at Marković for having urged Rukavina to take a sentimental and remorseful position in the courtroom, thus avoiding all nationalist tirades, and creating the impression that he was, at worst, guilty of a temporary act of discontent. He still had to explain where they had gotten the arms and for what purpose. A naïve story about how they had to defend their livestock against wolves simply didn't stand up. My own warnings that this explanation was senseless, and that Rukavina should therefore openly declare himself a "nationalist revolutionary," bore no results. I appealed to them to acknowledge that they were organizing because of the plight of the Croatian people, but this was rejected as useless. Denying the uprising established a link of sorts between the regime and the accused. Rukavina agreed to admit that, as a Croat, he was dissatisfied. His nationalism was the only thing he would never reject. And he agreed to stand by it at his trial.

It's strange how the threat of death removes barriers between people! The guards disliked Rukavina because of his arrogance, not because he was a Croat. They were all Serbs from Serbia, and their hatred of Croats was something acquired rather than intuitive. But now they were all attentive to him, even kind. Everything was forgotten: religion and politics. Rukavina himself had softened. He no longer blamed Serbs for all the evils of this world.

He slept that night, but it was a restless sleep. He woke up often, smoked and talked. He recalled small lyrical details from his childhood and youth. He said that he hated the thought of being touched by the executioner's hand, of having the noose slipped round his neck; he would prefer to be shot.

However, he bore up courageously. He was calm and friendly. Though he had not held up well before the police or during his trial, now that it was time for him to die he felt no fear and was resigned to his fate.

The following day, a lawyer came to draft the appeal for mercy, which was written in the most humble language. I urged Rukavina to change it. He said it was up to the lawyer. If they had already made up their minds to execute him they would do so anyway. If they hadn't, it meant they had sentenced him to death so that the King could give amnesty to him. Anyway, he decided to stick to his lawyer's advice. Perhaps he was right: the short-tempered King might take his head on account of one word he didn't like. The lawyer also brought encouraging news: Rukavina would almost surely be pardoned, because the Archbishop of Zagreb had traveled to Belgrade to intervene with the King on his behalf.

During the next few days enormous quantities of excellent food were sent to Rukavina. In keeping with Communist terminology, Rukavina said the food was donated by the Zagreb "bourgeoisie," which, judging by the excellence of the food, was enjoying a political revival.

A few days later, Rukavina was again ordered to appear before the court. We knew that he would be pardoned and we were happy. It all ended well: the man remained alive and so did the state. We Communists concluded that the regime didn't dare execute him out of fear of stimulating further discontent among the Croatian people. For a while Rukavina favored closer co-operation between Croatian nationalists and Communists. But when relations between the two groups grew strained, he withdrew, like so many hard-bitten Ustashi ideologists. But he always felt friendly toward me, perhaps because I had been with him when he was under sentence of death. Our prison leadership took advantage of this friendship, and whenever they wanted to win the Ustashi over for some joint action, they asked me to negotiate with Rukavina. Rukavina never rejected my positions, but I could never be sure that he promoted them later at the Ustashi gatherings.

Upon the formation of the Cvetković-Maček government, he was released from prison, along with the rest of the Ustashi. In 1940 Maček put him in a concentration camp, and in 1941 Pavelić made him a colonel in the army. He didn't do exceptionally well under the Pavelić regime: a man of low intelligence, he loved a good time; he was too fast and sometimes indecisive. When he ran into Communists in the street during the war, his former prison mates, he did not report them to the authorities. However, he exterminated Serbs all over Lika, and with gusto, believing that to be his mission in life. He hated Serbs far more than Communists. When Zagreb was liberated, our authorities caught him and executed him. He asked for nothing, and he expected nothing.

21

If our relations with the nationalists were relatively good, our relations with spies never assumed any form other than that of mutual tolerance essential in prison. They had no means of interesting Communists in any of their activities. On the contrary, we found everything about them repulsive. They were men without any ideals, at least by our standards. They had no scruples and no ideological framework to guide their actions other than material gain. Not even their opposition to the state of Yugoslavia, which they were so busily undermining, could bring us closer together.

One of these groups was important, both in size and in the nature of the business it was engaged in. Most of its members were former officers in the Austro-Hungarian army who in 1918–1919 joined the army of the newly formed state of Yugoslavia. Eventually they were released and pensioned off, but they maintained contacts with their former garrisons, both Yugoslav and Austro-Hungarian. This led quickly to various forms of espionage. The information was dispatched to Austria, to Hungary, and indirectly to Italy.

The leader of the group was a certain Mićić, an intelligent man, but one full of remorse and lacking in the will to live. The thwarted career of a professional army man might have played a role in making this man a spy, but there were more profound reasons, such as moral disintegration and disillusionment with society. It was hard to determine exactly what had prompted Mićić to espionage. His colleagues found their justification in a certain loyalty to their youthful ideals, but he didn't even have that. He kept silent in his self-destruction and helplessly awaited his sentence, a man who could neither escape justice nor summon it.

Another man in this group, a red-bearded officer of the former monarchy, was an altogether different type from Mićić. He was never rattled and never lost the inner harmony of a man who enjoys good food and the strength of his body, and for whom espionage was one of the more noble of life's occupations. He realized that his sentence would be determined independently of his position —in terms of the prevailing political situation, over which he had no influence one way or the other. The only thing he could do was not to provide the authorities with material for a heavier sentence. He would not try to fake or plead with anyone; on the contrary, he would stand up through the whole procedure, attempt to make it as short as possible, and return to a relatively normal routine.

The group also included a young Italian from Split. His contact with the group was entirely superficial, but the prosecution wanted to show that "our state" was being sabotaged by both Italy and Hungary. He was the only one who had confessed nothing. He defended the interests of his country and the ideals of the Fascist party, of which he was a militant member. His surname had been Slavified at one time, and then again Italianized. He felt himself to be an Italian with all his being, a missionary of the Roman and Italian civilizations. He was a handsome, intellectual man, very much aware of his gifts. In Split, he had been the central figure in the Italian propaganda campaign for Dalmatia. For many years the regime had been trying to catch him in an act of espionage. They finally succeeded by using a woman who had transmitted to him an insignificant message from Mićić's group. But this was enough to prove him guilty.

The young Italian hated us Communists. Nevertheless, he showed a certain respect for our courage and our faith in ideals. His behavior was correct, inasmuch as behavior between people forced by circumstances to live under the same roof had to be correct. He never engaged in ideological or political disputes with us, because he thought his own ideas far superior. He believed us to be primitive Balkans, a fanatical sect which would be annihilated in the great conquest by the empire and the fascist ideal. This originated not with his political ideas, but, rather, with his national upbringing— a characteristic of many Italians who believe in the superiority of their civilization. But since this man had integrity, his feeling of national superiority took the form of belief in the advantages of his ideology.

The Yugoslav government had very poor relations with its greedy neighbors, who supported all sorts of terrorist groups, each with its own vast spy network. As a result, spies were treated unmercifully. Mićić and the man with the red beard were sentenced to death by hanging. They said that Mićić had a hard time dying because there was so little of him left to pull down on the rope, whereas the red beard went fast because of his bulk. The young Italian got a long prison sentence, but he was released, along with his whole group, when the Stojadinović government came to power and established close ties with the Axis Powers.

There were also three Bulgarians at Ada Ciganlija. They were not nationalists, but poor peasants who had come to Belgrade in search of bread. They had large families to support, so they had agreed, for a relatively small sum of money, to place three or four infernal machines in various government offices. They were brutally tortured by the police, although no one was killed. Their offense could not have been more clear or simple. They were accused of having plotted to sabotage state property, of having deliberately planned the action out of their profound hatred of the state, and of having received large sums of money. They signed whatever they were asked to sign. Thus the Belgrade regime had found innocent victims for its political ambitions, mobilizing public opinion against foreign aggression and further justifying the existence of the dictatorship. Such grim business deals were often concluded in Belgrade and Sofia. An agent of the Bulgarian secret service had found these simple-minded poor peasants and had thrust them into a great international game.

Needless to say, the peasants had no idea that they had suddenly become the object of such complex political machinations. They thought of themselves as simple, hard-working people who had transgressed the law, for which they received a good beating from the police. They missed their wives, homes, children, and mother earth. The most difficult thing for them in prison was sitting around, doing nothing, though thinking evil thoughts. But the guards, also peasants by origin, quickly discovered in them excellent workers and very skilled gardeners. Before long, green beds of all kinds of vegetables lined the prison walls, and the Bulgarians praised the earth on the island, pointing to the large expanses of it under the willows. The earth was like velvet; it needed no fertilizer and no water, only hands!

That summer everyone had plenty of vegetables, and the Bulgarians were happy too. At the beginning they were watched carefully, but as time went on only one guard was posted, and he sat close by in the shade reading newspapers and dozing. It never occurred to these people to escape. Where would they go anyway?

They were far from their homes, and there was no way of getting there except by train. Besides, they had done wrong and it was only right they should do something for the authorities.

Two of them were mature men, while the third was fairly young, just married. When we asked him jestingly whether he missed his bride, he would lower his dark eyes and blush. He was frail and looked ill; he "hurt inside a little" since the police interrogation. They felt sorry to see their young companion rotting away in prison—no children yet, no fruit trees, no cattle, and his bride waiting for him at home.

They had no visitors, and they hardly ever received letters. Their families couldn't send them food because they didn't have enough to feed themselves.

They had court-appointed lawyers for their trial, which lasted much longer than it should have. The authorities dragged it out and dwelt extensively on every detail, which the newspapers in turn blew up, although as a rule trials in this court were not publicized. To everyone's astonishment, all three men were sentenced to death. They were no longer allowed to see each other. They awaited mercy for a few days, and then suddenly understood that something terrible had happened, that they were tools in some horrible game played by unknown powers.

At one end of the prison there was a special building, built like a barracks and used for storage. It was high enough to accommodate a gallows. The three of them were hanged there, huddled together and lost in a world that did not understand them, and which they did not understand. They were buried secretly in the swamps of the island, which eat up human bones in no time.

22

Several groups of Communists also passed through Ada Ciganlija, including a group of Slovenians composed of Boris Vojnilović, Boris Kidrič, Lidija Šentjurc, and Venigerholc. We "Balkanites" found it hard to understand the Slovenians. They were not beaten, but they confessed to the police anyway and betrayed their comrades almost as easily as the Croatians, Serbs, and Bosnians, who were beaten as a matter of course. Beating and torture were rare in Slovenia; when beating was needed to extract a confession, Belgrade policemen were usually imported. Even this practice, frequent at the beginning of the dictatorship, diminished under the impact of public opinion. The Kidrič-Vojnilović group was exceptional in this respect. On the whole they stood up very well, and the charge against them was not based on evidence provided by their comrades, but, rather, on the word of the police.

Venigerholc was assigned to my room. During the war he changed his name to Dragić because Venigerholc sounded too German. He was young and dark and intelligent.

Kidrič was a slender young man with a large, strong head and bulging blue eyes. He was mature for his twenty-one years but he had a bizarre sense of humor. His manner and dress betrayed his bourgeois upbringing, although like so many young Communists from bourgeois families he did his best to reject it by using dirty language (borrowed from Serbian, needless to say). Kidrič's "guilt," according to the indictment, was secondary and he was released, perhaps due in part to his father's connections and influence.

Lidija Sentjurc was not guilty of any serious "crime" either. She was a strong woman, rather short, dark, with large eyes and a broad smile. The whole group was cheerful, reliable, and competent. For us Balkanites contact with these even-tempered and intellectual Slovenian Communists was both pleasant and valuable. It was an active reminder of a large Communist family at work all over the country, regardless of differences in language and history. In fact, our friendship with them developed very easily, more easily than with the Croats. They accepted our somewhat primitive and vulgar ways, which they may have interpreted as an example of "Communist simplicity" and "camaraderie," and we, for our part, in their presence, suddenly stopped swearing, so as not to offend their European "suaveness" and "good manners." The Slovenians were less aggressive than we in direct contact with the "class enemy" (the guards and prison administration), but stronger in theory. Our approach to Communism was more emotional, theirs more intellectual. These differences, because we basically sought the same results, brought us closer together.

The most severely punished of the group was Boris Vojnilović, who was young, intellectual, and completely absorbed in one thought, one idea. He formed opinions quickly and was given to sudden enthusiasms. He came from a poor family and spurned Kidrič as a child of the bourgeoisie, but he also envied him his superior culture. The group was compact, but there was a certain amount of tension between the two of them: Vojnilović claimed that Kidrič was avoiding revolutionary activity, and Kidrič was convinced that Vojnilović had committed a series of blunders which had led to their arrest. Kidrič was basically right. Vojnilović's passion was conspiracy and secrecy. He had smuggled a letter from the Central Committee into our prison by stuffing it into a tube of toothpaste. He also brought in a number of party publications. He was a young man determined to take great risks.

There were also two rather large Bosnian groups, from Sarajevo and Tuzla, in our prison. For them the stay at Ada Ciganlija was a vacation, a chance to catch their breath. The Court Detention House in Bosnia had no newspapers or books, and they were beaten regularly. To maximize pressure on them, at Ada Ciganlija they were questioned by the same policemen who had beaten them earlier.

Both groups were undermined by mutual accusations and quarrels, and deeply demoralized, yet they had no intention of renouncing Communism. They felt a more personal bitterness because of a certain lack of camaraderie and solidarity, rather than disappointment with Communism itself.

Much of the tension in one group was generated by Milan Gavrić. High-strung and very intelligent, he was in conflict with himself as well as with everybody else. He was upset by his relatively poor showing with the police, and eventually he had a nervous breakdown. However, he remained closely attached to the movement and loyal to Communism. He later wrote to us from prison saying that among lunatics he was a "lunatic Communist." On his release, his condition improved, but he continued to be distraught.

Srdjan Prica was also in this group, but according to the plaintiff's statement, his involvement was secondary. Simple and modest, he was nevertheless aware of his tall good looks and he walked with his head up. His light hair was always neatly combed and he was quick to show his strong white teeth in a friendly smile.

A worker by the name of Risto headed the Sarajevo group. His showing before the police was not very good because, contrary to widespread belief, he thought he had had no choice of action. Finding himself isolated from the group, he decided to withdraw still further into himself.

Ivan Marković headed the Tuzla group. He didn't stand up too well with the police either, but, in contrast to Risto, he understood the harm that a betrayal can generate. He was sentenced to ten years, but escaped from prison in 1941, along with all his comrades. He never got the opportunity to prove himself—he was killed in combat.

I feel it is important to emphasize the difference between, for instance, Marković and Risto. I never knew a single Communist who behaved badly upon arrest and who did not repeat it during his next arrest, in spite of all the ideological and personal preparation he underwent in between. It is as if there is something deeper, inborn, so to speak, relative to fear or courage when one is left alone, between four walls, in the hands of an enemy. This courage has nothing to do with the kind of courage one displays in wars or during hunger strikes. One's ideological and political convictions obviously play a role, but not the most important role. Definite convictions are necessary in order to follow definite ideas. But how individuals react in struggling for them depends on their psychological and moral characteristics.

And such characteristics and values cannot be judged until a suitable opportunity presents itself for revealing them. The very best opportunity for testing them is the experience of police torture, with all its complex and insidious psychological and physical pressures. A man is alone, with himself and his enemy. The enemy exerts pressure on him to betray his idea. The enemy makes all kinds of promises; he even says the "comrades" will never learn about what passes between himself and his victim. Furthermore, the enemy insists this would be no "betrayal" in the conventional sense, but, rather, a kind of loyalty to traditional values and relations. In such situations the inner strength of a man is put to the test. I have always considered my own behavior in prison, under torture, the highest form of courage. Today I am not nearly as convinced, although I continue to regard this form of courage very highly. Personal courage, the courage to defend one's own opinions and ideas to the bitter end, is the greatest courage of all, and the most human, at least here, in this country, where there is so much physical courage and so much personal cowardice.

Pasaga Mandžić was also with the Tuzla group. He was a strong, heavy-set young man. He held up badly before the police, but didn't seem terribly "torn" by this, because he was cheerful by nature. In contrast, Leonid Banker reacted angrily at each reference to his behavior with the police.

Ahmet Kobić, a peasant from the Tuzla group, was brought into my room. He was a blend of several epochs and several characters. Like most Bosnian Moslems, he had fought on many World War I fronts and had come home disenchanted. He joined the Communist movement after World War I, when the party was still legal. He ran a mill, and had a nice plot of land, so it was injustice, rather than poverty, that attracted him to the movement, the teaching of the Koran more than of Marxism and Leninism. He read a great deal and was considered a man of wisdom in his village.

Following the ban on the Communist party, he spent years spreading his own brand of Communism free of any contact with the illegal groups and enjoying the reputation of a just and truthful man.

His own people criticized him as an opportunist and a wisecracker. There was some truth in that. Kobić opposed the distribution of pamphlets, the formation of party cells and committees. Why bring complete strangers together? One of them squeals to the police and we all go! Free of all this, he successfully gathered together his peasants, not into one group, but a dozen, telling them what he felt they should know, and interpreting Communist pamphlets his own way. Although he didn't believe in God, he saw nothing wrong in going to the mosque and bowing in order to stay close to his peasants. Thus his vast experience as a popular agitator was now in conflict with the revolutionary schematics. No revolutionary organization could ever be built up on the basis of his method and positions. But without his kind of experience to go on, the organization could not take root among the masses, which meant, in effect, that it could never grow.

Kobić was disappointed by the behavior of the "proletarians" before the police. He once said, half in jest, that it was no wonder that he, a peasant, a small landowner with retarded class consciousness, didn't behave right; but it was surprising that the city proletarians, strong as steel, proved to be such miserable weaklings.

He was willing to give up everything for an idea, but he also loved his family passionately. It was important for him to prevent the arrest of his son and to keep him from rotting in jail somewhere. He talked about his wife in a crude way, revealing the intimate details of their relationship. But in this apparent frankness there was deep secret tenderness, primeval, like his love of earth. They were two beings joined forever in a life they didn't share.

Kobić's small eyes were full of peasant humor and circuitousness. Sometimes he was naïve or aggressive, sometimes wise and cunning, but with his friends he was always gentle and honest. However, none of his machinations worked with the police, and they beat him until they got what they wanted. He might have been more effective if that traitor Kadić had not given the police a detailed account of what everyone was doing. He not only betrayed all his comrades, but he also participated in the actual arrests, since he was a committee member and as such well known in the organization. Thus men found themselves in the position of being not only charged with various offenses, but also denounced and incriminated and worked on by a "responsible comrade." This was enormously damaging to their morale, especially since they were mostly young and inexperienced people.

The trial of my group, which took place in the late fall following the Bosnians' trial, was the same as all the rest. Gojko Terić represented me along with Vladimir Simić and Tripko Žugić. Bora Prodanović, a Communist lawyer appointed by the party to defend Communists, advised us not to cause scenes in order to avoid long-term sentences. The trial passed without any revolutionary tirades and statements, attended only by a few close family members. From the benches agents stared at us blankly. Among them were some who had tortured us during the investigation. A Slovenian poet by the name of Gradnik was one of the judges. He had the reputation of being relatively strict. None of the judges suffered after the war for their participation in these trials. By and large, therefore, we were consistent: we were after only our wartime enemies and active opponents.

We had to wait three days for the verdict. Our group, reduced to six people, would gather in the yard to sit and talk, in spite of the bad weather and the wind blowing down the troubled river. We suddenly felt warm and friendly to one another. All the hostilities and insults were forgotten and pushed aside. We were particularly attentive to Beška Bembas, a frail lovely creature, and the only woman who hadn't been exempted from the trial.

The sentences were stiff. Stajkić and Jovanović each got six years, I and two workers got three years, and Beška Bembas got eighteen months. In retrospect, they were relatively lenient with me. Of course, they had no proof, except for my handwriting. It may have been that, or the interest a number of influential people had taken in me.

We didn't appeal the verdict. We waited at Belgrade's Glavnjača for several days to be transported to the penitentiary at Sremska Mitrovica. Beška Bembas was sent to a prison for women in Požarevac.

23

Every Saturday, on the other side of the Sava, at exactly twelve noon, a vague red form would emerge from between the little houses on the riverbank. Then it would stop. The form was actually a red sweater that would then get buttoned up—a row of shiny square buttons. I couldn't see either the opening or the buttons from that distance. But I knew they were there. I knew and saw the pale thin face and the round small eyes framed by thick, dark curly hair. That was Mitra, my woman. We had been in love for a long time, for as long as we'd known each other, and she came to wave from a distance, to me, to my hands outstretched between the bars. I could see her, all of her: a slender figure, her skirt blown by the wind. She could see only my hands; the rest was darkness behind the bars. She knew my window—the last one on the right. But as time went on, other prisoners got used to the girl in the red sweater, and they waved to her from their windows. She liked it, and I didn't mind it. She knew which hands were mine.

Later on, she came with wives and girl friends of other prisoners, but she was always in a red sweater so that I could instantly recognize her. She didn't miss a single Saturday, always exactly at noon, and always alone. That was our time, ours alone, arranged spontaneously. She would stand on the riverbank for a while, then look back, undecided as to whether to go or stay. I'd watch the red sweater receding against the background of houses and towboats, toward Belgrade, the red sweater that concealed her thin body and emphasized the soft and easy slenderness of her figure. There was an orange reflection in it. It was actually that orange reflection that I saw. It gave color to her pale face and to her eyes, and to her thin arms and slender fingers, as if she were sitting in front of an open fire. That was how she came and went.

What prompted this young girl, not very beautiful, but striking, and with a fine mind, to call so regularly on her comrade in prison? To write him letters which only the two of them understood and which echoed with cries of the soul, and the body, whose longings could be quieted down by no one else's caresses?

Our love had a somewhat different beginning from the usual love affair between young Communists. It was love from the first instant. That is to say, I knew I was a Communist, and she knew she wasn't, and we fell in love not because we saw things alike ideologically, but because we couldn't keep away from each other. At first I thought she found me attractive because of my reputation as a young writer. Other people, particularly women, thought so too. Having sensed that, she ignored, even underestimated, that side of me. At first I was angry, and then pleased—our relationship was developing unencumbered by any strains, uncomplicated and pure.

But I was sorry she was not a revolutionary and a Communist. I made an effort to explain to her the new "Communist" relations between men and women, to make her aware of her bourgeois traits, but she seemed to be paying little attention. Obviously I was responsible for her decision to join the movement; yet I am sure my intellectual arguments had little to do with that decision.

At first we didn't find each other very attractive physically. I didn't think her at all good-looking. She was too thin, her shoulders too narrow, her breasts too small, her forehead too high and serious. On her throat there was a large black birthmark. Actually it was rather becoming on her white skin, but she didn't really know what to do with it. She objected to "physical jokes," hard squeezing, wrestling, and nudging. That would make her angry, but not for long—like a child who has been spanked by someone he loves. Her real anger was intellectual in character, caused by a disappointment, a sudden knowledge of unpleasant things. But in her relations with me she rarely got angry, and even when I drove her to it, she relented quickly. She didn't have "pride" and she easily admitted her "mistakes," so we'd be friends again, so happy was she to bury her head in my shoulder.

And yet she was not really a gentle and forgiving person. She never gave herself completely in any situation; she was her own person. Her mind was all too complex and bright for her to be able to do that. She always understood that our most recent quarrel was not the last, that our most passionate kiss was not the most passionate, and that though she might adjust she certainly would not change. And as our love grew, so did our fights; we never gave in to each other. Her thoughts always remained elusive to me, while she found my impulsiveness impossible to reach or understand.

As a young revolutionary I took pride in my "lack of prejudice" in sexual matters—sex was of interest only inasmuch as it satisfied a physical need. But not in my relationship with Mitra. In reality I treated her with consideration and kindness, asking nothing of her, never threatening her virginity in any way. Once I did something rather coarse. I suffered on account of it for months, and she never brought it up again. In tacit agreement we decided to drop the whole matter. I made fun of her bourgeois virginity, but I made sure not to hurt her feelings. There was something contradictory in this, of course, between my professed view and my intimate joy, which I couldn't even admit to myself, that she was virginal and pure.

And she, like the rest of the girls who have settled their accounts with their patriarchal upbringing but haven't become wild in the process, allowed herself to be kissed, and learned to return kisses and ask for them. But that was the line she couldn't cross. The world of passion and love-making beyond that was not only a secret for her, but didn't come up as something necessary or wanted before she got married. We kissed each other, on hot days and cool nights, until it was almost painful. But these kisses were always a trifle innocent. I was not after her as a woman, but it was to her I always returned from all my journeys, to Požega in the winter of 1932, to Sandžak in the summer of 1933. And yet I looked forward to her embrace, knowing it would bring us both joy. Passion between us matured slowly, modestly, and through the knowledge of its inevitability, through caressings that went on for months.

Our relationship began in the form of sharp intellectual cynicism on her part and wild moodiness on mine. We had a quarrel, and then arranged to meet the following evening to settle it. A few days later we could no longer keep away from each other, we could no longer live without our arguments and clever quips, our walks late into the night, without the love that suddenly blossomed, transforming the whole relationship as she was about to leave for her vacation. She was now really close to me, in everything, and I knew we had to see each other, immediately, before the long hot summer was over. I followed her to the village where her sister and brother-in-law were teachers. I looked for her in the village. It was a market day. On the bare hill everything was in motion, people at the fair and the wind in the crowns of the old oaks. I took her hand and led her away. We sat down behind a thick tree trunk, away from the crowd. In front of us stretched round hills and mountains into bluish distances. She was still thin, but her cheeks had a healthy glow. We were alone and happy.

Of course, she had boy friends in school whom she didn't give up when she met me. Once she made up her mind to get married she would break off relations with other men, or that was what I thought she thought. But that wasn't so.

In the fall of 1932 a young Communist by the name of Dobrosav Simić, with whom Mitra had been in love when still in school, came to see me. He was in love with her, and as "comrades" we couldn't be rivals in love. He was indeed a good, honest man. The two of them were a lot alike, in the movements of their bodies and in their careful speech, but he didn't have her inner strength. In 1937 he was arrested. He made a poor showing with the police and was expelled from the party. During the war he was given minor responsibilities in spite of his superior intelligence. But he continued to fight, and finally disappeared in one of the offensives.

In the fall of 1932, though, we were both young revolutionaries, and as such happy to make personal sacrifices for each other. Following long conversations, about which Mitra knew nothing, we decided that we should both break up with her. We thought that this was the most honest and revolutionary approach, since she was behaving like a real "bourgeois" type, trying to catch a husband. We wrote her a joint letter explaining our decision.

I felt terribly empty and bitter. It was as if the whole city had disappeared. I tried desperately to concentrate on my political activity and catch up on my reading, but I couldn't; it took me hours to read two or three pages.

Mitra apparently received our letter with relative calm. However, a few hours later, in class, she suddenly had a fit of hysterics, convulsions, and uncontrollable crying. Her classmates took her home. She stopped crying, but her body was still stiff and her eyes stared blankly. The next day her sister asked me to see Mitra. She would arrange for me to enter the house without the knowledge of their mother and brother. I agreed, although I felt I shouldn't, because it meant betraying a friend and a joint decision, betraying Communism itself. I found her in bed. She didn't speak; she simply took my hand and began to cry. Then she said: "So long as you are here!" It made her feel better automatically. Her love for me had grown more unbearable, not greater.

The next day she was up and around and she came to see me in my apartment. We made up. But for a long time I felt that our reconciliation meant a betrayal of the idea, of the party. My loyalty to love had triumphed. I was only a revolutionary, not completely versed in the art of dogma.

Mitra came from a poor family. Her father, a minor railway official, had died of typhus during World War I. Her mother was a widow at twenty-four with five children—a son and four daughters. They lived in a two-room basement apartment in Užička Požega, Serbia. Her mother was young and beautiful and hard-working, and she got all her five children through school. She was a real Serbian woman, with an instinctive knowledge that rebellions and prison leave children in women's hands, to raise them through their own effort, and their own self-denial, in order to prolong the family name and the life of the Serbian nation.

Mitra grew up thin, but wiry and tough. They never had enough to eat but they were all excellent students, who had good taste and upbringing, and natural good manners, which you don't even find in the children of the rich. One of my most precious memories of Mitra and her sisters is of a stay with an uncle, a peasant who was relatively well off, and had plenty of fruit and corn. But Mitra was a city child in every way, and she loved the village only as a place to go on vacation.

With this kind of background, it was only natural that she would take her time before joining the Communist movement. It was hard for her to accept the reckless and casual attitudes that we young Communists spontaneously assumed in our attempt to separate ourselves from a world we had to destroy in order to survive.

Mitra was greatly influenced by her background, but she also had something of her own: a quickness and independence of mind, and above all an iron will to fight for every ounce of life. I never heard her complain. Life was something that had to be lived and fought, and the harder one fights the better it is. Therein lay the strength of this slender, graceful, cautious, and intelligent woman.

Sexual relations between men and women in the party were still being treated lightly, a hangover from prewar Serbian social democracy. In theory, at least, it was what was known as free love. Changing women, sleeping with other people's husbands and wives, taking out whores were acceptable. Solid marriages, particularly where children were involved, were respected, but that was due less to socialist theory than to inherited "bourgeois" morality. The fact is very few people practiced what they preached, and they lived in the usual way. A lot of popular literature dealing with the sexual captivity of youth came from Germany, including Aleksandra Kolontai's book, which put forward the "glass of water" theory: the sexual act is a basic physiological need, like drinking a glass of water, which was mystified by the ruling class in order to turn women into slaves and private property. Freud's psychoanalysis, which reached us as a vulgarized theory rather than a scientific discovery, merely served to strengthen such thinking. I also stood by that theory. On the other hand I felt disgust at the thought of using that approach with Mitra. And I simply couldn't stand the idea of her doing something like that—automatically eliminating my reasons for selecting her to be the person I was to love and spend my time with. Our friends appeared to feel that way about us too.

In spite of all my theories, our relationship was developing naturally. I tried to convince her from time to time to shed her "bourgeois prejudices," not because of my theories, but because I suddenly felt a desire for her. I wanted to go to the end or else break it up. As winter approached this conflict grew sharper. The reason for this was clear, but neither of us came out with it for fear of appearing "dirty" and "selfish." I tried to tell her that if we were to remain faithful to each other in the "bourgeois" fashion, we had to give everything to each other. How could she "save" herself for someone who would marry her? Were we in love because we wanted to get married, or because we met and understood each other? I sounded as if I were making an attack on her innocence. I was disgusted with her and with myself. Then we had still another quarrel. I thought that perhaps I should never tell her what was on my mind. But that was impossible, because by now our kisses had become a prelude to the passionate longing of our bodies. She may not have been aware of it, but desire had matured in her too. She was experiencing a profound internal transformation—deciding to give herself to the man from whose influence she would never be able to extricate herself. She may have thought of various obstacles until she made up her mind, but once that was done, nothing could stop her. Her body was ready for such a decision too. She didn't know that. I didn't know it either. But it was happening, secretly, in the act of our caresses, in the sweet pleasure of putting a hand inside the shirt of the man she loved.

After a quarrel she came to my room and stated flatly that she could not, and would not, postpone it any further.

The time was late fall. November was still beautiful in Belgrade. I walked her to her house. She was happy.

Our relationship suddenly assumed a new dimension. One evening she said: "I know this will sound bourgeois to you, but I'd like you to marry me." I felt then, as I do now, that one can be in love many times and with many women, but it is always only a revival of one's first love.

We had already built up a world of our own and a language of our own, movements and looks which only the two of us understood. One day, I remember, we ran into a friend of hers in the street. We were happy from satisfied desire. While her friend was chattering away, the two of us looked at each other in a way that said: We belong to each other now and we will always belong to each other. She said to me one day: "I like to have you looking at my body, particularly my back, my waist, everything." She was happy to be mine, she was happy to know I was hers alone. We were not just lovers. We felt we were together at a time in history that we had to serve with everything we had, including our love. We no longer made dates. I knew her schedule and she knew mine. Her flat was on Georges Clemenceau Street, now Lola Ribar Street, in a new building that was separated from the sidewalk by a fence lined with young trees. She would stand in the window around eight o'clock in the evening as I walked past. In the morning she would come and see me around ten. Or we would wait for each other.

Now all that was interrupted. Although most of my thoughts were preoccupied with her, I felt it my moral duty to release her from her obligations to me. I told her in a letter that she was free, and that she should not torture herself with the bourgeois concept of "faithfulness." I wanted to sound as revolutionary as possible, and as free of "prejudice." She didn't comment, which I interpreted as hesitation. Later in prison, I realized that other men had used a similar approach. Although I've never been jealous, I felt sad that this most beautiful dream of my life would thus come to an end. I was sorry that the idea of freedom of men and women to choose, which I had adopted and forced on her, would gradually make her sink into the ordinariness of life, inevitably wounding something the two of us created. Of course, there was male sorrow and pain in this too, but more than anything it was the sorrow of seeing the inevitable destruction of love and happiness in her.

My revolutionary awareness had matured, but the shadow of pain was cast on my words and my thoughts. Determined to be separated from her in order to fight, I couldn't give her up or forget her. She had already become a sickness that plagued my youth and my life.

The Idealist

People whiled away time in prison as best they could. The same was true of the island prison, although the party's orders were explicit: study Marxism-Leninism and other party literature, waste no time. For the two months that I was alone, I wrote all the time. I completed a short novel, *Black Hills*, dealing with the life of a poor Montenegrin family. A lot of it was autobiographical. While writing a chapter about the imaginary death of my brother, I wept like a child. In the first part of the novel there might have been some literary devices, but the second part contained very few. However, behind all this literature and sociology was concealed my love for Mitra, my hope that she would read it and find me in it, thus bringing the two of us together. The judge gave me permission to have the novel taken out of prison. Jovan Popović was the only person who actually read it. Stefan Mitrović kept it in his desk drawer for months, and the police confiscated it before he ever read it. Popović was favorably impressed, which doesn't mean the book was any good. But there was something in it, a certain tragic quality that is ever present in Montenegrin life. I also wrote ten short stories, which were lost. They were weak, written under the influence of "social literature." These stories also expressed my love for Mitra. The soul of a revolutionary is no less human than the soul of any other man.

All through the summer we gazed at the sunburned bodies of men and women on the beaches of the Sava River. The women looked beautiful, healthy, and slender. Of course, I was aware that this passionate impression reflected desires born of prison isolation, and that only one body was actually beautiful, because it belonged to me emotionally as well.

On a cold winter morning I trudged along a muddy road to my penitentiary. I was to stay there for two and a half years. I thought of the Good Soldier Schweik: I was not nearly as badly off as I might have been, and the two men who were with me were in a much worse predicament. I didn't feel sorry for myself. And I wasn't afraid. On the contrary, I was filled with pride, and a cheerful curiosity, mixed with bitterness, because I would get to know the side of life that was tested by everyone in this country who was worth anything. On our left were the uniform sentry cottages with shabby fronts and wilted flowers in the windows; on our right were the gray fields. In front of us were the red buildings and chimneys of the penitentiary. I was smoking my last cigarette, the last smoke before the gates opened before me, and I crushed the cigarette wrapper and tossed it to the ground. I grew angrier with every step. The void and bitterness of losing Mitra filled me with a sorrow that was beyond expression. Laughing artificially, we huddled together. We were leaving one life to enter another, entirely different from the one behind us. This new life would forcibly cut off the old one, although it would continue within us like a bitter and incurable void.

As the gates closed behind us I felt instantly reconciled to the loss of Mitra. I was too strong to cry, and too devastated to think I'd be able to reconstruct the world of our love or heal the wound inflicted on the joys I had with her. In the palms of my hands I felt the silky warmth of her thighs. In my dreams I could smell her, although there was no dew there, and no moonlight, and no warmth from the sun. But her image was receding painfully, and of her body I recalled only the lankiness, which was whipping me, not allowing me to forget it. Can one forget a past life? Yes, or so they say. But I couldn't forget Mitra. Whenever I thought about her I felt a certain tension all over. Something was being released from every cell.

One youth was thrown into prison. And a lot of dreams were cut short and buried. But my passion for the revolutionary struggle and my love for a woman, component parts of my youth, were not dead: the former was strengthened by the experience, evolving from a passion into an intellectual awareness, and the latter grew into a profound sorrow which only I knew. In prison there were men who for years had only one image before them: the revolution. All else was destructive. The revolution was something tangible, something I was proud of; my love for Mitra grew less tangible, but was hidden deep in every drop of my blood, in every corner of my soul.

Meanwhile, Mitra was fast becoming a Communist. I sensed that from her letters, and I was glad. She was a "comrade" in the true political sense of the word. My arrest obviously removed the last vestiges of hesitation. Having lost me, she started looking for happiness in the world to which I had belonged. She never tried to cheer me up by telling me all would be over soon and we'd be together again. That would have been too banal. We were so saddened by our separation that we couldn't think of the future. We were anxious to see each other, but she was not allowed to visit me as my "fiancée." I had a photograph of her in that red sweater and a tight silk skirt, but I rarely looked at it. In my thoughts she was alive and warm, a constant memory and pain. If I had lost that image, I would have been completely crushed.

24

In Yugoslavia in the 1930's, the so-called "Irish system" of prison sentences was in force. It was considered the last word in legal methods. This may well have been the case, but if so, the legal science hadn't advanced very far, or its application in Yugoslav prisons was incredibly awkward. The idea was that as the prisoner's behavior "improved" he would have his sentence eased, and after he had served half of his term he would gain the right of conditional release or parole. Theoretically, the system was a good one. But in Yugoslav practice it turned the prisoner into an even greater slave. He was constantly being offered better terms on condition that he be good and obedient, "truthful" with the management, *i.e.*, its informer. Even after the prisoner was conditionally released, his status could easily be reversed without any court ruling, at the discretion of the local authorities. These good angels had it in their power to bring the sinner back to hell for a simple misdemeanor. The inhuman nature of the whole political and social system turned the best of intentions into punishment.

Obviously, none of this applied to Communists. We were never conditionally released. We didn't ask for it and the authorities didn't give it to us. We never renounced Communism. We were clearly incorrigible. Renunciation was considered a shameful betrayal, and it was rare indeed for someone to ask for mercy. We Communists served a full sentence.

When the January 6th Dictatorship came to power, only a dozen or so Communists were in prison. At first they enjoyed relatively liberal treatment. However, as the number of Communists in jail began to grow, the regime treated them as they did hard-core criminals, which resulted in clashes with the authorities through protests and hunger strikes.

The 1932 hunger strike brought considerable improvement to Communist and nationalist prisoners, but by the time I arrived, at the end of 1933, conditions had again deteriorated. The Communists had just ended a hunger strike in which they had been defeated. After the strike, they were transferred to the so-called "Youth Building," which consisted of a large structure with group facilities, and a smaller one with solitary cells. Both structures were relatively modern, with wood floors, toilets, sinks, and low windows.

On arrival, we were thoroughly searched. All our belongings were confiscated, with the exception of underwear, socks, and toilet articles. They gave us baths, haircuts, and new clothing which didn't fit. They took our particulars and gave us numbers. We were now prisoners, subject to the strict regimen that prevailed in this building of solitary cells.

The cells were relatively spacious, the beds comfortable, and had we been allowed books and occasional human contact, the first three months would not have been so hard to take. However, everything was forbidden. During the morning walk no conversation was allowed. We had to take our caps off every time we passed a sentry. Outside of this walk we spent all of our time in our cells, but we were not allowed to lie down.

Each prisoner develops his own system of survival in solitary. Fortunately, thinking, infinite in its combinations, instantly becomes his most powerful comfort and support. The solitary prisoner quickly separates himself from his own thinking, and begins communicating with "himself" as if "he" were a long-lost friend, not a part of him. With this splitting of his personality, a man begins a dialogue with himself, which assumes different forms, depending on his personality. Peasants talk of harvests and cattle, intellectuals of discoveries and philosophy.

One grows feverish from exaggerated empty thinking. Sudden laughter and sorrow overwhelm the prisoner when he runs into people again, as well as a feeling of shame because of all that thinking in which all things tend to become weightless—walls crumbling as if made of ashes, bars melting and evaporating. The prisoner welcomes every change: a new day carved into the wall, the knocking on the wall of a new neighbor, the arrival of the sentry to pick up the laundry.

The senses are tense and they quickly become sharp. In this deaf loneliness, squeezed between four walls, a man thinks because that's the only thing left him. And his impulses are stronger and more direct. He no longer is inhibited by his conscience; in fact, his conscience gives in gently and gradually. I had a dream that I was smoking a cigarette three yards long; I couldn't inhale because my chest was cracking up. I woke up. The sentry was smoking in the corridor. For a time sparrows chirped in front of my window. One morning they were gone, and I missed them. The walls were covered with drawings of nude women with large hips and bosoms. Some of them were just breasts—two circles with dots in the center. Or of women's organs—a large ugly insect with a lot of legs. Also a lot of straight little cuts, check marks for days spent in prison. Someone made three hundred and sixty-five cuts, all the way from the ceiling to the floor. Did he continue? Or did he simply stop in desperation? Some of the drawings were quite nice. Now the drawings of women—were they real or just of any old females? Some looked real—the one with eyelashes all over her face, the one with a long, pear-shaped earring, the plump one with a pearl in her hand. It doesn't really matter, I thought; I'll draw a woman's head, round, with a small chin and tight lips, and a thin neck on thin shoulders. Not very sensual, but mine.

The sentries watched over us like priests over sinful souls. Even at night they would sneak around barefoot or in soft shoes in search of victims—men pouring their souls out to their fellow-sufferers, often complete strangers, on the other side of the wall.

Perhaps the whole point of solitary confinement is to force the prisoner to think his "sins" over, to think his whole life over, and to recall, as if in a distant and implausible dream, the "beauty" of his previous existence—fresh colors, good food, beautiful countryside, and friends. But I, and this goes for most of my Communist friends, experienced no repentance, no longing for the past life, except as a physical desire for good food, the countryside, and friends. I spent my time in jail concocting the most fantastic revolutionary schemes and adventures. Often I did it in installments; in between I thought of other things, but they were always secondary. While destroying me in one way, solitary confinement strengthened me in another: my belief in Communism, though in an unreal, dreamlike form.

The sentries caught me "in error": climbing up on the window, whistling, talking during walks or during cleanup. No prisoner could help committing such "digressions." On several occasions I was slugged hard. After a month we were transferred to the solitary cells of the Youth Building, where slugging was not practiced as a rule. The prison administration didn't want to get implicated in any illegal beating that could lead to the intervention of the Ministry of Justice and be used for propaganda purposes. Even so, I was punished twice for talking through the window with comrades from group rooms. Punishment was pronounced by the prison director, a certain Bralović, who was notorious for his strictness. He asked me whether I'd broken the regulation, and when I answered that I hadn't, he laughed sarcastically and said that meant the sentry was lying.

The position of the director of such a large institution as the one at Mitrovica was an important sinecure, and was usually given as an act of great favor and trust. The regime used the prison from time to time for a discreet settling of accounts with some "awkward" enemy. The position of director meant a good salary, free housing, a horse and carriage, prisoners as house servants, furniture from prison workrooms, and food from prison supplies. Rumor had it that Bralović was a friend of King Alexander's, and it was obvious that this tough man enjoyed a lot of authority. He was a Serb nationalist, a lawyer by training, strict, and ruthless when necessary in his treatment of prisoners.

It was a tremendous advantage that the prison was under the jurisdiction of the Ministry of Justice, rather than the police, as is the case today. The Ministry of Justice was concerned that regulations be observed, and was a little more liberal with regard to political prisoners than Bralović himself. This also meant that the prisoners were spared systematic provocations and maltreatment, or the indignity of being "re-educated." The prisoner had to serve his sentence, observing the prison regulations and "house routine," and outside of that his person was respected. Even Bralović had to stick to the regulations. He was a conscientious civil servant, whom the mechanism of state had rendered cruel, and as a matter of duty he saw a criminal in each prisoner, and in every man a potential convict. But in spite of his cruel acts, Bralović believed in order: rules were observed, food and laundry distributed regularly, cleanliness was on a very high level. His presence was felt everywhere and at all times.

When the war ended he was in retirement, but he was executed anyway; obviously we didn't always stick to our principle that people were to answer only for crimes committed during the war. It was one of those senseless situations in which revenge took precedence over political interests.

Dr. Rogulić, the prison physician, was a conscientious and humane person. During the hunger strikes he kept the authorities informed of the exact state of health of the striking prisoners. He made sure that when the strike was over the prisoners were fed properly. Of slow movement, stout, he rolled through the corridors, always ready for a joke. He was a wealthy man in his own right, a "bourgeois," but we appreciated his humanity and warmth. This kind of man and physician was indeed a rare thing in prisons, particularly in contrast to doctors such as Šantal, of Lepoglava, who gave the hunger strikers a strong salt solution, so that, in addition to the excruciating pain of an enema, they suffered from wounds in their intestines for months.

In this kind of a system, and with this kind of administration, solitary confinement offered possibilities for maltreatment and foul play without essentially breaking the prison rules.

For example, the two Communists who had attempted to assassinate King Alexander—Stejić and Čaki—had been held in chains in solitary cells for years. They both became mentally ill. Čaki said that during the fourth year of solitary confinement he noted a change in Stejić. He came across him during the cleanup period, and Stejić told him that he had discovered an ointment which desolves iron bars and that he would soon escape. Stejić had been in solitary for seven years, and Čaki for five. He was finally moved to a group room, and his condition soon improved. Whenever we had heated discussions, he would jump up and plead with us to make friends, evoking the names of Lenin and Trotsky. And with no amount of persuasion could we make him accept Trotsky's "betrayal."

The story had it that King Alexander often asked about Stejić, as if out of a personal concern. This may or may not have been true. Stejić, for his part, hated the King and was sorry to have missed him. Although he accepted the party's critical attitude toward the attempted assassination, deep down at heart he found personal justification for his action. King Alexander was his personal enemy. He always referred to the King by his nickname, "Šaca." And so, he would say, if it hadn't been for Pašić, who screamed at the driver to speed up, he would have got "Šaca." He was sorry the King had been killed later in Marseilles: somebody else had managed to do what he had wanted to do. The assassination was a fixation with him, and became even more so in the long years in solitary.

I myself have observed that people who have spent a number of years in solitary confinement give it up reluctantly. After a while they enjoy losing themselves in their fantasies. The wide range of man's imagination makes it possible for him to remain human in circumstances that deprive him of everything human.

25

Like most communities in which people live in a special way, prison greets its new prisoners with practical jokes, which are annoying, but reflect the prevailing atmosphere of warmth and camaraderie. However, this bright mood is quickly destroyed by conflicts, personal hatreds, nervous tensions, cynicism, and that political separatism which shakes up the Communist collective—otherwise seeming so unified to the outside world.

When I arrived in the group room in February 1934, there were some one hundred and twenty Communists and fifty nationalists. The number of Communists grew to as high as two hundred and fifty, while the number of nationalists remained stationary until the amnesty granted by the Cvetković-Maček government. A group of some twenty Communists was transferred from Lepoglava to Mitrovica, but they had a separate room in the Youth Building.

I was in room No. 2, on the third floor, which was occupied exclusively by intellectuals. Ognjen Prica referred to it as the idiots' room; we were doing too much thinking, he would say. But that was an exaggeration.

On the very first day, Oskar Davičo briefed me on the state of affairs in prison. He did it secretively and with a smile that reflected both kindness and naïve cunning. Of course I knew of Davičo. As a young teacher in Bihać, he had organized a sizable group of local workers, and was sentenced to five years. He was badly tortured. His preoccupation with the more perfidious details of torture reflected his literary frame of mind and his interest in the unusual, dark, and subconscious aspects of human nature.

Oskar Davičo in prison was quite different from the public image

162

of him today, although for those who know him closely he remains one and the same person.

He was nicknamed "Moska," which means "little Jew." I believe it was Ognjen Prica who gave him this name. Prica was extremely fond of Daviço. The nickname became so popular that Daviço himself adopted it. He was one of those Jews who made good-natured fun of the petty, commercial, and cautious spirit of his people. There was nothing anti-Semitic in the name Moska; in fact, there was no anti-Semitism among the comrades.

Daviço was short and frail, but aggressive. He had a handsome face and was very popular with most of the Communists in prison, though he was superficial and sloppy in his study of Communist literature. On several occasions, in group debates, it was obvious that he hadn't read the material at all, or only superficially. He did read Marx and Engels, but no more thoroughly than any other writers. Generally speaking, he didn't read much. But he wrote a lot. His drawers and bags were full of notebooks with verse in small, thin, and not very legible handwriting. He worked his texts over several times, discarded previous versions, which I felt were sometimes better than the final product. He suffered from inflamed eyelids, which prevented him from working at night; the lighting of course was feeble.

He was hard-working, but in his own way: he worked carefully on his own stuff and superficially on the party's. The truth is, the party's program of ideological study was tremendously boring for an intellectual, not only because of its very low level, but also because it was repetitive. We went over the same material every few months: trade unions, antimilitary activity, the national question, party organization. These few topics were discussed over and over again, following the same prescription derived from the Moscow party school.

Daviço was as active in propagating revolutionary ideas as in writing poetry. The two were one in his mind. Propagating revolutionary ideas among Communists sounds absurd—like spreading Islam among hard-core Moslems. Daviço, however, was on the extreme left among the Communists, and that faction was the most aggressive with regard to the prison administration, engaging in adventurous and immature activities that would put the whole group in an uncomfortable position. Ognjen Prica, to the far left himself, called this group *"vahabiti,"* after the Arabic Orthodox Moslems, for whom drinking a glass of wine was sinful, though the massacre of innocent children was not. The *vahabiti* never existed as an organized group. They were simply the more aggressive, leftist prison group. Within this leftist framework, each went his own way, and they all disassociated themselves from this name. But as an idea of often ill-timed and impetuous action, *vahabitism* definitely existed, and Davičo was one of its leaders.

In contrast to other leftists, Davičo rarely spoke at gatherings, and when he did, he was brief and fairly remote. He was repeatedly criticized for his Surrealism—which Davičo denied every couple of weeks, only to reveal again in some way that he still had not been able to "see through" and "shake off" the "nonsense" he had absorbed in Paris. Even though he was not much of a speaker, he liked to use certain short phrases, the kind that suddenly light up the situation. And he was often able to find the right phrase.

Davičo's sloppiness, his reluctance to wash himself or his dishes, his untied shoes, and particularly his unabated Surrealism, provoked gossip among right-wing Communists. But on the left, even though criticized for his "bohemianism," unthinkable among Communists, he was accepted with secret sympathy. And indeed, there was something very attractive in his virtual unawareness of the outside world. Of course, one's views of opponents, as well as friends, are nowhere as twisted as in prison.

Davičo's leftism was dogmatic, but in a special, poetic way. He was impressed not only with words and heroic deeds, but also with faces. He told me, for example, that Mihailo Ivić's eyes glowed with a real fire. For Davičo this was proof of Ivić's political virtue. His political arguments were always in terms of images and aphorisms. There was some powerful, secretive passion in this small, frail man. In personal relations he was the exact opposite of everything he represented in public life. At public gatherings he often gave the impression of being scatterbrained, whereas in personal contact he was captivating. He saw the future of both the party and the revolution in terms of the faction to which he belonged. Yet it was hard to tell just how clearly he saw that future. The poetic experience of the revolutionary struggle and the vision of the revolution were primary; everything else was secondary.

I was already a leftist, so Davičo's job was to explain relationships rather than win me over. And anyway, "persuasion" was considered unthinkable—this was a form of "factionalism"! Davičo undertook this job on his own initiative. Before long I was embroiled in passionate internal struggles, much more than was necessary, and thus my impression of prevailing conditions was unrealistic.

Davičo and I remained close and intimate friends until the end of my term. Our closeness was not based only on our politics, but on our emotional and intellectual approach as well. I showed him my writing, and although his reaction was always positive—that's the way he is—I sensed that he didn't really like it. He never pushed his own work on anyone, but he gladly showed it if asked to do so. He was an unusually sensitive poet. He loved words not for their sound but for their meaning. He often said that our language should be "broken," "bent," because it was too "logical" and too "peasant-like," and as such unsuitable to the complex modern idiom.

Davičo was also very close to Ognjen Prica, Marko Orešković, and Žarko Zrenjanin. His relationship with Prica, himself an intellectual of significant proportions, was based on his intellectual and poetic preoccupations. His relationship with Orešković and Zrenjanin, both typical revolutionaries, was necessary to him because of his revolutionary mood.

He was not the kind of person who expressed his affection for people directly or often. He always operated within a small circle of friends. He was reserved, perhaps even a little unstable, but he always remained consistent in his basic loyalties to the revolution and to poetry. I knew a number of Communists who were better revolutionaries than Davičo, some with considerable literary skills, but they quickly gave up literature in favor of party ideological and revolutionary pursuits. Only Davičo remained a poet, seeking, in a magic way, to reconcile the two. For most Communists his poetry was both incomprehensible and unacceptable, which made them doubt his dedication to the revolution.

Throughout my life as a Communist, I always felt a sense of guilt toward the party for one reason or another. No sooner would I forget one "sin" than I would come up with another. Every Communist I knew had the same experience—that goes for even the highest-ranking functionaries, absolutely without exception. They felt guilty either because of some political slip-up, some ideological activity, a secret passion for women, or failure at a police interrogation. I might even go so far as to say that the better the Communist, the more intense the feeling of guilt. This phenomenon can be explained in terms of the party's dogmatic and sectarian character. But there was one more thing: the constant conflict between one's instincts and the nature of Communism, which seeks to subjugate man completely.

Davičo suffered in prison. He felt guilty both as a poet and as a revolutionary. He was constantly criticized for not being able to shake off Surrealism, for wanting to "reconcile" it with Marxism, for wanting to "complete" Marx's brilliant teaching with bourgeois decadence. Also, he couldn't forgive himself for his contact with Sima Marković. Although this contact was minor, and chiefly out of ignorance, of course, he could always be reproached for it and his party membership questioned.

Sima Marković was a bad name in prison because his positions had been criticized by the Comintern and quoted as an example of "opportunism," a "remnant of social democracy" in our ranks. Even his former supporters gave him up in prison. There, in that enclosed space, where words were given enormous weight, any attempt to defend Sima Marković was considered counterrevolutionary. Any association with Sima Marković was a deadly sin, even if committed out of ignorance.

This applied, of course, to DaviČo too. But I don't think that was why he became a "leftist." He was a natural leftist, in the way he thought, in the way he experienced life.

DaviČo didn't play a significant role in the life of the Communist collective. He was, for me, an interesting and dear person, but not an important one. And he never thought of himself as important; he was very modest in his party pretensions.

Ognjen Prica was also an outstanding person. I soon became friends with him, but without the kind of secretive intimacy that I shared with DaviČo. Prica was greatly respected by the prisoners and the prison administration, which considered him our ideological leader. And he was the strongest Communist intellectual in the prison.

Prica, who graduated from the University of Vienna, had been a professor of mathematics and philosophy. He spoke four major languages fluently, he wrote in German with ease, and he was well versed in Greek and Latin. But his extensive knowledge was poorly organized. He was an improviser. As a speaker he was sometimes quite fiery, and in the heat of passion he could express beautiful thoughts. His writing, on the other hand, was awkward, dry, and forced. First and foremost, he was a revolutionary, and ideologically he played a significant role, particularly among the workers. He instructed them in the general outlines of Marxism, as well as in mathematics and physics.

He had always belonged to the leftist faction. The workers respected him for his knowledge, and for his steady position during strikes. In ideological matters, his opinions were decisive, but in interparty conflicts he did not occupy a foremost spot because these conflicts were among former functionaries, primarily workers. It was generally considered that the role of the intellectual in the movement was a secondary one. Some people, like Kraš, came out openly against intellectuals; he claimed they could only play a secondary role in the movement. This feeling grew sharper as some of the intellectuals joined the enemy faction.

Prica was aggressive and proud, a tall, impressive-looking man. I found him witty, colorful, and well spoken. He talked freely about his wild adventures with women, probably somewhat exaggerated in the prison bleakness. His rich imagination and his sense of humor kept him going at all times.

He enjoyed playing practical jokes on people, and they paid him back in kind. They took advantage of his extreme absent-mindedness, which was legendary. When he got out of prison, he was a little less absent-minded, although he tended to carry slips of paper in his pockets, which could get him in trouble with the police. His wife checked his pockets carefully at all times. In prison it was his comrades who had to make sure he wasn't walking around with any material that might implicate us.

It took many years before the ideological indoctrination in prison finally took shape and assumed the form of a firm philosophical footing. I can't exactly say that Prica helped shape the methods of indoctrination—forming study groups and lectures based on the level of knowledge of individual members. This was done individually, by workers and intellectuals who needed Marxist training. But Prica was the chief ideological figure, always capable of explaining everything. He followed developments closely, and although not dogmatic by nature, he was adamant in his defense of the principles he considered essential for the Communist party. Long before *The History of the Soviet Communist Party* was published we had solidified certain basic components of the movement in prison through growth and internal struggle. Leninism, *i.e.*, Stalinism, was absorbed at a very rapid rate. We also established certain final Communist "truths," without which the internal solidification of the Communist party could not have occurred. A lot of credit for this goes to Prica, a flesh-and-blood revolutionary, who subjected his heart and his knowledge to the cause.

When he came to prison, Prica was a familiar figure to the narrow circle of the party leaders. When he left, he was known to the whole party. His intelligence and wit, his attractive personality were widely appreciated. Many years of dogged struggle and the luminous quality of his revolutionary mind did not go unrewarded. Prica was trying to turn the prison into a Communist university, with himself acting as "dean"; without this the project could never have survived. He served on many party committees in prison, but he never sought party positions. When he was executed in 1941 he was still working as a party intellectual in various semilegal publishing organizations.

Žarko Zrenjanin arrived one day to serve a three-year sentence. We became good friends, in spite of frequent quarrels, mostly over chess. We were both equally bad at it: my triumphant laughter annoyed him, and his teasing me by holding his nose with his two fingers and then blowing annoyed me. He suddenly gained weight in prison. He was nicknamed "Pig"—not because of his weight, but because he had promised us a whole pig from home. That pig never arrived. He was a teacher, but he looked like a peasant, or a worker who had been "educated." His strength was not his intellect or his wit, but, rather, his straightforwardness and kindness, and his spirited and bold mentality. He was firmly and unequivocally on the left. But since everyone talked against "factionalism" and "recruiting," and since Zrenjanin indulged in these things like everybody else, he would say jestingly to me: "What else can you do, short of letting the opportunists take over?"

The Communist community in prison was divided into the party organization and the collective. All party members were in the party organization; all political prisoners willing to contribute money and food and abide by group decisions were members of the collective. But if the nationalists were in the same room with the Communists, they would join the Communist collective. There were a few Communists who were not party members; some were expelled because of the way they behaved before the police, others never had their membership clearly established for one reason or another. The Central Committee was the sole legitimate agent in expelling people from the party or accepting new members. In case of obvious treason, the prison party organization had the right to expel temporarily, as well as to administer penalties. All party members were automatically members of the collective. The collective usually held meetings, elected quartermasters (in charge of food distribution) and other functionaries, and made decisions regarding current problems without prior consultations with the party organization. Leaving the collective, or the party organization, for that matter, did not automatically preclude party membership, but it certainly provoked a lot of hostility.

The most prominent Slovenian was Stremecki. He had been in prison for three years. A group formed around him, not merely by virtue of nationality, but also because Slovenian Communists had a different mentality, different habits and views. They were more moderate and more reserved in their political position and more civilized in their personal relations. No such differences existed between Serbs and Croats.

Stremecki would state his position in a short speech, then sit down on his bed, a smile of resignation on his face. He knew he would be attacked as an "opportunist" and a "capitulator." This deeply hated man was in fact disciplined and persistent, good-natured and loyal. But his virtues faded quickly before the allegations that he was stifling the aggressive spirit and the "bolshevization" of the cadres, suppressing the struggle with "ideologically alien" and hostile elements.

However, in spite of the gap that existed between Stremecki's group and the rest of us, the atmosphere was not particularly hostile. The major attack on Stremecki did not come from Serbs and Croats, but from the Slovenians, mostly young men formed under the dictatorship, whose reactions to political conditions and interparty relations were very similar to our own. They were against all conciliation and ideological compromise. The attacks on Stremecki gained further momentum a year or two later when a new group of Slovenian prisoners joined forces with the other Communists. Upon his release from prison, Stremecki worked hard and fought bravely. He was killed during the war—which proves the academic nature of those prison arguments.

These men were the dominant characters in the intellectual and social life of the room. But we didn't seek to model ourselves after them. We all wanted to be with the workers, to become simpler, like the workers, in our views and our thinking. Daviço carried this conviction to poetic heights, which infected a number of people, including me. Prica was not a romantic in this respect, although he also believed that the working class should assume a leading role. Our room was important because of the size of its vote, but all major decisions were made in rooms No. 10 and No. 6. The former contained the most prominent functionaries, the latter a number of party members such as Moša Pijade, Andrija Hebrang, Milutinović, and Keršovani. The actual center was room No. 10, which was in the throes of a painful and wretched conflict, both political and intensely personal. The whole collective suffered the consequences of this struggle.

The strict regimen imposed as a result of a lost battle with the prison administration served to intensify mutual accusations. The goal of the administration was not merely to make physical conditions insufferable, but to break up political contacts among Communists. Joint food distribution was forbidden, as well as communication between rooms. Prisoners were taken out for walks room by room, and were not allowed to talk. The exchange of books was forbidden. Minor offenses, such as looking out of the window or neglecting to greet the sentries, were strictly punished. In spite of this, we managed to maintain contact between the rooms, even distribute food received from home. We placed the food in candy jars, which were sent from room to room through the sewerage system. There is an unwritten law in all collectives: the new arrivals do the "dirty jobs." Shortly after I arrived I was assigned the job of distributing food through the sewerage system. We would wrap the food in paper and put it in the jar. The person who opened and closed the tin, and operated the string, was not allowed to touch the food, because his hands were dirty. Some of us were squeamish at first, but very quickly we got used to it and didn't mind eating food that had traveled through such unsavory channels. The most awful part was the string. It quickly became stiff and had a strong odor. Every prisoner also immediately learned the alphabet used in knocking messages on the wall. I often worked on long and urgent messages, such as results of discussions and new proposals.

26

Following an unsuccessful hunger strike, the party organization underwent a period of "learning from the experience." Disputes had to be settled among a number of individuals in this sinister and wild drama, complicated by questions of revolutionary honor, vows, and personal passions.

In prison, one could speak freely and vote on all issues. No one was ever reproached for his views or the way he voted. This was the undisputed right of every individual, passed down to us as part of the tradition of the workers' movement and our political life. There were occasional reproaches here and there, but they came from one's intimate friends. Half in jest, Davičo and Zrenjanin reproached me a few times for allegedly having given my support to "opportunists." Using high-pressure methods to win people over to one's point of view outside of the regular meetings was unthinkable. Such maneuvering was unacceptable because it was unprincipled and factional.

All these rules notwithstanding, there was a lot of factionalism. But it was done on the sly. People with similar views had formed groups. In this respect the leftists were a little more active, and I'd say a little more ruthless. On the other hand, the rightists were more persistent in their positions, and more consistent in their voting. The left wing was in a state of confusion, whereas the right wing gained considerable clarity with the arrival of Moša Pijade from Lepoglava. The line between the two groups had not as yet been clearly defined, but it was definitely being formed.

The causes of confusion were numerous, but the most significant was the final disintegration of the so-called "Ivić line," complicated by the personal conflict between Mihailo Ivić and Petko Miletić.

Before his arrest, Ivić had been on close terms with Petko Miletić, an underground activist and a member of the Central Committee. Ivić was a very able underground operator himself, with good Central Committee contacts. Following a successful hunger strike in 1931, Ivić was asked by the Central Committee to put prison affairs in order. The party leadership in prison felt there was no need for such action, because the situation was under control. They questioned the need for a "commissar" at such a time. But since they didn't have the courage to attack the Central Committee, they turned fiercely on Ivić.

In prison all feelings ran strong, for the Central Committee, for party unity, for the Soviet Union. Letters from the Central Committee were few—one every two or three years—but they were used as the basis of endless disputes long after they had become obsolete. Every word was twisted and turned, interpreted a hundred times over. The same was true of the letter that had given Ivić supervisory authority over the organization, made him in effect the undisputed judge of the party organization with veto power over its decisions.

The conflict between the leftists and the "moderates" played into Ivić's hands. The moderates, led by Josip Kraš, maintained that so long as prison conditions were relatively acceptable there was no point in undertaking risky action. In fact, the prison should be turned into a Communist university, they said. Josip Kraš was a baker from Zagreb and a professional trade-union functionary. In spite of his pretentious knowledge and extensive but erroneous use of foreign words, he had a very direct way of approaching workers. They sensed in him a man who would never abandon them, and who dealt with their problems as if they were his own, making compromises when necessary, but also fighting when necessary. Obviously, so long as the prison problems involved fighting for survival, Kraš was able to give good leadership. But the new and more complex circumstances required a person with broader views. A simple direct man, he was also stubborn and tight. He didn't have much use for intellectuals and believed them fit to follow, rather than to lead, in the movement. It is understandable that such a man would not exactly get along with Prica, a clever European intellectual, and that Prica, in turn, couldn't help making fun of Kraš for his use of learned phrases and his primitive attitude toward "scholars." Prica thought Kraš a narrow-minded "trade-union" leader, lacking an aggressive spirit.

Prica and Kraš were at two extremes, but their differences would not in themselves have led to a major conflict was there not already a lot of friction.

It was Mihailo Ivić who introduced a dynamic note into the conflict by attacking his opponent for "opportunism." Otherwise it would be impossible to explain why Kraš, along with some twenty workers, the bravest and most honest of the prisoners, suddenly left the party organization. But they remained within the collective, abiding by all its decisions and maintaining solidarity on all matters pertaining to the prison. Kraš's group was held together not by any inner cohesion, but, rather, by its hostility to Ivić. Having separated themselves, they were accused of "factionalism," a grave sin in the eyes of the party. They thus risked expulsion, but that didn't stop them.

Ivić believed that the prison administration was in a flexible mood and that a new hunger strike could win further benefits. Of course, he buttressed his arguments with "facts," as was the custom in our prison debates: the favorable international situation, the strengthening of the Communist movement in the world, the reputation and success of the Soviet Union.

In spite of his unscrupulousness in internal struggles, Ivić was not without certain redeeming qualities. He was a Bosnian who had moved to Belgrade. He joined the party after World War I, and resigned from active duty in 1924 for reasons that were not clear, and which he defined as a "special assignment," which could have meant activity in the army or working for the Soviet Secret Police. Both jobs were a mark of honor in the party, so an air of secret admiration had built up around him. In any case, the police lost sight of him. In fact, he got a job with the National Theatre in Belgrade, which involved looking after the furnace and checking the building over every time the King visited the theatre. During the first year of the dictatorship he stayed put, but following the devastating 1929 raids, he became a leader of the Communist organization, displaying a great knack for illegal activity. Of medium height, he had a powerful chest and sinewy hands. In prison he grew a mustache, which drooped on both sides and made him look oriental. Politically, he was somewhat uneducated, but he was very bright. He was an excellent speaker, full of passion, folk picturesqueness, and revolutionary terminology. Witty, cynical, bold, he exercised a triple appeal: a tribune, an adventurer, and a magician.

The discussions about the proposed strike coincided with the climax of the conflict within the party organization. The "Ivić faction," which was in the majority, accused the "Kraš group" of "opportunism" and "desertion," and the latter, in turn, accused the Ivić faction of "adventurism." As usual, there were serious moral accusations on both sides, poking through the past, unearthing "old sins."

Ivić's committee employed a maneuver which would have been normal for a Communist organization under different circumstances: he put pressure on new party members to vote for the party majority in the collective. Thus the strike was initiated on the basis of an ersatz majority, and none of the nationalists were ever won over.

Petko Miletić had just arrived in prison. His position on the strike was ambiguous. He was for the struggle, but he wanted to activate people outside the party organization, Communists and nationalists alike. In the party organization he voted against the strike, and in the collective he didn't vote at all, which could have been interpreted as breaking party discipline. He claimed he was new to it all, and thus managed to get away with it. For Kraš's group this was a first hint that the Central Committee didn't really approve of the way they had been treated. It was a blow to Ivić, from a personal friend and a man who had the authority to jeopardize his position. Ivić attacked Miletić's position as indecisive. Miletić did not respond to the accusations. Quietly he laughed to himself, suspecting the future course of events.

To top this off, the party strikers, and Ivić's committee itself, made a weak showing during the strike. In order to undermine the morale of the striking prisoners, the prison administration had put them in solitary confinement. An attempt to feed them by force was thwarted by loud noise and banging—a demonstration that was supported by the nationalists and the criminal prisoners as well. But morale had already been damaged by the chaotic state of the organization, and above all by the ersatz majority. Ivić's own behavior during the strike was not exactly exemplary, although the accusations that he was a strike breaker were not true. On the fifteenth day the frail remnants of the strike committee authorized Prica to negotiate with the authorities to end the strike on the best possible terms. They offered the restoration of prestrike conditions, but without the collective and without circulation between rooms. Before Prica came back from the negotiations, Ivić had asked for a plateful of beans and had started eating—a great stomach! At that point Prica arrived. A fierce debate followed in the party organization as to whether or not Ivić had been a strike breaker. Actually both were true. He had not started eating until the decision was reached, but he announced the decision to the others before Prica had returned. Prica himself felt that although Ivić may have acted incorrectly, he was not a strike breaker.

Kraš's group, partly out of spite and partly because they were all strong men, stuck it out until the bitter end. In fact, Bukovac continued for two extra days because he didn't believe the guards when they told him that the strike had ended. Ranković became so weak that he was carted off to the hospital on the thirteenth day in a semiconscious state.

The end of the strike did not automatically ensure the end of Ivić. Many people believed that this kind of fighting was essential to improve the prison conditions that they considered unbearable and undignified. They recognized the possibility of defeat, but the working class suffered many defeats, yet continued to exist.

The situation had certainly been complicated by the arrival of Petko Miletić. He was preceded by a tremendous reputation. The newspapers gave elaborate coverage to his trial, perhaps because of the big campaign conducted abroad to save his life. He was the first Central Committee member to be arrested but not executed by the dictatorship. The police also spread stories about Miletić's heroic endurance; no amount of torture could break him, they said. Miletić himself was rather generous with stories about the tortures he had suffered. And indeed he had been tortured. His heroism in combination with his membership in the Central Committee made a great impression on us young comrades in particular. For us the illegal Central Committee, in contact with Moscow and the international Communist movement, had magical powers.

Behavior before the police, as I have mentioned before, was a frequent point of conflict among the comrades in prison, but never the chief cause of political differences. Rather, it was introduced as a personal element to substantiate an argument.

At that time good behavior meant not revealing the names of other people, and confessing only to the evidence presented against you. There was not a single Communist who had not confessed to something under torture. But they were not expelled from the party, not even if their actions were considered wrong and they personally weak. On the other hand, those who "gave away" everything were expelled. By and large, they were so unstable that, having rattled out everything they knew, they would then urge other prisoners to do the same in an effort to ingratiate themselves with the police. Due to our irregular contact with the Central Committee, it sometimes took many years for expulsion to go into effect. Thus, for example, Jovan Veselinov and Otokar Keršovani were still party members, even though the former, as a member of the Central Committee of the League of Young Communists, and the latter as a member of the Regional Committee for Serbia, held up poorly before the police. Svetislav Stefanović, also a member of the Central Committee of the League of Young Communists, had a similar experience. He was arrested immediately upon his arrival from Moscow in 1934; he didn't behave satisfactorily before the police and was expelled from the party two years later.

Petko Miletić arrived with the laurels of a man who had never confessed to anything. Moreover, he claimed that no minutes were taken during his interrogation because he considered any communication with the "class enemy" undignified for a Communist. Like the Comintern's, his position was that any form of confession was a betrayal. We were familiar with the official position, but we did not insist upon it because of the position a large majority of our Communists had in fact taken.

Miletić's behavior before the police gave him an enormous moral margin over every prisoner—he rightfully reproached them, if not for outright betrayal, then for not having been able to defend the honor of Communists and the Comintern line before the class enemy. There were several comrades, such as Pijade and Hebrang, who had not confessed to the police at all. But they had been arrested before the dictatorship, and they were not beaten. Miletić could not formally reproach them with anything, but he could always suggest that if they had been tortured, they might not have held out. Their "opportunistic" position with the prison administration illustrated his point. Many Communists lived in dread fear of having their true record exposed, and as a member of the Central Committee, Miletić had the authority to start poking through the past record of any party member.

This authority gave him a considerable advantage over Ivić. Until the conflict with Miletić, Ivić's behavior before the police was considered good. He had confessed only to the evidence others had given against him. Since he had been in charge of correspondence with the Central Committee in Vienna, the police had asked him to write letters inviting Committee members to return to the country on urgent business. Ivić did it, but he let them know by code that he was in prison. No one came back from Vienna. Ivić did not keep these letters a secret. But it was impossible to determine whether his story about the codes was true. And this became *the* issue in his conflict with Miletić. However, these accusations failed to turn Ivić's supporters against him. His record with the police was no better or worse than anyone else's. But Ivić was driven to unreasonable acts by the accusations. It was rumored that he assaulted Miletić with a chair.

Ivić's supporters considered this whole affair a great misfortune. In the conflict, the Kraš group disintegrated, the majority siding with Miletić. Following the strike, his whole group had rejoined the party organization, but it no longer acted as a unit, because the defeat of its chief enemy was now a certainty. The beast had to be driven into the ground, and Miletić was strong enough to take care of that himself.

There was a personal element in the Ivić-Miletić conflict of which few were aware. After Ivić's arrest, Miletić continued to drop by Ivić's home on his frequent trips from Vienna, and out of this developed an affair with Ivić's wife. Among Communists this was not considered an act of immorality, or a cause for anger or separation. But for a proud individual like Ivić, it represented a serious blow, particularly because it involved a close friend and a high party official. He understood, of course, that his wife's "error" resulted from the common morality of the times and from the desperate loneliness the wife of every Communist experienced. This loneliness was all the greater for Ivanka because of the small number of people in the movement and her isolation from Ivić due to the deeply conspiratorial nature of his job. She loved him, though, and she tried to prove it with her letters and her visits. Although he never reproached Miletić for his relationship with Ivanka, Miletić must have sensed the special male anger of Ivić's reactions. For Miletić this was only further proof that Ivić was a "crazy bourgeois" to whom a woman is more important than the party and the revolution.

Early in the spring of 1934 Ivić was officially reprimanded for the errors committed during the strike. It was interesting to watch his faithful followers, among them Daviĉo. They mourned him—and then they got over it. Eventually they realigned themselves behind the new leftist leader, Petko Miletić. It was indeed impossible to defend Ivić's failure in the strike, but most people could not turn on him as a man and as a comrade. Thoroughly beaten, Ivić gradually retreated and concentrated on ideological activity. It soon became clear how little he knew, but how quickly this clever improviser could learn. Of course, he was always with the leftists.

In 1937, when Miletić's influence in the party and in the Central Committee was at its height, Ivić was expelled for his behavior be-

fore the police and for factionalism. Following his release from
prison in 1940, he went to Belgrade. Ranković was against re-
establishing contact with him. Accounts were being settled with
unsound elements, and Ivić certainly belonged in that category.
Ranković told me in 1947 that Vujković, the head of the Belgrade
police, who was handed over to us by the Allies as a war criminal,
claimed that after he got out of prison Ivić had agreed to work for
the police. But there was nothing to substantiate this claim, and it
can easily be assumed that Vujković, aware of interparty struggles,
wanted to ingratiate himself by maligning an enemy of the top
party officials and offering them his "treasury of great secrets."
The fact remains that, even though rejected by the party, Ivić was
arrested by the Germans and executed with the first group of Communists. It is hard to believe that the Belgrade police would have
allowed such an important agent to be sacrificed in error. But for
the few Communists who bothered to think about Ivić, he ended as
a traitor.

Shortly after Ivić's execution, his wife was also arrested, which
virtually destroyed her, after a lifetime of sacrifice for the movement. Not only had a beautiful relationship been demolished, but
the man she loved had been defeated by the very essence of his
life—expelled from the party to which the two of them had given
everything, including their love. She disappeared in the whirlwind.

The climax to this particular story was the revelation that Petko
Miletić had not stood up to the police nearly as well as the official
teaching dictated. It turned out that his claim to having confessed
to nothing and signed no minutes was simply not quite true. But
this was disclosed much later, in 1939, long after Petko had been
expelled from the party as a "Trotskyite" and a "factionist." The
lawyer Bora Prodanović was instrumental in uncovering this information. Until 1936, Prodanović had glorified Miletić as a hero.
Then they had a quarrel. Miletić referred to Prodanović as a "petit
bourgeois lawyer," a "pet of government ministers," all the more so
because Prodanović was a friend of his enemy Moša Pijade. Then
Prodanović turned on Miletić. He didn't deny that Miletić had
shown courage before the police, which any "mule" could do. But
when Miletić's followers claimed that he had never signed the minutes of the interrogation, Prodanović, who had been Miletić's lawyer at the trial, produced the minutes of the interrogation signed by
Miletić. Regardless of Prodanović's views of the official "theory"
of approved behavior before the police, or Miletić's behavior, for
that matter, he knew that these minutes were the best means of

bringing about Miletić's downfall. With the assistance of Judge Job, he photographed the police record of Miletić's minutes and gave them to me to pass along "where necessary," *i.e.*, to the Central Committee, of which I was a member.

Miletić managed to acquire a false passport and, with the help of the Soviet Consulate in Istanbul, he managed to get to Moscow, where he hoped to clear up his case with the Comintern. In spite of Tito's protests, Miletić was received by the Comintern. Then the photocopy of his interrogation arrived. Tito later told us that as soon as he had handed in the photocopy, Miletić "disappeared." We never heard another word about him, nor did we exactly try to find out. His arrest by the Soviet Secret Police assured us that he was an "enemy," which we automatically interpreted as meaning a spy or a Trotskyite or something similar.

Of course, the story of Miletić's "treacherous" behavior before the police spread fast in prison. I distributed a short résumé of his interrogation among his few close friends, which was sufficient to destroy him as a man and establish him as a traitor.

However, this too was an exaggeration.

It is true that the authenticity of the police records cannot be disputed: the signatures were those of Miletić and Vujković. Yet there was nothing in the record to suggest that he was in fact a traitor. Miletić didn't denounce a single man, and certainly not the organization. He confessed to the evidence against him. There was some question whether he had actually revealed the addresses abroad, in Vienna and Budapest, which were quoted in the minutes. But in view of the over-all interrogation this really didn't matter.

Thus, Miletić was far from the hero modeled on the social theory and his own preaching. From the point of view of the police, who gained nothing of consequence from him, his stand was heroic. As far as the official Moscow party view went, Miletić's stand was "undignified," "weak," but of itself not necessarily deserving of expulsion. But when he turned up in the role of an unjustly maligned hero, the sudden divulgence of the true facts apparently was the last straw, and gave the Soviet Secret Police a good reason for moving against him.

27

Within the prison Communist cell there were many internal conflicts. Major discussion of "opportunism" and "adventurism" was often generated by some minor run-in with a sentry or demand addressed to the authorities for an improvement in conditions. But as regards the larger theoretical questions—the revolution, the problems of Marxism—there were no major conflicts. The pre-1929 party members had already gone through a factional struggle. And for those who had become members since 1929, factionalism was an evil that they knew about but would rather not experience. In keeping with the Comintern's "Open Letter" of 1929, factionalism was criticized as the party's greatest disaster and crime. This position was adopted by everyone, regardless of what stand they took with respect to pre-1929 conflicts. This meant virtually unconditional submission to the Central Committee.

It goes without saying that neither the left nor the right wing of the party ever referred to itself as such. On the contrary, both acted in the name of "bolshevik consistency," "flexibility," and party discipline. In intimate conversation left-wing members occasionally referred to themselves as leftists, but the right wing considered the word "rightist" an insult. The truth is, these denominations didn't reflect real positions. On many points the leftists were further to the right than the rightists, and the other way around. Generally speaking, one could make the following differentiation between the two groups: the left wing favored a more intense struggle with the prison, whereas the right wing favored a more reasonable approach. The significant and complex element in this differentiation was that the rightists were mostly older Communists, whereas the leftists were younger men who had become politically active under the dictatorship.

In spite of these differences, the party organization was, within the framework of established rules and notions, internally democratic and externally unified. The minority bowed to the majority, and the committee elections were free. For new party members, prison was a valuable experience. It meant mixing several party generations, from all parts of the country, as well as from the Soviet Union. In this closely knit place, in this strange family of men, they felt themselves part of a world movement composed of many revolutionary crosscurrents. The new men had been educated in an antifactional tradition, in the spirit of loyalty and obedience to the Central Committee. This explains their relative success in operating a deeply secretive organization.

However, the arrival of new prisoners introduced new problems.

Following Ivić's downfall, the leftists, as I have said, finally acquired an authoritative leader in Petko Miletić. But with the arrival of Pijade and Hebrang from Lepoglava and Maribor, the right wing also acquired leaders with a great deal of authority and experience. The difference was that Miletić understood clearly that he had to rely on the young aggressive generation that developed under the dictatorship if he was to succeed in prison, or outside of it, for that matter. It was obvious that soon the left wingers would constitute the backbone of the party. Their mood was different, they cared little for intraparty squabbles, they felt strongly about the struggle against the enemy. Their life had taught them that only complete and undisputed discipline and total ideological, intellectual, and spiritual loyalty to the cause of the revolution and Communism would produce results. Any exaggerated reasoning, discussion, respect for form were equivalent to "liberalism" and "wavering." They sought to bring the factional dispute to an end in order to strengthen the struggle against the enemy. They didn't care much for democratic processes. They wanted action. They were looking for strong leadership, and Petko Miletić looked like the man who would give them strong leadership.

He was a Montenegrin who had gone to Hungary before World War I to work and ended up fighting in the Hungarian Commune of 1919. When he came back he joined Dr. Vukašin Marković, who had returned from Russia to work for the revolution in Yugoslavia. After two years in Montenegrin forests, and a lengthy stay in prison, Miletić went to Russia, where he attended party schools. During the Comintern's reshuffling of the Central Committee, he joined the leadership that replaced the ones of 1928 and 1930. The leadership of 1928, in power when the dictatorship took over, spread the senseless slogan of "armed uprising" as answer to the dictatorship. The party paid dearly for this slogan, which separated it from the rest of the opposition and from the people. The leadership that followed was not much of an improvement. It wasn't until Petko Miletić took over that the slogan of "armed uprising" was withdrawn. However, his leadership continued in the sectarian and narrow tradition.

Miletić had a complex personality. He was a rebellious peasant who had not thoroughly digested proletarian revolutionary learning. His political education in Moscow, in which he had not distinguished himself in any field, further reinforced his impatient, tough, and rebellious spirit by oversimplified dogmatism. He had also learned the importance of intrigue in political struggle and thus freed himself of any idealized notion of the Communist movement. But none of this changed him fundamentally. He remained a Montenegrin who verged between adventurism and heroism, a typical product of a culture rich in extremes. Below his gloomy brow was a pair of dull green eyes. But when he spoke, one sensed a man of action, a man who had seen the world. In spite of his oversimplified picture of it, he had a great knack for maneuvering and plotting, particularly on the smaller issues of everyday party life.

His early experiences in the forest had left a profound impression on him. He scanned everything with great caution—as if he might run into a trap any minute. He thought of illegal party activity as a sort of rebellion in the cities, and not as a scheme for reaching large masses of people through political action.

He spoke often, and with great respect, about the Montenegrin leader Dr. Vukašin Marković, and praised him as a fighter rather than a politician. Marković came from the village of Piper, was educated in Russia, and took part in the Russian revolutionary movement as a simple dedicated fighter. In Montenegro, where he spent some time as a rebel in the mountains, he had become a legend. It was said that he set the Piper forests afire when the people went after him. But the people didn't condemn him for that. In the absence of medication he prepared treatments from grasses for the peasants. He treated them with great respect, and followed their patterns himself. On the other hand, people who came back from Moscow spoke of him with derision: he wrote letters to Stalin every time he was displeased with something, he agitated in Russian villages on his own initiative, and for many years, in Moscow, he slept fully dressed, with his boots on. The "class enemy never sleeps"! Tito also spoke about him with derision, but he respected him too. This eccentric folksy revolutionary from Piper was clearly outpaced by the times. Later he became the victim of senility, which took the form of increased revolutionary passion. He left a beautiful legend behind him, an inspiration for the awakening of revolutionary forces in my own times.

In his simplified, primitive, and arrogant treatment of relationships and ideas, Petko Miletić perfected the manner of his teacher, a man of great rebellious energy and fanatic dedication. Miletić generally supported the left wingers, but when leftists made unpopular decisions, he was quick to pronounce himself neutral. Thus he managed to maintain his position and protect his reputation. The leftists sensed this and held him at bay, but not for long. His strength was growing and they could embark on policies only if he would go along. Gradually he became their leader.

In the April 1934 crisis, however, his role was insignificant, as was the party leadership's. The incident itself was minor, stemming from an argument between a prisoner and a guard. In response a whole roomful of prisoners demonstrated from a window in support of their comrade. The other rooms joined in, and in no time there was a tremendous noise of shouting and banging with tin dishes.

That was in the afternoon. At night we discussed our course of action for the next day. The prison administration would obviously take appropriate countermeasures; they could not allow such action to go unpunished, particularly since they had gained the upper hand in the hunger strike. To initiate another hunger strike would have been senseless. We had just lost one and the men were exhausted. So we resumed our demonstrations the next day, and sent a delegation to the prison authorities with a list of demands.

They would not even listen. They feared that the incident would turn into a major uprising, and they were determined to squash it, with force if necessary. On the third day the gendarmes occupied the prison yard and the corridors.

Our demonstration immediately stopped. To keep up our morale, we continued singing revolutionary songs into the evening, which the prison administration had always tolerated. But this time they decided to use it as an excuse for revenge.

They abolished all privileges for two months: no visits, no parcels, no letters. The comrades in room No. 6 were interrogated, tried, and sentenced to two additional years.

The rightists criticized the demonstration as disorganized, senseless, and harmful to the point of being ridiculous. We should have channeled our anger into a hunger strike, they said, a form of rebellion accepted by the whole world, rather than engaging in immature "revolutionary competition" and "hysteria."

However, we leftists felt that the demonstration had expressed our "revolutionary" spirit and forestalled administration attempts to institute a regimen based on beating and brute force. As for the lengthened prison terms, these were the inevitable sacrifices of the proletariat and its avant garde. Prison conditions were indeed hard. Besides, our dignity was now threatened. The practice of having to take one's hat off and hold one's head down when talking to guards was reinstituted, as was the practice of forcing a roomful of prisoners to leap to their feet when a guard entered. Bitterness was growing, and it had to be expressed in some form. The argument that the proletariat had to make sacrifices was accepted by everyone. Both the leftists and the rightists sentenced to additional years in prison bore their punishment with dignity. This was all the more beautiful in that the punishment was imposed on comrades with long prison sentences. Pijade grumbled a little, not so much because of the years added to his original sentence, but because of the "*vahabitski*" nonsense that led to it.

In this matter Petko Miletić played a two-faced role. At first he was not very enthusiastic about the demonstrations, but when the leftists began gaining ground in defense of their action, he gradually took up the cause, and rose to the top.

28

It was the month of June, but a damp, gray day. Behind the prison walls it might easily have been late October. The afternoon walk was over and we were enjoying the "quiet hour." Suddenly the jail-keeper, Babo, rushed in and called out a list of names. We were ordered to get packed and to line up in the damp sooty yard: some sixty Communists and thirty nationalists—prominent "leaders," intellectuals, and disobedient "loud-mouths." The regime had made a careful choice. We were not told where we were going, or when. When Babo called out our names again, Ivić responded with the German *hier*, to remind Babo of his long and loyal service to the Austrian monarchy. Not a muscle moved on Babo's thick purple face. For us, Ivić's witticism brought cheer in an otherwise gloomy day.

When night fell, the gendarmerie took charge of us, and the column moved awkwardly in rows of six. We were pushed into cattle cars. After prolonged whistling and maneuvering, the train finally pulled out. It was late at night. We looked out a little window. We were headed north. A town was at our left, and deserted fields to the right. All the way to Slavonski Brod we fretted that we might be en route to the Zenica Prison, reputedly the toughest in the country. But we left Slavonski Brod, and that meant we were going to Lepoglava or Maribor. We didn't much care which.

We saw a little of the scenery: square canvasses of fields and hills, groves with small white houses tucked into them, interlaced with the grating on the cattle cars. In the late afternoon we were unloaded and we started walking into the hills, blinded by the green glow. The column moved along a rutted road in the direction of the penitentiary, which was about a mile from the station. In the distance was an odd mixture of an old monastery and sharp modern barracks.

The closer we got, the more clearly the two buildings came into view. The Lepoglava Penitentiary consisted of the old Pavlinski Monastery, at one time a well-known school in Croatia, and the new penitentiary across from it. These two buildings were fenced off, and they stood out from the rest: the monastery with its baroque tower, and the new building with its rows of similar windows. We were herded, by the dozen, into the group rooms of the new building. There were no toilets, and we had to use a bucket in a corner of the room. In addition to the workshops, the church, the administrative offices, and these group rooms, the building, of concrete, iron, glass, and brick in the shape of the letter X, also contained four hundred solitary cells. The builders were sparing with everything except the iron bars and the solid walls. The cells were just about as wide as my arms stretched out with my fists clenched, a little over five feet, and about five feet long. Most of the prisoners were serving their second term. All communication in the workshops and church was strictly forbidden, and we looked crushed as we spoke in whispers. The rest of the prisoners lived in the former monastery, mostly in group rooms, relatively bright and spacious, but with thick walls and rotting floors. In the yard of the new prison there was one additional building, fenced off with iron bars, for the mentally disturbed.

The view was not nearly as monotonous as at Mitrovica. The skies were brighter, livelier, more varied. Every Sunday groups of peasants, in white dress, came down the hill by the side of the prison wall, on their way to church. The eyes of the prisoners followed them from the time they appeared on the top of the hill until they disappeared behind the walls. These short knotty peasants, weary from work and misery, looked ruddy-cheeked and happy, and the girls in their wide skirts and starched blouses looked bright-eyed and cheerful.

On the very first evening we were pleasantly surprised. Instead of the stricter regimen we had expected, the situation was much more relaxed. We were allowed to eat together, and we could mix freely in different rooms. We took joint walks, and on Saturdays we were allowed to spend the night with a friend in another room, in exchange for someone else of course.

The food, however, was very poor—sufficient but badly prepared. The bread was soggy, half-baked; the meat bad. At Mitrovica, on the other hand, the food had been clean and tasty, the meat lean, and the bread—a mixture of corn and wheat bran—tasty and well baked.

Even so, we ate well. Many famous Communists were with us, including a few from well-to-do families. Red Aid sent money and packages, mostly to well-known comrades. A number of sympathizers also sent food, and there were days when we ate virtually no prison food. At Mitrovica, where we got no such aid, we had all starved.

The regime's policy was to single out the leaders and rebels and offer them better conditions. Fresh groups of prisoners were expected, and the regime hoped to save them from ideological "education." Although we should have been pleased with our new situation, many of us were not. Two groups were formed, differing on the question of relations with the prison administration. One group was less tolerant of the "class enemy," more dogmatic in the struggle for Communist goals, and it was supported by those who recognized that it was this group that would ultimately dominate the party. There were also some who, like Petko, used this strategy to strengthen their own position.

The right-wing group, which was larger, was going through a similar experience, and for similar reasons. When it came to drafting a course of action, the left wing was stronger, but in concrete action, it was in the minority.

The Prison Committee recognized this balance of forces, and it was controlled by the moderates. We made a special effort to keep the leadership of the party organization secret: each room elected a delegate, who was also secretary of the party organization, and these men in turn elected the Committee. But we knew who the members were anyway. The chief figure was Stanko Paunović, a young worker from Niš serving a long-term sentence. He spoke well and had a pleasant face. He looked more like an intellectual than a metal worker, and he stood out with his intelligence and wisdom. He wrote correctly in tiny careful handwriting. I have never met a man who learned so easily and quickly, and was at the same time so modest. He enjoyed a great reputation. He never got involved in group conflicts and gossip. Although consistent in his position of never giving in to the prison authorities, he was not trusted altogether by the leftists. The right wing respected his wisdom and common sense. Indeed, he knew how to maintain a "neutral" position in the most complex circumstances.

Paunović had one "weakness." He wrote verse in secret, which he gave to intellectuals to read, in the hope of getting some help. His verse was regular, as in a school assignment, but had no soul, which was true of other "worker" poets as well.

Salaj and Keršovani, two other members of the Committee, also took neutral positions. But they were insecure and weak, with their own motives for choosing the middle of the road. Paunović was against all clique policies, and favored a reasonable but aggressive position toward the prison administration. Basically, Salaj and Keršovani had no position of their own, nor were they too anxious to engage in the struggle. They carried the burden of not having stood up too well before the police, and Keršovani was still a member of the party organization only because orders for his expulsion had not yet reached us.

Salaj was short, dark, and not very bright. He was talkative, but one could easily throw him off with a few sharp remarks. Although he flared up quickly, he was always careful not to insult anyone.

Keršovani was a fairly typical Slovenian from the coast, dark, stocky, and good-natured. When he emigrated from Italy he was a nationalist, but in Yugoslavia he quickly joined the left wing. He was a gifted journalist, the most hard-working intellectual I've ever met. He never wasted a minute: in the morning chaos of making beds and cleaning up he would grab a book and read a page or two; he would do the same after supper, in fact until the last of the feeble lights were turned off. He had kept a pile of notebooks written in small, pretty handwriting. He was familiar with the major world languages, and was learning Hungarian to be able to read Croatian history. He had a large and well-organized stock of knowledge, and was able to write on any subject at a moment's notice. In the course of the year in Lepoglava he wrote a booklet called *The Agrarian Question*, for ideological studies in our collective. It may not have been an original contribution, but it was full of quotations and facts, and a diversity of views. He was also working on a history of Croatia. His wife, a ballet dancer, had abandoned him for Martinović, Secretary of the Central Committee, but his father-in-law, Dr. Silović, continued to visit him and send him books from the Zagreb Library. Keršovani had a fine, rich mind, but it was not a basically creative one because his Communism was not revolutionary. In 1940 the Central Committee instructed me to inform Keršovani that he had been accepted by the party. But he refused to join, stating he was unsure how well he would hold up before the police. That was proof of great self-knowledge and honesty, but also of weakness. By our standards, his decision amounted to breaking relations with the party. It was also painful proof that a long term in prison didn't re-educate everyone, but only those who wanted it. Keršovani withdrew into his own thing: intellectual activity with the aim of helping the working class, but on his own terms. Nevertheless, he respected party orders and did as he was told. He worked largely on legal publishing jobs, conscientiously and promptly. When he was executed he was still not a party member.

With this divided composition, the Committee could have no authority. Even though everyone accepted its orders, and the Committee in turn conscientiously attended to its daily business, real power evolved outside it.

At the very beginning, a fairly unimportant incident took place that helped define relations with the prison administration as well as within the collective.

Some two weeks after our arrival, during the afternoon exercise, the guards flung two mentally ill prisoners to the ground and beat them so brutally that even had they not been insane they would have had to scream. Partly inspired by the sheer brutality of the incident, partly by our own bitterness, a few of us shouted in protest. The guards stopped our exercise and chased us off into our rooms. Then a violent argument took place, all the more violent and painful in that the Prison Committee took no stand.

The following day Djordje Jovanović, Petko Miletić, Boris Božić, a frail young man from the Slovenian littoral, and I were asked to appear before the authorities.

The director, a certain Spasojević, was being replaced that very day by Učitelj, a fat, senile old man who gave us the usual lecture: we should respect authority at all times and stay calm. Djordje Jovanović took the offensive from the start: he pointed out that it was the guards who had created disorder by acting against the rule that forbid the beating of prisoners. Učitelj was clearly bored by the argument, which involved philosophy and law, and asked Jovanović to promise not to behave like this again. Djordje was evasive. Another argument. Učitelj asked Petko the same question. Petko tried to evade the answer too. Another argument. Then he asked me. I answered briefly: "I'll promise you nothing." The old man was enraged. "I'm the authority, I'm the authority!" he screamed. "Where do you think you are?" He gave each of us two weeks' solitary confinement.

Two weeks on top of the two months! Several times comrades from adjacent rooms left pieces of bacon for us in the garbage, but even so we were still very hungry. Cramped in tiny little rooms, overwhelmed with cockroaches in the summer heat, we were completely cut off from the outside world.

My room was the last one along the corridor. The room next to mine was empty. One afternoon the lock squeaked, and a prisoner was shoved inside. We began knocking on the wall. He gave me his name, where he was from, the length of his sentence. He said that he was a political prisoner, and of course I didn't believe him. I was surprised and delighted the next morning to learn that the "criminal prisoner" was Alexander Ranković.

I had heard about him long before this, and I had met him while we were being transported to Lepoglava, but I didn't know he too had received additional punishment.

Ranković was thin and pale. It was rumored that he had been consumptive but was now cured. He was a quiet, withdrawn man, without a sense of humor, but fond of a good joke all the same. There was something pleasant in his blue eyes and in his smile, which created dimples on his cheeks. He had peasant features— short, strong hands and broad feet—he walked with his legs wide, and he spoke slowly. From time to time he would flare up, but never lost control. He was concerned with honor, and even more so with his reputation and appearance. Quick, penetrating, and measured in everything, he belonged to the aggressive group, and was greatly respected by the workers for his tough, consistent position.

There was something subtle and careful in everything he did, in spite of his toughness and vulgarity. His behavior before the police was not bad, but not heroic either. He was arrested with the group of Andrejev and Gruber, which was uncovered shortly after the establishment of the dictatorship. They were brutally beaten and sentenced to long terms. Ranković got five years. He had joined the movement prior to the dictatorship as a very young worker, but his major political development occurred in prison, under the January Dictatorship. He was nearing the end of his sentence, but this was his first chance to study. He read diligently, but slowly, mostly popular pamphlets, and studied Russian and Esperanto.

I met this man under strange circumstances, never suspecting that we were to spend more than seventeen years working together, fighting together, developing an exceptionally strong and sincere friendship, and, following this, becoming such bitter enemies.

It wasn't until after we had served our sentences in solitary that we ran into real trouble. A number of people were against our "insane" stand and they considered my reply to the prison director a provocation. Party punishments were proposed. However, the left wing objected to this on the grounds that the party punishment on top of the "class enemy" punishment would mean turning the party organization into a police organization. They went so far as to reproach Petko Miletić for his ambiguous reply to the prison director. But this clever man, who had a knack for drastic expression, quickly defended himself: the majority in his room, following Pijade's suggestion, had forbidden him to take a "provocative" position.

The right wing ridiculed our solidarity with the lunatics as senseless. The leftists claimed that if we hadn't protested against such measures, the guards would be beating us now.

This seemingly insignificant incident quickly defined two basic camps; the Miletić and Pijade room was the center of both. Actually, Hebrang was the true leader of the right wing.

Pijade was already gray and had an impressive paunch. Apart from this there was nothing old about him. He had a typically "Semitic" appearance. His head buried in his chest, he wore glasses which he alternately moved from his nose to his forehead, and he had an unusually expressive face. He was a very popular person. His passionate nature, brilliant speech, his sense of humor and satire, his knack for swearwords, his funny appearance were all captivating.

He worked very fast and nervously, always crowding more work into a given time span that he could possibly accomplish. He never planned; he always lived "in a hurry." He had finished his translation of *Das Kapital*, and we were already studying from the first volume of the published work. He said he was going to take a rest following *Das Kapital*, but he never even slackened his pace. If there was nothing to do, he was quite capable of writing long tracts on something very insignificant, accompanied by sketches, drafts, proposals, all done neatly and conscientiously. It was fantastic energy in a small but resilient body that expanded luxuriously in all directions.

All these qualities notwithstanding, Pijade had little of the great Communist leader in him. His thinking was too lively, too much subject to momentary impressions and passions. A revolutionary in both spirit and temperament, he lacked the necessary solidity for all forms of struggle. He had translated *Das Kapital*, and other important Marxist works, but he was no ideologist. His public appearances and lectures were enjoyable, full of picturesqueness and passion, but, like his articles, they had no depth. In contrast to most of the leading Communists, he never subjected his private life to the dogma, before or after prison. He was moderate in his eating and drinking, but not so in his relationships with women, an inconceivable extravaganza for a leading Communist. Innocence was required, even if superficial, and Pijade was much too outgoing to conform.

He was criticized for not having held up too well in the hunger strike he led, for having given his paintings to the prison director to ensure a somewhat easier time for himself. These charges were probably true, but they were by no means the basis for the leftist attacks on him. No, the reasons were in Pijade's own personality, in his lively mentality, in the fact that he did not go along with the aggressive current. Thus one of the most passionate and lively leaders of the old left had become the target of the new left. In internal party struggles he was bitter and aggressive, had a long memory, and was persistent to the point of blindness. He would sometimes withdraw, and then spring back again. His withdrawals were always accompanied by ardent admissions of "mistakes," until he recovered, of course, and attacked again. He was not secretive or double-faced, but he was always passionate.

Although Pijade was in almost constant conflict with the leftists, he was not hated by them, nor was he considered their major opponent.

That role belonged to Andrija Hebrang.

Hebrang was employed by a private firm, but prior to that he had done physical labor. He was nicknamed "Fatty" and "Kuljo," both having to do with his obesity. Of medium height, very fat, with a ruddy face and low forehead, Hebrang ground his strong teeth in his sleep all night long. He had been arrested before the dictatorship, tried under the dictatorship, and sentenced to ten years. As a member of the Regional Committee for Croatia he supported the so-called "Zagreb line," which opposed both left and right factions. Josip Broz, then the Secretary of the Zagreb Local Committee, also adhered to the Zagreb line. The two of them were in fact good friends, and Hebrang often referred to him as a serious, solid party worker. In lectures on the history of the Yugoslav Communist party, the Zagreb line was emphasized as a positive element. It was said that in 1928 a Comintern delegate stated that the only traces of serious Communist organization were to be found in Zagreb. In any case, Hebrang was a strong man, and he stood up staunchly in all struggles. In contrast to Pijade, who would occasionally show friendship, or jest with the prison authorities, Hebrang's behavior was always serious, even a trifle arrogant.

He didn't have many friends. He operated with a small number of good, serious men. He didn't spare Pijade either, when Pijade made blunders, although he was exceptionally warm and attentive to him. He was tough, dignified, courageous, and he never backed away from conflict. Nor was he afraid to be in the minority, or altogether alone, for that matter.

Like most Communists, he was not a particularly good speaker. His delivery was cold, dry, concise. His language had no color, but it inspired confidence with its sparseness. He was of above-average intelligence, and what difficulties he had in learning were overcome by his iron will. He spoke German well, and read a little English and a little Russian. His knowledge of political economy, although reduced almost exclusively to Marx, was thorough. He took slow careful notes on everything he read.

Serious-minded, quick to blow up, but never out of control, stubborn and patient, a skillful conversationalist, with a clean past and considerable experience, Hebrang was well suited to play a significant role in the struggles among the factions. In fact, no man was better suited to assume leadership of the right wing. He was the equal of Petko Miletić in every respect. Although the latter had a sharper sense of intrigue and conspiracy, Hebrang was more adept at organizing people for action.

The only person to wage a consistent struggle against Miletić three or four years later was Hebrang, although it was Pijade who finally emerged at the head of the right wing. Hebrang never for a moment allowed himself to be overwhelmed by Miletić's "heroic" behavior, his high position, his aggressiveness, his energy, and his growing authority. On the other hand, Pijade, under pressure, often made "self-critical" statements. I was a witness of one such "penitent act." Pijade looked like an unhappy old man, about to burst into tears. It never so much as crossed Hebrang's mind to justify his acts, and he never repented. This may have indicated a certain inflexibility, but once he plowed a field, as they say, he stuck to the furrows.

The sharp conflicts of the future were in their initial stages. Personal relationships between the chief protagonists were still reasonably good. The unity of the organization, although muddied here and there, remained firm. The large marjority remained in opposition to factional scheming. I didn't participate in this warfare, although I was with the left, and Davičo and Zrenjanin had to "work" on me whenever some important issue came up. Davičo was more conspiratorial, full of whispers, allusions, and half-spoken words, whereas Zrenjanin was tougher and more direct.

Future events fit well this scene of unresolved contrasts, this unity in spite of differences, favoring now one, now the other current.

29

The whole collective, including the nationalists, was engaged in intensive ideological study. This was perhaps the first time that conditions favored us: we had plenty of literature and food. As a result, some of our internal differences faded away. In my room, the majority opposed all "outbursts," and the working atmosphere was excellent. Outside of ideological topics, discussions were brief.

Djuro Pucar was the party secretary in our room. He was very close to Hebrang, consulting him on all important questions. The three leftists in my room, Zrenjanin, Djordje Jovanović, and myself, found these "factional" consultations infuriating, even more infuriating than the firm way in which Pucar conducted his meetings. We had frequent run-ins with him, me in particular, and this hostility couldn't be erased.

He was basically a good-natured man, but quick-tempered. His appearance was tough. His small blue eyes were set deep under his powerful brows. He had irregular teeth, a strong jaw, a big nose, and bony arms and legs. This blacksmith from Bosanska Krajina rightly deserved the nickname of "Bear." He didn't care much for this nickname, although he had a sense of humor. He flared up easily, but he never swore and he never told dirty stories. There was childlike innocence about him, quite common among our men from the backward mountain regions. He came from a very poor family, and as a worker he had had the hardest and toughest jobs, unlike most Communists, who had taken easier, well-paid jobs. Learning was hard for him, but he could absorb certain basic notions in a simplified form. He was a strong man, and from the first instant inspired confidence.

The leftists, of course, considered him a great opportunist. But in action he was decisive and courageous. Some time in the spring of 1935 he was selected to bribe a guard to buy us newspapers and tobacco. We went out for our regular walk, and Pucar paused to give the guard one hundred dinars, which was a fortune for us. Once the hundred dinars were in his hand, the guard said: "Now, let's go to the office." Pucar grabbed the guard's hand, seized the hundred-dinar note, and ran out into the yard. Several guards followed him and there was a great commotion. Pucar passed the hundred-dinar note to me, I passed it to Andrejev, and Andrejev swallowed it in no time at all. This started off a violent argument. Obviously when a third party was in question, solidarity prevailed among us Communists. Petko Miletić took the initiative: he said the guard was a "provocateur," that the story of the one hundred dinars was made up out of whole cloth. They chased us back into our rooms. Pucar became a hero. I suddenly felt affection for this man with whom I had had so many arguments.

By and large the workers were far more orderly, cleaner, more precise in their work, and more disciplined in discussions than the intellectuals. The same was true of Pucar. He had a fabulous appetite and was capable of consuming two large portions of some miserable-tasting beans. For this man, authority was always essential, and one principle was more sacred than all the rest—party unity. He might have "meandered" a while, attaching himself to Hebrang, but that was because he believed that Hebrang was there to defend that sacred principle. Later, when Petko Miletić took over the party organization, Pucar sided with the majority, but at heart he accepted Miletić only insofar as he identified him with the party; when the struggle turned against Miletić, he couldn't wait to change sides.

For me and my comrades in prison, Pucar was an example of how false our prison notions of people were.

Risto-Rile Kolicić, a worker from Niš and a member of the Stanko Paunović group, was an altogether different person.

Intellectuals were never exactly a highly priced commodity, but Kolicić's hatred of them was almost pathological. Short, dark, with a hard face and eyes, Kolicić looked like many men from his part of the world, and he had many of their characteristics, which are commendable, but which in prison were intolerable: a parsimoniousness that verged on stinginess, and neatness that verged on primness. For years he had been the best quartermaster in prison. He always distributed justly: he could cut a lump of sugar in four equal parts. But our collective was "rich," and in his role as quartermaster he was eminently unsuitable. Besides, it was ugly to see him accumulating piles of rancid bacon for "lean" days. He was mean and quarrelsome. He had no friends. Djordje Jovanović often passed gas rather rambunctiously, which was a cause for instant quarreling. He claimed that, unlike Kolicić, he couldn't divide it neatly in ten parts. We laughed, and that made Kolicić angry. He hated me because I had found out that in his notebooks, while copying quotes from Engels' *Anti-Dühring*, he often mistook Dühring for Engels. I teased him about it in public, for which he never forgave me.

Cramped into small spaces, men in prison get on each other's nerves with various habits—sniffling, making noises while eating, chortling. Kolicić provoked a lot of people by giving them "lessons" in "good habits." He considered it his sacred duty to impose his own standards on others. Thus small quarrels spread, like wildfire, across the whole prison.

Upon his release from prison, in 1940, Kolicić refused to contact the party. It pleased me to think that I had anticipated the failure of this homebody to participate in the revolutionary struggle upon his return to freedom. Ranković didn't hold much faith in him either, although he never suspected Kolicić of such cowardly "withdrawal." Having spent a long time with the revolutionaries, never having betrayed them in any of their struggles. Kolicić returned to his own world, to live the rest of his life aimlessly.

The fate of an expelled party member in jail was quite moving, even for us Communists. While a whispered party meeting was being held in one corner of the room, the rejected soul would sit on his bed in another corner and pretend he was unaware anything was going on. We passed no "secrets" on to him, and almost everything the party organization did was considered "secret." But he would still try to be a Communist and force himself to demonstrate that he was "improving." Of course, he was aware that, compared with us, he had lost control over his fate. He simply had to accept all of our decisions, some made by men who had committed mistakes more serious than his, but were not punished—for God knows what reasons. These men suffered not only as prisoners, but as slaves of their conscience, a hundred times more, a thousand times more than the rest of us. They felt they were still loyal Communists, and yet this loyalty was not recognized. They were constantly hitting their heads against the wall of an organization which rejected them every minute of the day, simply because they lived with it and next to it.

Dr. Branko Bujić was a case in point. He had been arrested in

Sarajevo, along with Ognjen Prica, and expelled from the party because of his unsatisfactory behavior with the police. Prica respected him and treated him kindly, even though he considered the punishment justified. Bujić's problem was all the greater in that he was intelligent and understood his position, and he never suggested there was any greater importance in his views than they actually merited. He had spent several years at the prison in Zenica. This had been easier for him, because at Zenica there was no compact party organization of the kind we had at Lepoglava.

Bujić was an uncommonly hard-working man. Unlike most of our outstanding intellectuals, he concentrated on economics. Of all of us, he knew *Das Kapital* the best. He was a good lecturer, able to analyze the most complex problems and explain them concisely and clearly. But he was not a good speaker. This reserved, withdrawn man, with a young-looking face, small dark eyes, and thin eyebrows, looked like a Catholic monk in the depths of some monastery, dedicated to a special task by which to expurgate his sins. But unlike the monks, and the majority of us Communists, Bujić's views on the world's economic developments were not dogmatic. Generally speaking, the economist whose views were accepted as final pronouncements among us in prison was Varga. Of course, Bujić accepted Varga, but he didn't ignore the non-Soviet economists. He was the first to "discover" Sternberg, and he never dismissed "bourgeois" economists. His girl friend waited for him ten years, and they got married upon his release from prison. Before the war I used to run into them quite often in Belgrade. He had a job with a publishing house called People's Welfare, whose owner, Bajkić, an economist and a bourgeois, had a knack of discovering able people, regardless of their ideological leanings. I tried to involve Bujić in some semilegal party activity, but he refused. He never said anything against the party; he simply maintained that as a nonmember he should be engaged in legal activity. When the war started, he was in Sarajevo. He was killed by the Ustashi, who could not distinguish between party and nonparty members.

I wrote little in prison: one poor short story, *"Pleme"* ("The Clan"), and a poem commemorating the anniversary of the Paris Commune. I kept a notebook with observations and comments (later taken from me by the Cetinje police) on sexual "incidents" among the prisoners. One couldn't help but notice an occasional exchange of passionate looks, or one man watching the beautiful parts of another's body. It never occurred to Prica that he might become a homosexual, but he never concealed this aspect of our existence, and Daviĉo was constantly discovering certain "tendencies." Similar sensations were experienced even by those with less delicacy and education. Almost without exception, everyone practiced onanism, and, as someone once wittily remarked, we could be divided into those who admitted it and those who didn't. Some were quite out of control. In spite of the many conscious and subconscious expressions of such tendencies, there was only one obvious homosexual relationship. But all of this, of course, was almost immediately suppressed and forgotten by the individuals involved. One friendship, or, to put it more precisely, one love affair, in spite of its innocence, created constant food for thought.

In prison, friendships were broken far more easily than they were made. There was a great deal of affection and solidarity, and a determination to do everything for one's comrades. But the really great personal friendships were few. There was one, however, which after a momentary crisis cleared up with a new and more beautiful glow. That was the friendship between Radivoje Davidović-Kepa and Mita Aleksić. They were both from Vojvodina and they had known each other before they were arrested. But their love did not blossom until they were behind the prison walls.

We had all sensed something unnatural and "abnormal" in this friendship, and the "psychoanalysts," such as Djordje Jovanović, claimed the relationship was erotic in essence. Far be it from these two to have been homosexuals. But they had a relationship which no two lovers in freedom would have been able to embue with so much tender detail and genuine feeling: they helped each other make beds, they lent each other clothing and socks, they saved tasty morsels of food for one another, they used the same bar of soap.

Aleksić was tense and distraught. He read, but retained nothing, just whiled away the time. He was quick-tempered and nervous, but with moments of great tenderness and eternal sorrow in his deep green eyes. He was always considerate and sweet to Kepa, although quite straightforward when he found it necessary to reproach him for something. He had a long face and light skin, thick wide sensual lips, short hairy arms and body. He didn't care much for anybody, except himself occasionally and, of course, his friend. He never told stories with erotic overtones, and all hell would break loose when someone made an allusion to his relationship with Davidović.

He was the best chess player in prison. His ability to play chess so brilliantly was all the more strange in that he was unable to concentrate on anything else. But he had an instinctive knowledge of all future moves, and he felt, rather than understood, the game. However, he was able to explain his every move, as if his mind came back to him during those chess games, and he would radiate a noble inner glow. He never got angry when he lost, but he was overwhelmed with a secret sweet joy when he managed to "squash" some pretentious opponent. He played with his friend only rarely, as if in jest, as men do when teaching children. Although proud and vain, Davidović didn't object to being treated this way.

When Davidović was imprisoned for his four-year term, he wasn't yet nineteen. By his own shy admission he hadn't known a woman, nor had he yet loved a girl. Nearsighted, slender, and pale, he hardly had any beard or mustache and he still spoke in a voice that suggested change. I don't mean to imply that this young man was still in puberty, but only that the process of maturation had been somehow thwarted. His prison term was extended from four to fourteen years: two years for writing slogans on prison dishes, four years for the possession of propaganda literature, and another four years for singing at Mitrovica. He seemed to feel that he was doomed to a long and hopeless term in prison which he should endure by using as little as possible of his own energies. Not that he was lazy or greedy. On the contrary, he was hard-working, neat, and clean to the point of obsession. But he seemed to have forgotten his youth, intentionally and consciously avoiding passionate dreams, or anything that would remind him of women and love.

In this respect his friend Aleksić was the exact opposite. He loved to read histories of morals, amply "illustrated," and books dealing with the philosophy and psychology of sex. Davidović shied away from any such literature. I've never met anyone in whom the absence of life experience was felt as much as in him. With his dry dogmatism and literal adherence to the written word, be it Marx or Lenin, he often sounded funny. Of course, he was responding to an environment that was basically dogmatic.

Their relationship, innocent, strange, and transparent, lasted for many years. They had beds next to one another, and if by chance they happened to be put in separate rooms, they pleaded with the guards to put them back together again. They owned everything jointly, including their lives. Like lovers, but without physical love. It was hard to tell in this relationship which one of them was older, or superior, which is true of all great loves. In organization, cleaning, and so on, it was mostly Davidović. In making decisions on "important" matters—their attitude toward the outside world, or protecting and defending their reputation—it was mostly Aleksić. Yet it was always a harmonious union.

But life eventually separated them. According to some law, a person who commits a crime in a prison must serve his term in that same prison. So when Davidović was transferred to Lepoglava, Aleksić had to remain at Mitrovica. Aleksić joined the great escape of the Mitrovica prisoners in 1941, and I ran into him at Užice in December—the same old Aleksić, lost, sad, and incapable of doing a really serious job. He was soon killed. Davidović continued to serve his term at Lepoglava. On July 13, 1943, a Partisan unit, in a surprise attack, captured the prison and burned it down, freeing a lot of people, including Davidović. I saw him in Croatia. He was happy, although he had a hard time adjusting to life. He asked me about his friend. I told him the truth.

Autumn came rather suddenly, and found the unity of the party organization growing. The nationalists joined us in the collective, drafted an educational plan, and asked us to be lecturers. The situation looked good, and we felt that a kind of stability had been attained.

But one cold cloudy morning, the guards were wearing black bands on their sleeves, and black flags were fluttering in the wind at the church and over the office buildings. We began speculating: the Minister of Justice? The Archbishop? No one dared hope it was the King. My room was the first to learn the news. The chimney sweeps told us: King Alexander had been assassinated at Marseilles.

We had to take a position. Following Lenin, we condemned "individual terrorism." Consequently we had to condemn the King's assassination. I must admit, though, that in spite of Lenin there wasn't a man in prison who wasn't happy to hear the news. We felt personally avenged for the tortures we had suffered. In analyzing the political consequences of the event we came to the most varied conclusions. The Prison Committee gave its own analysis, condemning the assassination in spite of its possible disintegrating effect on the top echelons of the ruling class. The nationalists, on the other hand, had no mixed feelings. Rukavina kept twisting his mustache and smiling. He behaved as if he had been given wings. He was sprightly, the stiffness that followed his police injuries was gone, his stride was long and decisive.

Soon the prison administration took strong measures against the nationalists. They separated them from us, abolished all their privileges, and the most militant among them, like Šime Balen, were put in solitary. Balen spent that whole winter alone in an unheated cell.

His ears froze, but he stood up courageously. He considered himself a Communist, and we certainly treated him as such. Even so, he never questioned why, as a Communist, he had to suffer because someone fired bullets at the King in Marseilles.

It's hard to tell why the authorities took such extreme measures against the nationalists. Of course, for the director, the jail keeper, and the instructor, all Serbs living in the heart of Croatia, it had been a simple matter of revenging the King. But more likely they were following Belgrade instruction. At any rate their attitude to us Communists seemed to soften.

This was the point of the sharpest and the most serious conflict within the party organization. The leftists claimed that the attack on the nationalists required immediate and extreme action—a hunger strike. The other side was against action. The conflict ended in a rotten compromise: we were to register our "protest" with the prison authorities. The leaders were given instructions not to "provoke." The arguments were sharp; accusations included "objective treason" and "objective provocation."

We helped the nationalists by sneaking food into their cells. But some of us felt that this was the wrong thing to do. I recall now that we felt rather guilty enjoying privileges which our comrades-in-arms didn't have.

The elections of May 5, 1935, marked a turning point in our prison life, and the beginning of the end of the January 6th Dictatorship. The party organization decided to draw up new demands, particularly regarding the nationalists. Our list of demands was fairly long, but the authorities agreed to almost all of them. The leftists were suddenly gaining ground. We were again put together with the nationalists and placed in the old monastery building. The rooms were kept unlocked; we were able to circulate freely and spend eight hours outdoors. Dead walks were abolished, restrictions on receiving food were removed, the number of letters was increased. We were still not allowed newspapers and tobacco, but in the old building that was no problem.

An unbelievable change! We were separated from the outside world only by the walls and faded uniforms. No one paid much attention to the guards any longer. It was the beginning of the summer, and we all basked in the warm sunshine, in the baroque yard full of plaster saints. But our love affair with the administration was short-lived. This time, I dare say, it was largely our own fault.

30

A new person appeared in the collective, who won warmth and kindness from us all. It was "Uncle" Čaki, who, along with Stejić, had taken part in the attempted assassination of King Alexander in 1920. The prison administration granted our request that he be released from solitary confinement and moved in with us.

His life, wasted among the four walls, and his story, forgotten in the wake of larger events, have always been for me the most awesome and magnificent picture of my country and of human fate in it.

Like Stejić, Uncle Čaki had spent his first years in solitary confinement, in chains. But Stejić was young, and Lajoš Čaki, a Hungarian from Vojvodina, was an old man, worn from years in American coal mines and a lifetime as a dayworker on the estates of Vojvodina. He had been moved from prison to prison, and was kept mostly in solitary confinement, with the Bible as the only literature allowed him. By now he was mentally disturbed and he asked for no other book.

It was hard to tell how he was built, or what his coloring and movements had been, because he was almost transparent. His bones showed under the thin creases of his skin. He had passed seventy, and his thin hair and mustache intensified still more his extraordinary frail whiteness. He had suffered a stroke, so he could only walk a short distance with a cane.

In fact, he looked like an apparition, but when he spoke, one could tell that he still breathed and thought in terms of a life and a world which had once been real. He was a strange mixture of religion and revolutionary struggle. He urged us to believe in God and he preached the justice and equality of his Bible: Love all men, even those who hate you; conquer everything and everybody with love, or, still better, win over with goodness. But when he spoke of his former life, he would forget about God and his Biblical truth, and he'd sound like a revolutionary in old-fashioned language and thinking, but hard and adamant toward the enemy of his class. His old hatred had almost disappeared because he no longer saw that enemy as a firm reality. All that was left was the memory of the enemies he had had to fight. The present was peace and forgiveness; the past, rebellion and struggle. Between these two extremes there was no bridge, no reconciliation, as if he were split in half, with two men speaking with one voice, but in two different languages.

We were determined to establish a "definitive" explanation for Čaki's nervous breakdown. The leftists defined it as a form of Christian Communism, and the rightists as an expression of religious insanity. Čaki himself saw nothing tragic in his fate, and although his thinking and speech were often unclear, he considered himself perfectly normal. Indeed, he was living the blessed life of a child, complaining only of physical discomforts.

Every morning, in good weather, several of us would place this heap of skin and bones on a blanket and carry him into the yard. But he couldn't sit in the sun. Indeed, the sun seemed to be melting him with its glow and heat. For him, the sun was no longer a source of life and joy. So we put him in the shade, where a group of mostly young comrades would gather around him, and he would reminisce about one thing and another, as if piecing together an enormous picture: the formation of socialist organizations in the United States, agricultural workers in Hungary, the Second International. Although unfamiliar with Lenin's teaching, he saw in him a magic prophet who fought for the poorest of the poor, from villages, mines, and factories. More than in any other person I knew, Čaki was a reflection of the objective crosscurrents in the working class and among the poor peasants who followed Lenin. Lenin, whose single-minded energy and force embraced this spontaneous movement of the masses, gave it ideological content.

He talked of the assassination reluctantly. But he mourned Stejić as if he were his own son. He knew of Stejić's insanity, never suspecting his own. He appeared to have found "forgiveness" and "redemption" for himself, and he never appealed to the authorities for anything, because he considered it undignified. A revolutionary and a Christian lived in him side by side. Why was this? Perhaps he had retreated into his childhood, thus becoming a Christian again, and into his youth, thus remaining a revolutionary.

The Idealist

Čaki was pleased to be among his own people at last, although he recognized very few of us. Pijade stood in front of him, and Čaki gave him a blank look. Then he slipped Pijade's glasses back on his nose, and recognized him. "Moša, Moša," he cried, embracing him. However, Čaki's good fortune didn't last long. He was not to die surrounded by his family of comrades. We were transferred back to Mitrovica; he remained at Lepoglava. He drowned in a bathtub. Whether this was due to the negligence of the prison nurses or to another stroke, we never knew. Nor did it matter. He had stopped existing long before he actually died.

As if intoxicated by its achievements, the party organization was coming under the influence of Petko Miletić and other leftists. Boris Vojnilović, a relatively young man with little experience, had become one of his most important and loyal supporters, a kind of spokesman for Miletić, and the two of them were involved in constant scheming. The left wing was on the offensive, and it was obvious that the next leadership would be leftist. Petko avoided taking the title, probably preferring to work behind the scenes.

This spiritual blindness, which continued to puzzle me, was a symptom of the Stalinist, totalitarian passion that endowed leaders with values they didn't possess: theirs was the last word in everything, including the social sciences. But that was merely the beginning. Intelligent, knowledgeable men everywhere were in retreat before the leadership principle.

In fact, the right wing was in full retreat. Its prognostications, its caution, proved irrelevant in the new postelection mood. Besides, a public campaign was being launched, for the first time, on behalf of the prisoners. The new premier, Stojadinović, was himself making "democratic" statements. Aware that it had lost a great deal of power, the prison administration imposed certain minimal limitations. If we had chosen to negotiate we might possibly have reached an agreement. However, we couldn't wait for an excuse to rush into action, and that was that.

We hadn't prepared ourselves for this struggle at all. Petko Miletić's group couldn't win a majority for a hunger strike, so they decided on a spontaneous demonstration. Again we were banging and shouting. We understood that this was an inefficient way of fighting and that the confrontation had to be widened. We submitted our demands for radios, newspapers, visiting, unlimited and special medical care. But the authorities, obviously determined to settle accounts their way, would not listen. We would not give up easily either, particularly since the internal struggle among us was beginning to dominate our lives.

The nonpolitical prisoners were also forming a movement. Their position had always been hard, and we urged them to action and gave them leadership. The most prominent among them was one of the two Marković brothers, notorious burglars from a respectable Belgrade family. Our contact with the nonpolitical prisoners was complex, but even so we maintained it successfully through an elaborate signal system, in which I myself participated. They were a colorful group. Pickpockets were weak, and they "squealed" on people; the peasants were longing for a conditional release; and the burglars were ready for anything. The majority favored action, and their leaders were not fussy in the methods they employed to activate support—threats and beatings, a rug over the head, and then hit as hard as you can.

The authorities may have been indifferent to us, but they couldn't afford to be indifferent to the criminals. Their strike paralyzed the prison itself. At the height of the summer season, in the fields several hundred men refused to go to work. There was no one to attend to the pigs and cows. The workshop and auxiliary buildings were idle. They thought of setting them on fire, but we prevented it. We also saw to it that the power plant, the hospital, and, of course, the kitchen continued to function. This factory of human suffering couldn't operate without the assistance of its victims.

The prison administration was now in an exceptionally difficult spot. Its own machinery was unstable, and quick to yield if the alternative was bloodshed. The guards were mostly local people, loyal to Radić, and now to Maček, and as dissatisfied as the rest of the Croats. Their sympathies were with us, although they warned us not to go to extremes. Several offered to do us favors. Our traditional attitude to the guards was stiff, but now we called them our brothers and workingmen. We demanded freedom for Croatia. We activated the nationalists, who, in turn, promoted solidarity with us. Eventually, we had more authority in the prison than the administration. A message came from a group of Zagreb lawyers sympathetic to us: Don't go too far, hold fast where you are. But to most of us these were the warnings of "petit bourgeois intellectuals and opportunists." Besides, Lenin hated and scorned lawyers.

Hastily, we formulated a series of demands for the criminal prisoners: limited working hours, better food, the abolition of dead walks, and more. But the authorities didn't budge. The guards stood their ground. They were not tough; they just made sure no one escaped. The prison administration refused to receive our delegation, a good pretext for more demonstrations. The nonpolitical prisoners joined as if they were under orders.

Some two or three hundred peasants showed up in front of the prison. We shouted greetings to them and they waved back to us. Stirred up by the elections, they were demanding action on the political prisoners. Croatia was in opposition. The prison authorities, mostly Serbs, felt engulfed.

But how far could we go and how would it all end?

In spite of our power, we understood the senselessness of the situation. How could we possibly be both prisoners and supervisors of prisoners? The majority was mesmerized, but a few were uncomfortable. No one had the courage to admit it, not even the rightists, excepting perhaps Hebrang. Even so, he participated in the demonstration of power. The nationalists, who had just been released from a very strict discipline, stuck by us. In fact, they decided to form joint study groups with us. They were no longer in separate rooms, but scattered among us. Juco Rukavina, a future Ustashi colonel, addressed the gatherings with: "Comrades, Comrade Lenin teaches us . . ." And none of his people ever reproached him for this. Šime Balen, whom we rightly considered a Communist, emerged as the leader. Unity was greater than ever.

The evening before the confrontation, we held a general meeting to determine what course to take in case the authorities attempted to put us in solitary cells. We decided to lie down and force them to carry us away.

We sensed that the enemy was preparing an attack; tension was building up. Someone had to yield if a collision was to be avoided. And neither side appeared to be giving way.

Several days passed.

And then one morning, before dawn, we heard the clatter of boots, screams, shouting, cursing down the length of the corridor. Normally, the rooms were never locked, only the doors at the end of the corridor. We all rushed to the doors, but they were locked.

There were six rooms along that corridor, and each room had ten to thirty beds. The first one was the smallest, and the best; our older comrades, including Pijade and Čaki, stayed there. The third room was a corner room, and the largest, containing most of the Communist and nationalist "big shots," but the room arrangement no longer had the same significance as before, simply because we were allowed to mix. But in terms of organization the arrangement of rooms was still important. We tried knocking on walls. But apparently our neighbors knew nothing either, and they were next to the leadership room. We rushed to the window. The guard in front of the factory stood calm, at the usual spot, as the corridor echoed with screams.

What was going on? How long was it going to last? The guards were emptying the rooms in some brutal way. But how? Our comrades were obviously putting up resistance. The guards were cursing them, tussling with them. The voices were muffled. We had never heard such howls from our comrades. Perhaps it wasn't they, perhaps it was the guards yelling like animals. Perhaps we were just imagining things. No, no, that was a scream generated by pain, and the yelling of guards was very different.

We heard the next room being attacked. The screams were closer and more distinct.

We decided to implement our earlier decisions: we lay down on our beds and waited in the gentle summer morning.

Suddenly the door was flung open.

Like a fan, the handle of which was held by the commanding officer, a dozen gendarmes spread into the room, bayonets pointed at each one separately. The officer screamed orders "in the name of the law." We were still lying on our beds. Moma Djordjević jumped up, pointed his finger at the officer, and yelled: "I object!"

All of this, as well as the action that followed, went very fast.

Moma was small and thin; he couldn't have weighed more than a hundred pounds; he suffered from all kinds of ailments. His deep blue eyes looked sad in his yellow face. He had been expelled from the party because of his unsatisfactory behavior before the police, but he bore his misfortune heroically, and was always in the front ranks during a battle. He may have thought this would gain him membership in the party again, but what he wanted more than that was to live and die as a Communist. He had a fine intelligence. By profession a teacher, he was an excellent lecturer. But these qualities were gradually decaying, burning up in his frail body, and just before the end of his long term he succumbed.

Now, a gendarme picked Djordje up with the butt of his rifle and passed him on to another like a rag. He was a toy for those well-fed, wild fellows from Lika and Kosovo. In a split second they turned on the rest of us, brandishing knives, howling, swearing, grinding their teeth. Everything quivered in a deadly vertigo.

Pounding us mercilessly, they ordered us to stand up back to back, with our arms outstretched. My neighbor Boris Božić, a young fellow from the Slovenian littoral, and I found ourselves back to back. A gendarme stood on my bed. He was angry because he was unable to align our arms (I was the taller of the two), and he hit me on the neck with his fist. I shook my head. That angered him, and he struck me in the abdomen with his boot. He chained our hands together, and with a hard kick on the legs turned us toward the door. Tied in pairs, we were being pushed out into the corridor, where another shower of blows from rifle butts awaited us.

I knew that rifle-butt blows were not painful or dangerous except in particularly sensitive spots such as the head and the spine. Intuitively and consciously I tightened my muscles and lowered my head.

We had to go down a flight of worn stone steps into a long corridor which led to the arched doors that opened to the outside yard. This complicated route may have been three hundred yards long, if not more.

Božić was tied to my right arm. He was younger and weaker, and had less experience. Blood was trickling from behind Božić's left arm, sprinkling my shirt. I couldn't determine how deep his wound was. He touched it and was howling in pain. There were more gendarmes on the right side, five or six of them in a semicircle. We plunged through still another shower of blows. I got through this massacre fairly well, but Božić got a terrific blow between the shoulder blades. He stumbled and I lifted him up with the chain. We rushed along the corridor and down the stairs. The gendarmes were panting behind us, and a couple waited on each landing to give more blows.

The gendarmes knew little about the fine points of politics. Banging us on the head, they screamed: "You're for Maček, are you?" In the election campaign Dr. Maček had been the major opposition symbol. It felt humiliating to be beaten on account of a bourgeois politician, and I said: "I'm not for Maček, I'm Communist!" "That's worse!" they roared. Then, Božić fell down from a new and painful blow. He was screaming. And then a strange thing happened: three gendarmes turned on us, but aimed most of their blows at Božić—so infuriated were they by his yelling.

Božić fell to the ground once again, and two gendarmes leaped on us from the back. Covered with blood, Božić was screaming that he had a broken bone. I dragged him along the corridor for some two or three yards. I saw another blow approaching; instinctively I ducked, the butt brushed my shirt, and missed my spine. The worst of the guards were at the yard door. They beat us again, and then thrust us into the heap of prisoners already in the yard. They picked out individual prisoners, including Božić and myself. Božić again got it worse than I did.

We had had two permanent guards assigned us, both of them Serbs, and very different: Žunić and Picajzla. Žunić was heavy, good-natured, a conscientious man who loved people and bore us no hostility. He felt sorry for us, even when it was simply a question of minor discomforts, a cold or bad food. Although he favored law and order, he didn't like to see people punished. In contrast, Picajzla was impatient, mean, and full of hatred, particularly for us intellectuals, because we showed lack of respect for him.

All flushed, with his cap pushed back on his head, Picajzla now stood at the door, pointing out the "worst" among us.

The yard was a sorry sight. Some prisoners were sitting on the ground, some stood clustered together, half-naked, bloody, their faces swollen. Moša Pijade was sitting on the ground, huffing and puffing; Ivić stood up, straight and proud, as if under a banner. Hebrang was calm, but angry—his lips tight, his jaw protruding. Suddenly I found myself face to face with Davičo. Tears were streaming down from his bloody eyes—tears of bitterness and sorrow for his comrades. He whispered in my ear: Petar Živković must have assumed control again. But I doubted that. No, it didn't have to be that necessarily. It was frail, sensitive Davičo being unrealistic in his evaluations.

Finally the last couple of prisoners from our room were brought into the yard. Three gendarmes walked toward Ivić.

It was always harder for me to watch someone being beaten than to be beaten myself. I always felt that it was harder for that person to take the beating than it would be for me.

The three gendarmes turned on Ivić with the butts of their rifles until he fell to the ground. Then, as if on orders, they removed the bayonets and started beating him with the barrels, on his chest and back. He didn't howl, but simply released a loud groan now and then, his powerful chest rising. At last he fainted. The gendarmes then turned on Rukavina. They gave him the same treatment, except that Rukavina hopped and groaned after every blow. He didn't faint, although he was weaker and got a beating that was harder. When they were through, one of the gendarmes wound Rukavina's mustache round his finger, first one side and then the other, and pulled it out.

Žunić brought a bucket of water and poured half of it on Ivić's chest, the other half on Rukavina's. Ivić managed to sit up, supporting himself on his arms, and Rukavina got up to his feet, leaning on a comrade's shoulder.

We wondered which one of us was going to be next. Personally, I was ready for almost anything. We thought it was Petko's turn next. With his cap pulled down to his eyes, he squeezed himself inside a little group of people. But the sergeant, a large man with a dark mustache, gave a sign to the gendarmes to stop. The roll call began. Two people were absent! Čaki and Boljević.

Čaki had been beaten. Every time he tried to get back on his feet, a fresh blow leveled him with the ground. The gendarmes learned too late that he was paralyzed. They left him in the corridor, sprawled on the floor.

The prisoners in Boljević's room had piled beds and benches against the door in an attempt to bar the gendarmes' entry. Then a corporal by the name of Božić fired two bullets: one hit Boljević in the shoulder, going through his back and out at the other side. Boljević collapsed instantly, opening the way into the room for the gendarmes.

Originally from Montenegro, Boljević had been a worker in Belgrade. He had been tried with Ranković, but sentenced to a short term. Highly tense, he engaged in constant plotting and was a good fighter. Sharp and quick to anger, his small green eyes burned with hatred for Pijade because Pijade made fun of him. A close collaborator of Petko Miletić, he was eventually expelled from the party. It was rumored that in 1941 he joined the Chetniks, but that turned out not to have been true. In any case, he eventually joined the Partisans. Now he holds a civil service job in Belgrade, lives a quiet life, and has gained a lot of weight. Moreover, he has the courage to greet me in the street, which may mean that he is dissatisfied with the regime, probably because it's not "truly Communist."

Professor Milan Mijalković was the first and only person to come to Boljević's rescue. He was the kindest man among us, and one of the finest people I have ever met. A mathematician by profession, he had a fine feeling for people and personal relationships. He thought of the revolution as, above all, a human act, the beginning of eternal happiness and equality among men. His motives for accepting Communism were profoundly idealistic. In this there was something of Svetozar Marković's late-nineteenth-century populism. Mijalković was outside all factionalism. He was the only man truly liked by everyone in the collective. He was our quartermaster. In that capacity he introduced the principle of apportionment of food in accordance with state of health. His concern was inborn, as if he were created to look after people. When he was released from prison, Mijalković returned to his native Jagodina, and came to Belgrade in 1940. He was a close friend of Spasenija Babović, member of the Regional Committee for Serbia. However, he had "sinned" with a woman in Jagodina, an aggressive widow, and received harsh party punishment. Spasenija Babović didn't abandon him, but at the beginning of the war he had no party functions.

For this man, helping Boljević was not a question of duty. It was his nature, an irresistible urge, like the struggle for survival, or the fear of death. Only the blows of a rifle finally separated him from his wounded comrade. Covered with blood, there he was among us in the yard.

Following roll call they separated the Communists from the Croat nationalists, the two groups going in different directions. A small, wrinkled gendarme tied my hands to Davičo's. He asked us if he'd made it too tight. I replied bitterly: "Who cares. Make it as tight as you like!" Davičo whispered: "Let it be! Don't say anything!" The gendarme shouted an obscenity at me, ran his fingers over the chain, took out his key, and loosened it by one link.

The sun was up when our battered column left for the station through the yellow fields. This time we were being loaded into third-class carriages, probably because nothing else was available. The train passed through green hills, fields, and woodlands. The scenery was new and beautiful and bright, but in our bitterness the world looked joyless.

It wasn't until we were on the train that beads of sweat appeared on Ivić's face.

Keršovani pulled his glasses out of his pocket; he had guarded them carefully, risking anything to preserve them. This man who went to sleep and woke up with a book couldn't see a thing without his glasses. A moment later a gendarme grabbed the glasses from his nose and tossed them out of the window. Keršovani's eyes were stunned, lost. He didn't even go though the usual motion of rubbing his eyes when his glasses were removed.

The gendarmes continued to provoke us. One of them said: "So you Communists are for an independent Croatia?" Djordje Jovanović quipped: "Well, it all depends." I considered this a departure from the party line. On the other hand, I didn't like the silence either. I said: "Yes, we are." "And an independent Bosnia? Serbia? Montenegro? Slovenia?" And I kept answering yes to the whole list. Then he mentioned Macedonia. I said yes. He said he would make me pay for Macedonia that night. When the gendarme had gone, Ivan Milutinović said, not without irony: "Djetić"—they called me Djetić in prison—"intends to win the gendarme over to Communism."

But the major provocation didn't take place until early in the afternoon, when our carriages were taken to a deserted yard outside of Zagreb, to wait for the evening train.

In broad daylight, Corporal Božić beat up Djordje Jovanović, Mesud Mujkić, and Boris Vojnilović. Djordje Jovanović got it because he had told a gendarme that we would bring them to court for such treatment, which was reported to Božić. Božić ordered Jovanović to take back his threat. Jovanović refused. A shower of blows came upon him. In the end, Jovanović yielded. This was sensible, if not courageous.

On the other hand, Mujkić was beaten by mistake. Božić was looking for the man who had helped the wounded comrade, *i.e.*, Mijalković, and he got the two of them mixed up. Mujkić desperately tried to explain he wasn't the one. Božić grabbed him by the neck, bent him over, and beat him on the back. Mijalković wasn't in our carriage, or he would undoubtedly have intervened.

Vojnilović's offense was similar to Jovanović's. But Božić was an imaginative gendarme, and he beat everyone in a different way. He put Vojnilović's head between his legs, grabbed his neck, and pounded him on the back and in the groin. It was painful to watch. Many comrades, particularly among the rightists, were impatient to see how well one of the most extreme leftists would pass the test. And indeed Vojnilović passed it with flying colors: he didn't scream, nor did he take back his words. The hysterical gendarme finally gave up, cursing him.

In the other carriage there were similar incidents.

Anxiously we waited for nightfall—which would take us south. We expected to be tortured during the night, for it was clear that the gendarmes were preparing some activity. They were whispering and pointing at various prisoners.

I was in the group with Ivan Milutinović, a thin, bony Montenegrin, who had been a follower of Sima Marković—the right wing at the university. In prison the rightists erroneously considered him their man. He was simply a sensible, disciplined, steady person, average in everything except in his character, which was outstanding. There was something of the old-style Montenegrin in him: he kept his word, and he spoke openly and without suspicion. This gave him a good deal of prestige among the prisoners.

We consulted as to what course to take if they should start beating us up again during the night. At Milutinović's suggestion, we decided to try to reason with the gendarmes when they attacked, and help the person under attack.

But they didn't attack. I didn't sleep, which was usual for me in tense situations. Nor did Milutinović. But some of our comrades snored, waking up briefly at stations. At dawn they escorted us from the station to the Mitrovica Prison. Back again to Mitrovica, from which we had been taken, as punishment, to Lepoglava. The mist rose from the dark fields. The men were comforted by the rain, which eased their wounds, as we quickly approached the prison walls like ghosts.

The nationalists had been shipped to Maribor, and then they followed us to Mitrovica. The nonpolitical prisoners were dealt with immediately following our departure. The guards "worked on them" for two days, even more brutally than on us. There were two dead. Our belongings were sent on after us, in great disorder, but everything was there, to the last item.

31

One might assume that the gendarmes' attack dampened our fighting spirit and brought to the fore leaders who had promoted moderation. On the contrary, upon re-entering Mitrovica our desire to win was greater than ever. Of course it was hard to defend the Lepoglava excesses, and the left wing felt it best not to revive the issue. But conditions at Mitrovica were so bad that even Pijade and Hebrang found them unacceptable. The desire to struggle already existed among our people at Mitrovica, but the leadership, headed by Marijan Stilinović, felt that the time was not right. Our arrival stirred up all the latent forces that favored immediate action.

The first step was the merger of the party organizations and the election of a new committee. The leftist groups, encouraged by our arrival, turned on Stilinović, citing the better conditions at Lepoglava as a result of our positive action. Stilinović had been with the movement a long time, and this was his second prison term. He was an extraordinarily pleasant young man. There was something painfully warm in the fine lines of his face and in his dark eyes. He was later expelled from the party because of his unsatisfactory stand before the police. He was a good friend of Pijade, and remained so even after Pijade was isolated by the Miletić group. With our arrival the world around him collapsed, even though he was only partly to blame. For following the King's assassination, Dragoljub Jevtić headed a new government, notorious for its cruelty and its determination to maintain the political system of the January 6th Dictatorship.

At Mitrovica we found many new comrades. Most of them were good fighters, although inexperienced in intraparty conflicts. They all joined Petko Miletić and the left wing.

Krsto Popivoda was among them. This was his first time in prison. He came from Subotica, where he was studying law. Young, strong, tall, he struck everyone with his healthy and simple freshness. Showing a row of white teeth, he said: "If I had known I wasn't supposed to tell the police anything, I wouldn't have." Indeed, his statement was so simple and firm that we believed it. Following his arrest in 1937, his physical and psychological constitution changed, a result of the exceptionally severe tortures he endured.

Moma Marković was also there. He had stood up very well before the police. Even though a student, his knowledge of theory was no greater than that of his fellow-workers. But he worked exceptionally hard, as if to make up for it. He was direct, although not without cynicism. We quickly became close; I appreciated his simplicity, which I myself have always lacked. Both Krsto and Moma were typical examples of the new generation, which thought in simpler terms and was more inclined to action.

Jovan Marinović was now with us. Following my arrest he had been very active. His behavior before the police was not bad, although not all that good either. Boris Ziherl was there too, immersed in books, not belonging to any faction. Rumor had it that he said he hadn't participated in a strike because, as a theoretician, the party wanted him protected. He was not particularly outstanding except in his knowledge of Marxist literature and in his faithful, and monotonous, interpretation of it.

In the intraparty struggles surrounding the election of a new leadership I became aware that Petko Miletić was a factionalist. He knew that I was on good terms with the younger Belgrade comrades, particularly the students. One day he asked me to work on Slobodan Škerović, who had been elected room delegate, and to advise him to vote against the "opportunists." I had just met Škerović. He had been arrested in Belgrade on his arrival from Prague, and he knew a lot of my friends, including Mitra. He spoke about her with an intimacy that could only hurt me, but he also said that she was one of the most active women in the movement, which could only make me proud. I gave Škerović Petko's message, but I felt terribly uncomfortable—as if I were doing something wrong and ugly. Strangely enough, Škerović took my message in stride and firmly promised his support. Later he told me that he too had felt uncomfortable, although he had voted as I had asked him to. Škerović was later expelled from the party for his poor stand before the police. When he was executed in 1941, he still hadn't been readmitted, although he had a positive attitude and was loyal, dutifully carrying out all party assignments.

For a couple of days I was bothered by Petko's factional game, in which I was now involved. When I couldn't take it any longer, I decided to talk to him. It was not an easy decision, because I anticipated a tough reaction, and because an idol of mine—and he was one—was beginning to falter. Also, I felt that unless I told him honestly what was on my mind, our relationship would become intolerable. When I told Petko that I didn't think his pressure tactics were right or acceptable, he smiled vaguely. "You're right, of course. But what can you do, allow the opportunists to win?" This seemingly innocent exchange altered my attitude to Petko. I saw him more soberly and critically, although I continued to respect him as a "hero" and a "fighting man." The battles that were before us suppressed within me the significance I attached to this event. And yet I never forgot this episode or Petko's vague smile. As the conflict with Petko assumed wider proportions, I recalled details from this conversation and it occurred to me that he didn't really like anyone, even his collaborators, in spite of his alleged concern for them. He liked flattery and his legendary image. He always thought in terms of his final goal—full control of the party—to which he sacrificed himself, his comrades, his ideas, fanatically believing that he was destined for a historic role. This rendered him a man without a soul and without sensibility, but a man of infinite energy and will.

No one seriously denied that conditions in prison were intolerable, or that action was necessary. The only question was timing. The situation outside was in our favor: a campaign was being conducted for more humane treatment of prisoners, as well as for an amnesty. Even Maček made vague statements in support of this campaign. The well-known leftist writer Miroslav Krleža had published a pamphlet on the subject. Our families had hired lawyers to bring pressure on the Ministry of Justice. International humanitarian and leftist organizations were activated.

Inside prison, preparations were going well. In spite of old differences, there was unity in action. Everyone agreed that a hunger strike was the only efficient form of protest. We felt confident.

The one remaining problem was winning over the nationalists. Relations with them were now further complicated by a change of heart that occurred upon our return to Mitrovica. The group that came with us from Lepoglava had found people at Mitrovica who were already molded in the new fascist image. They were under instructions not to co-operate with us Communists. In fact, their narrow nationalism had become a fierce chauvinism, colored by the Hitler-Mussolini ideology of the "corporate state." Life in prison moved slowly. But political developments in Europe were moving at a fast pace. Hitler's victories had given a new impetus to the Ustashi faction in Croatian public life. While it hadn't yet assumed mass proportions, it offered prospects of victory. Overnight, so to speak, the nationalists separated themselves from us, and the handful of Radić followers wavered between us and them, afraid to offend the "Frankovci" (after Frank, the founder of the "party of the rights," later the Ustashi) as patriots, and us Communists as socialists. Of course, with the change in the Comintern's policies regarding fascism, we came to believe in the idea of Yugoslav unity, and in its defense, which in itself was sufficient to create a profound gap between us and them.

Stilinović's committee definitely deserves credit for this early realization that the Frankovci had become fascists. At the time, however, his position on this question was used against him: he had "made up the theory" because he was against fighting, and he had no use for a "united front" with the Croatian nationalists. But we quickly learned that Stilinović was correct. Even so, it didn't occur to anyone to withdraw the charges against him.

We began agitating among the nationalists. And it was very rough going, even though they also hated the Belgrade government and they didn't want to see the Communists get all the credit for the prison struggle. The participation of the nationalists was most important: it would ensure us the support of Croatian public opinion, including Dr. Maček, who was at the head of a powerful legal movement. I was asked to have a personal talk with Rukavina, with whom I had had a good relationship. Rukavina was reluctant to meet me, but he couldn't refuse and he couldn't reject co-operation —so he promised me his support. I have no idea how I looked to Juco Rukavina, but, for my part, I could just barely recognize him, and I wondered how we ever could have been close friends. All I could see now were his instability, his boastfulness—a former officer fit to be a tool of reactionary forces.

Prica's "victim" was Dr. Tot. He was not a Frankovac, but, rather, a "Radićevac," from bourgeois and civil-servant ranks, for whom the peasant movement was merely a tool in the fight for Croatian national independence. Tall, flabby Tot was an important administrator. Involved in terrorist action and underground activities, he was tortured by the police and sent to prison. He stood up well before the police, but in prison he was reluctant to act. However, once he promised his support, one could absolutely count on him. He judged people in terms of their civil-service rating, a hang-up from his Austro-Hungarian days. He tolerated Communists, but opposed them ideologically. Upon his release from prison, under the Cvetković-Maček government, he was appointed director of an important bank. Prica ran into him a couple of times and reproached him for his compromise with Maček, but Tot claimed there was little else one could do. Under Pavelić, he was a government minister. He awaited the arrival of Partisans in Zagreb, but his hopes for friendship with his former Communist fellow-prisoners misfired—he was executed.

Our action among the nationalists and the Radićevci meant little more than winning them over, but winning Rukavina and Tot meant a lot.

There were two other great "masters," Stjepan-Stipe Javor, from the older generation, and Cerovski, from the younger. Cerovski was a bank clerk. He was the chief Ustashi and fascist ideologist among the Frankovci. Undaunted by our greater dialectical skills and knowledge, he enjoyed refuting Communist ideas. He felt that he didn't have to give in to logic and facts because "the power of blood" and "race" were decisive. It may have appeared strange that this narrow-minded man could so easily and simply have convinced the Frankovci of the virtues of racism and corporatism, but actually it was part of a natural evolution from Frank to Pavelić, particularly since fascism was flourishing and the Serbian central dictatorship was still in power. Clear and firm in their nationalism, the Frankovci embraced fascist ideas overnight. In a simplified form these ideas appeared to be a continuation of some dark, primordial force. Cerovski was Pavelić's chief of police in Zagreb at the beginning of the war, and I never bothered to find out what happened to him subsequently.

Stipe Javor was a Frankovac of the old school. He was over sixty, and although he had weak lungs and had been tortured by the police, he still looked strong and healthy. Nothing in his appearance suggested that he was once a small merchant. He looked like a peasant from Lika or Dalmatia—hard, rough form in unfinished stone. His political manner was slow and reasonable, suggesting a man of great experience. It was rare for a man in his position to give himself to rebellion. It was impossible to cheat Javor or "get" him through sentimentality. In fact, it was impossible to convince him of anything. He weighed everything in his old-fashioned mind, and that took time. But once he made a decision, he never wavered. He had that traditional hatred for Serbs, particularly those Serbs living in Croatia, and he probably hated all other foreigners as well. Now it was Serbs who stood in the way of a Croatian state; before them it was the Hungarians, and before the Hungarians it was the Germans, and so on back to the twelfth century. The right of Croatia to independent status was the only idea in his head and the only idea he believed in. Javor's record was without a single blemish, and he was the major link, for the nationalists, with the movement's past.

These two men, so different in everything, dominated the nationalist camp. Eventually they decided in our favor—Javor, to help the "Croatian issue," and Cerovski because he was caught off guard and managed to suppress for a moment his ideological hatred of Communism.

There was another strange man among the nationalists. He was Marko Ozanić, one of the most determined fighters against the prison administration. A waiter by profession, and stupid-looking, he was nevertheless a man of great energy and devotion. He belonged to that generation of young Croatian dissidents (later known as Ustashi) who had responded to the dictatorship of King Alexander with bombs and revolvers. In an exchange of gunfire with government agents, Ozanić had missed his man. If he had not missed he would have been hanged, which he didn't think such a great disaster. "One has to die sometime," he would say. Ozanić lived in our collective, sharing both good and evil. The Communists considered him their man. But they were dead wrong. He liked the Communists because they were loyal to one another, helpful, and stable, whereas his nationalists were unstable, dissident, and selfish. Outside of this, however, he showed no interest in Communism. He may even have grown to like Communists over the years, but his hatred for Serbs never abated. Occasionally he would say: "I might consider becoming a Communist if only they would turn against the Serbs." This hatred was so strong that no amount of Communist reasoning, to which he was daily exposed for so many years, could quiet it. He accepted the Serbian Communists only because he assumed that in becoming Communists they had ceased to be Serbs. This assumption made it easy for him to explain his relationship with us to his people. Yet at this time he too kept himself separate from us; the nationalist camp was stronger, and there was no reason for Ozanić to remain outside it. In action we Communists could still count on him, though, and on this occasion we got his help. But, eccentric and stubborn in all things, he represented no one but himself. When Pavelić came to power, he settled for a restaurant at the Zagreb railway station. For a former waiter, this was no mean achievement. But considering his years as a political prisoner, this reward indicated a certain dissatisfaction with the official Ustashi policies. I have no idea how this strangely individualistic person ended up. He disappeared, in flight from the movement with which he was able to share everything except ideas.

It was late autumn when we decided to go on strike. A joint committee was elected, and Communists and nationalists joined forces. Someone proposed that we should take a little sugar during the strike, but this was rejected. The fight had to be clean: the administration might discover the fraud, and thus discredit the whole operation. Also, once the principle of the struggle was breached, the whole concept might fall apart. All food was to be refused and handed over to the guards.

I was elected head of the strike committee in our ground-floor room. This meant that I had to maintain contact with the Central Committee, located on the top floor. Perhaps they selected me because I was young and strong—climbing three flights of stairs three times a day on an empty stomach was no easy task. It was also, of course, an expression of confidence and recognition, which made me feel proud, and I was certain that I would last until the very end.

The administration was aware of our preparations, but remained totally passive. We interpreted this as a good sign, although there were skeptics who claimed that it was not. Throughout the strike no pressure was exerted on us, none of the rules were changed. We remained in joint rooms, circulating freely during the day. Exercise time was announced at the usual hour, the meals were brought in on time. The guards did their duty and stuck to their schedule, and we stuck to ours. This discipline facilitated the strike. We were able to help our weaker comrades by giving them water and emptying the urine, and we were able to threaten strikebreakers when this became necessary.

I had already participated in several short strikes—the longest had lasted for six days, at Ada Ciganlija. It was started by Dimitrije Jovanović, and I had joined more out of solidarity than out of conviction. That was a particularly painful strike because I had no water for three midsummer days. I burned from the inside, my lips were cracked, my tongue sticky, I felt horribly dizzy. Finally, a guard brought in one of the strikers to tell me that water was allowed, and I began to drink.

Like most of my comrades, therefore, I knew exactly what to expect from a hunger strike.

The greatest craving for food occurs on the second or third day, when the body begins to rely on its own resources. Like all other things in nature, the body is very rational: first it uses excess fats, then minor muscles, and finally the bone marrow and the brain. These hunger strikes never last long enough to cause death directly, but there were deaths by indirect cause. For example, Javor died shortly after the strike from a lung ailment exacerbated by his weakness.

A hunger strike is one of the toughest forms of struggle. Once the crisis of the first few days is over, hunger becomes an intellectual awareness rather than an irresistible craving. The stomach has stopped functioning, and the body has begun to draw on its own resources. Since man is the only creature aware of death, he can use this awareness to curb his craving for life. One loses about a pound a day, but this varies from individual to individual. Having survived the first few days, one can easily go on until death itself, provided one has the courage. One feels no physical pain, just growing fatigue, and long ghastly dreams. Unbearable breath continuously circulates from one's mouth to one's stomach, and nothing in the world can stop it. On the third day tobacco changes taste and one can no longer take it. Suddenly getting up on one's feet causes one to faint. Thus we learned to rise slowly, in stages.

Although a hunger strike is largely a painless struggle, in which the will and the mind play a major role, it is nevertheless a most unequal fight. Obviously, if it comes to dying, the weakest will go first. Every man hopes he is not the weakest, but very quickly, after the first five or six days, the weakest are separated from the rest. They feel death to be closer than do the rest. Even more painful, others see it coming on them. For example, Jordan the Macedonian, a frail, consumptive worker, was one of the weakest in the whole collective; by the sixth day he could no longer get up on his feet.

The administration was prompt in offering us food and a chance for exercise, and four of us, myself included, decided, out of sheer spite, to take a forty-five-minute walk every morning. On the tenth day there were only two of us left. I was aware that each movement taxed the body unnecessarily, but we were determined to show the administration that we were well. I recall how hard it became to endure such a long walk—we took special pains not to slow down the usual pace too much. I felt dizzy and waited with longing for the church clock to strike the half-hour and for the sentry to take out his big watch to check the time; that meant just a few more minutes. Often I would read during my walks. I retained practically nothing of what I'd read, but it made the time go faster. The circular concrete path seemed to get smaller as time advanced, and I felt as if I were going in circles, faster and faster, in a state of semiconsciousness. The weather was dull. Even though I was warmly dressed, I was cold. On the eleventh day the Central Committee forbade the two of us to take our walks: our weaker comrades found it irritating. Besides, the authorities might think our men could go on indefinitely.

After five or six days the prison physician began calling on us daily. He went from bed to bed, as in a hospital. On the tenth day, after examining Jordan, he said: "You are very weak, but you can last a few more days; don't worry." This humane man, Dr. Rogulić, made similar remarks in other rooms as well, indicating to us that the authorities were inclined to forgive. This bit of encouragement gave us new strength. There was no wavering in the collective, although some were losing courage. The problem was not merely one of physical weakness. Morally, Jordan was one of the strongest among us. During a hunger strike the sense of smell becomes particularly sharp. On the sixth day someone sniffed around and found traces of lard in excrement in the latrine. The following night the culprit was caught; he was a nationalist. While he was asleep we found half a cup of lard in his drawer. The room committee decided to ignore the whole incident. Indeed, the bitter and nervous men would have spread the rumor fast had not the committee specifically forbidden it. The following day, I told the Communists in the strike committee about the incident, and we agreed to maintain absolute silence on the subject in order to avoid conflict with the nationalists, who had been against the strike to begin with. The nationalists generally stood up well in action. The lard incident was an exception.

Of course, some men talked about food with great gusto, although I don't believe they felt a real craving for it. Particularly among the young, it represented an intellectual awareness of hunger rather than the activity of the glands. The dishes they selected were always very delicate, specialties of their region, or something they had eaten in their childhood. Žarko Zrenjanin, an indomitable fighter, loved to talk about food. Relatively heavy at one time, he was quickly melting away, and it was as if, with his talk of food, he was trying to make up for the loss of weight. The Central Committee put a stop to this kind of talk—a few people found it irritating. Those who enjoyed such talk had to gather in the latrine. That's where a lot of other time-killing conversations took place. In our rooms silence was maintained for those who were lying flat on their backs, consciously approaching death.

The prison administration showed no sign of giving in. On the thirteenth day they asked to see Prica, but he refused unless the whole committee was also asked. An hour or two passed. Some said he should have gone; we'd know what they were up to. But the committee approved Prica's position and there was renewed determination to fight. The whole committee was then asked to appear before the administration. Our demands were met, with the exception of radio and newspapers. The committee then gathered together a larger committee, and we decided to end the strike that afternoon, the thirteenth day.

We received our first food in the evening, with doctor's instructions. It wasn't until two or three days later that we started receiving normal meals. Then we had a new "crisis": an unlimited craving for food. We kept on eating, filling our stomachs until we could barely walk, but it still wasn't enough.

The struggle had not been a particularly hard one. It was a protest full of defiance and heroism, and particularly showed solidarity among prisoners. The abolition of dead walks plus daily time outside, tobacco, special medical attention, unlimited food parcels, new clothing, visits from relatives and friends were the benefits we gained, and they were effective until the war broke out. Our relations with the guards and the administration were substantially altered: we didn't have to show them any special signs of respect, and they didn't humiliate us.

That was our last hunger strike in prison, and the last major confrontation. From that time on, the intraparty squabbles originated from broader causes than our struggle with the prison administration.

32

As circumstances altered, so did our ideological education in prison. The basic assumption was that Marx, Engels, and Lenin were correct in everything they said and that the purpose of our ideological study was to understand them as well as we possibly could. It wasn't until later years, 1934 and particularly 1936, following the Trotskyist trials, that Stalin was considered an absolute and undeniable authority and a major Marxist author. In contrast to his predecessors, Stalin was unusually simple and to the point, which was well suited to the needs and thought processes of the average Communist.

I recall that even people like Davičo and Prica—and I, of course—with broad education and with a subtle sense for stylistic precision, were delighted with the "crystal-clear" simplicity and "beauty" of Stalin's style. Davičo, who had a graphic way of describing things, said that Stalin had transformed Hegel's foggy dialectic into a work of mathematical precision. Prica especially appreciated Stalin's "skill" in combining philosophical principles with everyday party practices. And I liked the simple structural design of his works. Of course, we made other subtle pronouncements: Marx was baroque, Lenin passionate and powerful, Stalin monumental. Working-class Communists understood Stalin more easily than anyone else, and, therefore, liked him. However, both workers and intellectuals found in Stalin something more important than simplicity and beauty of thought and style: they found a philosophical, ideological, and political basis to explain the world and justify their own actions. And for an organization increasingly centralized, and increasingly tied to the Soviet Union, Stalin was the most suitable ideologist. When I arrived in prison there were men from the older generation who saw Stalin mostly as a gifted organizer, but by the time I left everyone thought him a theoretician and practitioner of genius—that is how fast the process of ideological "Stalinization" was taking place. The true idolatry hadn't yet swept us. We thought of him as a great genius, not yet as a divine being. But a solid foundation had been laid for later adoration and belief in his infallibility. Trotsky was considered a man who had "deviated," and possibly even a counterrevolutionary, but no one thought him a traitor or a spy.

There were two constants in our ideological education: the acceptance of the revolutionary Leninist side of Marxism and loyalty to the Soviet Union, which subsequently triumphed in the ideological acceptance of Stalin's theories. We believed that the Soviet Union had discovered the right way. Moreover, the character of Yugoslavia's revolution was determined by the Comintern: the first step was a bourgeois-democratic revolution similar to the February Revolution in Russia—destroying feudal remnants which not even the most skillful dialectician could discover in Yugoslavia. During the war, this scheme of things stood in our way, putting us in the ridiculous position of fighting for a revolution while constantly awaiting the "second phase," *i.e.*, the revolution itself.

Our dogmatic acceptance of Marxism was so great that in the midst of a complex argument someone would suddenly ask whether anyone could recall a quotation from Marx, Engels, or Stalin that might help end the dispute.

Acceptance of Marxist-Leninist theories was proof of one's revolutionary awareness, but it couldn't make a true revolutionary out of a person who wasn't one to begin with.

Other Communist theoreticians, such as Kautsky, Plekhanov, Labriola, and even Rosa Luxemburg, were virtually rejected, although an odd intellectual here and there considered them as partly usable material.

The third characteristic of our ideological activity in prison was a mechanical acceptance of the Central Committee line. This experience was largely transmitted by new functionaries, and it was quickly outdated. In addition to this, we were instructed in useful techniques regarding illegal activity: conspiracy, codes, chemical ink, means of multiplication. Several men were real masters in this craft. A number of Slovenians excelled in technical "innovations." Courses were offered in subjects such as trade unions, women, and youth. Taught in a simplified form, they had been prepared by Kocmur several years earlier, based on what he had learned so well in various courses in Moscow schools. Kocmur had been expelled from the party because of his poor stand before the police. But unlike many who had experienced this fate, he seemed unaffected. He was egotistical and sturdy; he had a good memory, but no depth. Even so, for many years his writing served as staple material for practical political education. Workers and intellectuals found the complex Hegelian-Engels dialectic and Marx's political economy hard to comprehend. The literature was available only in German or in Prica's popularized form. Kocmur's simplified analysis was satisfactory until 1935, when our demands grew more sophisticated. The level of the lectures rose and party assignments were more complex. Ideological activity began to grow and differentiate among individuals. Direct "sources," Marx, Engels, Lenin, and Stalin, had been smuggled from abroad.

Ridiculous situations arose in our ideological education, and mine was a case in point. The "Kocmur program" was simple enough for an intellectual to go over once and comprehend it completely. I went over it six times, and Davičo even more. To refuse participation in study circles was considered "hostile" and an expression of "contempt for the workers," who, of course, needed to be helped. This killing, monotonous study of one and the same topic was time-consuming, even if it weren't for endless internal disagreements. However, it was useful for the uneducated in that it settled in their heads the basic principles of Marxism and gave them guide lines for practical political activity.

Ideological study therefore served a useful purpose: peasants and workers were introduced to books they were able to read on their own. This literature, of course, tended to create a schematic picture of society and man; yet this was essential to Communist revolutionaries. Actually we didn't look at it that way. We accepted it all as a final scientific explanation, and the "Kocmurian" vulgarizations as inevitable and essential popularizations, useful in practical work for the lower intellectual levels. I was not an important theoretician in prison. I showed no particular passion, or talent, for it, even if I quickly understood even the most complex problems. It was shortly before my release that the leadership noticed my interest in the national question and my understanding of it, and they appointed me lecturer on this subject in my room. I showed a certain facility in interpreting Stalin's and Lenin's views on the national question, but I did no research on my own. I even became the leader of the study circle. My true personal interest continued to be fiction, but I hardly managed to do any reading at all. I managed to learn French and Russian, enough in any case to be able to read in both, the former in two months and the latter in three. Later on I improved my Russian by translating Gorky, but I forgot much of the French because of ·disuse. The English language was not considered valuable because so little original Marxist literature was written in it. At first people were studying mostly German, then later Russian.

In any case, what I personally learned didn't come from good or bad study circles, but through my personal initiative. My own feeling is that the ideological re-education in prison did not come primarily from lectures, but, rather, from the collective life of Communists, from the accumulated knowledge of the entire membership, the common belief that Communists were an avant-garde community, called upon by history to reshape the world and to liberate it from misery, wars, and exploitation. Through daily life in a collective which believed in this, adjusting one's own relationship to harmonize with this belief, a young Communist adopted and absorbed into his blood this feeling of the party and of the world Communist movement as something very special, and of Communists as people with a "special make-up." Solidarity, a fighting spirit, dedication to the ideals of the working people and to the efforts to improve their lives, all multiplied and strengthened the obligations with which we arrived in prison. There was something else too: in this crowded space, in a community made up exclusively of Communists, we were building up our—closed Communist—world, in a far more intensive and complete form than the party organizations outside. Communists outside shared their lives with other people; we lived with ourselves. Needless to say, none of us understood clearly what was happening. We were fully convinced that we had a scientific ideology, and that as the avant-garde of the working class we were automatically its essence, the end result, the most progressive and noble people in the world. Our Communist world was to us the real world, the rest was something "backward," "capitalist," "bourgeois," "foreign," something that simply had to be changed and reformed.

We were not taught the Biblical "truth" that a just life in this world prepares a man for the next. We were taught something far greater: to expect a paradise in this world, not too far in the future either, but in two or three generations. That was what revolutionaries, better and older than we, told us, that was what people who had been to the Soviet Union and seen the "truth" in practice told us. And we believed it. Misery and despair were all around us, and the more unbearable life became, the closer we were to the new world. Our truths were daily confirmed by the misery and suffering of millions of people. They were life truths, our very life. That's how we saw them and felt them, living in them and for them. The more passionate the idea, the easier it was to accept it. This in turn intensified our moral and spiritual obligations to the movement. There was no greater and more shameful betrayal than abandoning this Communist world. It meant ending one's existence as a man.

Living in a fighting collective, under the watchful eye of the enemy, under such an intellectual atmosphere we built up not only an external party discipline, but a much more profound internal one as well. Implementing decisions was not sufficient; anyone could do that. One had to transform oneself so that at any time all of one's actions could be measured in terms of the interests of the revolution. This didn't mean giving up one's private life. We were not ascetics, in theory or in practice. Differing personal lives, of course, had to be made consistent with the party life. Gradually, a series of moral precepts was established for us Communists—not a set of rigid rules and regulations, but a sense of what was in keeping with the party interests, as interpreted by those who ruled the party.

None of this assumed final shape in prison. The long and painful process of bolshevization was under way, and I fell right smack in the middle of it. The image of the Bolshevik, a man completely committed to the revolution and the party, hovered continually before our eyes. The image was not of a real Bolshevik, but one from propaganda pamphlets, which we fully accepted because we had to win.

We received most of our information about life in the Soviet Union from comrades who had been there.

I must say, though, that the comrades who had attended the Moscow political schools were not particularly respected in prison. They had been selected often on the basis of the factions they belonged to, or through personal connections and influence. Of course it was nice to be educated in Moscow as a party functionary. In return, however, Moscow required some of its students to return to their country for illegal party work. But the lessons learned in Moscow often contradicted our own experience. Filled with perfect schemes, the newly arrived functionary would then be beating his head against the wall of our imperfect reality. To make matters worse, most of them stood up badly before the police. Moral and spiritual courage and a conscience were not things they could learn in Moscow. This marred their reputation, and we all felt that there was something rotten about the comrades educated in Moscow.

It gradually became clear that a true revolutionary Communist could not be transplanted, that he had to grow from a seed in the national soil. He could absorb theory and general experience from Moscow, but he had to "rework" these theories, and find new realistic forms for them, to be able to resist the blows of our enemy, who was also a specific product of our environment. When it came to generalities, his mind might be "Russian," Bolshevik, but the hands had to be Yugoslav.

Of course, our Moscow-educated comrades learned one lesson well: to stay away from factional conflicts. If one of them belonged to some faction or other, which was usually the case "up there" in Moscow, he had to give it up. The trouble was, however, that the leadership often changed, and as good party members and opponents of factionalism, they had to switch rides often. This created a cautious type who followed the party majority, *i.e.*, the Central Committee. All our Moscow-educated comrades shared this characteristic.

The most prominent among them were Jovan Veselinov, Svetislav-Ceca Stefanović, and Mesud Mejukić. They came back in that order, were promptly arrested, and joined us in prison. The result was that we were able to get a continuous picture of conditions in the Soviet Union. All three were eventually expelled from the party because of their poor stand before the police.

Veselinov was from Vojvodina. He was pleasant and gentle, although not exactly direct, a trait obviously acquired in the Moscow kitchens. He learned easily, simplifying somewhat the Marxist-Hegelian dialectic, sometimes to the point of vulgarization. He sang revolutionary songs beautifully, and was a fairly good speaker, although his fiery outbursts sometimes sounded phony. He was neither creative nor courageous. That was also a characteristic acquired in Moscow—waiting for directives from "above." He could tell stories well, and we would often gather around him in the evening to hear his impressions of the Soviet Union. Stefanović also talked well. He was handsome and popular with comrades. He never made up his own mind about anything. He always waited to see which way the discussion was going and what his comrades would say—his comrades "up there," that is. Before leaving for Moscow, Veselinov had been a "right winger," and Stefanović a "left winger." But they were both now "on the line," able to change their minds one hundred per cent overnight when necessary. This kind of "discipline" hadn't caught on yet in prison, but the fact that no one, except for a few intellectuals, objected to it was a sure sign that it soon would.

Mujkić, on the other hand, was deeply unhappy and lost when he was expelled from the party. He was a metal worker from Bosnia, a poverty-stricken Moslem who had moved to the city in the hope of survival. He was a man of great passion, but morbid and withdrawn, accentuated by his gloomy physiognomy—heavy lips, thick brows, low forehead, and thick bristly hair, like a boar's. He said everyone in Moscow thought he was an Armenian. Having risen from darkness and misery to party heights, it was hard for him to accept his sudden expulsion. For Mujkić the party was like a mother, like air and water, without which he couldn't live. He injected into his reports the faith of a worker who never had a single second thought about the "first socialist country" and the "fortress of the international proletariat." Upon his release from prison in 1937, he got in touch with me in Belgrade and asked me to send him to Spain. I understood that he wished to regain his party membership with his blood, and I sent him off. There he was killed.

Reporting on collectivization in the Soviet Union, Veselinov and Stefanović emphasized the success and the prosperity that it had brought to the villages. They also cited details that revealed all the cruelty that accompanied collectivization—cruelty if one didn't see kulaks as the bitterest counterrevolutionaries. Mujkić was full of such detail, but for him the liquidation of kulaks was something taken for granted.

Of course, they saw things that were not very happy, but they would not have dared talk about it—not because we would proclaim them the "enemies" of the Soviet Union, but because they didn't want to kill our faith. They granted there were certain drawbacks, but these were temporary "remnants" of the "class enemy," or products of a momentary economic "backwardness." They painted the transformation of Russia in the most vivid colors. They were mostly men from the lower classes, still uneducated, for whom Moscow's Communist universities were their first taste of the world, their first taste of a good life, often their first theatre performance, or their first love.

We asked them all kinds of questions, mostly to do with the concrete forms of life: love, marriage, schooling, kolkhozes. These men didn't see everything clearly, but they didn't lie. They saw a whole world erroneously because they couldn't grasp it otherwise. This was the world of their imagination, and they pictured it falsely to those who, in turn, didn't dare believe it different from the way they wanted it to be. If either of them had known and understood conditions in the Soviet Union, their own ideals, the whole purpose of their lives, would have been undermined and lost.

Following our break with the Soviet Union in 1948, I listened to Stefanović and Veselinov portraying only the negative side. Something snapped and removed a film from their eyes.

In prison, even under the most difficult circumstances, we celebrated various anniversaries—May 1, the October Revolution, the Paris Commune, Women's Day—usually in the form of a lecture. But with improving conditions, the celebrations assumed a more formal character. In 1936 we initiated publishing activity—prison magazines, mostly political and ideological, and occasionally something humorous. The anniversary editions looked more formal— red lettering in the titles. Also, our quartermasters gave us extra food.

Indeed, prison was an important, perhaps the most important, school, not only for ideological and political preparation, but for our spiritual transformation, which was stronger and more lasting. It helped create men who had only one objective, men who were unwilling to accept the role of history's observers, a role that seemed undignified once history pointed the way to the final freedom and brotherhood among men. An ordinary man, a non-Communist would gladly accept such an "undignified" role. But among us Communists, who had already stepped on the revolutionary path, such a role was reserved only for cowards unable to perform their human duty in society. Choosing one way or the other was a question of consciousness and honor. For a man who was a Communist there was no alternative. Prison prepared us for one way, the Communist way.

33

A person about to leave prison suddenly becomes loved by everybody. And he feels the same way about those he is leaving behind. Quarrels and hatreds are forgotten and forgiven, and he says good-bye warmly and directly, as if nothing had ever happened.

Behind the prison walls, we didn't feel the spring. But I knew it was in the air, and that the date of my departure—April 23—was close by. Time went both faster and slower than I had expected, slower because I had to start a new life, and faster because I had to leave friends with whom I had shared evil and good, despair and hope—life itself. True enough, I didn't much care for Pijade, who always had that bored expression on his face, but he spent many years of his life giving our movement a translation of *Das Kapital*. What hadn't he thrown underfoot and sacrificed? Our differences were a mere trifle in terms of a life which, for the sake of an idea, had buried itself behind prison walls with only one thought—how to help the struggle outside. Now they wanted him to translate material from the Seventh Congress of the Comintern, as if we didn't have younger comrades to do the work, and he worked late into the night, under a feeble light, to enable departing prisoners to "mull over" the most recent literature and prepare themselves for the battle outside. He asked me to help him, but I couldn't do as much as I wanted: I was leaving, and I was anxious to get acquainted with the most recent developments. He cursed me with gusto, but without hatred. Pucar laughed and grabbed me so hard with his enormous paws that my bones were cracking. And Prica wrote a funny epigram in our magazine:

> Here I'm suffering torture
> And in my suffering studying Marx;

233

I shed tears by the litre
That's how much I miss my Mitra. . . .

I went from room to room that afternoon, kissing everybody. Some had tears in their eyes. Did I? No, one must control oneself—that simply wasn't done among us Communists.

The last night was to be spent in solitary confinement, and at dusk I was already alone in a solitary cell. Time stopped. I heard every sound. I paced back and forth. I sat down. They brought me here, on my last night in prison, to think about my "crimes" before I became a "free" man again. Instead I felt waves of desire in my chest to repeat, not once but a hundred times, what I had done before, and what I had done here, within these four walls, among my comrades.

But why couldn't I settle down? Why was I pacing back and forth? Why did I hear every sound? Supper was over. They were washing dishes—DaviČo had probably forgotten to rinse them, and there was no one to remind him to do so. They were singing—Veselinov led them. Beautiful singing. Prica squeaked a little with his thin voice. Somebody was mad, wanting them to stop singing because it was time to go to sleep. Who was it?

Silence quickly took over. Only the guard and I were awake through the night. Since the big strike, the guards were no longer allowed to yell under our windows every half hour: "Attention!" But I heard him anyway, walking up and down the concrete path. I was walking too. So that was it? Yes, until the morning. My comrades were at last asleep. But I'd wake them up. I'd shout: "No, I won't betray you, I won't forget your affection, or our dreams and suffering. Don't worry, don't doubt for a moment. I won't, I won't . . ." But I chose to be silent instead. Silence is stronger. If only they knew how powerful that silence was and how full of vows. Silent tears filled my eyes. I was weeping and waiting for dawn and for freedom.

They brought my belongings—a suit and a few other things, all packed up and creased, but in good condition and smelling of mothballs.

Now I had to finish up the usual routine of a political prisoner: exile to one's birthplace, to my parents' home in Bijelo Polje. Everything that had happened to me since the first days of the student upheavals was typical of all those Communists who had worked under the dictatorship, particularly intellectuals. The form was my own, but the path itself was typical. Exile was the last step of the treatment, and I was about to begin a new phase of my revolutionary activity.

The Idealist

The police kept me at Mitrovica until afternoon. They tied me to a thief and shipped us both off to Belgrade on the afternoon train. I had served my full term, and as such was not dangerous, and the thief was no serious transgressor, so the gendarme agreed to untie us at Zemun, one stop before Belgrade. Suddenly I felt overwhelmed, by colors, smells, shapes, everything. Women in spring coats and hats, strange fashions. And the bridge across the Sava, suspended on an invisible thread. And many more lights, and stars in the sky. I passed by the University; the square in front of it looked smaller. Karadžićeva Street, where we held our first demonstrations, was so short and had so few houses that I simply couldn't understand how we ever managed to get away. Glavnjača prison was the same. The gendarmes were the same, though there were a few new men.

I felt as if I had spent those three years in a troubled dream. Time was still strong within me, but it was gradually fading away. For months I had difficulty adjusting to the new routine. It was as if I had been thrust out of life, and I kept returning to the physical state of that troubled dream, the bygone dark times which had pulled me out of life, but which lasted within me. I absorbed many new impressions, but for a long time I spontaneously rejected everyday routines.

After a couple of days at Glavnjača I was told to go to the political division of the police to get the decree on my exile. My lawyer came with me; he made a fruitless effort to get permission for me to see Mitra, and to travel without a gendarme. He chatted a few minutes with someone, and I waited for a "big shot" to sign the decree. The Chief of Police, Dragi Jovanović, came by. Before he came here he had held this position with the Zagreb police. He was tall, heavy, well dressed and groomed. In the corridor there were several frantic young men, Ljotić supporters who had embarrassed the government with their disorders. Jovanović slapped them around a little and told them to be off. He asked me about Svetislav Stefanović. They were from the same town. Jovanović was on his way to Zagreb to track down a Central Committee instructor. Who should it be, lo and behold, but the son of Uncle So-and-so, the father of Svetislav? He had known him as a baby. Leaping from topic to topic, he cursed the Communists: "They've organized a Communist university in prison! Serves everybody right. That's because they are under the jurisdiction of the Ministry of Justice rather than in the hands of the police. We'd have none of that." He knew about our strike and the concessions we won, and, showing off, asked me what Marx said in *Das Kapital* about workers on

235

strike. Though I had studied Marx carefully and memorized a lot of things, I didn't know what he was referring to. I knew that he was bluffing his knowledge of Marx—which policemen and reactionaries in high positions often did. So he proceeded to explain Marx to me: when workers go on strike, capitalists let them stay out so long as it is in their interest to let them stay out. "And it is in 'our state' interest to let the Communists strike to the bitter end, until they die of hunger." He would let a few of them die, which would bring down the number of strikes considerably. He wouldn't let me say a word. But I couldn't resist answering his question as to whether I had "educated" myself in prison. I said I wasn't exactly among the worst. That infuriated him. He ended his speech with a threat: he would personally take care of me if I came back to Belgrade, but he would see to it that I never did. He could tell that I "hadn't come to my senses" after all. I thought to myself: They named this policeman "Šalov" (Crazy) because he talked so much and was so hot-tempered. But the description wasn't altogether accurate: he also possessed a certain imagination and ingenuity, lacking in his predecessors.

The following morning I was in Užice. The local police locked me into a small concrete cell which had no chair and no bed. In the afternoon, I was on my way again, accompanied by a young gendarme. We immediately struck up a conversation. The new party line offered vast possibilities for agitation, even among gendarmes: defense of the country against Germany, democracy, and so on. My guide was confused. We were walking through Višegrad at dusk, looking for the local jail, when this young peasant said: "After what you've told me, I feel sick at heart. I'd like to toss this rifle away."

Even I found the Višegrad jail shocking: dark, damp little rooms, tiny windows, and low ceilings; unswept for years, perhaps since Turkish times; rotted timbers; rags, old shoes, and God knows what strewn all over. There was no light. It was impossible to stand up or walk, let alone lie down. Fleas jumped all over me, as if each step awakened thousands of them. In the dark, I stumbled on a huge iron stove. I worked my way up to the top, and sat down. The fleas can't get me here, I thought with relief.

On and off through the night, I heard a woman wailing. A Moslem peasant woman, they said, accused of having murdered her mother-in-law, rotting away, with a child at her breast, in this darkness permeated with fear and vermin.

The next day I felt weary. The district policeman, a Moslem, had seen many exiles like me, and had got into the habit of squeezing a few coins out of them. When I asked him to get some food and a newspaper for me, he didn't give me back my change. I decided not to make an issue of it, and he let me spend the day in the prison yard. A branch full of purple blossoms hung over the wall, and from the window of the house next door a young woman was shaking rugs. She may not have been beautiful, but to me she looked sweet in her simple innocence. I told her I was a persecuted student. I asked her if she would lend me a rug to lie on for a few dinars. She agreed, provided my guard, Mujo, agreed. Mujo agreed to anything that involved money. These corrupt paupers were a godsend in certain circumstances, and I had a marvelous rest, lying on the rug in the yard all day.

That night I had a lamp, for which I had bought fuel with my own money. The fleas were not nearly as aggressive, perhaps because they were unaccustomed to light. In the middle of the night a drunken young peasant was brought into my room, brimming over with energy and fury. He yelled, cursed, and threatened he would let them have it the next day—with the knife that he had on him. He wasn't drunk, but he was high, as peasants often get on market days. They can stand on their feet, and they are in control of themselves, but they are quick to start a quarrel. Anyway, my roommate cursed everybody, the District Chief, gendarmes, government ministers. He was a member of a Chetnik organization, he said, and they had forgotten his help during the election battle against the Catholics and Moslems. I felt uneasy. What am I going to do if this ignorant, hard-core supporter of the regime finds out that I am a Communist? He might very well assault me. Physically he was stronger, he was a peasant, and drunk besides, but he couldn't be more skillful or faster than I. But that knife? To give myself time, I advised him against using his knife to settle accounts with the policemen, although they had done him an injustice. He whispered that in fact he didn't have a knife at all, he was just saying it to scare the gendarmes. I felt better and told him that I too was arrested, "innocent before God," for my politics. Suddenly he fell silent. He understood that he was faced with a new enemy, a terrible enemy, with whom he would not be able to make peace, even when sober. I thought of the terrifying medieval darkness and fury raging in the souls of our ignorant and backward peasants. Who will ever be able to fight the darkness in that peasant, fight his hatred of men, of neighbors of a different faith and name, of Communism? I am one of those who chose to wrestle with the darkness and evil in this peasant lying here next to me, this man who doesn't know what to do with all that energy and blood except destroy, until he has destroyed himself in his bloody and cursed preoccupation with hatred and annihilation.

The stationmaster at Rudo would not allow me to wait in his station for the bus to Plevlje. I had to walk some fifty miles, but I was not chained and that was good. I knew the road leading through this deserted, mountainous region. The gendarme, a tiny little man, slung his bayonet over his shoulder and followed me at a proper distance. He rejected any suggestion that we stop a truck, and he refused to talk to me. The river Lim seemed restless in the muddy valley, different from up there at Berane. In my youth it was playful even during the most serious floods. But the Sutjeska, in whose ravine we soon found ourselves, that was my childhood. There must be trout out there, with golden eyes and low fins on their firm slender bodies. I felt the clean mountain air, the fickle skies, and the clear smell of my home.

But I didn't feel like walking, and carrying my suitcase and blanket besides. We were approaching the mountains. Why was this gendarme so dense? This was the first time he had ever accompanied a Communist, a former long-term convict. Who knew what he was thinking? Was he afraid to be alone with a Communist in the middle of nowhere? I sat down by the road. He pointed the bayonet at me and ordered me to move on, but I refused. It was within my right to decide how I would go—on foot or on a truck. All I had to do was pay for his fare. I felt a little nervous, and lit a cigarette. I offered him one, but he refused. Silent tension grew between us. His rifle was ready. I asked him to turn the butt away from me. He said nothing. Was he afraid, or had he made up his crazy mind to kill me? Whatever the case, I was determined not to give in. Suddenly a truck screeched up. I ran out, stopped it, and jumped in. The gendarme was too small to jump up onto the truck. He handed me his rifle first, and then reached up his hand. In the truck he was a different man. He cheered up and started talking. Obviously he had been afraid, and this was a great relief.

The Police Chief of the Plevlja District was a certain Vujišić, originally from Kolašin. A lawyer by training, he was a good-natured, intelligent man. He knew my father well. A member of the Ljuba Davidović Democratic party, he was one of those rare policemen who stuck to the law and tried hard not to use force and violence. He received me kindly, and expressed anger at the Belgrade City Administration for having kept me locked up overnight.

He was aware that there were a number of Communists among the students, but he would stir up as little trouble as possible. He ordered me to spend the night at the police station, and he asked me to take the side streets to prevent the young from gathering around me.

The gendarmes gave me an excellent lunch. They made a circle around me, as if I were a wild beast, or a magician, asking me all kinds of questions. I talked and talked. They brought up Sima Marković, who had also been here in exile: a brilliant man, but lost to the world because he was a Communist, and making them work hard besides by climbing those craggy mountains all the time. At sundown I found myself again in the hands of Moslem policemen, who were also keen on money, but not greedy, like Mujo in Višegrad.

Early the next morning I got on the bus that was to take me home. I saw the familiar shapes of the mountains and the brilliant, resonant spaces that enclosed them. The willows and alders were green along clear full streams, the meadows saturated with spring waters and grass; the shoulders of the mountains breathed with the pale green glow of the spring.

The bus stopped in front of the post office, which also served as the district administrative office. The gendarmes frisked me and, in spite of my protests, confiscated my papers. The District Chief, a tall handsome Montenegrin with an imposing mustache, was unpleasant and aggressive. A few curious heads peeked out at me from the post office, but no one greeted me.

My father had come into town every day to wait for me. I ran into him on the main street. He looked lost, forgetting to kiss me and biting his lips to stop himself from crying. Two girls ran into my arms, but I didn't know who they were: my younger sisters, grown up and changed in the three years. Not that three years is so long, but children grow fast, I guess. We walked slowly down the main street. People looked at me from the shops, but they didn't greet me. Three years ago, when I left town, they waved to me cheerfully. Now they looked with fear at the notorious Communist and convict. I felt those looks and that fear, but it didn't bother me. In fact I was proud. I raised my head and slowed my stride.

My older brother was waiting for us on a hill below the house. I recognized the rocking of his broad shoulders from some distance away. I ran to him and put my head on his chest. He was sobbing.

Aleksa had a harder time than I. He was not allowed to go into town. On market days the gendarmes would chase him away from the meadow by the road to prevent him from talking to the peasants. Hardly anyone came to visit us at home. It was a life full of spite, concocted by the idle gendarmes, who had little opposition in this god-forsaken, frightened town. Quick-tempered and worn, Aleksa had spent all this time waiting for my occasional letters, then crying over them. And, loyal and persistent in his love and in his idea, he waited for the day I would come home.

My mother was sobbing silently as usual. She had dropped what she was doing, rinsed her hands quickly, and rushed down the alley the minute she heard our voices. Suddenly all those sweet names she used to call me when I was a child came bubbling out.

In the midst of all this joy and tears, I understood clearly and unequivocally that this episode had brought to an end a phase in my life.

Some seven years earlier I had left my native village to go into the world. I was confused and afraid I would get lost in it. Now I felt that the world was so clear to me that I would be able to influence its destiny.

Book Two

THE PROFESSIONAL

1

Even before I left prison it had become obvious that the party line had grown obsolete and had to be changed. In 1933, when I was imprisoned, the dictatorship still stood on firm ground, but in 1936 it could barely depend on its own organization. The police sensed this change. They realized that the struggle against Communism had to be conducted more carefully lest the Communists successfully exploit the popular hostility against the government.

I was aware of the enormous potential in this situation, but I also sensed the limitations of party life and its activities—following well-trodden paths which led nowhere, or, at best, to heroic sacrifice.

At Bijelo Polje the party organization consisted of my brother and a couple of peasants and craftsmen, getting together in secret and reading illegal literature. Actually they were not formal party members. Their activity assumed no organized character. The typical forms, such as trade unions and young people's organizations, common in big cities, did not exist here. But there were other grounds for organization: peasant get-togethers, summer parties along the river Lim, patron saint days. A real party organization had to be set up, not large, but strong, and made up of high-school and university students and other young people with strong antifascist feelings. About half of the population in the district voted for the opposition candidate, all the machinations of the authorities notwithstanding. Obviously it was possible to make the transition from archaic party groups to a mass movement based on antifascist democratic slogans.

My brother was partly to be blamed for this isolation. He spent more time fighting the gendarmes than organizing and agitating. He was forbidden to go into town, but the night was his, and a number of people had the courage to visit him. The ban might have been lifted if he had been persistent or had relied on the mood of the masses, particularly the youth.

My brother and I hadn't even completed our discussion of what steps to take when a wave of arrests spread through Montenegro, and swept him up too. His contact in Kolašin, Muro Tošić, was arrested, but my brother hoped that Tošić would not denounce him. My brother's experience was more limited than mine: betrayal is never the result of logic, but of inner weakness.

I had been home only a few days when, dressed in silk shirts and with slippers on our feet, my brother and I took a walk along the stream. As we were walking back slowly, we spotted Dobrana, our middle sister, running across the field, ducking under the bushes. Breathless, she told us that the gendarmes were looking for us. She had managed to slip out unnoticed. We had no time to find out what it was about. We had to run. We rushed down into the valley, crossed the river, and, running from one clump of trees to another, got up the hill on the other side and into the forest.

My brother had gained a lot of weight, and had a hard time running. I had to pause every so often and wait for him. We quickly reached the forest and surveyed the valley from a clearing. There wasn't much going on. The usual late-evening village commotion, people calling people, the cattle mooing, axes banging. Night was descending fast, we were cold, it started raining. We decided to look for a place to sleep.

It was late when we knocked on the door of Ilija Bulatović and his cousin Vuksan, in the village of Okladi. Ilija belonged to my brother's group, but Vuksan didn't want to get mixed up in Communist affairs. Like most peasants, he was discontented, but not ready to participate in the Communist organization. However, we could count on him for that one night. A simple sense of hospitality made him give us food and shelter. Of course, that "shelter" turned out to be the woods. They brought out some supper and a few rugs and placed them by the house in the woods. But we couldn't fall asleep: excitement, dampness, and the cold held us in a state of tension.

We had to find out why the authorities were looking for us. The next day we received a message from our father, who had gone straight to the head of the district office for information, that the authorities were not looking for me, but for Aleksa. We decided that I should go home and my brother would remain in temporary hiding. But where? And with whom?

The Professional

Our neighbor, Mijajlo Milošević, who was rather well connected, offered my brother shelter in his attic, if he found no other place. That was risky. On the other hand, the place was safe—the authorities would never suspect Mijajlo. We finally decided to take advantage of the offer. At night, my brother crawled into the house, and the following morning I reported myself to the district office.

The District Chief of Bijelo Polje was a man by the name of Blažo Višnjić. By Montenegrin standards, he was very handsome: dark with large eyes and a thick mustache, a powerful presence. As a policeman, he paid little attention to regulations and he ruled his little duchy with an iron hand. He ran after women with the same violence and brutality, as if his police authority were transferable. He used the stick only on rare occasions. Slapping and kicking was more his style. His hatred of my brother and the local Communists was passionate. At the beginning of the uprising in 1941, my brother and the Bijelo Polje Communists tried to locate him, to take revenge for the many indignities suffered at his hands. But they never found him. He was killed in the spring of 1942, as a Chetnik. By then my brother was no longer alive either, but he would have been disappointed to hear that this "class enemy" had been killed by someone else.

Gradually I was beginning to absorb this hostility. In fact, I was intoxicated with hatred for this particular man, whose gendarmes chased youth off the beaches, dispersed village gatherings, made unreasonable arrests, slapped people around, opened mail. His violence was growing intolerable.

My feeling was that both the Montenegrin authorities and the local Communists had not changed during my prison years.

The simple-mindedness and violence of the authorities should have favored the growth of revolutionary activity. But Montenegrin Communism had not yet reached that level. It leaned heavily on the traditional pro-Russian sentiment of Montenegro and a great bitterness toward Belgrade for its neglect. On the whole, its leaders were ostentatious and nonconspiratorial, given to rash actions. They showed great courage in fist fights with gendarmes in pubs, but systematic torture between four walls was an altogether different matter. Very few among them could take that. The ensuing police raid exposed these weaknesses. The Regional Committee betrayed the membership. Even so, the local authorities were unable to disentangle this Communist knot. The Belgrade police eventually took the matter into their hands, moving headquarters from Cetinje to Dubrovnik, where they were free of pressure from influential Montenegrins.

This was the first major raid in Montenegro. Rumors of police torture made their imprint. The remaining party members, most of whom fled into forests, convinced a group of enterprising peasants to march on Cetinje and demand the release of their people. They were met at Cetinje, near Belveder, by a cordon of police and a hail of bullets. Several were left dead and many more wounded. The event spread fear and aroused much bitterness, even among non-Communists.

The arrests, the bloodshed at Belveder, and some fifty Communist guerrillas created a tense atmosphere. Sooner or later the government would have to step in.

In midsummer I was summoned to Cetinje to straighten out my military obligations. My civil rights had been suspended—including my right to vote and the right to serve in the army—but a military checkup was still necessary.

This was my first trip as a free man. Chitchatting on the bus and in cafés, meeting old friends, gazing out at forgotten scenery, all of this was a new experience and made me consider the new political situation and its possibilities.

The Communist guerrillas were considering a flight across the border into Albania. I stopped the Kolašin group, of which my brother was a member, from going over. I don't know why they wanted to go to Albania, which was also under a dictatorship. They would be thrown into jail and shipped off to fascist Italy. They had to find a solution within their own country.

I started circulating a petition demanding that the guerrillas be allowed to turn themselves over to a court, that is, to avoid police interrogation and beating. But without assistance from the Cetinje and Podgorica comrades the petition's impact remained limited. The only support I could get was from students who were home from Belgrade on vacation. They were very enterprising and had a sense of discipline, so lacking in Montenegro. Everywhere I went, Communists and sympathizers gathered around me. I had been in prison, I had stood up well in prison, and such credentials were a carte blanche among Communists. Krsto Popivoda had also been released from prison; I asked him to meet me at Cetinje.

At Cetinje I met Peko Dapčević, a student and a member of the local committee. This was our first meeting. He struck me as a strong, cordial, and self-confident young man. He and Popivoda instantly understood what I had in mind: a way of overcoming the

morbid "Belveder" atmosphere. They got a few well-known bourgeois politicians to work for the petition, and thus to put pressure
on the Belgrade government. They counted particularly on Nikola
Djonović, a Montenegrin lawyer in Belgrade, and Tripko Žugić,
of Davidović's Democratic party, and Gojko Terić of Jovanović's
Peasant party.

It soon became evident that the Cetinje bourgeois politicians opposed the petition. But we decided to go ahead anyway. This was
our way of restoring contact with the people.

For this reason alone the petition deserves attention. Such methods may have seemed opportunistic, but they were necessary. The
petition was finally successful. The regime agreed to our demands,
and the guerrillas were allowed to go straight to the courts. Most of
them were set free, including Blažo Jovanović and the Lekić
brothers.

Something funny happened during my military checkup. The
doctor quickly looked me over, pronounced me fit, and a commissioner asked me why I was so late in registering for military duty. I
was already twenty-five. I replied that I had been in prison. For
what reason, he asked me. For spreading Communist propaganda, I
replied confidently. The Commissioner stepped back, as if touching
fire. Silence reigned. In confusion, the Commissioner started looking over my papers. An old corporal broke in: "And your father is
an honest man!" "What makes you think I'm not an honest man?" I
asked in anger. The corporal was embarrassed: "No, I only meant
your father. I don't even know you."

The trip to Cetinje provided a new insight into the world.
Dapčević's group was a good reflection of the Belgrade student
movement, that great source of young revolutionaries—bold, able,
and self-sacrificing.

I began to organize my brother's group. I started an underground
newspaper, which I wrote and printed myself. Not a single copy of
it is left. It was antifascist in character, and four pages long. The
illegal press had a special power: it gathered together the strongest
people and held them together regardless of what was said. Va-
cationing students were also organized in groups. My younger
brother, Milivoje, an agricultural student and a party member, was
there. With their departure in the autumn, my opportunities became more limited, and life rather tedious. I had to think of some
way of altering my sentence of exile.

I didn't feel well in the damp climate of Bijelo Polje, but not
badly enough to require treatment elsewhere. Still, a physician

agreed to recommend a thorough physical examination in Belgrade, on the basis of which I received permission to leave. Actually I had the impression that the police couldn't wait to get rid of me. The clerk who was in charge of me told me that he would celebrate when I left. Another one wanted to know if after all my suffering in prison I was still a Communist. I replied without hesitation: "Yes." They liked that, and they said: "That's it, brother, be open about it."

But I didn't believe the police, and while en route I kept expecting to be stopped and taken back.

Apparently they were planning to do something: at Peć the police had made inquiries about me. So I got off the bus before we reached town and hid out in the flat of Miladin and Mihailo Popović. I finally got out of Peć in a limousine belonging to a Belgrade funeral home, on its way back after having brought a corpse down to Peć. Who would ever think of searching a hearse? The driver was also taking a suckling pig, which squealed and climbed over me all the way.

The Belgrade dawn was bright, the beginnings of a beautiful autumn day. Mist hovered above the roofs and in the golden treetops. Needing some clean air, I breathed deeply and felt the freshness. I was happy and excited. I walked toward the center of the city. I wasn't sure where I would find a place to stay.

2

For a couple of weeks I stayed with the author Alexander Vučo. I got all kinds of medical certificates, which turned out to be fairly simple because I suddenly came down with pleurisy. I enrolled at the Law School, found an apartment, and reported to the police. The police had, of course, been looking for me; the following day an agent came by to check on the address. Thus I legalized my position and received the right to reside in Belgrade, which would not have happened if the police still wanted me exiled.

Radovan Vuković was party leader and secretary of the Regional Committee for Serbia. I knew most of the regional and local committee members personally, but I didn't know exactly what functions they had, though Vuković indicated that he himself had a very responsible position. Now that I had legalized my position, I was ready for a party assignment. Naturally I turned to him. But I never got around to undertaking the assignment he had in mind for me: to edit the party publication *Komunist*, which assignment would have made it possible for me to pursue my own literary career at the same time. In November a series of police raids swept the country, and quickly spread to northern Serbia.

The party organization functioned more or less as before, in a set, schematic way. Outside of the University the work consisted in gathering Communists together; there was no significant contact with the masses. They followed a routine procedure: a regional committee was organized, which in turn selected the local committees. At the same time they worked out the "technique," an apparatus which distributed literature, served as contact, and was in charge of typewriters and Multigraphs, the most conspiratorial part of the organization. The technique usually consisted of one man attached to every committee, usually an able and reliable man. The regeneration of the organization always began with the arrival of an instructor or a Central Committee member from abroad, who got together with the handful of Communists left over after the raid, and gave them specific assignments. In fact, only the skeleton of the party organization was revived, but not its activity among the masses. Mass involvement often developed independently of the party. For example, in the summer of 1936 the Belgrade construction workers went on strike. The party organization had nothing to do with the strike and couldn't even establish contact with the strikers. The construction workers displayed great courage, and a number lost their lives in clashes with the police. Cedo Minderović commemorated the occasion with a poem, "We Build Houses Up to the Skies," which was very popular reading at leftist gatherings before the war. But the local committee had nothing to do with the strike. Obviously, to have been at the head of this strike would have been more significant than all the abstract schemes originating in Vienna or Paris.

Vuković understood the weakness of this method, and of the organization it produced. He realized that such an organization could at best last five to six months before the police would get it. "And then comes your turn," he would say to me, "to take over and start from the beginning."

Indeed, there was an element of doom in all this: no sooner would we put together an organization than the police would get hold of a thread, usually at or near the top, and unravel the whole net. Many raids were the result of effective infiltration of our organizations abroad, but the majority were carried out by tailing compromised Communists. And so it had gone on for years. It was more important for the Moscow instructors to report on how well the organization was set up than to get some real action going.

Vuković never concealed his displeasure with the Moscow instructors. They didn't hold up too well before the police either; the Communists were still stinging from the 1935 raid, in which Mitrović, the chief of the so-called "national bureau," denounced everyone all over the country. They spent a great deal of money besides, and made advances to the wives of sympathizers in whose homes they stayed.

Faced with the choice of being branded a liquidator or a rebel against the system, Vuković grumbled but did what he was told.

In my last conversation with Vuković I resisted his fatalism. I felt one could function differently, although I wasn't sure just how.

We also discussed the problem of how one should behave under police interrogation. I maintained that one should confess nothing. He felt that some charges might be admitted, and added: "I know I'll tell everything."

The following evening Vuković was arrested. He was the only one who never divulged anything, even though he was an epileptic and was brutally tortured. Consequently, the University, with which he worked, remained unbruised, the contact with the District Committee at Kragujevac was spared, and so was the "press." Vuković was a great revolutionary at all times.

As always during police raids, a panic set in among the few remaining sympathizers and party members.

I was the only well-known Communist who was likely to be swept up. Overnight I became a person to whom everyone turned for assistance. I was like an address which everyone knew and which was easily accessible. It made sense: I had been in prison, and had been known before that. Masleša, the only other person with such qualifications, had been arrested on some minor charge.

First we had to take care of what was left.

Through Dr. Savo Strugar I met Lazar Kočović, who had an apartment in an unostentatious villa belonging to a former sympathizer. Kočović had himself been a party member until 1929, and he had not severed his spiritual ties with Communism. He was willing to aid every reasonable undertaking, particularly with men he knew and trusted. His apartment served for many years as a hiding place for underground activists. It was also used for the district consultations, attended by Tito, between March 27, 1941 and the German invasion several weeks later. We continued to use Kočović's apartment during the war, until 1944, when Buha, a member of the District Committee, betrayed him. Following the most terrible torture, Kočović was executed.

Krsto Popivoda and Moma Marković were hiding in Kočović's apartment. But they were not the type of men to sit idle while in hiding. They were the new kind of Communist, active and uncompromising in all their activities. Yet they were very different temperamentally. Popivoda was proud and quick, and Marković cautious and deliberate. We used to send compromised comrades abroad, but now that was out of the question. All foreign contacts had been severed. Besides, we didn't favor flight.

All the same, something had to be done.

The comrades from southern Serbia, having lost contact with Vuković, had automatically lost contact with the Central Committee as well. The most active member in southern Serbia was Žika

Djurdjević. His sister, Slavka, was a very good friend of Mitra's. It was thus easy for Ziva to get in touch with me. I discussed with him the possibility of sending Popivoda and Marković to Kragujevac. Popivoda and Marković were delighted with the idea, and after some six weeks of hiding in Belgrade, they left with false papers to do party work in areas with which they had little familiarity.

Thus life imposed a new form: not flight from the country, but underground activity within. Conditions were giving birth to a new type of Communist—a professional revolutionary—not the kind sent over by Moscow, but our own.

There were many sympathizers in Belgrade, which made it easy for us to get small favors—apartments, financial aid, storage. Belgrade University gave us exceptionally strong support with both men and money.

The raid had not caught Vukica Mitrović and Djuro Strugar. Vukica had just come back from Moscow and legalized her position. She was working for the trade unions, whereas Strugar, still a student, was an instructor in a workers' party cell. He was the only remaining member of the local committee. The other members had been arrested.

Vukica, Strugar, and I became the local committee, self-appointed, out of immediate and practical need. At first, we didn't think of ourselves as a committee; we simply took over what was left of the old organization and continued to function in it as individuals. We had as yet no contact with the Central Committee. There was no other leadership. Ranković joined us in the spring of 1937; the following summer we became the local committee, and later the Regional Committee for Serbia. Vukica Mitrović, Ranković, and I remained members of the Regional Committee until the end. However, in order to distribute the work load, Strugar rejoined the local committee in 1938.

I realized that we would not be able to follow the old forms or wait to be approved by the Central Committee. Besides, I felt that the party organization could not be built up by gathering together a few odd Communists here and there to discuss the usual pamphlets honoring May 1 and the October Revolution. Such an organization was an easy prey for the police because it had no basis in personal confidences and friendships. As a result, the members didn't feel compelled, by feelings of personal friendship, to hold up strongly during police interrogations.

It was perhaps a blessing for us that we had lost contact with the

Central Committee, located in Paris, because we would have been under the discipline of a preconceived plan of organization. Political work in Serbia was being conducted by Sreten Žujović, a member of the Central Committe, whose pseudonym was Stojan. He was in Serbia when the raids began, but later he managed to flee the country, and soon ended up in Paris.

Mitra knew that Žujović was in Belgrade, and when the raids started she was determined to find him. But she didn't know his true name. He was staying in Senjak, in an apartment belonging to a cousin.

Mitra had told me that she was going to see a "comrade from abroad"—so that if she was arrested, I'd know what it was all about—and asked me to accompany her. We walked up to Senjak along the streetcar tracks, and decided I should wait for her at the tram stop. A half hour went by, an hour, an hour and a half. I was sure she had fallen into a police trap. Suddenly, after almost two hours, I saw her elegant, slender figure walking down the steep street, accompanied by a stylishly dressed young man. I was sure he was a police agent. They passed me. Mitra showed no signs of recognition. They got on the tram, and I followed. Mitra paid her fare, and the man showed his pass. Now there could no longer be any doubt: Mitra had been arrested. She gave me a few nervous glances, and we understood each other. I got off the tram at the London station and immediately called up her sister Zora. She in turn called their brother Živan, a *Politika* correspondent with good connections among the ruling circles. He went to the City Administration, and two hours later, after a brief interrogation, Mitra was released.

3

Of course, we might have survived the raid had not our "legal" political activities also been affected by it. The opposition groups—Maček and the Serbian Bourgeois party—were very active. In Serbia the youth responded well to popular-front slogans. Throughout the country trade-union activities and strikes were on the rise.

Veselin Masleša was in charge of our legal activities in Belgrade. He enjoyed a good reputation as a publicist and had good contacts with the bourgeois politicians and intellectuals. The Central Committee favored an "alliance of the working people," which would later evolve into a "party of the working people." The party of the working people had to be composed of politically well-known people. Thus it was natural that Masleša and Ljuban Radovanović, a university professor and a Sima Marković follower, were in charge. Their activities were semilegal, and the police knew them well. Their impact was not great, but they were very useful. They were able to engage a large number of bourgeois politicians in our campaigns. Hitler was knocking on the doors of Europe, and antifascist activity was gaining momentum, absorbing the energies of different groups—nationalists, democrats, and people of many ideologies.

Just before the raid I had been asked to contact the Montenegrin bourgeois politicians, many of whom lived in Belgrade, with a view to possible joint action in Montenegro.

The most important and interesting among them were Nikola Djonović and Tripko Žugić, both lawyers. From his youth Žugić had fought for the unification of Montenegro and Serbia, and was a member of Davidović's Democratic party. Within his party, he was of the left. He was a staunch opponent of the dictatorship and a zealous defender of Communists on trial. Yet there was a note of naïveté in his democratic convictions. He believed that bourgeois democracy was based on some inherent quality of the human race. He was devoted to Ljuba Davidović, a feeble old man who had one rare virtue: in this country of corruption and fraud, his hands were clean.

Djonović didn't join Davidović's party until the 1938 elections. In contrast to Žugić, Djonović was very well informed. He followed British social theories with great curiosity. For our conditions, of course, these theories were quite unrealistic. It was amazing to see this powerful man display such a keen sense of realism in dealing with small practical matters, both in his professional life and in politics.

But neither Žugić nor Djonović clearly reflected the main currents in the democratic bourgeois parties. They were to the left. The political complexion of Montenegro from which they drew their support was more radical than that of Serbia. Thus they were useful in the antifascist struggle we Communists propagated.

Our relations with the Ribar-Plećević group were reasonably good. Plećević approached the Communists cautiously. On the other hand, Dr. Ivan Ribar increasingly favored co-operation, partly influenced by his son Lola. Ribar's position in the Democratic party grew weaker, and his conflict with its leadership sharper, incurring the moral crises, intrigues, and plots so common in such situations.

The popular front with the bourgeois parties never materialized. We Communists consistently used the front's slogans, seizing every opportunity to make our views known. The bourgeois politicians took advantage of our energy and skill in organizing meetings, and we used the meetings to promote our line. But there was no genuine co-operation.

Culturally and ideologically co-operation assumed more specific forms, particularly in the magazine *Naša stvarnost* (*Our Reality*), originally conceived by Masleša. He was close to our two Surrealist writers Vučo and Matić. The Surrealist group, however, was in a state of disintegration. Jovanović and Davičo were in prison. Marko Ristić didn't rule out work with the Communists, but was quick to make excuses, and he had reservations about the Trotskyist trials.

As always during police raids, Vučo's flat was a source of news, rumors, and fears. Vučo and Matić performed many favors for the Communists, providing money, carrying materials, escorting illegal activists, giving them shelter. When Popivoda was denounced, I took him to Vučo's flat. They gave him shelter, of course. During the raids, they were in a state of great tension, wondering when someone would expose their role to the police. They would sit up late into the night in Vučo's apartment, expecting the police to knock on the door, looking out of the window at every sound. And it would go on until interrogations were over. Vučo took it all with a combination of apathy and good-natured fear. He never refused me financial assistance. Yet he insisted on maintaining his legal status.

Matić was more nervous than most of us. He kept finding signs of police surveillance. His wife, Lela, a rather masculine-looking blonde, was bolder and more effective, and she frequently helped us out. Vučo's wife, Lola, was also helpful—not out of revolutionary devotion or conscience, but, rather, with the same unobtrusive simplicity with which she recommended dresses to customers in her salon. Lula was an unusually beautiful woman, who knew how to enhance her loveliness with good taste. She made frequent trips to Paris to keep up with the latest fashions. There she contacted the Central Committee for us early in 1937. For this purpose I used chemical ink, on the pages of a novel, which this elegant lady was to take with her on the sleeping car, and I gave her instructions on how to treat it.

In addition to Matić, Vučo, and Masleša, the editorial board of *Naša stvarnost* included Jovanović, Ristić, Jovan Popović, and Radovan Zogović.

Jovan Popović behaved like a man whose time had passed. He had been active in leftist literature during the most violent years of the dictatorship, and had been the editor of *Stožer* when the Surrealists were engaging in their wildest extravaganzas, even attacking Marxism. And now, suddenly, the Surrealists were fashionable although they still hadn't renounced their earlier views. Under the popular front we had to co-operate with these anti-Marxists, which was alien to this man who was a "pure Marxist." He had received his ideological and literary education from German "social" literature, a literature that attached such great significance to the "awakening consciousness" of the proletariat. Now such views were pushed into the background. We had to work with "bourgeois" and "art-for-art's sake" writers. There was something tragic in Popović's situation. The editorial board tolerated him, but took little notice of his views. By nature withdrawn, he retreated still further into himself. He co-operated, but only because the party ordered him to.

The Professional

On the other hand, Zogović didn't feel defeated by the popular front policy. Not that he had much confidence in Vučo and Matić, but he accepted them as men with whom the Communists had to co-operate. However, on the question of publishing "Great Serb" writers known to be ideological opponents of Communism, there was sharp disagreement. Vučo saw in the popular front a whole new ideology, an intelligent recognition by the Communists that there were other progressive men around as well. For Zogović it was merely a question of tactics.

Masleša took a broad view of the popular front, and he was genuinely enthusiastic. He was the soul of *Naša stvarnost:* he settled conflicts, he cleared up disagreements, he took care of Zogović's temper tantrums. But he couldn't smooth it all over. He was arrested twice, and in his absence the conflicts grew more violent. But the magazine continued to appear and was very well received. The public thought of it as a Communist publication. The popular front idea did much to convince people that Communists didn't oppose democracy and that they had achieved a certain ideological tolerance.

The situation at the University was so complex that it needed daily attention. We had a hard time during the last few months of 1936 and the first months of 1937. I can't recall any specific details. All I can think of is running from meeting to meeting, from contact to contact, from dawn till late into the night. And it rained all the time, and I was always wet, in a hairy coat made out of a blanket that Vučo had given me. I had no income at all except from an occasional article or so, and sometimes I accepted something from Mitra, reluctantly. My belief that the situation would improve in the aftermath of the raid proved an illusion. It was the other way round: the continuous growth of the party demanded more energy from all of us. This proved the old point that the more one does the more one can do.

4

The spring of 1937 was marked by two important events: the appearance of Tito, the leading member of the Central Committee, and the arrival of Alexander Ranković.

Having no contact with the Central Committee, our local organizations improvised. Red Aid, or People's Assistance, as we now called it, was broadening its activities. We were beginning to infiltrate the trade unions. We decided not to set up street cells composed of professionally unrelated people, but to create party organizations based on social groupings. Most societies already had leftist groups, not yet solidified or connected with the party, which fought for the Communist line. It was a question of selecting the best amongst them. Bogdan Novović, for example, a bank clerk and an old leftist, was already performing, among the bank clerks, the function he would have performed as a party member. This group was gradually weeded out and turned into a party cell. There was no longer anything secretive or unnatural in their acting as a group in their professional organization. We didn't get Central Committee approval for this form of activity even after Tito's arrival in Zagreb.

We had received a message from Zagreb that spring that a "comrade from the Central Committee" had arrived, and that we were to send someone there to meet him.

Vojislav Srzentić, who delivered this message, was fairly well known as a leftist, active in the party of the working people, a semilegal party group. He was cautious and very selective about his contacts. He was one of the most active and able people in the bank clerks' association. We both went to Zagreb. And there we met Tito.

That was my first encounter with him. It took place in a small modern flat belonging to a musician, a fairly well-known leftist. Tito impressed me as a strong man, but not a careful listener. I didn't know much about his conflict with Gorkić, the Central Committee Secretary, to whom the Comintern had given the veto right in the Committee, but I didn't like Gorkić's political thinking. For him the popular front was synonymous with the United Opposition, which rejected co-operation with Communists. Furthermore, Gorkić opposed the illegal party organization and his pamphlets contained certain inaccuracies damaging to the reputation of the leadership. In my correspondence with the Central Committee I brought up this point. I never received a reply. I also brought it up in my conversation with Tito, but he circumvented the question, and I had the painful feeling that all was not well in the Central Committee. Tito's position on one basic question was very important: he didn't discourage the creation of illegal organizations; he said only that they should be established cautiously and gradually. Our local committee, still formally unrecognized, could thus take over all business matters and act as a real local committee, gradually evolving into Serbia's leadership. Tito inquired about our contacts with Montenegro, Bosnia, and Macedonia. Belgrade was in a good position to make these contacts, and Tito issued directives that we pursue those contacts. There were no party organizations in Macedonia and Bosnia; we had to evaluate the situation and look for people. Tito asked about the possibility of sending men to Spain, and he wanted to know our financial picture. We had no financial problems. He also mentioned that the Central Committee planned to relocate inside Yugoslavia. I felt the move was premature, not for political reasons, but because of the police, though I was aware that it was impossible to conduct a day-to-day political struggle through sporadic correspondence with Paris.

In short, even though nothing was resolved at the meeting with Tito, he encouraged us to proceed on the road that we had chosen and that had been imposed on us by circumstances.

Tito's image seemed familiar somehow, like something out of a distant dream. I couldn't get it out of my head. Finally, on the train going back, I recalled that I had seen his portrait in prison, painted by Moša Pijade. That was Josip Broz! At our next meeting I felt it my duty to tell him how I knew his name. He attached no significance to this knowledge, and smiled cautiously. There was something beautiful and human in that smile.

At our second meeting Tito asked if we had a competent worker in the Belgrade leadership who could join us at our next meeting.

He obviously sensed our major weakness: in contrast to Zagreb, we in Belgrade had a poor standing in the trade unions and generally among the workers.

Tito also asked me to bring a politically mature youth.

I asked Tito to send us a copy of the Central Committee proclamation on the occupation of Austria, which placed the antifascist struggle on a much wider basis, calling on the supporters of the Jereza, the ruling party, to join in the common struggle. I approved of the proclamation. Tito attached special significance to it, signifying the "final" elimination of the sectarian spirit among Communists.

The worker I recommended to him was Alexander-Leka Ranković, who had just returned from the army. The youth was Ivo-Lola Ribar.

Ranković's arrival was extremely important for our organization. I heard that he had come back from the army from Pavle Kovačević, a predictatorship Communist who had known Ranković for some time. The next day I rushed to the address he gave me.

Ranković lived with his wife in a small simple room in a one-story house, entered from the yard, a fairly common arrangement in Belgrade. The room was clean. It had a bed, a wood stove, a small fir table, and a washstand. He was waiting for his dinner, which his young wife, Andja, was hastily putting together. I was anxious to tell him about the situation, but he didn't want to talk in front of his wife. He was more conspiratorial. After dinner he suggested that we take a walk.

As soon as we were in the street, he took my arm and asked: "How are your contacts with the party?" I laughed. "I'm the contact!" I said.

Ranković was very cautious in his approach to party work. He had joined a trade union, managed to become a functionary, and was promptly removed from that position by the police. Even so, he maintained active contact with the union leadership, some of whom were Communists. During the dictatorship a lot of them were removed from their posts. They found refuge in the social-democratic unions, whose leaders tolerated Communists but kept them out of high positions. Thus, while Communist influence was rapidly spreading, the leadership remained in the hands of the Socialists. This arrangement lasted until the beginning of the war. Then the membership turned radical under Communist influence, and increasingly isolated the Socialist leaders.

Even so, we in Belgrade were never able to develop a broad and spirited trade-union movement. The police exercised daily control, freely roaming through the plants, and watching over even the most minor meetings. In Zagreb the case was altogether different. The national character of Croatian resistance automatically created better conditions for union activity. Police agents were treated as employees of the Belgrade government, that is, as Serbian nationalists. Whereas the atmosphere in Zagreb was such that people in authority were afraid, and ashamed of their roles. Strikes in Croatia were more frequent, better organized, with less bloodshed and bitterness, than in Belgrade. In Belgrade the trade unions served more as a source of party cadres than as a forum of the working-class struggle. In Belgrade our activity thus assumed the shape of a firm party organization, and in Croatia that of a mass movement.

Ranković was important not only because of his cautious doggedness, his exceptional sense of detail, his Communist strength and determination, but also because he favored infiltrating the ranks of the workers in a far more intelligent, enterprising way than any of our other workers.

Thin, fair, and reserved, he was relentlessly energetic. His political horizon and perspective were limited, as was his knowledge of theory, but he had an unusually well-developed sense of what was essential to the party in complex political situations. He was a born organizer, but not of the petty, practical kind: he had the ability to use the organization as a weapon to further a political aim.

As I look back today over this whole period, I see that the party organization in Serbia would have developed even without Ranković. Yet there was no man more highly qualified to do the job. With his arrival, we proceeded with unflinching confidence. Though we never managed to have more workers than civil servants or students in our ranks, we did manage to tear ourselves out of that constant circle of small craftsman-worker Communists, burdened with social-democratic "prejudices." Ranković was not the sole organizer in this field, but he certainly was the most important and the most reliable.

He joined our committee and was made its secretary partly because of the tradition that workers serve in that capacity and partly because he was the oldest party member. He had recommended me for the post, but I didn't accept, trying to make myself free for the pursuit of my literary career. Ranković quickly became the central person in the party organization.

At the next meeting with Tito, Ranković was present, along with a couple of Slovenes and Croats we didn't know. It was a consultation session: we discussed political issues rather than significant decisions.

As for Lola Ribar, he had just become a party member, but was known as a student activist. A few months before, he had taken a trip to Paris to attend an international student gathering and he had asked me for instructions regarding his role. He spoke French very well, and he was fairly fluent in German and English.

The League of Young Communists of Yugoslavia (SKOJ) had no leadership and no secretary. In the summer of 1937 Ribar was appointed secretary. This explained why Tito had asked me to recommend a young man.

If I had known what Tito had in mind, I would not have recommended Lola Ribar, although Tito's choice proved not only bold, but also correct. In Belgrade we had a number of tested comrades in the youth organization, like Djoko Kovačević, Vladimir Popović, and Cvijetin Mitjatović. In their eyes Lola Ribar was little more than a bourgeois sympathizer. His sudden rise to power put him in the difficult position of giving orders to men who were both older and more experienced than himself, and above all more party-oriented.

My own reservations regarding Lola Ribar soon vanished. In the course of working together we became friends, and we remained very close until his death.

Tito left again for Paris. A little while later Žujović arrived.

I didn't know Žujović. He asked Mitra to meet him in Užice. We decided it would be good if I went along. He was staying in a little house belonging to Miša Jovanović, a member of the local committee.

Žujović's position on party organizational tactics was like Tito's, but even more decisive, particularly regarding pace. The organization in Serbia was to be divided into two parts, and the existing local committee in Belgrade was to become a regional committee. There were no political differences between Žujović and myself; he was able to answer my inquiries about Gorkić fairly convincingly. No one on the Central Committee objected to the creation of party organizations, but the question was how to make them function.

The meeting with Žujović lasted the whole day. The actual business part went fast, but there was no end to our political talk.

I liked Žujović. He was an open, emotional man, an adventurous spirit, and so handsome that women turned to look at him. A purebred from Šumadija, he was solid and determined to see things through to the end. In contrast, Tito was sincere but reserved, with a self-confident revolutionary hardness. Žujović was a man of passion and quick enthusiasm, direct, and easy to make friends with. They both had quick reflexes. Tito had greater stability; it was practically impossible to win him over if he had already formed an opinion, whereas Žujović might give in. Tito spoke little; Žujović bubbled over with arguments. They both dressed well. Tito's elegance was ostentatious and cheap, *nouveau riche*. Žujović's was more relaxed. They both stood up well before the police.

In the course of several months Moma Marković and Krsto Popivoda had set up party organizations throughout southern Serbia. Žujović asked me to join him at a meeting with the two of them at Kragujevac to draw up a new course of action. My presence was intended to synchronize relations between the two regions.

We held the meeting in a flat in the center of town belonging to a certain Tasa, a stonecutter. At one time, long before he had become a Communist, Tasa had acquired a little wealth, and along with that a paunch and the confidence of the authorities. However, the renewal of opposition activity had stirred him up. His caution and timidity notwithstanding, he was flattered to have such important things taking place under his roof. Popivoda lived in his house, and Tasa's daughter was his girl friend. Moma came by often, and Žujović was staying with them temporarily. I spent the night there, as did Žika Djurdjević. Tasa's wife prepared tasty Serbian meals for us and she viewed this gathering of men with false names with both concern and good-natured kindliness.

The organization in the southern part of Serbia was now far ahead of ours in the north. Popivoda's and Marković's achievement was gigantic. They had made the rounds of the small towns and villages, working through sympathizers, but also discovering new men and new possibilities. This was their most significant contribution. The police spies and provocateurs had narrowed their activities to former Communists, which meant that we had to isolate ourselves from them and look for new people. But here we ran into certain differences of opinion with Žujović. Popivoda, Marković, and I felt that the former Communists were a hindrance in setting up new party organizations, which could be put together only by fighting their opportunism and indolence. Žujović, on the other hand, was against alienating them, and for making use of them in legal activities, such as the proposed party of the working people and contacts with the bourgeois opposition parties. This very important, critical point remained unresolved. Popivoda, Marković, and I firmly believed in the bolshevization of the party; we believed that nothing could be accomplished without an ideologically unified, disciplined, and illegal party. We learned this both from the courses taken in prison and from practice. We were not burdened with Moscow schematics, and we were unfamiliar with the Central Committee and Comintern discussions. Žujović didn't object to such an organization, but he favored the legalization of party activities, which meant putting the opportunists and liquidators to work on our legal activities. Žujović was less familiar with local conditions. He operated through the illegal channels, but when they were not available, he worked with former Communists. They were afraid to lose their prestige; they opposed the new people as too young and too unstable, lacking in political perspective. But they themselves wanted no part in the illegal organizations.

The dictatorship had succeeded in making a profound gap between the masses and former politicians, among them former Communists, and left the masses unto themselves, simmering in spontaneous protest, ready for action. Revolutionaries were the only people able to give them leadership.

Žujović may have seen us as "sectarians" who didn't understand the Comintern line regarding the popular front. We, in turn, saw him as a man who gave in to the opportunists and liquidators. Even so, our relations remained cordial. He was a member of the Central Committee and we were obliged to adopt his positions, but we were always able to state our case and he listened.

However, it was not in the cards for Žujović to resolve these differences, which were later to assume such vigorous proportions in debates throughout the country. Unexpected events were in store for us, which may not have eliminated the conflict, but they certainly changed our roles in it.

5

From the very onset of the Spanish Civil War, Yugoslav leftists talked about going to Spain to fight as volunteers. The party encouraged it. Tito and Žujović emphasized its importance, stating that Spain could serve as an excellent training ground for party military and political cadres.

However, the project turned out to be a very complex one. First of all, the police controlled the issuance of passports and made it impossible for the well-known leftists to leave the country. Illegal routes were limited and difficult—Austria and Switzerland had to be crossed without any documents.

Even so, we sent people.

The Paris Exposition proved a suitable solution. A lot of people were going there anyway. We had to make money available, as well as an address in Paris from which they could organize the entry into Spain. I was in charge for Serbia, and I helped a lot of people get to Spain, among them the journalist Sveta Popović, and Blagoje Nešković and his wife. But many simply went to Paris for the exposition, made their own contact, and left for Spain. We received money for this project from Paris in French francs. Tito gave me the first payment, a relatively small amount, and Žujović the second.

The Central Committee was dissatisfied with the slow and scanty shipment of people to Spain. They were anxious to score a quick and sudden success. Tito told us that Gorkić was planning to have a ship pick up volunteers directly from the Montenegrin coastal villages, which would have taken care of several hundred people in one fell swoop. Montenegro was a good choice, because the movement was strong there.

One day Dr. Dušan Kusovac sent me a message to come and see him at his office. He introduced me to a slender, red-haired woman, a foreigner, who was trying to get in touch with Ljubo Vušović concerning the ship to Spain.

Dušan Kusovac was a well-known gynecologist who provided women in the movement with abortions at no cost, helped the movement financially, but worked only through people in whom he had full confidence. The police knew that he was a sympathizer, but also that his involvement was as much due to family loyalty as to political conviction. His brother Labud was a well-known Communist, in exile in Paris. Dušan saw Communism as a dark conspiracy, and he delivered his reports in whispers, with exaggerated gestures of secrecy. The factional struggle, in which his brother played a major role, was for him only an enjoyable intrigue. Committees, organizations, and leaders came and went, and Dušan Kusovac survived many a turbulent year, always maintaining contact, and, as luck would have it, never attaching himself to anyone who would betray him for the favors he performed.

Anyway, I warned the woman not to act outside the party, and explained to her that Vušović was a complex man. But she rejected my warnings and asked to be put in touch with him immediately. I didn't know Vušović too well, but my feelings about him were largely negative, as they were about most of the older Montenegrin Communists, who boasted a lot, accomplished little, and were more concerned with their own image than with the organization. He had no knack for conspiracy, and his activities had become a public secret in Belgrade: everyone knew that Vušović had a lot of money, that he was giving it freely to people to go to Montenegro and from there to Spain. In Montenegro the news of his operations spread like wildfire. Montenegrin Communists took to the road, marching off to the sea, with a song, to board the ship to Spain.

Later Tito claimed that it was Gorkić's fault that the ship was discovered. I don't know if this was true, but the Montenegrin authorities certainly knew what was going on. The peasants were dispersed and arrested; the ship searched; Adolf Muk, a member of the Central Committee, arrested, along with the woman Kusovac had introduced me to, and I in turn had put in touch with Vušović.

The whole job had been done sloppily. Vušović relied more on his acquaintances than on the Montenegrin party organization. Indeed, the Central Committee in Paris didn't put much trust in the party organization either. Ranković and I had been skeptical of the project from the start—I even more than Ranković, because from my Montenegrin contacts I understood the superficial, nonconspiratorial nature of the operation.

Adolf Muk was transported to a Belgrade jail, where he promptly told the police more or less everything he knew about the old party organization in Belgrade, which had already been liquidated by the police. Fortunately he knew nothing about me and the new organization. Vušović could have pressed charges against me because I had put him in touch with the woman, but he held up bravely. And the woman, identified as Braina Fos-Rudin, stood up heroically in spite of police torture.

This incident triggered a fresh round of arrests. The Popović brothers were the first to go. Nenad Popović's arrest came as a surprise, because he was a proregime journalist. His brother, Dejan, was the editor of *Vreme* (*The Times*) and an intimate friend of Milan Stojadinović, the Premier. No one had ever suspected Nenad of being a Communist, including me. Letters and important messages were sent to his address, and the only person familiar with this detail was Radovan Vuković. Dejan, on the other hand, was known as a leftist sympathizer. But the brothers couldn't reveal anything, because they didn't know anything.

I sent several messages to the Central Committee in Paris concerning Muk's conduct. But orders came for us to conduct a campaign throughout the country to save him. International public opinion was aroused. Students printed a pamphlet on the subject, but I put a stop to it before it was ever distributed. Out of ignorance, Lola Ribar encouraged the campaign for a time. Vujković and his policemen gloated over the ridiculous situation. Muk's betrayal dealt a serious blow to the Central Committee's prestige, and the campaign to promote his heroism was an even greater threat. We stopped it wherever we could, but Paris continued to promote it.

The police didn't spend time on Muk; in less than a month he was handed over to the court. I immediately got in touch with him, through secret channels of course, requesting a report for the Central Committee on his conduct in the police investigation. Muk responded with a letter in which he tried to justify himself in a way that was as undignified as it was incomprehensible. He said he felt it wiser to admit what he knew than to suffer torture. Djoko Kovačević, Secretary of the University organization, was on his way to the Paris Exposition, and we sewed Muk's letter into the lining of his overcoat. He delivered it to the Central Committee, and they finally then stopped the idiotic and shameful campaign.

Djoko Kovačević possessed all the characteristics of a Communist revolutionary. I've met only a few people like him in my life. The revolutionary Communist organization at the University had thrust to its forefront this man who reflected its true character: he was dedicated, quick, and fiery, an unusual and complete fusion of dogmatism and practicality, a straightforward fighter and leader. He and I had worked together for some ten months and had grown very close.

After delivering the message, Kovačević left for Spain almost immediately, in spite of my objections. There he excelled. When Tito asked for someone to represent us at the Communist Youth International, Lola Ribar and I both recommended Djoko Kovačević. Our recommendation was accepted, and Kovačević was to be recalled from Spain. But he was killed: one of our comrades accidentally shot him.

A second serious blow, following Muk's betrayal, was a police raid in the southern part of Serbia.

I had made arrangements with Krsto Popivoda and Moma Marković to conduct our correspondence in a chemical ink. A few days after I had gone to Bijelo Polje to visit my parents, where I intended to stay for a month, I received a letter from Marković telling me of the police raid in Serbia. I was in danger, and I left for Belgrade.

The police followed me, but they lost track of me at Berane. I spent the night in the home of Vuksan Cemović, a leftist friend of mine. The following morning, some distance from the village, I got on a bus bound for Peć. At Andrijevica, while the bus stopped for the mail and passengers, several gendarmes crossed the market place, and asked me to accompany them to the main district office. They left me alone in a small room. I opened the window, determined to jump out. But Andrijevica is built on a cliff, and the district office was over an abyss. Also, I soon realized they were not treating me as a prisoner, and I began to protest my detention: my bus would leave, I would be late. The bus driver had been ordered to wait, they said, that they only had to check on a few points. I heard them talking on the telephone. Everything ended well: the police merely wanted to know whether I was among the passengers. I continued on my way to Peć, and from there to Mitrovica. At Mitrovica I boarded a train, and before long I was in Belgrade.

Mitra and I went into hiding. We were the only two people threatened. For two weeks we stayed in Divčibare. We had just gotten married, and those were beautiful days in spite of the tension: a plateau in the mountains, gentle sunshine, a brook and fields, a modest attic room in an inn. No one knew us; we were much like the rest of the guests: quiet leisurely people who had come to relax and enjoy themselves.

The raid in southern Serbia had been extensive. Not a single organization was spared.

Žika Djurdjević, a member of the Regional Committee, was largely responsible for it. Žujović, in turn, was responsible for Djurdjević's membership in the Committee. Obviously it was a mistake to have familiarized an untested man with the leadership of the organization. But such errors of judgment were natural. Djurdjević came from a well-to-do merchant family. He and his sister were both hard-working activists as well as good people, sincere, kind, and generous. But there was something in their upbringing that was too soft for the severe tests of a revolutionary struggle. Djurdjević knew a lot; he revealed what he knew, and hanged himself in prison. Had he done it before he confessed, he would have won our respect. This way, he was remembered only for the shame of his betrayal, and not for the suicide.

On the other hand, Krsto Popivoda and Spasenija Babović displayed courage and endurance that were beyond belief. They couldn't conceal very much, because Djurdjević had already told all. But they refused to corroborate his testimony. There had been Communists before them who had confessed nothing, but none had been tortured quite so brutally. Their heroic conduct marked a turning point in the conduct of Communists under torture.

In this connection I recalled two discussions with Masleša. Before the Popivoda-Babović case I had tried to convince Masleša that it was possible not to confess to anything, and he argued that "some" charges had to be accepted. After the Popivoda-Babović case I reminded him of our earlier discussions. He said: "Obviously there are such people, but they are rare."

Following the Popivoda-Babović example, the police never treated anyone as brutally. When they ran into such resistance they would give up. The police too had learned their lesson.

Meanwhile, Moma Marković had gone into hiding in Belgrade, from which we sent him off to Spain. But on the way, in Austria, he was arrested and shipped back to Yugoslavia. Thanks to his own maneuvering and his father's influence, he never reached the Glavnjača.

It was generally believed that our Austrian contact was denounced by Trilnik, who worked for Pavle Gregorić, party chief of Zagreb, following his release from prison in 1936. Trilnik's conduct before the police was entirely unsatisfactory. Gregorić was again arrested in 1937, and Trilnik came to Belgrade to get money for the Spanish volunteers. Money was all I gave him. I didn't trust him. He went to Paris in 1938 or 1939, and the party leadership denounced him as a provocateur.

In any case, the Austrian contact had served a number of people extremely well. For example, Marko Orešković used him successfully in his flight from Belgrade, where he had been hiding following a police raid in Croatia.

After the transfer of Popivoda's group to the court prison, I decided that there was no point in my hiding any longer. I returned to my flat, a small room on the top floor of a building on Majka Jevrosima Street, where I had already moved in with Mitra and where we were to live for two years. A couple of months after Popivoda's arrival at Ada Ciganlija, he sent me a message that Žika Djurdjević had mentioned me in his testimony and that I should go into hiding. But I decided against it. The police knew that I had returned to my apartment, but had decided to leave me alone. And what could they do anyway? The only person who could make serious charges against me was Žika Djurdjević. And Žika Djurdjević was dead. Obviously they were saving me for some other occasion. This was a warning of a kind—to be more cautious than ever. And I was. Mitra's case was similar. She was accused of having been my contact with Žujović at Užice.

The raid in southern Serbia had great practical impact. We were now faced with a whole set of new problems and responsibilities, not just for Belgrade, but for all of Serbia, and our committee automatically evolved into a Regional Committee for Serbia. We had lost virtually all contact with towns, and had to start from the beginning, making use of all kinds of people and situations, personal friendships and former party members.

The biggest blow, however, came from Paris. Lola Ribar came back in the autumn of 1937. He told us that Gorkić had been arrested in Moscow as an enemy of the people. The Central Committee was thus beheaded, and its entire membership cast under suspicion. The prestige of the Paris leadership had sunk to its lowest point. Ribar also brought orders from Tito: maintain contact with Zagreb and Ljubljana, consult regularly, and continue to inform Paris of our activities. Čolaković and Žujović, both members of the Central Committee, had supported the "Gorkić line" and were compromised. Tito alone continued to enjoy a certain respect, because he had opposed Gorkić and because of his proletarian background. Both in Paris and within our country, Tito was the only person in whom people had confidence and to whom they instinctively turned.

The activities of the Central Committee in Paris had come to a virtual halt. In Belgrade, Zagreb, and Ljubljana we took the position that we had to maintain discipline while waiting for events to resolve themselves within the Paris Central Committee.

The raids, the shipment of volunteers to Spain, Gorkić's arrest, all took place at the time of the Moscow trials, the time of conflict between the new and old concepts of discipline and unquestioned devotion to higher authority.

Beginning in the summer of 1936 the newspapers had been full of stories about the Moscow trials.

While still in prison, I accepted the view that "objectively" Trotsky was a counterrevolutionary. We carefully studied his "mistakes," following Stalin's formulations and positions. I was familiar with Trotsky as a writer and I could not deny him certain stylistic qualities. Bukharin was a similar case, though he was thought of more highly as an economist than a philosopher. But his "deviations," particularly on the "peasant question," were well known, and had been pointed out before, by Stalin.

But none of this could explain what was going on. Deviations were one thing, betrayal quite another. We had seen deviations and disagreements before, but very little betrayal—actually none. More profound explanations had to be sought.

The most difficult thing to explain was not the transition from deviation to betrayal, but the manner in which the Soviet leadership resolved these problems. No sooner would the confusion of one trial get resolved, and some kind of an explanation get accepted, than a new series of betrayals, still harder to explain, would come up. We thought: Ah, well, Trotsky has always been in opposition, so that's that. But then it was Bukharin's turn, and then Tukhachevski's . . .

There was no substantial support for Trotsky among us, but there certainly was a lot of confusion, and we had to do a lot of explaining.

The intellectual group associated with the magazine *Naša stvarnost* was not Trotskyite in character, but they accepted our explanations very skeptically, more out of a sense of discipline than out of conviction. For them the main thing was sympathy for the Soviet Union, the "major force of socialism"; everything else was secondary. These people were not burdened by Communist dogma, and they accepted the events without intellectual or moral trepidation. At the University there was some wavering and I had to hold a series of meetings with party members and sympathizers. Here we had to combine "factual" with theoretical and intellectual explanations. On the whole the workers had little interest in these developments. The leftist trade-union leaders sided with the Soviet leadership. The social democrats were triumphant, and scandalized by the inexplicable happenings.

Ranković, who had revived his anti-Trotskyite training in prison, accepted my explanations. He firmly believed that Stalin was right. The same was true of the other comrades in the leadership.

Marko Orešković's reaction was interesting. He believed that virtually nothing in the trials was true to the facts, but he was thrilled with the way Stalin finally took care of the factionalists and deviationists. When I told this story to Tito, Kardelj, and a few other people, they laughed with warmth at Marko's "nonsensical" explanation, which reflected their extreme devotion to Stalin and the party.

Orešković had an original mind. He was a worker, close to forty, in excellent health. We nicknamed him "Junk"—as a taxi driver he always referred to his car as a piece of junk. Tall, fair, and strong, he was a mixture of a peasant and a proletarian fighting his way through life. In the expression of his feelings and thoughts he was direct to the point of crudeness. He liked to eat a lot. He also liked women and they liked him.

He had left his wife, Jela, a small, dumpy, illiterate woman, who had waited for him faithfully while he was in prison. Marko gave a simple explanation for this: he had lost all sexual interest in her. He said to me: "I could sleep next to her for a year, as I do next to you!" We had put him up in the apartment of the pianist Jelena Nenadović, with whom he eventually started sleeping.

An unusual, strong relationship developed between this cultured, refined woman and this direct, strong man, for behind Marko's tough directness there was an understanding of complex, deep feelings. He liked her and they got along well. He had no objections to her appearance either; in fact, he claimed that she had a Venuslike body. As for her morbid psyche, he claimed he would cure it with his own health and inner strength.

When he came back from Spain, he lived in Zagreb with a beautiful young Jewess, a Communist, but from a rich family. He was criticized for having given in to a "decadent bourgeois." This made

Marko angry and he complained to Tito: "What do you want from her? She's dedicated. Tell her to cut off her finger, she'll cut it. Tell her to cut her hand off, and she'll cut it!" Tito sympathized with him. He had similar weaknesses himself.

While Marko was still in Belgrade we had begun a campaign against the sexual promiscuity that still prevailed among Communists. The trouble was that we found it hard to defend our cause with Marko's case in mind. He argued that he was not bound, by Marxism, to stay with one woman for the rest of his life. Stalin himself had been married several times! I granted him that point, but I insisted that nevertheless he should not change women like socks.

In effect the conflict was over his role in the party organization. Marko was very active by nature, and he couldn't bear to sit idle. We couldn't give him any party assignments because, following the raids, we had to be a little more subtle in gathering people together and teaching them, and Marko was not a subtle person. In his role as an instructor, he abused the local committee and threatened to exterminate them like cockroaches because they hadn't joined the construction workers' strike. He was partly right, of course. The organizations were isolated.

Unlike the local committee, which requested Marko's recall, the students were thrilled with him. They were excited by his restless revolutionary spirit, by his tough criticism of "bourgeois intellectuality" and philosophy. This was no accident: the local committee was rigid and had no contact with the masses, and the University organization grew out of youthful upheavals.

Also, Marko had expected to leave the country, on orders from Paris, but the chances of getting him a false passport had been reduced by the police raid. Thus we kept putting it off, which made him very angry. He accused me of "sabotage," and I accused him of "anarchism." The conflict between us reached such proportions that he threatened to beat me up. Finally, we organized his departure and I handed him the money and the addresses of the people he was to look up.

In Spain Marko proved himself a miracle of heroism and initiative. He was in fact a man for direct armed battle. Full of revolutionary passion, he was able to arouse the masses. After the end in Spain he wrote to us that the battle in the Pyrenees was lost, but that he was coming to Yugoslavia to start a new one. And he did come back. We met in Zagreb. Meanwhile, we had changed our assessment of each other and we were good friends again.

Orešković's case amply illustrates the problems we faced in the year 1937. We could not engage in underground activities. There were no party organizations outside of the University, and we operated chiefly through sympathizers and individual party members.

In Croatia and Slovenia the party organizations were in no better shape, but they were strong in the trade unions, and their contact with the masses was stronger.

Having traveled all over the country on party assignments, I realized that the new approach to party work was not merely a Belgrade "fabrication." It was evident in Croatia, in Montenegro, and in Slovenia, in a somewhat different form perhaps. Semilegal and legal activity of sympathizers was in evidence everywhere. Conditions had produced a new wave of discontent, and that wave in turn thrust forward new forces. Still stronger and fresher forces lay deep down. But to set them in motion we needed an extremely large organization and an exact and unwavering political orientation.

6

The arrest of Gorkić and other party leaders in the Soviet Union, the failure of the Spanish volunteer project, and the Moscow trials created a favorable atmosphere for those groups that disagreed with the official party leadership and the Moscow line.

However, all of us in leading party positions stood firmly behind Stalin. Indeed, this was a prerequisite for party membership, the standard by which revolutionary spirit was measured. We were the most active in setting up illegal organizations, in militance toward other parties and all forms of deviation within the party.

I must explain the expression "within the party." It didn't apply only to people who were active in the party, but to all those who were close to it, to the formerly prominent members now reactivated in the general revival of political life. Not one of them was a dedicated Marxist in the Stalinist sense.

In Yugoslavia in that era, Stalinism—devotion to Stalin personally, his ideology, and the Soviet Union—was synonymous with revolutionary spirit. This was not our own Stalinist observation; that was the way it actually was. People who didn't take that position would never have been able to bring about the revolution, because they would never have been able to set up its instrument—the party.

Today I refer to "Stalinists" and "Stalinism," but at the time such usage was considered improper. We thought of Stalin as the sole heir to Lenin and the sole representative of the only kind of Communism we recognized as right. Devotion to Stalin was for us the same as devotion to Lenin, the revolution, and Communism. The expression "Stalinism" was not used because it would have implied a separation of Stalin and Lenin. However, expressions such as "Stalinist strength" and "Stalinist clarity" were often used to define something positive and ultimate.

We also conducted a struggle against Trotskyites.

In Belgrade the only genuine Trotskyite was Nikola Popović. He had gathered around him a handful of intellectuals. We branded him a police agent, based on some irrelevant facts, which nevertheless were convincing to us. He was the author of a study—probably the only one ever written—on Tucović, which I thought very poor, all the more so in that it was written by a Trotskyite. He was executed after the liberation of Belgrade in 1944. I don't know whether there was any evidence proving that he was a spy, but his admission that he was a Trotskyite was considered sufficient proof.

There were certain developments at the University which we interpreted as Trotskyite. We reacted to them by organizing boycotts among the students. Such methods yielded excellent results in building up party discipline and in increasing ideological unity. We leading Communists considered this kind of sharp and uncompromising position useful and natural. We had automatically accepted the premise that the Trotskyites were police spies and agent provocateurs; we had accepted it by virtue of having unconditionally accepted Stalin and the Soviet Union.

The truth is, however, that there were very few Trotskyites among us. Even that handful that we had labeled as such in our Stalinist vigilance was exaggerated. Our problems came not from the Trotskyites, but from Petko Miletić, who was in prison, and from our people abroad.

Taking advantage of his popularity, Petko Miletić continued to exercise authority both in prison and outside. He had made contacts all over the country through people who were released from prison and were assuming an active role. Thus, still another center was being created, this one within the country, but no more realistic than the one in Paris. Gorkić's Central Committee may have leaned too far to the right, but the prison "center" was much too narrow and dogmatic on the other side.

When I took over in Belgrade, toward the end of 1936, I ran into immediate trouble with Petko's prison center. At first the conflict was not sharp or open. I still had great respect for Petko and his group, but I realized that his directives had nothing to do with reality, that they reflected the kind of abstract thinking typical of people in prisons. Ranković admired Petko, perhaps even more than I, but he saw the flaws in the prison line. We were in touch with the

Central Committee, and we thought it best to limit our contact with Miletić to the sending of food and literature.

From my own experience I knew that Belgrade's contact with prisons had to be constant and vigorous. It was important for us to know what went on and how well individual prisoners stood up. It was a simple matter of assigning the task to one person, something that had not been done before. We gave the assignment to Milica Sarić, the wife of Djuro Strugar, now the wife of Svetozar Vukmanović-Tempo.

She was a young girl who had entered the University after being released from prison. The youth group to which she belonged had been swept up by the great raids of 1936. The leader of the group, Butum, was a cynical, bizarre character. His stand before the police was poor. But that wasn't all. Once he realized his failure, he gave the police detailed descriptions of his sexual adventures with girls in his organization. The police interrogated everyone once again, not because they were particularly interested in all this dirty laundry, but to demoralize the students. They had also confiscated the love diaries of Jovan Popović's sister, in which she had faithfully recorded her intimate relations with an impressive number of men. The scandal quickly spread: the police asked the parents of some of the girls to appear, and related the whole story in detail before the parents and their lawyers.

The affair harmed the movement seriously. Our enemies gloated, and ordinary citizens were scandalized.

Such relations between men and women were contrary to my own views of Communist morality. They demoralized and repulsed some of our most spirited people, and destroyed the emotional health of many revolutionaries. While our heroes were by no means innocent in sexual matters, our cowards were dissolute or at best irresponsible and lighthearted.

The University party leadership was determined to improve this situation. The idea came from me, but the University group carried it out in a crude and cruel fashion, which so often happens. On their release from prison, the young men and women belonging to Butum's group were boycotted by their colleagues.

Thus Milica Sarić was included in the boycott although she had no contact with the group's activities. She was Djuro Strugar's girl friend. He asked me to help her. On our first meeting I sized her up as a person dedicated to the movement, sensitive, but overly delicate, a little vain. The University organization accepted her on my recommendation, and assigned her the job of keeping in touch with the men in prison, a task which she performed conscientiously for many years.

Contact with the men in prison was maintained through their families. With the help of a reliable worker, and following drawings she received from prison, Milica constructed cans with a double bottom, wide enough to hold our literature. The can itself was filled with honey, olive oil, or something like that. Many other similar devices were also used. She would then deliver these cans to the prisoners' families, for them to take on their weekly visits. For shorter messages chemical ink was used, a system that was being slowly perfected. The rule was that none of the families were to know anything about Milica, or the contents of the cans. Needless to say, they had their suspicions.

In Belgrade we immediately understood that the prisoners had to be told of Gorkić's arrest. Tito sent his approval from Paris for me to inform Petko Miletić and Moša Pijade, on condition that they keep it a secret. This secrecy was necessary not so much because anyone hoped that Gorkić would be cleared, but because we were afraid the membership would be demoralized, and because we felt the membership should have further briefing on all aspects of the struggle against Trotskyism. Above all, the police had to be kept in the dark, or they would publicize the news and make use of it for their own ends.

Instead, Petko Miletić used every bit of this information to solidify his position in prison. He stepped up the struggle against Trotskyism and opportunism, or, to put it more precisely, against all those elements that obstructed his own course of action. He seemed to have decided that the time had come for him to take over party leadership. His campaign assumed hysterical proportions, which no one could oppose as yet, and was fused with the efforts of the Paris émigrés in opposition to Tito and the remnants of the Central Committee. Labud Kusovac was particularly active in this direction.

Through his brother, Dr. Dušan Kusovac, Labud told Miletić about Gorkić's arrest, suggesting that the Comintern would soon have to do away with the present Central Committee, and that he, Petko Miletić, would be the sole hope for the party's salvation. In effect, he had no confidence in the Central Committee, and he urged Petko to start making his own decisions. Dušan related a similar message to me concerning a conversation his brother had with Petko, whom he had visited in prison. At that time the regime was relatively liberal and everyone was allowed to visit prisoners.

I immediately made out a report to the Central Committee; I also informed Ranković and the comrades in Ljubljana and Zagreb. It was clear that Petko, in co-operation with a number of émigrés, had initiated factional activities in order to gain party leadership. All of us in Serbia, Croatia, and Slovenia took the position that until further communication from the Comintern, we had to stand by the Paris Central Committee and Tito. The Central Committee had not been suspended, even though the Comintern had limited its rights by virtue of having arrested the only person who had veto powers.

But we in Yugoslavia felt the burden of intraparty squabbles far less than did the leadership in emigration.

We were preoccupied with the practical political aspects of party life to such an extent that we had little time for meditation and depression, so inevitable in exile and in prison. The lively political activity in the country made us realize that the situation at home was not nearly as gloomy as it appeared to observers abroad. Also we suspected that in resolving the crisis, Moscow may have made a few false moves. If the organization in Paris was rotten and infested with spies, here in Yugoslavia the party body was wholesome.

Tito and the Central Committee knew all this, but they were experiencing a far more complex emotional drama. They were more familiar with the method and manner of the Comintern in Moscow, which had sentenced them to temporary passivity. None of them had been in Yugoslavia between Gorkić's arrest in the summer of 1937 and the spring of 1938. In fact, we received no political instructions from them until the summer of 1939. We managed on our own as best we could.

Tito did make a very short trip to Yugoslavia in the spring of 1938, when he finally set up leadership inside the country. This was done without the official sanction of the Central Committee, which could not take official acts without the approval of the Comintern.

There were certain other changes as well.

Until that time consultations were fairly irregular, nothing more than occasional meetings of three bodies—the Belgrade, Zagreb, and Ljubljana organizations. Contact with the Slovenians was especially poor and irregular. Regular contact was not established until 1938.

The changes in the composition of the Yugoslav Central Committee were not great—as far as people or activity went. However, the relationship between this newly formed body and the one in Paris was not clearly established. Tito stressed the fact that the

Paris Central Committee had no right to interfere in internal Yugoslav matters. But we were to understand that the Paris Central Committee was the senior body, particularly when Tito participated in its decision-making. Tito was at the head of the organization in the country, although he was absent; he was the only man who still enjoyed the Comintern's confidence. The Comintern didn't know anyone else in the country, with the possible exception of Kardelj, except as gleaned from Tito's reports.

The establishment of a Central Committee within the country, without the Comintern's approval, was a very bold decision. The Comintern could have annulled it. In effect, Tito was consolidating a position that the national party had already accomplished.

We knew that this new body was the real leadership, that we were members of a real Central Committee, and that the one in Paris was going to last only until the Comintern formally decided to dissolve it.

7

In addition to Ranković and myself, representing Belgrade, the newly formed Central Committee included Lola Ribar of the Young Communists, Petrović, Žaja, and Kraš representing Zagreb, Kardelj, Marinko, and Leskovšek representing Slovenia. If I remember correctly, Kardelj, Kraš, and Žaja were absent for a while in 1938, and Marinko in 1939, when they were under arrest. Rade Končar joined the Committee in 1940, following the Fifth Conference, and Ivan Milutinović the same year.

If the Committee was unstable in composition, it was even less stable in performance. The absence of the key man, Tito, minimized its central position. But the basic reason for its weakness lay in the fact that the party had not grown sufficiently to require leadership in continuous working session.

Even so, this leadership made very important decisions, without the Paris Central Committee and without Tito.

For example, we decided to participate independently, as the party of the working people, in the parliamentary elections in the fall of 1938. This decision was reached at a meeting in Zagreb: Ribar and I represented Belgrade, and Kraš, Žaja, and Petrović represented Zagreb. The Zagreb representatives hesitated at first, but finally accepted our position. The Slovenians didn't show up at all, and we had no word from Tito in Paris. (He was either in Moscow or about to go to Moscow.) The Slovenians later adopted our position. The Croats, on the other hand, under pressure from certain intellectuals, decided against putting up independent candidates because they felt it would be wrong to undermine the "unity of the Croatian people" when there were good prospects for their autonomy and equality.

"Tagging along with the national bourgeoisie" hurt relations between us and Zagreb. In the spring of 1939, the Central Committee, and Tito personally, attacked the position of the Zagreb comrades as opportunistic. Having concentrated their activities on the trade unions, they had been very slow in setting up party organization.

I hardly knew Žaja. I had seen him only two or three times. He was a worker, with considerable practical sense but no vision. Petrović was very primitive in his views and in his approach. His political thinking was so muddy that we wondered how this man would hold up before the police. Yet there was something positive about him: he came from the lowest stratum of the working class, and no matter where he ended up in life, he would always belong to that class. Both he and Žaja were good union leaders, with all the virtues and faults that we, professional Communists, attributed to these people: slow in making decisions and inclined to compromises, but with an understanding of the immediate problems and needs of the masses.

Josip Kraš was of a similar mold, but he was much more aware politically, more enterprising and dogged. He was totally dedicated to the cause of his class. But he didn't possess the intellectual strength and inner drive needed to make independent decisions. In the final analysis he was no more than a trade-union leader. At a different time in history, a time of legal class action, he would have played a significant role in the party. But in the late 1930's he appeared somewhat old-fashioned—too slow and insufficiently bold in the struggle for the interests of the party.

By Communist standards, Kraš was too stubborn and unyielding. In 1940 he organized a bakers' strike. He was a baker himself. According to the Croatian Central Committee, he made a series of mistakes. Rade Končar, Croatian party secretary, was in such sharp disagreement with Kraš that he recommended his expulsion. Tito was uncertain and, since it involved an old personal friend, he sent me to investigate the matter. For hours on end we criticized Kraš and pressured him to admit his mistakes. It wasn't that he didn't want to do it; he simply couldn't. This emotionally wholesome and strong man finally burst into tears. "Kill me, comrades, but I can't confess to mistakes that I don't see as mistakes." Bakarić and the rest sided with Končar. And I understood that we were dealing with a man who was incapable of grasping the situation. I informed Tito of my findings, and at a Politburo meeting I opposed the expulsion. Tito was pleased to have the matter cleared up, to know that we were not dealing with an "enemy." Kraš received a severe party penalty. His heroic death proved beyond a shadow of a doubt his complete loyalty to his ideals and to his class, in the way in which we Communists understood it.

All three men—Kraš, Žaja, and Petrović—were dropped from the party leadership during the bolshevization period. They were simply bypassed when, in the spring of 1939, Tito finally formed our Politburo in co-operation with the Comintern. Tito had originally picked all three because they were the best men in Zagreb. But he didn't hesitate to drop them when the hour came to replace them with fresh talent.

Tito picked Ranković and me. He knew Kardelj from Moscow, and Marinko and Leskovšek were included because they were workers and prominent party functionaries.

Marinko was a miner from Trbovlje, the largest and most powerful workers' center in the country. We from Serbia, where the movement still revolved around small craftsmen and intellectuals, saw him in a heroic, romantic light.

Leskovšek had drawbacks which, by the standards of the time, were entirely out of keeping with Communist ideals: he liked to drink and he liked women. He was aggressive and bold in only one respect: he hated social democrats—perhaps because he had been one himself, and priests because he had been a Catholic. But he was very popular among the workers, and he treated the party as his own home and only possession. In essence he didn't differ much from us in Belgrade, since he favored decisive moves to build up the revolutionary party, which would take charge of all the activities of the working class.

Marinko was reserved and introspective, with a quiet sense of humor, shy and almost virginal when it came to personal matters. Leskovšek was loud, open, and had a wild sense of humor.

The Central Committee, composed in this manner, made a variety of decisions in all areas of party activity.

In the course of 1939 Kardelj became, next to Tito, the most important member of the Central Committee. This was not by any formal decision. But that is the way it was. The reasons were many. He was closest to Tito, from the days of their emigration, from Moscow. Politically he was the most skilled, possessing vast knowledge. He had taught in the Moscow political schools, and his knowledge of Lenin and Stalin was fresh and complete. In domestic and party affairs he was the most farsighted; he opened up the broadest possibilities, even though his specific prognoses, like everybody else's, proved unrealistic. In that respect he had an advantage over Tito too.

In 1939 this Central Committee evaluated, independently of

Tito, the character of the war that had broken out between Germany and the Western powers. That evaluation was identical to Moscow's. The Central Committee was by then a well-functioning body. It met often and made decisions on all matters. When Tito was not present, it operated as a collective leadership, and discussions were democratic and open, although we never took a vote. If someone expressed an opinion for which he gained little or no support, he would withdraw it quietly. Thus all decisions were basically unanimous. But the 1939 Central Committee was not the same as the 1938 Committee.

In the spring of 1939, at the time of Tito's trip to Moscow, the Paris Central Committee ceased to exist as a formal entity. The difference for us was not a mere formality, however. From then on everything was in our hands and everything depended on our leadership. We no longer expected assistance or advice from any source except, possibly, on rare occasions from the Comintern. Actually, the transfer of the Central Committee to Yugoslavia was a gradual one, which had been going on for some time, but the final decision was not reached until the spring of 1939.

Tito's position in the Central Committee was exceptional: he was the only person in whom the Comintern had confidence, and they recognized the composition of the Central Committee as he envisioned it. He had veto powers, although he never emphasized that. Not only was his word the most decisive, but he didn't tolerate long discussions and arguments, not even when his position was clearly based on ignorance or misinformation. That was the kind of relationship we always had with him. We accepted this relationship out of revolutionary discipline: the Comintern had given us a man in whom they had confidence, and his power and role were therefore exceptional. To oppose him would have meant going against the majority, expulsion from the party, isolation from all revolutionary activity. Though we sometimes grumbled about Tito's self-willed decisions and occasional lack of understanding, it never occurred to us to try to change that relationship.

Of course, the claim of today's official history that Tito had formed the leadership is false. But it is true that he was able to expel anyone he wanted to. Tito's personal power created a sense of discipline, party unity, devotion to the revolution, to the Comintern, to the Soviet Union. We were all pleased to be able to express these feelings for the man who, in spite of certain traces of willfulness, was so deserving as a revolutionary and a fighter for these principles.

No minutes were taken at any of the Central Committee meetings until 1939. At that time Lola Ribar started taking down minutes, and Tito gave exact formulations for all points he wanted recorded. These minutes were recorded on little slips of paper, which Tito kept. I know that some are preserved in his personal archives.

8

In the year 1938 there were still no party organizations in Macedonia and Bosnia. This concerned Tito particularly. We were also worried about the impact of Gorkić's arrest and the conflict with Petko Miletić, especially in Montenegro, where Petko had many followers. The Central Committee instructed the Serbian Regional Committee to make contact with people in those three regions, to send them literature, and help set up party organizations.

In the summer of 1938 I was dispatched to Montenegro, Kosovo, and Metohija. Metohija had a party organization, which was particularly strong in the town of Peć. Activity livened during the summer when students came home for vacation. The head of the organization was Petar Radović. Like most people who felt guilty because they had "witnessed their own weaknesses before the police," Radović engaged in frenzied activity. And like most people who were under Petko Miletić's influence, he kept running into "opportunists" and "liquidators."

My chief task was to explain Gorkić's case and, in this connection, to discuss the factional activity of Petko Miletić.

Miletić had not yet been removed from the party prison leadership, but the conflict with him was growing.

Radović himself was unstable, and factionally tied to Petko. It turned out later that he had not been straight in his dealings with me, and he was expelled from the party. In 1940 rumors reached us in Belgrade that he was working for the police. But that was untrue. He was living under the party boycott, unhappy and withdrawn.

During the war he proved to be one of the most courageous

fighters in the First Proletarian Brigade. In 1944, on the island of Vis, he took his own life. He was then commissar of the newly formed navy. He was apparently afraid that he might be expelled from the party again—this time because of his relationships with women. Ranković had been preparing to talk to him, but never got around to it. Radović was quoted as having said that he couldn't stand another expulsion from the party. In a letter Radović asked his comrades to forgive him, but did not give the reasons for his suicide. He destroyed himself, but he had absolved his revolutionary honor with his heroism and his blood.

The head of the Montenegrin Regional Committee was Jovan Marinović. He arrived from prison with authority given him by Petko Miletić, called a regional meeting, and got himself elected secretary. Blažo Jovanović and Kadja Petričević were also members. In fact, they were the three most important members of the new leadership.

Under Marinović's able leadership the Montenegrin party organization was recovering rapidly and his work would have been beyond reproach had he not been getting directives from prison. This had to end, and Montenegro had to be reoriented to the Central Committee and Belgrade.

The meeting itself, held one summer night in Cetinje, was a painful one. Following my report on conditions in the party, Marinović expressed his support, but without enthusiasm. Kadja was silent. Blažo Jovanović objected openly. "All this is well and good—we are dedicated to the Central Committee—but I don't understand how we can glorify them one day and attack them the next. How am I to explain to people that Petko is no good? I praised him yesterday, and folks were singing songs about him all over Montenegro! And what about Gorkić? Yesterday we were told that we finally had a compact and unified Central Committee, and today we are told that Gorkić is a spy! Today we are told that Petko is the Central Committee; tomorrow that he is an enemy! By God, I don't understand how people can change so suddenly, and I don't know what's going on."

Jovanović and I spent the rest of the night in fierce discussion. Every issue was taken up, although little was said about the work of the Regional Committee.

I had met Blažo Jovanović once before—a thin, pale young man, sporting a black mustache. He had made a good impression on me: dedicated to the movement, and still tied to his peasant background by gesture, speech, and way of thinking. He was the only one who raised objections to my report, but in no way did this cast doubt on his devotion to the party and the Central Committee. In fact, when Marinović was removed from his position as secretary of the Regional Committee, I recommended Blažo Jovanović for the post. Ivan Milutinović seconded it, and the Politburo approved it.

Marinović continued to function throughout 1939. I maintained that Marinović would not turn against the Central Committee, that he was a good and useful party member, even though he continued to maintain contact with Miletić. I had met with him several times in the 1938–1939 period, and every time he had assured me of his devotion to the Central Committee, though he felt that Petko was a courageous and able man. Basically I think that he was telling the truth. In 1940 Marinović was finally replaced, and later expelled from the party.

Marinović always lived under the erroneous impression that I was his chief enemy. He continued to feel that way even after the war, and particularly after 1948. At that time the UDBA (Secret Police) had information indicating a lack of decisiveness in his position on the Cominform. Old doubts floated to the surface; old "antiparty" elements were awakened now that the Central Committee was in trouble again. I can't say that I didn't approve the measures taken against Marinović, but I didn't initiate them. I always believed him an able and sincere man. I ran into him in 1954, following my own conflict with the Central Committee, but he didn't greet me. He still blamed me for all his troubles. I see now that he has finally managed to climb up the ladder. But he is mistaken if he thinks that this automatically means he will play an important role in the present system.

The conflicting impressions I got from the meeting in Montenegro were widened by meetings held subsequently with the party organization in Mostar.

The head of the Mostar organization was an old party member, a certain Pašić, a worker who had served a five-year prison term. He had revived trade unions and reactivated young people within them, but he had avoided the establishment of an illegal organization. He had, of course, set up the local committee, which functioned for the whole region.

I had a meeting with this committee. It was an unusual occasion. We met outside the town, at exactly midnight. We climbed up a steep mountainside. The night was clear and pleasantly cool, following the fiercely hot summer day in Mostar. Even so, we sweated and panted. We kept climbing for almost two hours. Finally we reached a stone tower, a former Austrian fortress.

The Professional

It was a pleasure to greet the dawn on the mountaintop. A sea of stone emerged from the morning mist, growing more immense and hard and quivering as the day advanced. But the first rays of sunshine brought tremendous heat to the bare rock. We scampered from the unbearable heat away into the shade of the walls, until around noon, but that too became hopeless.

I could understand why Pašić had selected this spot for the meeting. From this bare mountaintop we could see all around us and yet not be seen. We were safe here from shepherds and casual vacationers. But we had brought with us only two bottles of water, which vanished in no time. At noon the meeting was over, and we were stuck on this scorching mountaintop. In the endless valleys the air boiled and everything quivered, the rocky hills and the yellow fields. Only the tops of distant mountains stood serene in the white burning sky.

It was on that mountaintop that I understood the nature of our problem with Pašić. His exaggerated conspiracy, which brought us up there to the sun, was proof to me that he intended to steer clear of illegal activity. He insisted that the most important thing was to attract the masses, and I maintained that the masses could not be attracted without a firm illegal organization.

Thirsty, exhausted, oppressed by doubt, I started walking down the hill in the early afternoon to catch my train. But I was certain of one thing: conditions in Mostar were ripe, if not for Pašić, then for some other Communist, to organize a strong group. Pašić and the committee members stayed behind on the hilltop. If anyone were to spot this lonely "mountaineer" in the middle of a summer day he would think him a maniac. But I didn't worry about that. I must admit, though, that I had never before, or since, attended such a meeting.

As time went on, Pašić avoided contact with our Sarajevo comrades, allegedly because he was not sure of them. But it turned out we had other differences as well. Finally, he was expelled for refusing to accept party discipline. He was killed during the war, fighting bravely. In spite of his "weaknesses," he was without doubt dedicated to the party and to his class.

The Regional Committee for Bosnia was in its initial stages.

On the basis of a Central Committee decision, I selected two of the best party members from Belgrade University, Cvijetin Mijatović and Uglješa Danilović, and sent them to their native Bosnia in 1937 to work for the party. The Regional Committee for Serbia financed their mission. They received monthly salaries, not high, but regular. I was their contact.

Mijatović was aggressive and dogged, passionate and tough, Danilović cautious and soft, indefatigable and conscientious. Danilović was also given more to meditation than Mijatović, although the latter was entranced by literature, which was in some contrast to his coarse physiognomy and common expression.

They ran into formidable difficulties on that scattered and uncultivated territory. There was no organization except for a few sympathizers here and there, too frightened to give them food and shelter. Their visits to Belgrade, where the movement was thriving, refreshed their spirits. Though I was their contact, Lola Ribar usually attended our meetings, because we had to thrash out problems relating to young people.

In 1939 we sent Isa Jovanović, a worker and Ranković's brother-in-law, to join them, mostly to strengthen the working-class composition of the leadership. He was a fairly common man, not very bright, who had not stood up too well before the police. Awkward and timid in political action, he showed no signs of the working-class man's psychology, astuteness, class awareness, or collective spirit. Even so, he was a reinforcement for Bosnia: he had benefited from experience in an advanced organization, and in a simple-minded way he was totally dedicated to the movement.

In 1940 Borislav Kovačević was also dispatched to Bosnia. He had little initiative, but he was bright and intelligent. He lent a certain calm and seriousness to the committee.

Thus, over an extended period of time, a Regional Committee for Bosnia and Hercegovina was created.

In the autumn of 1940 I myself visited Bosnia, by which time the Regional Committee had already been formed. They needed help in purging the organization of antiparty groups, particularly with Vujasinović, who resisted illegal work and firm ties with the Committee. My talks with them led to a temporary solution: establishment of an organization in Zenica, where Vujasinović worked. We also got rid of Berta Papo and other opponents of the new party line.

When war broke out, the organization in Bosnia and Hercegovina was still undeveloped, but it was strong and pure. Many towns had no organizations, which was typical of the regions where the uprising caught on the most rapidly. In this respect Drvar was an exception. When the war came, Djuro Pucar became head of the Committee. He had just been released from prison. At first his approach to illegal activity was cautious, but he quickly gained respect in this backward environment.

The Professional

I set off for Macedonia in the middle of the summer of 1939. My very first impressions were painful. In Serbia, in Croatia, and particularly in Slovenia, one felt free in comparison with Macedonia. Dull silence prevailed in cafés and in the street, augmented further by fearful scenes of misery and backwardness. Gendarmes paraded in public places—on trains, at markets, and on the main streets. People were afraid to speak their own language; they were instructed to add the Serbian ending of "ić" to their names.

Skoplje had only two handsome buildings—the Officers' Club and a branch of the National Bank, symbols of money and sabers. An attractive complex of buildings was under construction on the right bank of the Vardar River, mostly one- and two-family homes. But this could not be compared to the "exclusive" neighborhoods which had grown up between the wars in Belgrade and Zagreb. The houses were built with cheap materials, and everything about them was flimsy and improvised. Beyond this was a neighborhood of the old type: wooden gates, fenced-off back yards, and narrow alleys paved with Turkish cobblestones.

The town of Čair, on the left bank of the Vardar, was a picture of misery, filth, and poverty which I had never seen before. The houses were of unbaked brick, put together with mud. There was no sewerage system, or plumbing. Inside, in the small bare rooms with no floors, half-naked children and adults milled around. Except for a few street lamps, there was no sign of modern civilization. The population was a mixture of Turks, Gypsies, Albanians, and Macedonians, a depressed, distorted, tight people.

At the University of Belgrade there was a separate Macedonian group within the framework of the National Students, the legal branch of the Young Communists. As a matter of fact, I had approved the setting up of this separate group. The Communist youth movement was in its initial stages at the University and it had to be given both organizational strength and national (Macedonian) breadth.

While in Skoplje, I stayed in the home of a Macedonian student. He was not a party member, but a reliable sympathizer, who lived with his mother in an old house. The two of us slept upstairs, his mother in the front room. Everything in that little house looked fresh and clean; every object reflected the care of a woman's hand: the large copper dish polished to a high gloss, sparkling glass, clean rugs. The mother knew, of course, that I was an important mysterious man, and that her son was taking a risk in involving himself in forbidden affairs, which are always connected with death in this country. But having set fear aside, she surrounded us with such quiet, humble care that for a moment I felt I was in my own mother's house, but without the Montenegrin noise and ostentation. Her son ran numerous small errands for me, took messages back and forth, arranged meetings. We talked late into the night, and he passionately absorbed the stories of Communism and the Soviet Union told him by this "all-knowing" revolutionary, who might even have been in contact with the inaccessible Central Committee. We always met at the beach, never in town, for reasons of conspiracy. This same student later joined the party and became very active. After the war he became a high UDBA functionary in Macedonia.

There were two men in Macedonia on whom I could rely: Duško Popović and Blažo Orlandić. I had met Popović in prison, and Orlandić in Belgrade.

Duško Popović came from a Serbian family, but he had adopted the Macedonian manner in his speech, his way of life, even in the most modest, tragic, and warm constraint so characteristic of this people. He had been arrested in an earlier raid and his stand before the police was rather poor, but he was highly ethical and I felt I could count on him. He deserves credit for the organization of the student movement. Blažo Orlandić was a Montenegrin, overly sensitive, narrow-minded, and courageous, even by Montenegrin standards. He was supposed to be my main contact. In fact, everyone thought him the major figure, and everyone turned to him for advice. But he lacked emotional and political depth, and he didn't have the ability to lead. However, at the beginning he was the only suitable person, because he was energetic and tough.

In addition to these two, there was also an active worker at Čair. After the war I came across a photograph of him: his name was Pitu and he had become a national hero. He lived in a cottage at Čair, except that his was cleaner than most. He had one of those elongated and emaciated Turkish physiognomies, so common in the Balkans, which reflect the continuous pleasure of tobacco-smoking and a deep concern with the evils of this world. In his case, this expression also reflected the profound and hopeless misery into which he had been born. His laughter was painful, and his faith in the better life that Communism would bring the poor had no limits.

I used these three men to form a local committee, which would gradually take over the organization of all of Macedonia.

The Skoplje organization was in its initial stages. I called on a couple of cells, I met with each party member individually, and discussed with them future possibilities and assignments. I was there for a total of ten days. The heat was unbearable. I informed the leading comrades about Gorkić and Miletić. There was no problem.

Mitra met me at Lake Ohrid, as we had planned. We lived for ten days in intense and powerful joy, surrounded by the miraculous blue water, sky, and the sun, in a simple, friendly, worm-eaten room of an old cottage, eating cheap southern food, breathing in the smell of fish from the streets and the lake, and enjoying the evening breeze that came from some unfathomable distance.

9

Psychological studies might have brought out the underlying personal motivations behind the struggle for a new sexual morality which we leading Communists launched in 1937. When I say "personal motivations," I refer to us "betrayed" men, including both Ranković and myself, each one in his own way.

Ranković just barely knew his wife-to-be, Andja, when she started writing to him, following the naïve concept that each comrade in prison should have a girl waiting for him. Eventually she became his fiancée. As soon as he was released from prison they were married. However, even this serious and fairly simple girl got caught up in the rather facetious approach to love that had taken hold among many Communists as the dictatorship shattered their ranks and their hope for a speedy victory.

We had inherited from the earlier phases of the Socialist and Communist movement the view that loyalty in sexual relations was a petit-bourgeois prejudice, based on proprietary relations—treating one's husband or wife as private property, and children as means for the preservation of property. Of course, we believed that the church acted as an agent of the ruling class in strengthening such "proprietary" morals.

For a movement that was building a radical image for itself, it was of course essential to shed the traditional morality and life style. Chastity and loyalty were considered, if not counterrevolutionary, then certainly old-fashioned, bourgeois. In deference to socialism, one had to get rid of these notions as fast as possible. Young people often made their choice on the basis of this very premise.

These concepts and relations were in continuous conflict with the simple human instinct for orderly, clean, and close relations in love and in marriage. Life itself imposed a simple and eternal human morality. And thus a new type of relationship was in the making: free in attitude and word, but with a secret "non-Communist" need for maximum fidelity. Thus there were many couples who lived together for a number of years, although they claimed they were always ready to part if . . . Such couples had a strong bond even though they were not legally married. In fact, their relations were often closer and warmer because they were based on emotional and ideological factors rather than on material ones.

These personal developments played a role in the formulation of a new position on the sexual life of Communists. But more important was an immediate political goal, related to a broader transformation: the evolution of a new Communist image, the revolutionary of the new type—an evolution already under way for two decades.

For this new revolutionary, ascetic sexual relations between Communist men and women were as essential as adopting the Leninist theories. It also meant doing away automatically with all petty intrigues and hatreds within the party. We strongly believed we were creating a new man and a new revolutionary—open and sincere in his relations with his comrades.

A change of partners was permitted only if relations between a man and a woman had become insufferable. All other "deviations," such as having relations simultaneously with two persons or a casual affair with one person, were considered cardinal sins.

Of course, the end result was by no means the idealistically pure relationships we had hoped for. In many cases, it simply meant that, being only human, Communists now had to conceal their sins. Even so, we did achieve something: a greater concentration by Communists on the revolutionary struggle, fewer affairs within the Communist ranks, and, above all, an enormous increase in the power of the leadership, which now had the authority to expel people from the party for serious "errors" in their relations with the other sex. Since many people were vulnerable to such charges, particularly when they first joined and had to dispense with their "petit-bourgeois" habits, they developed a sense of guilt—they could not be open with the party because if they were open they risked expulsion.

Beginning in 1937 we gave out only small party penalties, or none at all, for such violations. We were not particularly consistent, and our decisions often had a lot to do with how damaging a case was to us politically. Not even among the leadership were the principles of sexual chastity followed consistently—at that time, or at the time, for that matter. In this respect there were always high functionaries who were very free. As time went on, the principle was qualified more precisely: no Communist should do anything damaging to the party in his private life—sexual or otherwise. By and large we adhered to this principle.

Also, our attitude on the question of relations between Communists and non-Communist or "bourgeois" women was uncompromising. Djordje Jovanović once remarked humorously that the party had forbidden Communists to "caress" bourgeois women. The new rules also affected those who wished to avoid conflict with the party over their sexual activities by being absolutely fair with women inside the party, but enjoying a certain freedom with women outside it. We were a little more lenient here, and we would let them get away with it until such a case became a problem for the party.

I was the chief ideologist in drafting the new moral code, but Ranković was the one who adopted it and relentlessly carried it out. The rest followed suit. The Serbian organization was far ahead of the Croatian in this respect, and even more so of the Slovenian. Its influence slowly spread to the entire party. Ranković and I had thus formulated a policy that ultimately emerged as a general component of the entire Yugoslav Communist movement.

Ranković was away from Belgrade when the Belgrade University party organization uncovered information concerning the sexual exploits of a certain Paternoster.

Paternoster was one of the most spirited and aggressive of our students. In encounters with the fascists and the police he was among the most courageous and the most imaginative. Being willful and undisciplined, he had never joined the party but the party treated him as one of their own, and he accepted this. Fair, handsome, and masculine, Paternoster was a strange mixture of the bright and spirited, on the one hand, and the morbid and unhappy, on the other. He came from a poor, demoralized family; his mother may have been a prostitute and his brother a police agent. It seemed that he wanted to make up for this shame by his courage.

It turned out he was having two affairs at the same time, with two girls from Čačak, good friends, and both of them party members. He was involved in other relationships as well, but it was the rivalry of these two women that got the party embroiled in his case. We initiated an investigation, and in the process uncovered many similarly complex cases, full of lies, half-truths, plots, and counter-plots. We decided to impose a boycott on Paternoster. The determining factor was his failure to keep his promise to stick to one of the two girls, or, rather, the fact that he made the same promise to both girls.

The boycott of Paternoster produced a violent reaction among the party membership in general, mostly because of his reputation for excellence and his popularity as a fighter. The students felt that we did not have the right to judge him; he was not a party member, and the nonparty student group had not even been consulted. The student committee found itself isolated, and appealed for my help.

The meeting at the student cafeteria was attended by a large number of Communists and sympathizers. It was legal. I spoke at length about the "new morality." I also touched on Paternoster's case, proposing that the boycott be set aside, and that he be given one last chance for self-improvement. This was our only choice, if we were to get the committee out of an impasse and remain loyal to the principles of the new "Communist morality." My proposal was received very well by the student body, less well by the committee.

The ice began to melt around Paternoster. But before long he got himself into a similar predicament. A new investigation was ordered. At around that time he went on an excursion with his comrades. On the way back he fell off the train, "accidentally," and was killed instantly. That was the public story, but we knew better.

This incident produced considerable unrest among Communists and their sympathizers. But we took a firm stand: Paternoster had been in the wrong, he hadn't improved. Personally I didn't feel the least guilt over this case. Perhaps I could have prevented his final step, but we couldn't have given in to him indefinitely. We had to protect party interests.

The Paternoster case, which cost us Communists a lot of energy and nerves, and for which we risked losing a great deal of influence, was a turning point in our struggle against casualness in sexual relations. Defending Paternoster was the equivalent of turning against the party. I am not denying that this approach offended certain human sensibilities. But it was clear to me from the start that human sensibilities had to be sacrificed to those other, party, sensibilities. Moreover, I defended the thesis that there were no interests superior to party interests. Devotion to the party meant giving it everything. True Communists carried this premise out in both their personal and party lives.

In 1937 Mitra had a painful and complex experience, from which she emerged a good Communist. She got into a fight with Bosa Cvetić over the management of the women's groups, and the character of personal relations. As often happens in such cases, there was a lot of gossip, sharp criticism, bitter accusations, and blind hatreds on all sides. Both women were well-known Communists. Mitra had many advantages over Bosa: she was more intellectual, better educated, and brighter. But Bosa enjoyed the reputation of a good fighter, having made an excellent stand before the police. The two of them were magnets around which many women gathered, and men as well. The danger of a split was imminent.

The case had to go before the party commission.

Mitra's enemies used her private life against her. They brought up her behavior when I was in prison. It was a thing of the past, when different standards prevailed, yet because of our struggle against "sexual freedom" it appeared to be pertinent. At heart Mitra felt that she had erred against the party, because the party had given her freedom of choice, and against me, as a man. I myself was in a ridiculous and undignified position, not because I was living with a woman who had once been unfaithful to me, but because I had covered up for such a woman. This issue became a topic of endless and painful discussions in which I tried to reduce the whole issue to a simple fact that we were not good enough Communists because we allowed personal problems to occupy so much of our time. I don't want to underestimate the problems, but there was something "bourgeois" in them when isolated from the party. Mitra's lack of "sincerity" in personal matters, or, rather, her refusal to confess "everything" to me, I interpreted as proof of her limited "party awareness." Obviously, I may have also been reacting as a jealous male. But that was not essential. I was not jealous by nature, although I couldn't forget the innocent beauty of our former love. Communism had taught me that jealousy was a proprietary prejudice. The core of the matter was that I sensed a certain resistance in Mitra, something held in reserve, a world of thoughts and feelings which were her own, not belonging to Communism or to me.

Before her appearance at the commission, the two of us thrashed it all out, and she confessed everything, in a mood of uncertainty and passion. Her other relationship was the only one that had relatively deep roots, perhaps because she was faced with a complex moral issue. The man was also a friend of mine, and he had previously taken out her sister. The relationship had become public knowledge and she decided to go with him. But he was forced to leave Yugoslavia, and shortly thereafter I was released from prison. I managed to convince her to be less inhibited with the commission than she had been with me. She should, I said, reveal her very soul. There could be no secrets before the party because we were the party, its living organism.

Ranković was a member of the commission, and a very good friend of mine. Mitra gathered together her strength and told them the whole story. They didn't ask her too many questions. It was obvious that she had not concealed anything.

She received a party penalty and was given an "opportunity to improve." She did.

This was one of the first cases of interrogation and confession.

From that time on she was a good Communist and our relationship evolved without any internal problems. She could now begin to build up her party career, first as an instructor in the cell, then in the Regional Committee, and so on.

However, I had the feeling that she could never overcome a certain inner loathing for what she had been forced to go through, even though she had accepted the party both intellectually and emotionally. I myself had a heavy feeling about it. But I maintained that the party was right, that it was a Communist's duty to reveal every last feeling.

Mitra's case was a new experience for us. It was a test of the sincerity, openness, and dedication of party members. Supervision of our private lives was essential if we were to have a new party and a dedicated membership. It didn't mean constant supervision, but rather the *right* to supervise whenever the party's interests were threatened, interests for which we leaders stood and which we defended in the name of the entire membership.

10

In the winter of 1938–1939, Rodoljub Čolaković, a member of the Paris Central Committee, turned up in Belgrade for a brief visit. I had not known Čolaković personally, but I had heard of him, under the pseudonym of "Rudi." Čolaković moved about so cautiously that he seemed positively frightened.

He introduced confusion into our activities, and he and I got into an argument almost immediately.

His visit was actually contrary to Tito's instructions that all decisions were to come from the national leadership and from Tito personally. Yet Čolaković spoke in the imperative, in the name of a supreme body whose rights and authority we no longer recognized. One might have concluded from Čolaković's position that things had finally started moving in Moscow, and that the Paris Central Committee was again authorized to run the party.

Ranković and I were unhappy about the situation, although we had agreed to obey the Paris Central Committee, and Rudi, its representative. Ranković left all negotiations with Čolaković to me, in an effort to avoid meeting him.

In my first conversation with Rudi I sharply criticized the Paris Central Committee for not having purged the factionalists, and I gave him a full report on Labud Kusovac. He was unfamiliar with the Kusovac-Miletić situation, which strengthened my belief that he knew little about party life. He was trying to protect the authority of the Central Committee, but he was not very convincing.

The opinion I formed of Čolaković during this visit remained essentially unchanged through the years. He liked theory, but he had no depth and no strength. His book, *A Primer of Leninism*, was withdrawn because of certain "errors." He dogmatically absorbed theory from the Moscow party schools, quick to stuff reality into its forms. His knowledge of Marxism was considerable, if uncreative and bookish. But he was an honest man and he had a genuine feeling for the earth, the countryside, the language and customs of his native Bosnia.

In 1940 Čolaković returned to Yugoslavia to legalize his position. The police had not beaten him, and yet he behaved badly. He confessed to having been in the Soviet Union, which meant automatic expulsion from the party, because it opened the motherland of socialism to the charge of interfering in the internal affairs of other countries. He wasn't readmitted until the war broke out.

Paris was in no hurry to settle accounts with Petko Miletić, perhaps because the Comintern hadn't yet solved the problem of our Central Committee. But at home our attitude to Miletić grew more hostile every day.

At Ranković's and my suggestion, Tito agreed to replace the old party leadership with a new one. He also accepted our proposal of persons to be included in the new leadership, providing only that Moša Pijade be included, to which we had no objections. The new leadership was composed of Pijade, Popivoda, and Paunović. Popivoda was the least controversial. Ranković and I were less than enthusiastic about Moša Pijade. He was a bitter opponent of Petko Miletić, and thus we feared that he would create more tension. Ranković didn't much care for Paunović. He thought him "indecisive" in intraparty struggles. Tito didn't know either Popivoda or Paunović. Actually, the least controversial of the three—Popivoda —proved to be the worst: for a long time he couldn't accept charges made against Petko Miletić. He gave Pijade no end of trouble with his uncertainty and his complexities. Taking advantage of his naïveté, Miletić's followers attempted to form a new opposition and create new problems. Popivoda was eventually replaced by Mirko Bukovac, a simple worker recommended by Ranković and me.

The majority of the Communists in prison were under Petko's influence, and to them the naming of Moša Pijade, his chief opponent, "opportunist," "liquidator," and "capitulator," to head the party organization came as a complete surprise.

It has been generally assumed that Moša Pijade deserved a great deal of credit for the liquidation of the Miletić group. Of course, this wasn't true. It was impossible to get rid of Petko Miletić and his influence from inside prison. This is not to deny that Moša Pijade performed tremendous services in prison: resolutions, reports, investigations, conferences day and night. His manner was sometimes overly temperamental and biting, but he acted nevertheless, exercising tremendous influence in leading people away from Miletić.

Every week we were overwhelmed with his voluminous reports, which I just barely had time to read.

Pijade found out that Miletić was organizing an escape from prison in order to convene a party congress, seize the leadership, and "save" the party. There were also rumors that Miletić's people had tried to poison Pijade, that they were all a bunch of homosexuals, and other such accusations.

At the meeting of our Central Committee in the spring of 1939, a conflict arose over Petko Miletić between Tito and Kardelj, on one side, and me, on the other. Tito said Miletić was a Trotskyite. I associated this term with spies and provocateurs; I knew Petko personally, and I simply couldn't accuse him of such deeds. Kardelj countered by saying that there was, after all, no essential difference between the Trotskyites and Petko Miletić. Ranković was quiet, as usual, and held his opinion to himself. We all agreed, though, that Petko should be expelled from the party; and he was expelled as a Trotskyite.

However, that didn't automatically put an end to Petko Miletić. Upon his release from prison he came to Belgrade, where he wanted to meet with the members of the Central Committee. We finally decided that he should meet with Lola Ribar, a Central Committee member, whom Petko didn't know personally.

I also attended this meeting. Lola Ribar lectured him on his factionalism and antiparty activities. Ribar was young, and he looked young. He was fashionably dressed, and had bourgeois manners —I recall him putting out half-smoked cigarettes. Petko took a dim view of all this and was obviously disappointed that such a man was on the Central Committee. This proved to him, beyond a shadow of a doubt, that the party leadership was in a state of complete disintegration. He was guarded in his statements and demands.

Shortly thereafter he left for Moscow, via Istanbul, with a passport forged by Ivzija Cavtović, one of his followers.

Petko's presence in Moscow was awkward for Tito. A Comintern and NKVD agent, Belov, now known as Damyanov, President of the Bulgarian Presidium, tried to help him out. Petko was received by the Comintern, to which Tito objected. His case was not resolved until a photocopy of his interrogation, which I had sent through our Paris contacts, reached Moscow. According to Tito, Petko was then immediately arrested.

I always felt that, upon his return from Moscow, Tito suspected that it was I who had helped Petko get his passport. Perhaps in Moscow's atmosphere of persecution and suspicion, Tito remembered my reluctance to believe that Petko was a Trotskyite. He didn't know who prepared Petko's passport, or that it was I who had dispatched the report of Petko's interrogation to Moscow. As was his custom, Tito never apologized for these suspicions, but silently admitted later that he had been wrong.

After Tito's trip to Moscow, which took place, if I recall correctly, in the fall of 1938, we learned little about the arrests of Yugoslavs there. Tito had been told not to discuss the purges. He mentioned a few things to Kardelj, but very little to us. However, from his second and third trips, in summer 1939 and spring 1940, we learned a great deal more. Tito gave us the official version, which, by and large, is what he believed.

The Central Committee declared that all those arrested in Moscow would be expelled from the party, by which time many of these men had been in prison for two years, and others had been executed. Their expulsion was not even discussed at the Central Committee meetings; Tito simply made announcements in *Proleter*. Not that any of us objected. On the contrary, we were delighted that the Soviet Union had dealt a final blow to the emigrants. This was particularly true of Tito and Kardelj, who were more familiar with the situation in Moscow.

Tito didn't play an important role in the Moscow purges. That was his good fortune. The major wave was over, and he was out of danger, even if he had given some character references that hadn't quite corresponded to those of the NKVD.

On his first trip to Moscow Tito had been asked to write a number of character references for the emigrants. He told us, for example, that he had given Vladimir Čopić, a former party secretary, a good reference. Even so, Čopić was arrested. He felt that Filip Filipović, a factionalist, should never have been arrested, because he was too old. On the other hand, he told us that Flajšer, who represented our party in the Comintern, was a spy for the Yugoslav police, and that Kotur, an outstanding and fairly popular Yugoslav Communist, operated a secret radio station for a foreign government. He believed that Gorkić was an agent of British Intelligence, based on the "fact" that Gorkić had spent a couple of days in British jails. We also believed all of these stories. They were simply versions of what NKVD agents had passed on to Tito as confidential information. Tito may not have believed all he was told, but he certainly accepted the basic premise that factional activity was connected with espionage, that it benefited the enemy, primarily Hitler's Germany and Japan. We all adopted this position. The adoption of this view coincided with the victory of Tito's group in the party, the Trotskyist trials, the final rise of Stalin to power, and the imminent danger of war.

We were proud of our loyalty to Stalin, of our consistent Bolshevism. Becoming a Bolshevik was the ultimate aim of each party member, and in our eyes Stalin was the incarnation of everything Bolshevik.

Even so, we, particularly Tito, were aware that the purges had been carried to excess, that some people had been punished more severely than they deserved. After his second trip to Moscow Tito told us that the Secretary of the Comintern, Dimitrov, had admitted to excesses, but claimed that they had been necessary—to obtain a chunk of wholesome meat one had to cut away much that was rotten and decomposed.

The publication in *Proleter* of the names of the enemies, the rumors of arrests in Moscow, turned Ljuba Radovanović away from the party. He refused to accept the charges that Sima Marković was an enemy who deserved imprisonment. Old controversies suddenly flared up again. The efforts to gather together all Communist groups came to an end. We believed ourselves to be the most consistently Bolshevik group. And we were. It was the year 1940, and at Ranković's and my suggestion, the Central Committee expelled Ljuba Radovanović from the party.

That was virtually the end of the Sima Marković group.

The Central Committee was also threatened by the Marić-Baljkaš group in Split. Marić was an émigré in Paris who had worked with Kusovac, while Baljkas was an old and respected Communist leader in Dalmatia. Vicko Krstulović, a worker from Split, was outstanding in his efforts against this group, and he won Tito's admiration in spite of his poor stand before the police. This group was finally defeated in 1940.

11

As the dissatisfaction of the masses grew, so did our leadership role among them. We saw this as proof of Lenin's theory that the party strengthens itself through purges of opportunist elements. Indeed, the party organizations were growing stronger. Large-scale police raids had practically stopped. People were standing up better in police interrogations. Continuity was insured.

Our influence among the masses was still limited, but our presence was being felt. Our participation in political action far exceeded our numbers. The major source of our strength was the students. In Serbia there were few strikes. However, most of the trade unions had come under our influence or fallen into our hands. The central union organs were still controlled by the Socialists, but this was more because of their legal standing than because of their actual power. There were, of course, more strikes in Croatia and Slovenia, but political activity in Serbia was more lively. Until 1939, we had little effect on events, but, rather, merely projected ourselves into them. Someone else would call a meeting, and we would interject our slogans. We attended regime meetings, with the aim of obstructing them. We also took advantage of various international events, particularly visits by foreign statesmen.

Serbia had strong traditional ties to France, and with the threat of Hitler's Germany in the air, huge throngs greeted the French Foreign Minister on his official visit to Belgrade. Our own people were among the thousands lining the streets. But our antifascist and anti-German slogans injected a rebellious tone into the welcome. The police had to intervene. Several of our own people were arrested, but they were released almost immediately to avoid scandal.

Lola Ribar and Milovan Matić, who were active in the student peace movement centered in Paris, established contact with French officials in Belgrade. I can't say I was exactly pleased with these contacts but because of their practical advantages I tolerated them.

Nothing in the past had ever stirred the Serbian people as profoundly as Premier Stojadinović's concordat with the Holy See. Religion played an important role in this reaction, but basically the people cared little for their religion and their church. Fighting the concordat meant for them fighting the reactionary regime, the church, the pulpit, and the faith. The most reactionary nationalists were also involved because the Serbian idea was threatened. The situation was confusing in every respect. Masleša and I had our first skirmish over this issue. He opposed our participation in this struggle because it was reactionary. Maček was altogether passive. The Serbian leaders in the United Opposition were also inactive. Masleša felt that it was wrong for us to be at the tail end of the nationalist-chauvinist campaign. Our participation would not gain us leadership, or give us influence over the masses—because of our limited strength and the religious nature of the conflict.

My own arguments were much less subtle. I cited the example of the Russian workers' demonstration of January 9, 1904, led by Father Gapon, in which the Bolsheviks participated. My second argument—and the more powerful one—was that we Communists had to be at the side of the masses, with our own slogans and positions, regardless of our strength. In any case the issue was not basically religious, but national—submission to fascist Italy and the strengthening of reactionary forces.

But Masleša was not convinced. He only gave in when he realized that I would not yield. Ranković quickly agreed with me, which was always true when it came to political decisions.

It was summer and a lot of people were away on vacation. Even so we were able to gather together a couple of hundred workers and students for the confrontation between the bishops.

In fact, our participation had little influence. The regime grew frightened when it realized the depth of popular dissatisfaction. Stojadinović pulled back halfway. It was not a Communist victory, but the experience helped us revise the narrow view that Communists should take part only in strictly class conflicts. And the people realized that, even though we Communists were atheists, we were against the concordat, against fascism, and aware of the threat it posed to our national survival.

Our participation in the welcome given to Dr. Vlatko Maček on his arrival in Belgrade was based on similar calculations. It was one of the most magnificent spectacles of mass action and mass passion.

The Serbian contingent of the United Opposition had invited Maček to come to Belgrade. The idea was to demonstrate that only the democratic parties could establish contact with the Croatian people. Unfortunately, the agreement with Maček—a feeble communiqué—was only a faint echo of the mood and the energy of the masses.

Indeed, Belgrade, so full of chauvinism during the concordat crisis, greeted the Croatian leader with an unselfish enthusiasm that couldn't have been imagined in Zagreb, even at the height of Maček's political power. It was not the frivolous and organized enthusiasm of children in national costume, but, rather, the spontaneous commotion of simple people brought together by a genuine desire for freedom. Many had come from all over the country.

In this avalanche of people, we Communists practically got lost, and our slogans and speakers went almost unnoticed.

I watched the demonstration from the office of Dr. Julka Mešterović on Svetosavska Street. An enormous crowd of people was working its way up that steep street, toward the building in which Dr. Maček was staying. The double row of gendarmes guarding the building leaned backward, broke, and fell apart. Their uniforms merged with the colorful masses and disappeared. The noise grew louder. Cheering the United Opposition and democracy, they were begging Maček to appear on the balcony. At last he appeared. And as the climax to this rare moment of popular strength and feeling, he delivered one of his typically colorless and ambiguous little speeches.

Maček's speech and the whole false cordiality of the Serbian opposition leaders were old, worn words that had been repeated many times over, fading thoughts, from graying wooden men, all of it in such contrast to the fresh spirit of the masses. But the people followed because there was no one else to follow. The discrepancy between their mood and what the leaders were promising was enormous.

There was one form of political activity that we practiced at the University for a long time: the so-called "cultural evenings" to which students invited leftists, antifascists, and democrats to discuss current political events. Admission was free, and sometimes as many as five thousand people would gather. The speeches were not subject to censorship because the University enjoyed autonomy, but the speakers themselves were nevertheless careful.

Gradually we were gaining momentum among social organizations, particularly among groups of civil servants. I was put in charge of these activities, because it concerned intellectuals and because I was responsible for propaganda and agitation. Leftists were strong in the teachers' unions. They were represented by Miloš Janković. He published, at his own expense, the popular Communist pedagogical line of books under the imprint Budućnost (Future). I knew Janković very well, and I often used his flat as a hiding place. He was somewhat aggressive in his thinking, but unwilling to risk going to prison and being beaten. There was nothing wrong with that. On the contrary, one had to do one's best to avoid it. Such people had to be preserved for legal action.

Moma Marković and Radovan Zogović also worked with this group. Our objective was to bring all leftists in the teachers' union together under one leadership. Dragiša Mihailović, the most active member in the teachers' union, favored legal and public action exclusively, and broader co-operation with bourgeois democrats. We didn't object to that, but we did feel that a firm Communist group was essential, and we made co-operation with other groups contingent on equality for our group and an agreement based on specific antifascist, popular-front programs.

It became obvious that we had to look for support among the young. People like Janković were too slow and cautious, unable to follow the struggle through to the end.

Among the younger teachers the most outstanding was a certain Rakić. He delivered thundering speeches at teachers' congresses, which made him very popular with the still-embryonic left. But his anarchy and lack of discipline made him unsuitable for leadership.

We had to look for new people and we found them. They accepted the party line and adjusted easily to party discipline. That was how I met those many teachers who played such outstanding roles during the uprising in Serbia.

The work with the engineers developed along similar lines. Laza Simić was in charge of the Belgrade group, for which he performed various technical services. He was later wounded while manufacturing grenades according to a formula given to him by a Soviet agent. He was arrested, and executed, along with his wife, who came from a well-known Communist family, the Baruhs.

Our efforts among engineers shifted to a group of Sarajevo engineers led by Slaviša Vajnert. During the uprising he was known as Cica Romanijski. I got together with him in 1940. He was still not a party member—simply because the Bosnian party organization was so weak that it had not yet discovered him. He was tall, fair-haired, Germanic-looking, but with a Slavic softness in the eyes. He gave the impression of careful composure and high culture—the exact opposite of the wildly passionate man he proved to be during the uprising, the man who was able to mesmerize and entrance even the most backward among the Serbian peasant masses.

Thus our activity spread through various organizations and in various forms throughout the country.

The essence of this activity was to form a party group inside these organizations. The task of that group was to gather together all sympathizers, leftists, and radicals. They were to act together and strive to take over leadership.

Indeed, we would never have been able to achieve any degree of success had it not been for the growing atmosphere of discontent and the spiritual and political stagnation of the ruling class. Moreover, the international situation seemed to have confirmed our predictions. The people were seething with discontent, and both the party in power and the parties in opposition were being torn apart by the same kind of anxiety as the man in the street felt, who saw no improvement in sight, while fascism was devouring one country after another. In spite of official optimism, it was Yugoslavia's turn next.

12

The Regional Committee for Serbia functioned uninterruptedly from 1937 until the beginning of the war. Its core, consisting of Ranković and myself, remained unchanged. Vukica Mitrović was a member throughout this period, but her role was a secondary one. Other members came and went as they were needed. There were no basic changes or shake-ups.

Without new people and new methods it would have been impossible to maintain this kind of continuity and the thriving illegal activity of that period.

At the beginning, while the committee was still considered a temporary one, Djuro Strugar was a member. But Ranković and I decided that he was far too young for such responsibilities. At the right moment we transferred him to the local committee. But Djuro had pride, and he was somewhat hurt by this maneuver. Fortunately, he quickly got over it and became an even more passionate revolutionary and disciplined Communist.

Until the war Djuro worked for his relative Savo Strugar, a lawyer, who was obsessed with the solution of the Montenegrin question. To him nothing else mattered. For us young Communists, the national question, including the "Montenegrin problem," was simply an adjunct of our quest for power. But Strugar was closer to Montenegrin federalism than to Communism. He had no use for the United Opposition because it denied the existence of the Montenegrin question. He shunned illegal activity, although he hardly ever refused to meet with high-ranking Communists, and he never refused financial aid to the party.

He thought of his political career in terms of various legal possibilities, which was to our advantage. He wanted to run for people's deputy in the 1935 elections, but was rejected by the opposition and the government. Living in fashionable quarters, earning a handsome income, enjoying the reputation of a Communist obsessed with the issue of Montenegrin national freedom—this was indeed a strong mixture of several people and several epochs in one man.

Even so, Savo Strugar stuck by us Communists. Once people get attached to the Communist movement they cannot ever detach themselves, even if rejected by it. When I became a party member in the early 1930's, Savo Strugar was an eminent Communist. I was still on good terms with him in 1937–1938, but we made fun of his views and pretensions. After that we grew so rapidly that we were in conflict with him.

At first Djuro staunchly defended him, insisting that Savo was essentially an honest man. But as Djuro's involvement with the party grew, he acquired that mentality of exclusiveness toward everything non-Communist and that exaggerated dedication to everything that was so characteristic of that period. Consequently there was a certain parting of ways with his protector. This change coincided with the completion of his legal apprenticeship. Gradually he was becoming a professional Communist—for whom party activity was the sole occupation and the sole source of income. He was aware, more sharply than the rest of us, of Savo's petit-bourgeois attitudes, his pretentions. This was not merely a conflict between two generations, but of two worlds as well. Savo Strugar was still a Montenegrin Communist. Djuro Strugar was simply a Communist. As a man he had no faults. As a Communist he had even fewer. When he was arrested in the fall of 1941, he proved to be a miracle of courage. He left the police no record at all. After endless nights of torture, this tough young man was scooped up on a blanket and transferred to the death house at Jajinci.

Dragiša Mišović, a Čačak physician, was made a member of the Regional Committee by a Central Committee decision. He was very popular not only in his own area, but in the rest of Serbia as well: he attended to the poor free of charge, he was a distinguished intellectual, educated in France, he was warm and decent, willing to co-operate in illegal action, even if he did not actively seek it out.

I set off for Čačak to inform him of our decision. He accepted his appointment to the Regional Committee with dignity. He felt that much of our activity should take legal forms in co-operation with the United Opposition. He was exactly what we needed. He would be of little use to us in illegal action, but indispensable in legal activities and as a contact with other political groups. He was a member of that older generation of intellectuals, educated in the West, who identified Marxism with materialist philosophy rather than with aggressive action, and saw Communism as a new form of humanism rather than a new route to bloody revolution.

He was our candidate in the 1939 elections. Arrested by the police on some feeble pretext, he was detained in Belgrade, and while being transferred to Ada Ciganlija, he was allegedly killed in an auto accident. However, the testimony of police in the prisons after the war revealed that his skull had been bludgeoned and that the accident was staged.

Thus the most popular Communist in Serbia disappeared without ever having attended a single session of the leadership group which was to put into effect his ideals—ideals that were to us greater and nobler than anything ever initiated by man.

Blagojević attended only a couple of sessions. He was accepted upon his return from Spain, on Kardelj's recommendation. At first Ranković was enthusiastic about him, but he quickly cooled off. Blagojević proved to be reserved and intolerant, argumentative and lacking in collective spirit. Except for the fact that he was a worker, there was nothing about the man that qualified him to be a Regional Committee member. Worst of all, he really couldn't get along with anyone. We functioned almost as a family, a unified collective which thought and acted the same way, without necessarily having reached prior agreement. However, Blagojević proved a hero during the uprising. He was killed by the Chetniks in 1941, holding his head high. The Regional Committee was not his element. He preferred open military confrontation to delicate organizational maneuvering.

Upon his return from Spain in 1940, Koča Popović was appointed a member of the Regional Committee, on my recommendation, though I had known him only superficially before he left in 1937.

He came from a rich, though now bankrupt, family, and was a member of a Surrealist literary circle. We always teased him about this latter, particularly since he had a bizarre and intellectual sense of humor. He enjoyed the reputation of being a first-class intellectual among us Communists. He avoided illegal action, but this was out of a sense of its futility rather than out of fear. His trip to Spain meant a final break with intellectual Communism, an acceptance of Communist practices and the Communist movement. He described his superior, a Hungarian, as not very bright but having the advantage of accepting Communism as something simple and natural, in keeping with his way of life.

In the Spanish Civil War, in the superhuman effort of a people new to him, Koča Popović discovered fresh and unexpected beauty. He and I became friends immediately upon his return.

In Spain, and later on in the Spanish refugee camps in France, the situation was the same as in Yugoslavia: party purges; the fight against Trotskyite elements within the party. We maintained illegal contacts with the refugee camps through letters and parcels. Popović said that the Communist party of Yugoslavia was the only party that had successfully organized the mailing of aid to the camps. Something profound and fundamental was stirring within our people.

When Popović returned to Yugoslavia he found the same elements of simplified genuine Communism and simple human beauty, but in a stronger, more concentrated form.

For me personally, his presence was tremendously refreshing. I loved his stories about Spain. I enjoyed the lovely songs in that rich and colorful language, but, above all, I found him intellectually stimulating. Exclusive involvement with party activities, exciting as that could be, was limiting. My close relationship with Ranković was one of joint revolutionary effort, obviously very emotional and deep. But there was no intellectual intimacy, not even with Moma Marković or Svetozar Vukmanović, who were intellectuals. In the final analysis, they were practical party functionaries. My friendship with Radovan Zogović never quite satisfied my need for exchanging thoughts on a wider and more varied plane. Both Zogović and I were intellectual revolutionaries, Marxists. Koča Popović was that too, but he was also witty and charming, he had traveled widely, he knew a lot about music, he was familiar with modern literature.

In 1940 Popović and I took many long walks, often simply for the sake of the walks themselves. In France it was known as "*flâner*," or aimless walking, in which only an intellectual could find deep and intoxicating beauty. Together we prepared *Književne sveske* (*Literary Notebooks*) and the Resolution of the Regional Committee, and a lot of other things as well. He was gradually taking over a great deal of our theoretical and propaganda work.

And then Koča Popović was denounced and arrested. He was denounced by a worker with whom Ranković had put him in touch. Popović in turn revealed Ranković's name after a short beating. Other than that, he told the police only what he "had to," that is, information that emerged "logically" in the course of the interrogation and on which the police cruelly insisted.

As a result, Popović was expelled from the party by a unanimous decision. It was a great blow to us, because we all liked him so much.

I was asked to communicate the decision to him. We met at Alexander Vučo's flat. Of course, he knew why I had asked to meet him. He lowered his dark, intelligent eyes. His ordinarily calm face twitched slightly. I almost burst into tears. But I told him what I had to tell him.

Communicating this decision to Koča Popović was for me a much more painful duty than communicating the same decision to Veselin Masleša for the same reason, some time earlier. In Masleša I mourned an idealistic leader from my youth, a good man, an intellectual pillar of the party. But it was a sorrow I felt for the party. In Koča's case, I felt sorry for myself: I was deprived of a friendship that had fulfilled my intellectual and emotional needs.

I didn't see Koča again until the beginning of the war. He was staying with his "bourgeois" sister in a villa in Senjak, playing cards, engaging in empty talk with people who led small, leisurely lives. When I saw him again, this lively, quick-thinking man was half-dead, heartless, and mindless. I took steps immediately to get him involved in party action. He was definitely our man. We had to help him.

He joined the Partisans at the very beginning of the uprising. Under the pseudonym of Pera Posavski he became a company commander, and there, in the fields and among the peasants, he came alive again.

He had become softer, yet more disciplined. And again his good-natured humor made him popular with the leadership, and won him the right to make jokes at everyone's expense.

He advanced fast. He was a very able commander, although heroism was not his strong point, and he was devoted to the leadership. In his thinking he grew increasingly less independent. He began to enjoy ostentatious comforts. It was as if he had returned to his old bourgeois circle, though it was a new circle of men, men he didn't hate, because they were his own. There was precious little left of his personality, his intellect, and his poetry.

Koča's expulsion from the Regional Committee was an unfortunate incident, which was quickly forgotten in the inexorable logic of party life. Buha's membership, on the other hand, proved a grave error.

Buha became a Regional Committee member on the basis of the rule that there had to be a civil servant on the Committee. He was a bank clerk who happened to have stood up very well before the police. I cannot recall who recommended him. He was a colorless and insignificant person, a poor revolutionary, particularly when it came to questions of life and death. He lacked the strength, like most men, to choose death. Only men who believe in an idea unequivocally are capable of making such a choice. He was not that kind of a man. I felt this way about him even before his monstrous betrayal to the Special Police in 1943.

One day, not long after the beginning of the occupation, Ranković and I were walking down Čuburska Street (today Maxim Gorky Street) in the direction of Južni Boulevard. Ranković had seen Buha a short while before, and he seemed worried. Suddenly, as if reading Ranković's mind, I asked him: "Are you sure Buha stood up well before the police?" He replied that he wasn't at all sure and that the thought was often on his mind. But these doubts remained only doubts, and Buha continued to serve on the Regional Committee.

Miloš Matijević was a member of the Regional Committee for a very short time. He was dropped, but not for political reasons. He had no ambitions; he was simple and steady and utterly dedicated to the cause. He came from a very poor peasant family, and he remained poor. His mother and sister lived with him in a tiny little room in a Belgrade suburb, and depended on his meager earnings for survival. Ranković and I wanted to buy him a pair of shoes, but his feet were so wide that we couldn't find any to fit him.

This man, with his slow reflexes, his seeming ineffectiveness, his ignorance of politics, was the first to penetrate the working masses. It started with his distributing a party pamphlet to workers he knew personally at his factory. Pamphlets had usually been distributed in the streets, dropped in mail slots, or mailed. The effect of his bold action was stupendous: workers actually began seeking out the party. From that time on we distributed our pamphlets inside the factory, in broad daylight. Matijević often said that the further one penetrates the masses the better response one gets. That was true.

His experience proved what we had long suspected: we had to look for new party cadres among the workers. We had to make a bold break with our small group of enlightened artisans, trade unionists, and petit bourgeois.

Matijević was fond of Ranković and considered him his leader and his superior. He expressed the thought simply—it was like recognizing someone's physical superiority. Ranković, for his part, acknowledged this relationship. There was nothing condescending or insulting in Raković's behavior. It was a natural and respectful relationship on both sides, a friendship that remained unblemished for many years.

During the occupation Matijević was arrested and executed. He stood up courageously. He gave in on certain small charges, but never revealed any names.

Radoje Dakić became a Regional Committee member quite late in the game.

He was one of the new workers we had discovered. He had been a party member prior to our discovery and he had played a prominent role in the trade unions, but it was under our leadership that he grew and developed. A Montenegrin, he seemed to be a typical industrial worker, disciplined, decisive, with a strong feeling for order and cleanliness. Like most Communist workers, he liked to study theory, and, like most of them, he had very little talent for it. He made his mark with his persistence and strength. He loved people in a simple direct way, as a child loves his family, and not in the abstract way so characteristic of politicians, and of so many Communists.

When the war started he was in Montenegro. After our withdrawal he remained with the Partisans as Secretary of the Regional Committee, and he performed his duties staunchly under very difficult circumstances. His sentimental attachment to Montenegro must have suffered when he saw his people rising against the Communists under Chetnik leadership. Thus this bright and tireless fighter became embittered. At the same time he was succumbing to an illness, and quickly wasting away.

Dakić was typical of a new generation of worker revolutionaries —bold, simple, uncomplicated. They began joining in 1938 and were extremely pleasant to work with. They grasped things quickly and simply. There was something in them that the enemy could not bend or change. These people would win or die.

Vukica Mitrović was not a worker, although we sometimes insisted she was—to improve the social composition of the Regional Committee. She was also from Montenegro. She had attended Teachers' College, working in a factory at the same time. All of her family was Communist, but Vukica stood out with her fanatical dedication and retiring manner. When we got to know her better, we realized that she was very observant but too shy to express it. In Moscow she had experienced a great disappointment. While attending the party school, she got involved with a "ladies' man," who left her after a brief affair. Back in Belgrade she was arrested and severely tortured by the police. Gradually she recuperated and recovered her nerves, and she was very happy with her man in 1940 and 1941.

When it came to carrying out revolutionary assignments, there was something hard and unbending in this quiet, unobtrusive woman. At the end of 1941 she was arrested, and, needless to say, she disclosed nothing. On the other hand, her brother Ratko put himself in the service of the police. When the two of them were brought face to face, and he tried to persuade her to give in, she spit in his face. She was so weakened by police tortures that there was hardly anything left of her to take to the execution: a handful of bones and skin with wild dark eyes.

Vukica's martyrlike death upset us very much. When Mitra and I had a daughter, we named her Vukica, in memory of this courageous woman.

Spasenija-Cana Babović joined the Regional Committee upon her release from prison. She had stood up heroically before the police and we admitted her immediately.

She was unequivocal in carrying out Regional Committee decisions, but she never developed politically.

In public appearances, she spoke loudly and with a pathos for which she had to prepare ahead of time. She didn't much care for people in spite of her cheerful disposition and her jolly loud laugh. Her love was a "party" kind of love, if I may say so: she looked after her comrades and was concerned about their well-being in a head-of-the-household kind of way, more as a parent than as a friend.

She was a little on the heavy side, but fresh, with bright blue eyes, and beautiful. As a good Communist, she accepted the new party moral code, but she craved more freedom. After all, she had belonged to a somewhat different era. Her husband had died in prison. She had loved him, although she never forgave him his weak stand before the police, or the jealousy he expressed, justifiably, in his letters. She had gone to the Soviet Union in 1934 or 1935 to be educated. She didn't learn much, but she became more decisive and more disciplined.

Tito and Kardelj didn't much care for her. They knew her from Moscow, and Kardelj had good reason for a certain reserve. They had visited a Soviet kolkhoz together, and Kardelj had refused to eat the rotten meat served him. She accused him of "bourgeois" behavior. The matter got so out of hand that a report on it reached the Comintern. Kardelj admitted his mistake—just to get them off his neck, he later explained. But Cana was impossible. She attacked a certain Maslarić and me for our refusal to understand the motherland of socialism. Maslarić was stubborn. He refused to give in. "I'll eat shit for the revolution, if I have to, but not that rotten meat!"

Thus Tito was pleasantly surprised when Cana delivered a fairly calm and straightforward report at a consultation meeting of the Regional Committee held March 27–April 6, 1941. That was the brightest moment in her career and her greatest achievement. Ranković was in Zagreb working with Tito and Kardelj. I didn't want to take on the duties of the Regional Committee Secretary in his absence and I insisted the position be given to Cana. This awakened in her a sense of initiative. She asked for my help in preparing her report for the consultation. I advised her to speak without her usual rhetoric and helped her organize the material.

During the war she continued to make life complicated—harassing everyone with various tests of "party devotion."

Strangely enough, this courageous woman found air raids very hard to take. In fact, she was beside herself with fear. Also, she loved owning many dresses, a ridiculous idea under our circumstances. During the war her desire for life's finer amenities took the form of carrying coffee beans in her rucksack.

After the war she was much the same, which may prove that people basically never change—certain traits come to the fore, depending on circumstances.

Blagoje Nešković joined the Regional Committee at the end of 1940. I had been against this, but Ranković, with Tito's and Kardelj's backing, overruled me. My reasons were simple: he had been passive for some time during the dictatorship. My position didn't reflect any political reservations.

As a party member Nešković was unbending and crude, but not without a certain inner strength. It was very hard for him to change his position to suit the new circumstances. At the beginning, he always rejected new ideas, but accepted them eventually as if he had never opposed them in the first place. This was a result of his rigid thinking and the stubbornness of a man of great physical strength and iron constitution. He got his chance when the war broke out. He was left practically alone in Belgrade to guide the Regional Committee. In Spain he had functioned as a physician, and had distinguished himself by his courage and reliability. We didn't deny this even during our conflict with him over the Cominform resolution.

The Professional

Moma Marković joined the Regional Committee after an unsuccessful attempt to make his way to Spain. He was a steady, practical party worker, willing to accept new ideas, but not particularly decisive in new situations. This revolutionary, who had withstood the enemy's blows so admirably between four walls, was badly suited to battle, not to say cowardly, during the war. Actually, it was not cowardice, but the result of his inability to cope with new situations. And war is full of the new and the unexpected.

He was popular with women, although he didn't quite look the part. He had thin hair, a faded complexion, cold damp hands, but his face was very expressive. He tried to avoid Communist women; if he did get involved, he was no more constant with them than with any other "class." His adventures were a welcome relief in our basically ascetic life.

In contrast to Marković, Svetozar Vukmanović was fast-moving and full of nervous energy.

In 1938 he was released from the army and started looking for a job in the party. I knew a great deal about him, but I didn't know him personally. I felt we had to find something suitable for a man of his energy, and he simply wanted a job. My search went on for some two or three months. He felt that the party had no confidence in him, and he was in a state of great agitation.

Finally, Ranković and I decided to entrust him with leadership of the regional technical staff, which meant building up a printing press, finding people to man it, and organizing the distribution of printed material in the provinces. I myself had been in charge of the operation, without much knack for it, except for inventing new methods on which someone else did the follow-up work.

Vukmanović was the right man for this project. He was quick, bold, and indefatigable. We didn't often run into such revolutionaries.

In 1940, relations between him and Ranković grew exceedingly tense. Ranković was not pleased with something Vukmanović had done, and Vukmanović in turn interpreted this as "lack of confidence." I managed to smooth things over, and we agreed to send Vukmanović to the provinces to set up new organizations.

Vukmanović was fabulously effective in this mission. The operation of our printing press was impossible to imagine without him, and the results of his efforts were evident from week to week. He replaced people promptly and mercilessly when he spotted sloppiness or hesitation. And when he encountered an able person, he was very attentive, even kind. All printing, transportation of material, contacts, passwords were in his hands. We all helped out, but he was the driving force behind it. He quickly became a member of the Regional Committee.

He had no knack for ideology, and was easily carried away by great political dreams. He was a hard-core dogmatic, but more for practical than theoretical reasons. As soon as he discovered that a position was "against the party," he would automatically find it ideologically damaging and hostile. He would flare up suddenly and easily, and his yellow eyes would blink in fury. He didn't care much for food or comfort of any kind. His sole concern was getting his revolutionary assignment done.

Vukmanović was an excellent example of revolutionary energy. But he was ignited by the revolution, and burned up in it. What remained after the revolution was only the shell—soft, indecisive, without faith and ideas.

Ljubinka Milosavljević joined the Regional Committee as Regional Secretary of the League of Young Communists. This emaciated girl, nervous and not at all pretty, was fanatically dedicated to the party cause. Although she had never been arrested, we felt she would stand up staunchly before the "class enemy." She was often put in the awkward position of having to issue directives to people who were older and more experienced than she. Although she never achieved full security in her position, she finally got used to it. Her intelligence was not of the obvious kind; but intelligent she was. She carried out her party assignments with passion and complete dedication.

Most women in the movement, incidentally, were unattractive. In later years the party began to attract a few good-looking women, but very few. I'd say the men were more handsome on the whole.

Ljubinka was unhappy about her looks. Perhaps it was because her relationships with men didn't last very long. She was not promiscuous, but she couldn't stand being alone. She would get distraught over nothing, and she was sensitive to criticism.

Our collective was composed of colorful, diverse people, but we shared an inner striving for a common cause, a fanatic faith and dedication. There was something else as well, and much stronger than anything I have mentioned thus far: a warm camaraderie and love, of a kind customary in traditionalist families and religious communities—the more romantic, the more real; the more blind the belief, the more beautiful. Personal conflicts, differences in character, family background meant little in contrast to this inner link.

Once I said to Vukmanović: "You and I between us make one

good Communist," meaning his practical energy and my fresh ideas. I had a similar relationship with Ranković, Ranković with Vukmanović, and so forth.

We had a problem with the Montenegrins. There were too many of them on the Regional Committee, the local committee, and in all other leading positions. We Montenegrins were particularly aware of this, and it embarrassed us. But one day Ranković, following Tito's example, said that the important thing was not where a man came from but whether he was a good Communist. There were also too many intellectuals on the Belgrade committees, but we took a similar position on this.

Times and people had put together an impenetrable and compact community. The stronger the movement grew, the stronger our emotional and personal ties became. Indeed, the party's close ties with the masses would not have been possible without our own psychological, ideological, and personal bonds.

13

Our organization continued to improve. After two years of hard work, not even a big raid could have restrained us. The police seemed to be paralyzed anyway.

During the so-called "Czech crisis," large numbers of people demonstrated in front of the Czechoslovak Embassy. I myself was arrested and taken to Glavnjača.

The police treated all of us kindly, including Communists, so carried away were they by the patriotic, Slavic enthusiasm of the hour: our brother Czechs were on the verge of fighting a war; we would be fighting the Germans soon ourselves.

But in the course of the night the atmosphere at Glavnjača changed completely. These same people were suddenly transformed into wild beasts. Something serious had happened. Indeed yes: the Munich agreement had been signed. For us Communists it meant the end of the popular front and the coalition between the Soviet Union and the Western democracies. The authorities would take a sharper course with Communists. The bourgeois parties were discredited among us, and their faith in Western democracy was now under attack. But we felt no fear of the police, because we knew we would be able to resist.

The switch in police tactics demonstrated fully what a tremendous blow the Munich agreement dealt to the ruling class and to the general patriotic and anti-German mood that prevailed in the government and all the bourgeois parties. We Communists were the only consistently antifascist party. We realized we were going to be in a different position, but it also made us feel very strong.

I was sentenced to a month in prison, which was the maximum

sentence without a trial. But we engaged a lawyer by the name of
Životić, to buy off part of my sentence, and to have Ranković's sentence of exile to his birthplace altered. Životić's police contact was
Vujković, head of the anti-Communist division, and part of the
money went to him directly. This in no way softened his attitude
to Communism, nor did he slacken his persecution of us, but it
was a crack in the wall at least.

I was taken to the new City Hall. I suspected I would be interrogated, but Vujković started a "political discussion" instead. He was
thrilled by the Munich agreement: the Western powers had finally
recognized the Communist threat. He predicted a general attack on
Russia and the end of Communism. Gradually, we switched the
conversation to the behavior of Communists under torture. He said
that "the club came from paradise," and I retorted that he knew
very well there were people with whom a club didn't work. We
gazed silently at each other. He was threatening me, and this was
my reply. Finally he said: "Yes, indeed, there are such people."

A certain change had taken place in the mood of both of us:
Communists and our opponents. The police were no longer able to
understand our methods. They found themselves isolated. We felt
it, and we became even bolder.

Most police lived and operated in the center of the city. So we
transferred the heart of our operations to the suburbs. Meetings, in
groups of two or three, could easily be held outdoors. This simplified the problem of looking for places to get together. We walked
for months and years, from morning till late at night. I once remarked that for Communism, in our country, feet were more important than heads.

We were also improving our conspiratorial methods. We took
advantage of every loophole in the regime's controls and security.

At Požarevac one of our sympathizers owned a printing press,
and we printed our pamphlets there, including Stalin's biography.
A student helped us transport the material. A relative of his, a police officer assigned to the Belgrade railway station, allowed him to
bring in meat without paying duty. In one suitcase he had meat,
and in another illegal literature.

We needed a car for emergencies and for the transportation of
material. A relative of Marko Orešković, a mechanic, put us in
touch with a certain Franjo, a driver for the Red Cross. The advantage of having a Red Cross car was that customs control never
bothered it on leaving or entering the city. We simply called Franjo
when he was on duty, and gave him an address. We guarded this

car as if it were a precious possession. The person to whom material was being shipped never actually saw it. Franjo would park it in some secluded spot and carry the suitcases from there.

One day Vukica Mitrović and I loaded five or six suitcases in the car, got in ourselves, and off we went. To our surprise, we stopped at customs. I peeked through the window and saw Franjo talking with a gendarme. Then they disappeared. We waited for some time. At last they came back, and we drove off. Franjo said they were old friends and they had decided to have a drink together. That was all.

Franjo was a Croat, who had once been a Communist. Now he was beginning to be active again, but regretted it. Ranković forced the issue; he recanted but continued to function quietly and precisely, "like a German." He was denounced during the war, betrayed by Buha.

The value of his service to the cause could never be calculated.

His wife complained to me in 1953 about her small pension, some 6,000 or 7,000 dinars, not nearly enough to live on. I had the feeling that this woman had no idea of the extent of her husband's services to the Communist party.

Dr. Dejan Popović also helped us out with his car.

He was a handsome, pleasant, cultured man who had two passions: trout fishing and Communism. In the former he sought rest from city life; in the latter he believed he would find the cure for all the evils of modern civilization. Did not Communism mean the elimination from society of everything unnatural and superimposed, making possible the natural course of events, or the birth, at long last, of a completely unencumbered freedom?

Popović never lost his humane attitude toward life, not even during the most brutal war years. He was immersed in his own world, and yet he functioned as an excellent surgeon in the wartime slaughterhouse of men. During the Fifth Offensive, in June 1943, he was captured by the Ustashi in that very Bosnian village on the Drina River that he had so often visited as a fisherman, and there he was butchered. A woman, an eyewitness, said that he displayed a deep inner peace in his moment of agony. Was this a result of his faith in the natural world of beauty and happiness? Or was it the peace and helplessness that come over one when death appears inevitable?

Dejan Popović helped us out in many ways. One day he and I transported several suitcases in his car to Šid, where we handed them over to a physician's family by the name of Vukobratić. Dr. Vukobratić's brother had come down from Zagreb to take the material. The family asked us to stay for dinner, acting throughout as if they knew nothing about our dealings.

They were Serbs, well-to-do people, and they were all executed during the war except for the brother, who lost his life as a Partisan. He had a cottage in the woods near Zagreb, with a radio station through which we maintained contact with Moscow and which Tito often visited.

Transporting illegal literature and important people turned out to be a growing problem as the quantity increased.

Proleter was first published in Zagreb. Later it was done in Belgrade because Belgrade had better technical facilities. By today's standards our publications were extraordinarily primitive. But at the time, we all thought it a great success, and quite a breakthrough, when our May 1 proclamation appeared in red print. Our emblems—the hammer and sickle and the five-pointed star—were also particularly good when printed in red.

Svetozar Vukmanović organized our publishing activities, in consultation with Ranković and me.

The first printing press, operated manually, was run by Niko Vučković in Neda Božinović's apartment. But that proved dangerous because she was known as a Communist. We rented a small house on a side street, at the very end of King Alexander Street (now Boulevard of the Revolution). Blažo Janković and his wife occupied one room, and Niko Vučković the other. Just before the war broke out, we moved into another building (which is now a museum), outfitted to conceal the presses in a special room. The building also served as the Regional Committee hide-out, the only safe place during police checkups.

Niko Vučković was a special kind of Communist. He had little interest in either politics or political theory. And he liked women. Surprisingly enough, although he was not particularly handsome, women liked him too.

His special quality lay in his lack of discipline, his complete lack of feeling for collective action and life. And yet he was totally dedicated to the Communist idea. He had no use for committees or functionaries; he didn't believe in what they said, and he preferred not to listen. But he trusted the functionaries he knew personally, and was willing to carry out their orders. Vukmanović and I were in this category. Left to himself, to do a job for which he was personally responsible, he was excellent. But working with other people was another matter. He hated the cowardice, the small lies and intrigues so inevitable among Communists.

It was he who printed our pamphlets and *Komunist*, which he also wrote and edited, and later *Proleter* as well.

After the war he was expelled from the party because of his casual relationships with women, and at the Third Plenum he received a minor penalty for having disputed the accusation that I was a traitor. He is now serving a sentence in prison for embezzlement, of which I don't think he is guilty.

There was one moment of great love and loyalty in his life. That was the period in which he lived and worked with Brana Perović. Locked up together in that house, they became very close. But circumstances separated them: during the war Brana, who was young and pretty, continued to live in the printing plant, but with Nešković, whom she eventually married.

Mirko Sardelić did political work for us among engineers. He was full of complexes. His father was an epileptic, his brother a schizophrenic. Like the rest of his family, he was extraordinarily sensitive. He had an unusually fine feeling for conspiratorial combinations, but preferred to operate on his own. In this respect, and in his resistance to discipline, he was like Vučković. Sardelić helped us with a great many technical problems, and we used his little flat on Starine Novaka Street for many years. The front room, facing the street, was occupied by two Hungarians, and we used the kitchen facing the yard. Ranković and I both had keys to this flat and we used it often over a period of three years. During the war it was discovered by the police, and the Hungarian in whose name it was rented was executed.

Every morning Mitra and I heard a whistle under our windows at 10 Majke Jevrosime: Sardelić coming up to have coffee with us on his way to work. He whistled to make sure the police had not set a trap in our flat. We developed a warm friendship.

Toward the end of the war Sardelić joined our intelligence service. That was the only place where he could settle down while there was still time for intricate and grand schemes. When the organization became dull and schematic he grew restless. He turned to diplomacy, where he was well paid and displeased with himself and everything around him.

There was one flat where we were particularly careful. Only Ranković, Lola Ribar, and I knew of its existence. It belonged to a man by the name of Fingerhut, an announcer with Radio Belgrade. Because Fingerhut was not compromised, he was ordered, much to his distress, to remain passive—so that we could use his apartment. When Tito came to Belgrade he went straight from the station to Fingerhut's flat. Kardelj stayed there a number of times.

Fingerhut's end was tragic. He and his wife were Jews; he was completely adjusted to the Serbian way of life, whereas his wife, who was from Palestine, barely spoke any Serbian, and was simply lost. Fingerhut was killed during the war defending Yugoslavia, and she was liquidated by the Germans during the general clean-up of Jews in Yugoslavia.

I called on her at the beginning of the occupation. The unfortunate woman was waiting for her husband. She had no contact with anyone, not even us Communists, her only remaining friends. I gave her some money, but that was the only assistance she would accept.

Acquiring identity cards and application forms was a fairly simple matter for us, because a number of our people worked in various government offices. We even managed to get some unnumbered passports from the State Printing House. But putting together seals and stamps for counterfeiting official documents was a problem.

We knew only one man who could actually make them up: that was Djordje Andrejević-Kun, a painter. His work was extraordinarily clean. Some of his stamps came out better than the official ones, so we were deliberately sloppy in stamping the passports out of fear of giving ourselves away. Our passports were so good that Žujović was able to go to Paris and back using one of them.

Our need for stamps grew. Kun should have had an apprentice, but that would have required too much time. Thus his monopoly was further strengthened. During the war he made up all kinds of occupation stamps, without which a great deal of our movement would have been impossible.

Kun was not a party member. I had discovered him through my intellectuals. A quiet, serious man, he was just right for this kind of work. At one time he expressed hesitation about his involvement. He wanted to paint and we were asking too much of him. Of course, he said, he would do us a favor now and then. But Vukmanović and I had it out with him, and he worked even faster and more diligently than ever.

Our style of functioning had completely changed within a relatively short period of time.

We changed Red Aid to People's Assistance, both to make it sound more legal and to keep in the spirit of the popular-front vocabulary. The organization had in fact become half legal. This was a very important source of financing, but it was used only in exceptional situations. I put Oskar Davičo in charge. He was much too casual, and avoided responsibility by taking frequent trips to Zagreb.

In contrast to Davičo, Dragánče Pavlović was absolutely perfect for the job. He came from a family of Belgrade merchants who had once been very prosperous, and this gave him access to money-raising sources. But this was not his only reason for taking on the job. He was disciplined and conscientious, and also sufficiently broad-minded not to close off sources simply because of minor differences of opinion. He loved his comrades as men and as Communists.

Our money-raising operations had become so broad and so open that the police could no longer punish our contributors.

We raised as much as 50,000 dinars a month in cash alone. In Slovenia money-raising was poor, which Kardelj explained in terms of the national trait of frugality. We fared somewhat better in Zagreb, and best of all in Belgrade, which was very generous, and had now become the center of assistance for the whole country.

We made it a practice to call on our organizations regularly throughout the country. At one time I was in charge of Kraljevo, Kragujevac, and Čačak. It was in Kragujevac in 1940 that I met Mijalko Todorović and Lazar Koliševski for the first time. Todorović was secretary of the local committee, and Koliševski was secretary of a factory committee.

Our visits were very helpful. We got to know the membership and their problems. The organizations were given better form and direction, and we drew richly on their experiences. Our financial resources, our methods of operation, our organization, political line, and contacts strengthened and multiplied. We were moving fast. We didn't know exactly what lay ahead, but we suspected it was something great and exciting and, instinctively, we were preparing for it.

14

One night, a few days after the signing of the Soviet-German Pact, around two or three o'clock in the morning, Mitra and I were awakened by terrifying screams from the street: War, war! There was something horrible about that scream, something coming from the very bottom of the human soul, that has stayed with me for the rest of my life, even though my own view of the war was not characterized by horror or fear, but, rather, by the expectation of a new political solution for Yugoslavia that would emerge from the war.

I actually approved of the Soviet-German Pact, as did most of the leading Communists, with only a few minor misgivings. We had already trained ourselves to have absolute confidence in the Soviet Union and in the decisions of its government. But there was another, more profound, reason. Theoretically speaking, we Communists had not ruled out collaboration between the Soviet Union and capitalist countries. All the capitalist countries were more or less the same for us. We saw no fundamental difference between Hitler's Germany and the Western democracies. It was simply a question of how useful a certain country could be to us at a certain moment in history. And if one bears in mind the policies of the Western governments during this era, our position may appear all the more logical.

The news of the Soviet-German Pact was carried in the morning papers. Some intellectual leftist friends said that it could have both positive and negative results. I attacked them violently. I could see only positive results emerging for the Soviet Union, and thus for us Communists too.

I knew that an attack on Poland was inevitable, and that the Western powers would respond with a declaration of war. This, I thought, would create an ideal opportunity for the Soviet Union to spread socialism at the expense of the two warring sides.

Thus we welcomed the war several days before it actually broke out. Tito was abroad. Kardelj was in Slovenia. My job was to work out a political position for the Belgrade Communists and leftists. The basic issue, of course, was whether the war was imperialistic on both sides, or antifascist. If it was antifascist, it would be a "just" war for the Western powers.

We spent some time vaguely discussing these issues, but after September 1 there was no time left for discussion.

The University was in a state of excitement. The students, the source of our strongest support, were confused. We had been the foremost protagonists of antifascism, the popular front, a policy of national defense. Thus everything now depended on the interpretation we placed on the war. I was so overwrought I couldn't sleep.

The following evening, which was mild and gentle, I went to the student cafeteria to address the students. I had just come from a meeting of the Regional Committee; there we had decided to wait a while, even though everyone appeared to favor my position. Crossing Šumadijska Street I suddenly felt a change taking place within me, something bright and cheerful, as if I were being relieved of a burden. All things surrounding me grew light, playful, and soft. The street was like a river, its vehicles appeared to be rushing by like toys, and the pedestrians were unhappy ants drowning in the river.

In spite of the Regional Committee's decision to wait, I took the position with the students that the war was definitely imperialistic, and that we Communists could draw the proper conclusions from this. There, among the students, amidst all that excitement, it was impossible to wait. The bourgeois parties, and most of the press, were favorably disposed to the West, which was likely to influence the students and break up their ranks.

The news of my position on the war spread fast in leftist circles, and by the next day, September 3, everyone in Belgrade knew about it.

The trouble with my rash statement was not only that the Regional Committee had not yet taken a position, but also that the Central Committee hadn't even gathered to discuss it. Moscow maintained a mysterious silence, which awakened all kinds of fears. What if Moscow took a different position? Much later, it so happened,

Moscow took exactly the same position. But we couldn't wait for Moscow's decision.

Lola Ribar had just come back from Paris with the news that Thorez had stated he would defend his country if it got involved in this "just" war. Thorez had great authority with us. He was a member of the Executive Committee of the Comintern, and we assumed that he reflected Moscow's position.

Vlado Dedijer, who had started a weekly magazine, 7 *dana* (7 *Days*), asked me to write an editorial. I wrote one entitled "War," in which I took a very definite position. Then we read in *L'Humanité* that the French Communists had taken the position that since the war was in defense of France, it was therefore a just war. This rattled me a little, and I modified my position somewhat.

I had first met Vladimir Dedijer in 1936. He had a job with *Politika* and a reputation as a penetrating jouralist. Tall and strong, he looked like a sportsman, with pronounced cheekbones, protruding lower jaw, and an upturned nose. He was very attractive in his directness and aggressiveness. He didn't become a party member until 1939, but long before that he had carried out party assignments as if he were member.

All of his publishing activity was co-ordinated with the party, although the initiative for this came from him personally.

Dedijer always had one very special quality: he knew how to handle illegal publishing activity. He had managed to circulate the first and only issue of 7 *dana* before he ever submitted it to censorship. In 1940, in Zagreb, he published a monthly called *30 dana*, which consisted of reprints from the world press. It was a curious concoction, but it exercised a major influence, had an enormous circulation, and promoted our position. Yugoslavia was on good terms with Hitler's Germany at that time, and so Dedijer would simply give German and Scandinavian credits to Soviet news items. The censors passed everything that was not Soviet.

Dedijer also began bribing the censor—that is, the public prosecutor. He showed great skill in distributing "his" publications. He operated in Zagreb because Zagreb had greater legal scruples, and because, with Maček in power, there was less control over the press.

The war brought out Dedijer's great energies. In contrast to the bourgeois intellectuals, it was for him a decisive turning point in favor of the party and Communism, eliminating the last residue of uncertainty. Dedijer had married a girl from a rich family and lived in a luxury apartment building in Zemun owned by his father-in-law, a former minister in the January 6th Dictatorship. This may have removed him from us, but the war brought him back closer than ever. Their apartment was used as a meeting place, and Tito and Kardelj stayed there now and then.

The meeting of the Central Committee didn't take place until the middle of September.

Lola Ribar and I met Kardelj at the railway station in Zagreb. Our first question was: "Just or unjust?" He replied: "Unjust, of course." Obviously he had independently taken the same position on the war as we had in Belgrade.

Nevertheless, there was quite a bit of confusion in Zagreb. Maček had just concluded his agreement with the Belgrade government, and was taking power. There was a chance that he might give Communists in Croatia certain freedoms, and we didn't want to jeopardize that chance by sharpening our position on the war. Even so, the Zagreb Communists accepted the Central Committee position with discipline.

The most important element in that situation was the general mobilization carried out by the Cvetković-Maček government. Rumors had it that England and France would quickly overwhelm Germany, which meant that we had to be ready to march into Carinthia. Thus the mobilization had an anti-German character. The Central Committee stood against the mobilization, and against participation in an imperialistic war. Maček's position was vague, and for the first time the Croatian peasants resisted his leadership. In Slovenia the resistance was still greater.

Our position on the war immediately separated us from the bourgeois parties. Vilder's *Nova riječ* attacked us as "traitors," which was symptomatic of the change that had taken place since the beginning of the war. The popular front had obviously undergone an enormous transformation.

These changes had to be explained to the Communists and to their sympathizers. I wrote up our evaluation of the war in a paper called "The Theses of the Central Committee of the Communist Party of Yugoslavia," which the Central Committee approved almost without change. I had no apartment in Zagreb, so I did all my writing at the Café Zagreb. The Zagreb police didn't know me and I was fairly comfortable.

We sent our evaluation to Moscow.

Tito was asked to report to the Comintern in Moscow on our position. The Soviet position was not yet known. He told us later how proud he was of our firm independent stand. And he had every reason to be proud. In fact, we were the only party to take this position from the very start of the war, and we maintained it, with certain modifications, until the German attack on the Soviet Union of June 22, 1941. Our position was recorded in the resolutions of the Fifth Conference of the Communist party of Yugoslavia, held in Zagreb at the end of 1940. In 1946 I had this resolution reprinted in *Komunist*, along with Tito's report to the Fifth Conference, but Tito insisted on deleting the portions explaining our position on the "imperialist character" of the war, because it was "embarrassing today." I objected to that.

Historians will surely define the practical significance of our position on the war more clearly. At the time, we gave it a double interpretation: we adopted the line taken by the Soviet Union because it made us feel that we were working very closely with the first "land of socialism." Also, we understood that, under wartime conditions, we had to fight it out alone, that no other group would go along with our unequivocal support of the Soviet Union and our condemnation of the two warring camps.

I must add that we Communists were thrilled by the partition of Poland. We knew nothing about the secret agreement between the Soviet Union and Germany, and it seemed to us that the former was only taking territories inhabited by Ukrainians and Byelorussians. I appreciated very much Molotov's kind references to "blood and class brothers," that is, the Ukrainians and Byelorussians whom the Soviets "liberated" from Polish oppression. "Blood brothers" I took to mean national identity, and "class" to mean the common struggle against capitalism. This formula, I felt, reflected both the times and the real quality of the Soviet action. In any case, the Polish military regime was unpopular in Yugoslavia. The rapid disintegration of the Polish army, which both Soviet and German propaganda interpreted as proof of their rotten political life, was not without significance. But the main cause of enthusiasm among us Communists was that the Soviet Union had taken the field and was broadening the territory of socialism. And as the popular fear of Germany grew, so did the desire to strengthen Russia as a counterweight.

Our position on the war was modified in late 1940 and early 1941 to emphasize the right of national self-defense. This blunted the sharp edge of our position in the eyes of ordinary people. For them it was a simple question of whether or not Communists would rise to the defense of their country. On this point we grew more assertive each day.

Not that we ever thought our 1939 position against mobilization incorrect. We didn't think that way. We merely evolved with events. The 1939 mobilization was conducted under pressure from London and Paris, and to satisfy national aspirations. Besides, Germany and the Soviet Union were acting in concert at that time. In 1940, after the fall of France, differences between them began to emerge. Obviously Germany wasn't too pleased when the Soviet Union took the Baltic countries and Bessarabia. Moreover, the German-Italian threat to Yugoslavia was daily growing.

Even before Tito's return from Moscow we had understood that our opposition to the war and to mobilization might isolate us unless we also emphasized the need for national defense. Popivoda and Vladimir Popović committed a serious error by failing to understand this important nuance, and, as Central Committee instructors, caused severe isolation of the party organization in Montenegro. They still opposed mobilization in the winter of 1940, by which time we had not only modified our position but had started criticizing the government for not taking measures to provide for national defense.

While we were aware of this important nuance, it was Tito who defined it with precision and determination. He stressed that part of our position that dealt with the need for national defense. The Central Committee didn't disagree with him on this, but it was he who first stated that we Communists would have to fight the Germans without basically changing our position on the general character of the war.

The war in Europe had pushed up the cost of living, and created many other problems for the Cvetković-Maček government.

In Slovenia and Croatia resistance to the high cost of living was slowly developing. We in Serbia lagged behind. And we felt badly about it.

Partly in order to publicize our new position, and partly to channel popular discontent in our direction, we decided to organize a political demonstration. In this we Communists could rely only on our own forces. With the exception of Ranković and Dakić, the Regional Committee members were not to take part, to ensure continuity of the Committee's work. Ranković and three other comrades were to organize and lead the demonstration. It was set for December 14, at eight o'clock. They were to start walking toward Slavija, and from there to move along Makenzijeva Street, in the direction of Čubura, thus to reach the poor neighborhoods as fast as possible.

In spite of our agreement to stay away, I couldn't resist seeing the demonstration. A few minutes before it was scheduled to begin,

I found myself casually strolling at the intersection of Belgrade and Njegoševa streets. Traffic was moving as usual, and no police were in sight.

I ran into another "curious" stroller, Svetozar Vukmanović, who was hanging around for the same reason. We walked down the street, in the direction of Slavija.

It was a couple of minutes after eight o'clock. First I saw two or three people walking toward the center of the square. Then, suddenly, streams of people were following them. After a brief commotion, they returned in our direction, followed by gendarmes.

Obviously the police had been informed, and were stationed in buildings around the square. Three to four thousand people had shown up, not as many as we had expected. Bunched together, and pushed around by the police, the demonstrators were moving so fast that Vukmanović and I almost had to run to avoid being overtaken by them. When we reached Aleksandrova Street, we turned left. We looked back: the demonstrators had turned right and were walking up Aleksandrova Street. By that time they were scattered, their shouting uneven. From the center of the city a bus was approaching, loaded with gendarmes, guns, and bayonets. A whole garrison of police was stationed between the main post office and St. Mark's Church. The two of us turned back from the post office and walked over to the Tašmajdan Heath. We were under tremendous tension, increased by the dull echoes of distant gunfire, seemingly coming from several scattered points. It was as if every shot was fired at us, again and again. Finally we decided to go to my flat, which was nearby, and wait there for Mitra.

Mitra came back and told us what she had seen and heard. We went looking for Ranković, and found him at our alternate flat, at the appointed time, upset but not frightened: the demonstration had not gone as scheduled. Ranković was particularly enthusiastic about Rade Žigić, a civil servant, who had been exceptionally courageous. Žigić was still not a party member. In fact, we thought him a Trotskyite because he had once distributed a few Trotskyite pamphlets. Thrilled with Žigić, Ranković exclaimed: "We must accept him right away!" And indeed we did.

Our losses were fewer than might have been expected from all that gunfire.

Two days after the demonstration the government announced its decision to set up a concentration camp. Many prominent Communists were arrested in Belgrade, among them Lola Ribar, Ivan Milutinović, Moša Pijade, and Djordje Kun.

The demonstration of December 14 was the final indication to us

Communists that we were not to expect any better treatment from the Cvetković-Maček government. It put the stigma of murderer and tyrant on the government, and opened a deep gap between us. It ended our hope that Maček would alter government policies on civil liberties. Freedom for Croatia obviously had no great impact on the working-class movement, or on the citizens of Yugoslavia, for that matter.

The subsequent strike of the metalworkers, initially economic in character, assumed political overtones. The main trade-union leadership, under government pressure, refused to participate, which made the strike illegal.

In effect the strike was conducted by the Regional Committee. Dakić led the striking committee and directly managed union affairs. Ranković was also involved.

This was the first battle fought by the modern, highly qualified proletariat of Serbia. There had been bitter conflicts between workers and their employees before, but this strike demonstrated a new doggedness that was both wild and well organized. We Communists now recognized the full potential of the industrial workers.

All government efforts to negotiate a settlement remained unheeded, and the strike lasted almost three months. There was no way of replacing the workers. There was no reserve of trained people, and they could not be brought in from the provinces because no housing was available. When it became clear that the strike would spread, the government mobilized the striking workers and shipped them off to two garrisons. Although basically apolitical before this event, the workers sang the "Internationale" before leaving the station.

The workers were a source of uncontrollable discontent in the garrisons, and they were soon released. This finally ended the strike. Communist influence among metalworkers in Belgrade was established, and shortly after the strike the most prominent strikers all became party members.

Rumor had it that Prince Paul personally ordered the strike squashed. I don't know how true that was. The fact remains, however, that the Cvetković-Maček government acted crudely and unwisely. There were people in the government, like Srdjan Budisavljević, who favored a different approach. But they obviously had little power.

As German pressure grew, the new government began to split up. The leading core around Cvetković and Maček became ever more active in persecuting Communists. Even so, the concentration camp was dissolved, because it yielded no results other than a great deal of public opposition to it.

In the autumn of 1940, students organized a leftist gathering in Topčider. The police made a surprise attack, killing and wounding a number of students.

The police were unusually brutal in this attack. They shot women students in the back and hit them on the head with their revolvers.

Rifat Burdžović, who reported this incident to us, stressed that further demonstrations of this kind were out of the question unless the students were given arms to defend themselves. I managed to convince him that it was still too early for that. However, I realized that certain forms of action had to be ruled out now that the police had opened fire at such slight provocation.

We decided to hold half-legal conferences in apartments, with thirty to forty people. But they were a poor substitute for mass demonstrations, particularly among young people.

The government and its appendages were anxious to have it out with us once and for all. They no longer slapped us around for causing disorders. The times were on their side. A "new order" was being solidified in Europe. There was a deadly passion in these imitations of the mindless Hitlerian orgies. We Communists had to resort to more decisive measures.

15

The establishment of the concentration camp at Bileća was of great political and organizational significance for us Communists. Up till then we had had only a few professional functionaries. Now we were forced to produce them by the dozen, and they had to be supported chiefly out of party funds.

There were also the professional revolutionaries who came from Moscow. In fact, after 1937, many of us could be classified as professional revolutionaries. We were engaged almost exclusively in political activity, and supported ourselves by our own independent means, or with the help of sympathizers. Mitra supported me until 1938, when she was fired from her job in the library of the National Assembly. At that point I started translating the works of Maxim Gorky with Borislav Kovačević. And as late as 1940 I lived on this kind of thing. For my trips I collected from party funds.

At the University a special type of student was emerging, one who spent the bulk of his time in political activity, who postponed his exams from one year to the next, who gave up all professional interests and immersed himself completely in revolutionary activity.

We were familiar with the term "professional revolutionary" from Lenin, from the post-1905 history of the Bolshevik party, and it sounded sublime to us—a man who had no other purpose in life except the revolutionary struggle. But we didn't have the courage to adopt it for ourselves, even though it reflected our situation.

For example, Ranković had a full-time job in a tailor's workshop until 1938, when he started working only in the morning. Occasionally I helped him out financially. After a while he began receiving a small sum of money from the party. As late as 1940 the question of his salary had not been settled. In fact, the salaries of the Politburo members were not regulated until Tito's return from Moscow in the spring of 1940. At first, each was never more than 2,000 dinars a month. As time went on this was increased, and just before the invasion of Yugoslavia it was high—3,000 dinars. Tito's salary was still higher, 6,000 dinars, if I am not mistaken. He proposed his salary and we proposed ours.

As a result of the establishment of the concentration camp, dozens of Communists became professional revolutionaries overnight. This was a culmination of a long process which would have happened even without the concentration camp. But the concentration camp accelerated it.

Our major problem was finding apartments for so many people. We tried to solve it in many ways. Some stayed with their relatives; some crowded into one room. Others were sent to the provinces, which had enormous significance in the development of local organizations.

Thus all of us became true illegal activists with false papers. Some grew mustaches and wore glasses. I had a good identity card, which came from the journalist Dejan Lapčević. I used his name, but changed the photograph. This card entitled me to a seventy-five-per-cent discount on all railway lines, which I took advantage of with pleasure.

We began giving salaries to comrades in hiding; in Belgrade alone there were close to thirty. The pay was not high, but it was regular. Naturally, it was understood that the party had claims on all their time. They were at our disposal and we felt free to send them wherever they were needed, at a moment's notice.

The war had brought about a gradual change in our operating procedures, the rapid development of the party, and the establishment of a professional party apparatus. We were also organizing a work schedule for war itself. We set up our printing presses, found apartments, and obtained propaganda material.

It was not easy for us to cope with the new organizational problems, particularly since we were suddenly faced with serious political problems as well. One was the war in Finland.

If the partition of Poland was received in leftist circles with mixed feelings, the war in Finland was downright unpopular, and completely contradicted the image of the Soviet Union as a non-imperialist country. The argument that tiny Finland was a threat to the enormous and powerful Soviet state was completely unconvincing. This uncertainty in leftist circles was further strengthened by

Finland's vigorous and prolonged resistance. The contention that a "bourgeois" army was bound to disintegrate when faced by the Red Army proved wrong and naïve.

At that time Ljuba Davidović, the leader of the Serbian Democratic party, fell gravely ill. His dying words were: "What's happening in little Finland?" This was reported in the newspapers. These words made us Communists feel very bitter about the "bourgeois democrats." But among ordinary citizens, or the petit bourgeois, as we Communists liked to call them, there was a great deal of feeling for Finland.

We published a brochure dealing with Finland shortly before the war ended. Stefan Mitrović wrote it, and Koča Popović and I edited it.

The Soviet-Finnish peace treaty, which gave the Soviet Union only those territories necessary to the defense of Leningrad and Murmansk, was very well received, as was the statement that the Soviet Union had no intention of annexing Finland if its people were not ready for it. This pacified the petit bourgeois, and brought straying leftists back into the fold.

I myself didn't feel particularly disturbed by the war with Finland, but I can't say that I had the same enthusiasm for it as I had for the partition of Poland and the annexation of the Baltic countries. The organizing of volunteers in France to aid Finland, and the temporary truce by mutual agreement on the Rhine, served to convince us further that the Soviet government had not made a mistake in invading a peace-loving country. In constant conflict with the police, we Communists were trained to believe that the "bourgeoisie" was acting against the proletariat at all times. Thus even Finland must be a part of the "capitalist plot" against the "fortress of socialism." As far as we were concerned, Finland was a bourgeois country, and the Soviet Union had every right to "protect" its interests and to assist in the "liberation" of the Finnish people. We accepted, without reservation, the explanations put forth by Soviet propaganda, not because we had to, but because we wanted to and because we genuinely believed in them.

During the war, the Finnish issue was often brought up in discussions within the Central Committee. Finland's participation in the war on the side of the Germans further solidified our conviction that the Soviet Union had every right to "play it safe." But our discussion of the Finnish war, at the "highest level," was in itself an indication that something was bothering us, in spite of our blind faith. We had to work a little too hard to convince ourselves of the

Soviet Union's position. This question never even arose in the case of Poland and the Baltic countries.

Could this have been due to the heroic resistance of the Finnish people? I don't think so. At least not as far as I was concerned. I was convinced that the Soviet Union was right, but I was perhaps a little less convinced that its methods of operation were always the best. Nevertheless, my own powers of suggestion were so strong that there was no room in my mind for any other solution.

During the Finnish war a party conference was held in Slovenia. I addressed it in the name of the Central Committee. The conference was also addressed by a Comintern representative by the name of Šverma, a member of the Politburo of the Czechoslovak Communist party and of the Executive Committee of the Comintern, who was in hiding in Yugoslavia.

The conference, held in a mill, was well organized. But it was very cold, and since I was poorly dressed, it was most uncomfortable reaching the mill at night. Inside, it was warm and spacious. We slept on the floor. The orderly Slovenes had blankets ready for us and tea was served regularly.

The main speaker was Kardelj. As usual he had prepared a long and intelligent speech.

We were not allowed to applaud, so as not to attract attention. Šverma spoke with pathos, as if he were standing on a parliamentary bench. He didn't look at all like a revolutionary, not by our standards anyway. His views and his style of expressing them were also different—indirect, softer, and much more cunning.

Following the occupation of Czechoslovakia, he had moved to France. When the war broke out, he decided to go to Moscow, by way of Yugoslavia.

In Paris, Beneš had told him he didn't think it was such a bad idea that Gottwald had gone to Moscow; Czechoslovakia had to have people in the east too. Šverma told this story not without mild irony. He had a respect for Beneš that was completely beyond me; I thought Beneš a "bourgeois" politician whose behavior during the Munich crisis had been cowardly.

When Šverma arrived in Belgrade I put him up in Lazar Kočović's flat. I met him there several times to discuss plans on how to ship him off to the Soviet Union. He was in agreement with us with regard to the character of the war, but his views were not nearly as categorical as ours. That was hardly surprising: he came from occupied Czechoslovakia and he must have felt that in the struggle against Hitler there was at least a grain of something nonimperialist in his own country.

As time went on he and I became friends. He was a cultured, civilized man, with good manners and a sense of humor.

Šverma had a Canadian passport, and we sent him to the Bulgarian Consulate to get a visa. He was followed by three comrades in a car, in case problems arose. But everything worked out smoothly. He gave a sizable contribution to the Bulgarian Red Cross.

Then he left for Sofia, accompanied by a certain Mina, a Bulgarian student at the University of Belgrade, to try to get a visa from the Soviet Consulate. Mina got in touch with the Bulgarian Central Committee, but they refused to help, claiming that there were a lot of provocateurs in Yugoslavia and that they had no intention of compromising themselves. Mina called on Todor Pavlov, who was in correspondence with Zogović, and knew me by name. Pavlov went to the Soviet Consulate. Two days later Šverma was put aboard a Soviet ship at Varna.

As he was leaving Belgrade, Šverma had said to me: "See you in Prague after the war." I saw him again, in Moscow in 1944, when I was there as the chief of the Yugoslav Military Mission. But he didn't survive the war. He was sent to Slovakia, and in the debacle of the uprising during that very cold winter, he died from hunger and exhaustion. It was Slansky who told this story. His wife, also a prominent Communist, was sentenced as a traitor during the Slansky trials.

Šverma arrived in Moscow before Tito. He had seen our best organizations throughout the country. He had followed our political activities, read our publications, and participated in our discussions. He submitted a very favorable report to the Comintern, which, according to Tito, helped to restore Moscow's confidence in our party. This had been at such a low point that we had almost been dissolved, like the Polish party.

Tito said that an additional reason the Comintern decided against dissolving our party was the antifascist activity of our youth, covered favorably in both the foreign and Soviet press.

All this was happening while we were in hiding and preparing a polemic against Miroslav Krleža.

Our conflict with Krleža had begun as far back as 1938. The first sparks were created by Radovan Zogović, in a brief and nasty article in the magazine *Umetnost i kritika* (*Art and Criticism*), which he published in Belgrade and with which I, by and large, disagreed.

The conflict with Krleža was very complex. It set in motion the most varied elements and passions of the political and ideological struggle.

I had first met Krleža in the spring of 1938. Bora Prodanović, a Belgrade lawyer, had introduced me to him.

Prodanović was a party lawyer, engaged in organizing the defense of Communists. He did his job conscientiously, if a trifle automatically, and "in the name of the party." The great thing about him was his pipe, and his sallow face, seemingly saturated with nicotine. Prodanović was accustomed to a bohemian existence, which set him apart from the new generation of Communists. He was a bitter opponent of Petko Miletić and a great friend of Moša Pijade.

Prodanović and Pijade considered Zogović a provocateur in the conflict with Krleža, and they felt that my meeting Krleža might help soothe matters.

Zogović was the best-known leftist poet, who favored socialist realism. He and I had never been in agreement on the question of esthetics, because I was always hesitant in giving my support to socialist realism.

In his introduction to a book of drawings by Hegedušić, Krleža had risen up against "social literature." He was attacked by the leftists, with whom he settled accounts contemptuously and convincingly. Krleža was not involved in any party activity but every couple of years he met with illegal functionaries, his old friends. On the other hand, his literary activity was strong and leftist.

Of course, with his introduction to the Hegedušić drawings he risked a conflict with the party because the Central Committee stood behind the leftists who had attacked him. Instead, the new Central Committee apologized to Krleža. That was a fantastic victory for him, and unheard of for a Communist party. Krleža was the best-known writer in Yugoslavia, and in full intellectual force. The Central Committee's apology rubbed many leftist intellectuals the wrong way, but the conflict was liquidated and almost forgotten.

The new conflict with Krleža coincided with the Moscow trials. He was obviously hit hard by the trials, and began to have doubts. But he never admitted it because that would automatically have meant breaking with the left. He had no desire to do that; he felt he was a Communist. But in spite of himself, his writing reflected despair and lack of faith. This was sufficient reason for us to doubt him in turn, particularly at a time of such sharp struggles against all groups that opposed the party leadership. This leadership accepted orders from Moscow without any reservation, almost without thinking, believing them to be truly revolutionary and socialist. The party leaders were aware that in Krleža's circle jokes were made about the trials, doubt was expressed about Stalin's ideological greatness and the correctness of Soviet foreign policy. The circle around Vučo was not free of this feeling either, but they accepted the party position to a much larger degree. Vučo's older son quipped one day, after he was unable to get Radio Moscow, that perhaps the announcer had been executed, which was reason enough for Zogović to entertain doubts about Vučo himself.

An artificial hysteria was generated about the dangers of Trotskyism, but since the danger was basically nonexistent, the hysteria soon died down. Thus no one ever accused Krleža of being a Trotskyite.

Other, more serious issues, were also at stake. Krleža had been friends with a number of former leaders who had disappeared overnight. After the war Krleža told me that he simply couldn't believe that Čopić, Cvijić, and others were spies and enemies and that he was enormously upset by the whole idea. The new leadership was quickly gaining ground and demanding discipline in all matters, including ideology. Until that time, Krleža had been indulged by the party: he could write anything he wanted, he didn't have to work illegally, and he could create literary circles of his own choice. That was one side of the conflict with him.

The second difference was that Krleža maintained that we Communists shouldn't stress our uniqueness so much at the very time when the Croatian people were united in their national aspirations.

By resisting the new leadership and its policies, Krleža was also resisting the new party line: centralism, military discipline, and Leninist ideas in their Stalinist interpretation.

The Central Committee members—Tito, Kardelj, and I—never thought of Krleža as a true Marxist, but we felt that collaboration with him was possible. Tito showed the most patience in this respect; after all, they had been personal friends for a long time. But collaboration with Krleža was impossible because of his temperament and views. He was a Communist out of an earlier era, before the dictatorship. Although he hated social democracy, he steadfastly held to one idea—the role of a free and independent intellectual. By the standards of the time this was considered incomprehensible as well as taboo.

These issues were further complicated by many other elements—intrigue, passion, personal animosities.

My talk with Krleža in the spring of 1939 lasted for two whole hours. There were no specific guide lines, but we touched on all of the controversial issues.

Surprisingly enough, in conversation Krleža displayed none of the great erudition of his writings, but he used the same eloquent, fiery manner. He was already a little on the heavy side, bald, his eyes a muddy green, but his look was bright and penetrating. He didn't treat me condescendingly. He didn't think me very important either. He answered my questions with boredom, like a man who couldn't be bothered. Even so, we found a common language. He told me he didn't like Mayakovsky. To my comment that Stalin considered Mayakovsky "the greatest poet of the Soviet epoch," he responded sharply: "That's Stalin's taste." The Communists to whom I related this story thought Krleža's remark impudent, an effrontery, whereas I saw it as the caprice of a great and conceited writer who didn't know much about either Stalin or Mayakovsky. In any case, it wasn't serious enough to cross swords over.

Our talk was more an enquiry into each other's thinking than an effort to arrive at an agreement. Krleža was not exactly open, and neither was I. Even so, our meeting postponed an open conflict with him.

Before long, all of the Belgrade Communists had heard about our meeting. I addressed a large group of students and related it in detail. Our party organization was even more anxious to hear the news. I felt I would lose its support if I gave in to Krleža. Zogović accused me of having allowed myself to be "impressed" by Krleža. That wasn't true. But practical reasons for an open conflict still didn't exist.

I met Krleža once more, in Zagreb, in the fall of 1939. That meeting was colder and more reserved. He had obviously made up his mind to go his own way. I was sorry about that. But I also felt I had developed a resistance to him.

Krleža's old skepticism about the Soviet Union and the new leadership of the Communist party of Yugoslavia was revived at the beginning of the war. To him the war was a monster that had emerged from the dark depths of humanity, hungry for millions of lives. In these words of his there was the poetic strength of great prophets. He never mentioned the Soviet Union. He thus brought chaos to our ranks. His skepticism, not unlike that of Lunacharsky and Gorky in the history of the Bolshevik party, became the ideology of all the nonbelievers and "enemies" of the party. This skepticism brought all the old controversial issues to the surface.

Radovan Zogović proved incapable of handling the dispute with Krleža. For him the Central Committee's slow and cautious reaction to Krleža was a sign of ignorance, if not of fear. He requested an official party condemnation of Krleža, whereas I maintained that we should settle accounts with him ideologically, challenge his

Marxism, and let people draw practical political conclusions from that. Using this premise, Zogović again launched an attack on Krleža. But his writing was full of personal squabbles and attempts to prove who was right in all kinds of trifling details. This, of course, meant getting involved in an endless polemic and losing sight of the main objective, which was what Krleža wanted. He wanted to make this whole dispute appear a struggle against cultural barbarism. On some issues, such as Jovan Popović's poetry and some of Zogović's own writings, Krleža was absolutely correct. But that was hardly the point.

After his return from Moscow, and his recognition of the negative effects of Krleža's attacks, Tito agreed to a counterattack. I then put together *Književne sveske*, with Koča Popović's assistance, which was valuable, particularly in matters of style and logic.

Književne sveske brought our polemic with Krleža to an end. We managed to isolate him completely from the Communist ranks. From the very start *Književne sveske* was of tremendous significance for the party. Although these writings were naïve and dogmatic, they nevertheless served to strengthen the party ideologically, and marked the victory of the new leadership over all opposition. Krleža had become the opposition's rallying point. Now all that was eliminated, along with the rallying point. The subsequent settling of disputes with the remaining "leftists" in Belgrade was only an administrative matter.

After the war Krleža had a wide variety of explanations for his failure to join the Partisans during the war. He had been rejected by the Communists and he refused to join the reactionaries. In prison, after the Ustashi takeover in Croatia, a young Communist spit in his face and asked him what he, a "traitor," was doing in prison. "I cried," said Krleža. But he was in the Ustashi prison a very short time. He was released by Mile Budak, Pavelić's second-in-command, and the chief ideologist of the Ustashi regime. Following his release, Krleža called on Pavelić. Budak slapped him on the shoulder and said: "Don't worry, Fric; everything will be fine." Krleža never told us what was discussed at this meeting, and I was too embarrassed to ask him. Augustinčić did a bust of Pavelić, but, unlike Krleža, he offered a very simple explanation of how it happened: "They asked me to do a portrait of Pavelić and I did it." Krleža went into Dr. Vranešić's Sanatorium. Vranešić was a member of Pavelić's committee on racial purity and played a role in the extermination of the Jews. After the war our authorities executed him, in spite of Krleža's cautious intervention on his behalf.

On two or three occasions Krleža was invited to join the Partisans, but he didn't do it. He claimed that he was still upset about the argument he had had with us. That may well have been one of his reasons, but it was not altogether justified. Indeed, a few Trotsky-ites were executed, but Krleža was never in any danger of that. We certainly could have used his name. Later, Krleža said he was too embarrassed to join the Partisans because everything was over anyway. I personally think that it was also a question of simple coward-ice. He didn't want to put himself out for something he didn't altogether believe in. Besides, he is the kind of man who is physically repulsed by war and the horrors of war.

Krleža was a frequent topic of conversation among us functionaries during the war. We felt very bitter about him, and his friends. Their passive role seemed to have confirmed our position in the *Književne sveske*. In 1945 Krleža requested an audience with Tito in order to "rehabilitate" himself. Tito refused to receive him alone. He asked me to be present. We didn't want to be accused of having "cooked up" something with Krleža, because some people objected to this meeting. The essence of what Tito told Krleža was the following: "We had no choice, we had to create a unified party in order to save Yugoslavia, which, you, as an old Yugoslav, should have understood." Tito's position was determined partly by the current political mood—he was full of enthusiasm for "brother-hood and unity." But in his words there was also a calculated appeal to the ideals of Krleža's.

After this meeting Krleža and I often got together. Whenever he came to Belgrade he would first telephone me at the Central Committee. He had even made up with Zogović. There are some who claim that Krleža had finally accepted a philosophy whose essence he had rejected, but they were wrong. He still maintained his philosophical skepticism, but he was nonetheless convinced that a road to a new and happier life had finally been found. He often reproached us for not being more firm with "reactionary forces," which represented a "serious danger." Yet Tito's regime was essentially the kind he dreamed of and for which he fought.

He tried to explain his old conflict with the party as a series of unfortunate circumstances and misunderstandings. Both he and Ristić insisted that they were far from doubting the Soviet Union, Stalin, the trials, and our own party. They maintained this position until our break with Stalin in 1948, when all their old doubts were revived. They insisted, justifiably, that they had known all along what the Soviet Union was about. But they dropped this line of talk when they sensed that the Central Committee wasn't anxious to have them telling everyone how right they had always been. Krleža had never actually been expelled from the party, although his membership had been canceled during the war.

Krleža's case was typical of the destiny of a revolutionary writer in a Leninist, or, rather, Stalinist, party, as well as of the battles such a party had to fight on its road to power.

Oskar Davičo got involved with Krleža in the conflict with the party, and was expelled from it.

On his release from prison, the Regional Committee put Davičo in charge of Red Aid in Serbia. Unfortunately, he made quite a sloppy job of it—not because he didn't love the work, but because he was preoccupied with his poetry. His alienation from the party began with his friendship with Ristić and Krleža. He came from prison feeling hostile to both, but he was also drawn to them by his intellectual curiosity and his desire for something more expressive than the worn Moscow molds.

He had moved to Zagreb without the approval of the Regional Committee. In Zagreb he refused to accept party assignments. He had a big blow-up with his old prison friend Ognjen Prica, because of his Krleža-like stance. Prica said that Davičo had become deceitful and double-faced, that he said one thing and did another. That was very likely true. Caught between party positions and his own convictions, but remaining true to the revolutionary ideas of socialism, he had to fall into contradictions. He was expelled from the party without a serious investigation.

I was deeply hurt by Davičo's expulsion. I liked him as a man, I appreciated him as a poet, even though I criticized him for his "remnants of Surrealism." I don't mean to imply that I doubted the correctness of the decision. On the contrary: I opposed him more bitterly than anyone else.

In 1943, after the liberation of Split, Davičo joined the Partisans. As a Jew, he had had no choice but to seek refuge in Italian-occupied territory. He said he had sought contact with the party, but the Communists had refused him. I don't think he had been overly persistent in seeking this contact. Joining the Partisans at Split was not hard. Early in 1944 he came to the Supreme Command at Drvar. I said to him: "The war must be coming to an end if you've decided to join the Partisans." He was crestfallen and angry.

Ranković and I made up our minds to be kind to our old friend. We sent him off to our elite unit—the First Proletarian Brigade—to be "re-educated," and ordered him kept at headquarters and protected from getting killed. Suspicious by nature, Ranković implied that Davičo was something of a Trotskyite, although neither of us actually believed that. He had simply left the party at a critical moment because he was not ideologically strong enough and had not completely given up that "petit-bourgeois" (Ranković), intellectual (me) nonsense. In the Proletarian Brigade Davičo was courageous and well liked because of his knack for close friendships, his good-natured humor, his revolutionary passion, and his sympathy for great human drama.

Naša stvarnost came to an end with the Soviet-German Pact. Zogović proposed that a new Marxist magazine be started. I approved the idea, and soon *Umetnost i kritika* began appearing. The magazine didn't have a large circulation, about two thousand copies, but it paid for itself because Zogović worked very hard on it. He hired Velibor Gligorić as an assistant, but Gligorić's editorial role was negligible. He was not equipped to edit a Marxist magazine because he was neither a Marxist nor a party member. He had a reputation as a progressive literary critic and a name that could be used profitably with the censors. But Zogović ran the magazine. It was not easy to resist Zogović's aggressive force. With his exceptional sense of logic, particularly the logic of the language, Zogović left hardly anyone's manuscript alone.

Zogović was self-confident, but it was hard for him to accept new ideas. He was firmly convinced of his ideological superiority as a Marxist, and of his linguistic skill as a writer.

At heart, Zogović was a great romantic. And like all great romantics he was sectarian and dogmatic. A man of exceptional moral qualities, he loved truth, and was much harder on himself than on other people. But he was also egotistical. He loved man and the movement as abstractions, and so he was in constant conflict with our Communist movement. He couldn't believe that these very people, with all their faults, could carry out a revolution. And when the revolution was actually being carried out, it wasn't the ideal and pure revolution he had imagined. He was a very complex person, sick in his tight, orderly, and disciplined mind. Moments of fury and senseless anger, particularly where his women were concerned, would be followed by moments of tenderness and forgiving. He simply couldn't live without this inner turmoil.

Interestingly enough, Zogović couldn't live without close friends either. And there was always one to whom he felt closest.

From 1937 until the beginning of the war I was that friend.

Our friendship suffered a little during the war, but was revived later. It suffered a final blow during the conflict with the Cominform, when Zogović refused to join the Central Committee in its resistance to Moscow's aggression.

I was even involved in his personal life: his first wife left him, he left his second wife, and the third, Vera, an intelligent young woman, hadn't altogether reconciled herself to spending the rest of her life with him either. Day in, day out I went through the weary details of his life with him. He sympathized with me, but my problems were of an altogether different nature—an overcommitted party worker in constant danger of being arrested. That was by and large my personal life, with frequent and difficult psychological turmoil set off by conflicts within the party and outside.

I may have given Zogović moral support in coping with his problems, but he also gave me moral support, without perhaps suspecting it, because I was an important functionary.

Umetnost i kritika helped build up the party ideologically. It transmitted to us Soviet views on art and culture, in keeping with our goal of bolshevization. It helped complete our Communist image of the world.

Unlike *Naša stvarnost*, *Umetnost i kritika* was a purely Marxist magazine. Its title, like that of *Književne sveske*, served to conceal its actual substance—the struggle for Marxism and for ideological purity within the party.

The elite of our intelligentsia didn't much care for this magazine —it was too narrow and schematic. But it was well received by the intellectual revolutionaries and functionaries. Kardelj and I didn't like it much, but we thought it very useful. Tito found it acceptable. He even met with Zogović and his cell (Bane Vučković and Nikola Petrović), which gave them great moral support.

We protected Zogović and a few other well-known intellectuals from daily involvement in illegal activities. Some of these intellectuals feared such activity. But Zogović was always ready to confirm his beliefs with a personal act and commitment.*

* This was as far as I had got by June 13, 1955, the date of *Borba*'s attack on me for my articles criticizing the new Soviet leadership. In spite of this, I continued writing.

16

When Tito returned to Yugoslavia he found the party in good shape. Local leadership cadres, cleansed of hostile elements, had been organized throughout the country. I don't mean to suggest that all he had to do was to mount the horse. A good horse needs a good rider. And that he was. Even though he had lived in Paris, he had guided us in our activities and he always gave us support and the benefit of his opinion on all questions. Even when absent, he was the central figure—because we knew that he would eventually fill this role, and because, in the back of our minds, we always tried to act in keeping with his ideas.

On his arrival Tito introduced one important change: the Central Committee met regularly to discuss outstanding issues. Although we considered Kardelj the chief figure in Tito's absence, he had not functioned as the party Secretary. With the arrival of the party Secretary, the Central Committee members had someone to turn to. Indeed, both as a functionary and as a man Tito knew how to conduct business, how to treat people, how to take them firmly in hand. With his arrival our need for a more centralized leadership was finally realized.

At the first session of the Central Committee in Zagreb Tito and I had a fairly serious disagreement. We had already heard that he was bitter over our failure to send him a passport to Istanbul. He had had to wait there for two full months, exposed to danger, and finally arrived in Yugoslavia with the passport he had acquired in Moscow. With Kun in a concentration camp, we had had no one to make up the seals and forge the passports. We had other problems as well. Tito's wife, Herta, contributed to this unpleasantness by

351

suggesting that Tito, concerned about Trotskyite plots, suspected that the delay had been deliberate.

Kardelj managed to calm Tito down, but the meeting progressed painfully. Finally Tito turned on me personally. He asked who had issued a passport to Petko Miletić. Kardelj cautiously defended me. So did Milutinović. Ranković was silent, but I knew he would defend me if Tito went all the way. I was bitter, and didn't try to defend myself. When I finally spoke, I was so angry and so upset that I had tears in my eyes. At that moment I was ready to abandon the party. They all thought I might actually do it, and they tried to pacify me.

By the time the meeting was over I had composed myself a little. As I was about to leave Tito asked me to join him for a walk. As a rule he didn't move much around Zagreb, fearful that he might be recognized. I was sure he was going to apologize, and I began to thaw out. But he didn't do that at all. He simply chatted with me about all kinds of things, particularly my personal life. From time to time he would smile gently. There was something so human and warm in this that when we parted, without having exchanged a word about the incident, I was happy, a child whose father understood that he had administered unjust punishment but couldn't quite admit it. Ranković and Ribar were very pleased when, on the train going back to Belgrade, I related what had happened.

I had been the treasurer of the Central Committee, a job for which I didn't have much knack. Making notations on little slips of paper, which had to be hidden, of sums and initials, I had it all mixed up. And when the time came for me to pass this assignment on to Milutinović, I couldn't make head or tail out of the whole thing. On the other hand, Milutinović handled the job as if he'd been doing it all his life. While I was treasurer, my apartment had been burglarized, and the thief got away with 11,000 dinars. The man was subsequently caught, and admitted stealing the money. However, the police thought it belonged to the owner of the apartment, because I had lived there illegally. The newspaper carried the news. But neither this theft nor my treasury account (the cash on hand and the receipts not being consistent) produced a shadow of a doubt in Tito's mind. Nor did any other issue, for that matter, ever. Following the passport incident our relationship seemed to have changed. And anyway, it was not in Tito's nature to be bothered by such minor things.

During the war, I had many minor run-ins with Tito. There was nothing serious in that, though. They were personal squabbles, sometimes quite sharp, between short-tempered people in trying situations. He never cast any political doubts on my character. Nor did he ever use his authority to settle such personal arguments. But in political conflicts he did use this authority, and in such matters he was adamant, even intolerant. He never admitted he was wrong in personal or in political conflicts. He ignored them instead, stating implicitly that he "realized what it was all about," and that normal relations should be resumed.

In all our personal conflicts, and until the final blow-up, he maintained that special father-and-son relationship between us. He had a similar relationship with Lola Ribar, to whom I, in turn, felt like an older brother. Tito may have been politically closer to other comrades, and I know he was to Ranković, for example, but not in a family or "blood" sense. It was Lola Ribar and I who gave Tito the nickname "Stari" (Old Man).

The new leadership, which Rade Končar joined in the fall of 1940, was not only politically unanimous, but personally intimate and friendly. This leadership put a whole series of assignments into effect very quickly and efficiently. It was essential to complete the structure of our organization, because Tito wanted to schedule a party congress in the near future.

The Comintern's view of our party was also undergoing a change. Dimitrov told me in Moscow in 1944 that, just before Tito left for Yugoslavia, he had vowed to restore the honor of his party, which had been smudged by the factionalists. Dimitrov warned him not to boast and not to overestimate his possibilities, but Tito instinctively sensed the rising of the revolutionary tide in Yugoslavia.

First of all, we decided on a series of regional conferences during the spring and summer of that year, in Serbia, Slovenia, Montenegro, and Dalmatia. I was busy with other assignments, so I only attended the Regional Conference for Serbia, held in Belgrade.

Nor was I able to attend the All-Yugoslav Consultation held in June 1939 at Šmarna Gora in Slovenia, which further extended the unification, purging, and strengthening of the party. Tito was there, of course, and the conference demonstrated his wide support, enabling him to face the Comintern with self-confidence.

Tito, Kardelj, and I were in Zagreb before and after the Fifth Conference. We were not formally a secretariat, but in fact we played that role. It was not a collective; Tito made all the major decisions, following a review by us of major issue. Tito and Kardelj were closer in policy-making, because Tito considered Kardelj a more important person.

The three of us, with some help from Rade Končar, were responsible for the organization of the Fifth Conference. All the work was done under Tito's leadership. Tito and Kardelj were in charge of the political aspects of the conference, while I worked with Končar on the organization. But Končar ended up doing it all himself because I was asked at the last minute to prepare a report on the national question, as a substitute for the usual one written by Moša Pijade. My own assignment, a report on agitation and propaganda, was given to Boris Kidrič.

The Fifth Conference was attended by one hundred and five delegates. They were escorted in groups, and at night, into a villa that Tito had rented. Only one incident occurred: as one of the groups was being escorted along the tracks a railway guard fired a shot in the air, but it came to nothing. During the conference itself no one left the villa, except for Tito and his wife, who went back and forth by car. We slept on the floor, lined up like sardines, in a crowded room which was aired only at night. We also had to control noise and applause.

The conference reflected our unity and our fighting spirit, except for an argument I had with Šarlo, a Macedonian delegate who had been until then a member of the Bulgarian party. He asked that our position on the national question include the expulsion of Serb colonial gendarmes from Macedonia. I sharply objected: I was not against the expulsion of the gendarmes, but I was absolutely adamant on the subject of identifying them with the Serbs. I quoted Stalin in connection with the Russian colonists in the Caucasus. The argument was beginning to assume serious proportions when Tito stepped in. He supported my position with a statement that we had to approach this problem from the class point of view, rather than have proletarians go after proletarians.

Svetozar Vukmanović's nickname originated from this conference. His emotional speeches, frequently appealing for a faster tempo in party activities, made a good impression. We nicknamed him "Tempo" because he used the word often and also because no one knew his real name; he had for some time operated under a series of pseudonyms.

The Central Committee was elected by a commission made up of Tito, Popivoda, and one other comrade. In effect, it merely approved Tito's recommendations. I resisted joining the Politburo. A plenum was elected, which didn't actually meet until Stalin's attack on our party in the spring of 1948. The former Central Committee became the Politburo. Its composition remained unchanged. Tito, Leskovšek, Kardelj, Ranković, and I had been members of the Forum. Milutinović and Končar joined later, the former in

1939, and the latter at the conference, although he had already attended the meetings of the Central Committee, and it was common knowledge that he would be elected. This was the composition of the Politburo (without Končar or Marinko) for which Tito had received the Comintern's approval in 1939. On Tito's recommendation, Sreten Žujović was also elected to the Central Committee Plenum. The leading comrades, particularly Ranković and I, objected to this appointment. Žujović was very depressed, and his party work was fairly limited. But he cheered up again after the conference. During the war he was generally around the Politburo, and he attended all its sessions. This continued after the war. Thus, in effect, he was considered a member. The quartet of Tito-Kardelj-Djilas-Ranković was formed during the war, through joint activity and identity of views. We were not elected as a special body until the Fifth Congress in 1948, although we had acted as one since 1938.

I always felt that official party propaganda exaggerated the practical results of the Fifth Conference. I don't intend to dwell on that here. I would only like to mention what appeared obvious to us immediately following the conference.

We were fully aware that the Fifth Conference would finally solidify the Comintern's confidence in our party. To be able to hold an illegal conference, attended by such a large number of people, with so many reports and discussions, was itself proof of a consolidation of power that no other illegal Communist party had achieved. We knew it and we felt it.

A Soviet Intelligence man had accompanied Tito on his trip from Moscow. He had brought a radio with him; thus we were in regular contact with Moscow. Tito had also brought some money with him. The Comintern had been giving the party regular monthly financial assistance. But after Tito came back, this stopped. For one thing, it was technically impossible to get it. But it was not only that. In truth, for a year or two we had not received real financial aid from Moscow. Whatever money we had received from Moscow had been spent on our people abroad. In fact, our financial independence was such that we were able to give assistance to our Italian comrades, who had stopped in Yugoslavia on their way from Moscow.

Within the party, the Fifth Conference meant a confirmation of the new leadership, fresh encouragement to party members and their sympathizers, and knowledge that our party had become an invincible power.

We had also achieved another important goal. By publicizing the procedures of the conference we not only amazed and angered the police, but demoralized them as well, and made them recognize Communist strength. The conference also forced people to deal with the Communist party as a real power. We expected new faith in us and sympathy for us.

All our expectations were justified.

The decisions reached at the conference were not in themselves of any great significance, but they helped clarify the relations within the party and confirm the existing line.

Emotionally and morally, the conference prepared Communists for the contests ahead, although it did not prepare them for the manner in which future political relations would evolve.

The new leadership's power was further solidified. In effect, this meant unlimited authority for the new leadership, in recognition of its activities.

17

Following the Fifth Party Conference we continued to concentrate on organizational problems.

Tito, Kardelj, and I left for Bohinj, in Slovenia, to get *Proleter* and other publications under way. We were there for ten days, just barely long enough to get it all done. The weather was poor, so we couldn't work outdoors, and we would have been much too conspicuous in hotels.

Both Tito and Kardelj, particularly Tito, liked to hold meetings in mountain retreats, which combined comfort with obscurity. We had held such meetings before, and sometimes we would walk for two to three hours. But that was always during the summer. This excursion, intended for writing and discussion, proved impractical. We met with Tito only a few times.

Tito stayed with his wife in the Hotel Zlatorog, while Kardelj and I, for about the same amount of money, stayed in a peasant house in the village of Fužine. We felt it would be a little more conspiratorial that way. Bohinje was empty—it was the month of November—and our stay there was unusual. But for some reason we didn't attract the attention of the authorities. I don't care much for Slovenian cooking, so I ordered sauerkraut with sausages every day. Kardelj grew tired of this menu, but there wasn't much he could do about it—the landlady cooked only one dish.

On our return to Zagreb, we received disturbing reports about the state of the party in Slovenia. The reports were submitted by Kidrič, who asserted that most of the Slovenian functionaries were masked Trotskyites.

Kardelj didn't believe this, but it concerned an organization for which he felt a special responsibility. He couldn't quiet Tito's fears; it was true that the Slovenian organizations hadn't shown the inner strength or fighting spirit of the Zagreb and Belgrade organizations.

We decided that I should make a round of the Slovenian organizations. And I spent about a month working hard in the cold Slovenian winter.

In the Slovenian Central Committee the chief man, after Kardelj, was Kidrič, although the Secretary was Luka Leskovšek.

Kidrič had spent a lot of time out of the country, part of it in a Vienna prison. He made a short trip to Moscow, stopped in Paris for a while, and came home in 1937, when we started bringing people back to Yugoslavia. He had met Tito abroad, and he and Kardelj were childhood friends. I didn't know him at all well.

Slender, indefatigable, alert, he was always in motion. A man of great revolutionary passion and energy, he had a tendency to fly in a number of directions—always leftist. He had a powerful intellect and an ability to think things through, and he was always thinking, thinking passionately. In that sense he was different from the rest of the Slovenian comrades, who favored a cool, balanced approach.

Kidrič had a bizarre sense of humor. At times he could be quite cynical and hard, particularly to those he thought stupid and opportunistic. And yet he was very well liked by the top party leaders because of his enormous energy and his great love of his comrades.

His wife, Zdenka, on the other hand, was not popular with the top leadership. Even Kardelj couldn't take her. Cold, reserved, a little vain, not very good-looking, she was not a part of the Communist community and mentality. This reserved woman, with no sense of humor or joy, had a tremendous influence on Kidrič. He couldn't live without her. He was faithful to her because of his emotional dependence on her rather than out of moral scruples.

Unlike Kidrič, Tone Tomšič, another member of the Central Committee, was cold, calculated, sparse in his speech and in his humor. But when it came to technical and organizational details he had no match. The mechanism of contacts, apartments, printing presses, and other things functioned flawlessly under his leadership.

His wife, Vida, was also a member of the Central Committee. She was not very good-looking, with that purplish complexion so common among Alpine women, but she had a marvelous sense of humor and was always cheerful. She had a tendency to complicate matters, yet she got things done. She was hard-working and utterly dedicated.

Vida Tomšič fully shared Kidrič's suspicions about the Trotskyites in their midst.

Like the rest of us, Kidrič accepted Moscow's thinking on the subject of Trotskyites. In addition, he had a lively imagination of his own. The suspected comrades had been associated with Petko Miletić, and we identified this group with the Trotskyites. Kidrič felt that the work of building up the organization was going very slowly, and it was under the leadership of Petko Miletić's supporters. That was true. But this was an objective situation rather than a "plot," as it later turned out.

During my tour of duty, I found that the Ljubljana organizations differed little from the Zagreb and Belgrade groups. They appeared a little more relaxed, and certainly less strict with regard to personal conduct.

The best organization was in Maribor, headed by Zidanšek, a follower of Petko Miletić. Zidanšek was an extremely bright and able man, and it could hardly escape his attention that the control of the Central Committee had shifted. So he opened up both his organization and his heart. He fully expected to be replaced, all his work and trouble of three years down the drain. He was solid, straight, and to the point; he spoke little, but clearly. His reputation among the workers was steadily growing.

Having thoroughly checked out the Slovenian organizations, and following numerous discussions and meetings, I concluded that the situation in Slovenia was sound and that Kidrič's suspicions were sick and senseless. I met with the Central Committee members in a suburb of Ljubljana. We took a long walk: Vida Tomšič was crying; her husband, Tone, was depressed. Luka Leskovšek was upset, convinced that it was his fault that the "enemy" had undermined the organization.

It was cold winter weather. I stayed with a musician who lived on a godforsaken street in a Ljubljana suburb. His family was very poor, and, in spite of their protests, they were glad to accept the food I brought them. I held conferences at night, in freezing-cold weather, and came back to a freezing flat long after the trams had stopped running. But I got a lot of work done.

I left suddenly, even by my standards. In Zagreb I gave Tito and Kardelj a detailed account of my findings: Kidrič's suspicions were unfounded. Since the organization was sound, I began to suspect Kidrič of being a Trotskyite, and perhaps a provocateur. I brought that up too. Tito and Kardelj rejected this idea as ridiculous. I wavered and withdrew.

Kardelj reported my suspicions to Kidrič. Kidrič was hurt, and this lasted for a long time, even after the war. I felt badly, which made me try to get close to him.

Immediately following this incident, we had to deal with the Stefan Galogaža affair in Zagreb.

Galogaža was a writer and journalist who had performed great services for the party. During the worst years of the dictatorship, he found ways of publishing leftist magazines. Also, he was our "legal contact" with illegal activists from abroad. He found apartments for them and gave them money. In addition, as head of Red Aid in Yugoslavia, he was widely known among leftists, and obviously among the police as well.

He had begun his political career by volunteering for the Serbian army in the war of 1912. In the postwar era he became disillusioned with the national idea, and he started a magazine called *Kritika* (*Criticism*), which gradually assumed party positions. The January 6th Dictatorship brought him very close to the party. He was arrested several times and tortured by the police.

Galogaža liked to sit in the Zagreb cafés late into the night. He had turned sallow from coffee and cigarettes, which he consumed in enormous quantities. His yellow eyes looked large in his pale, emaciated face. For hours on end he would sit and chat with comrades at the Café Medulić, or at the Gradska Kafana.

Galogaža couldn't hang on to money for any length of time. He always spent freely, by treating comrades to drinks or "lending" money to them. Some of this money came from Red Aid funds. Of course, it was assumed that his position and function entitled him to such expenses. For years no one checked on him. But with the stabilization of the party organization, this item was put on the agenda.

It turned out that Galogaža was performing his duties as Secretary of Red Aid very amateurishly. This job could no longer be conducted at a café table; the money could no longer be given away casually, because the bulk of it no longer came from abroad. Red Aid—that is, People's Assistance—was now a complex organizational issue that demanded systematic daily attention. Galogaža was simply not up to this task, in spite of his efforts to organize himself and grow with the times.

Thus it was a great blow to him when he was relieved of his duties as Secretary of Red Aid. These duties were now entrusted to the Serbian head of People's Assistance. Galogaža liked to gossip and thrash out everything with comrades, and he couldn't keep secrets. This suddenly became a problem for the Central Committee. Galogaža was angry, and grumbled against the new leadership, whom he had continuously supported and all of whose members he knew personally. Tito and I felt sentimental about him, but Končar had it in for him. Galogaža was suspected of spending People's Assistance money for his personal use. There was no way of avoiding an investigation.

I was on the investigating committee, and this made Galogaža quite bitter—even if I had not been so persistent and unmerciful. We had known each other for many years, and on my frequent visits to Zagreb I always called on him. His house was a place where one could pick up all the party gossip as well as essential contacts.

Indeed, the investigation brought to light an extreme sloppiness in handling money. Even so, Tito managed to smooth things over a little, and Galogaža was given only a strict reprimand.

But his time was up. He belonged to a former era and an antiquated party style. Gradually, Galogaža was alienating himself from the party.

Tito was the only one of us involved in the activities of the Military Commission of the Central Committee. The other members of the commission were Mitar Bakić and Vladimir Popović.

Work in the army was considered exceptionally dangerous and confidential. It was assumed that the discovery of Communist organizations in the army would automatically draw death sentences. Several air force officers, some former school friends of Bakić's from Montenegro, sought contact with the party through Bakić, and so he became a member of the commission. Work in the army was to be developed with the help of these officers, and the commission was to collect all available information about Communists in the army. The commission's activities progressed slowly— only a few contacts were made outside of the Zagreb group. The war brought a stop to this project.

Among the officers Božo Lazarević stood out, with his energy, high spirits, and good looks. Dressed in a handsome uniform he looked every bit an adventurous type, decisive and effective. He had an affair with Bakić's wife, Ruža, who was a very good-looking woman, slender and strong. We were very surprised, because she had just gotten married, and we thought she was in love with her young husband. Ruža was not a party member. Bakić and Lazarević were working on the same party project and they were good friends, which complicated the matter further. It was impossible for us to proceed as usual and expel Lazarević. Our needs dictated a different solution. Lazarević was reprimanded, and Bakić made peace with his wife, who cried a lot and promised to reform, to which theory I also made a friendly contribution.

Bakić had served time in prison and he stood up very well. Freed by the court, he returned to his old job of checking movie house receipts. This job gave him free tickets to all the movie houses. So the two of us spent a lot of time in the movies. I don't think I ever saw as many films in a similar period. I was very friendly with Bakić, and when I had nowhere else to sleep he gave me a bed.

Mitar Bakić was strong, muscular, and very cheerful, with a sense of fun which was not without a certain rough cynicism. He liked to associate with high-ranking functionaries and to work on "special" jobs, but he was nobody's flunkey. He wanted to become a political writer, although he had no talent for writing or for theory. He tended to overestimate his capabilities, but in every other respect he was an honorable man, straight and controlled in his behavior within the party.

Bakić and I became friends partly because, outside of Ognjen Prica, I had very few close friends in Zagreb. Also, Montenegrins characteristically seek out one another in a strange environment, and the more isolated they are the closer they become. We remained good friends until my conflict with the Central Committee in January 1954. A year later, in January 1955, at the time of my trial, he asked me to return the hunting gun and fishing rod that he had given me as gifts several years before. In the meantime I had passed them on to other people. So I ended up compensating him directly.

During my stay in Zagreb we had a political conflict with Otokar Keršovani, which was not without significance.

France had already capitulated to Hitler. The Nazis were hovering over the Balkans. Britain appeared powerful in its determination. The two colossi, the Soviet Union and Germany, were continually testing one another. Keršovani wrote an article, published in *Izraz* (*Expression*), analyzing the balance of power following the German victory in France. He concluded that Germany had become the greatest military power in the world, and that a conflict between the Soviet Union and Germany was inevitable. In this battle the Soviet Union would have to rely on the Western powers.

Keršovani's article was criticized in party circles for its demoralizing effect. Kardelj and I were particularly bitter. I wrote a reply, in the same magazine, under the pseudonym V. Zatarac. My article was dialectically skilled and convincing, although, as it turned out, it was wrong in its fundamental premise. Of course, I maintained that the "first land of socialism" had to be stronger than Germany, that there was no possibility of war between Germany and the Soviet Union, that Germany was much too weak for such a contest, and so forth.

Keršovani was judged severely in party circles, whereas I won general admiration for my intelligent appraisal of the situation.

Suddenly one morning a ban was put on the trade-union movement. Our role in the trade unions, particularly in Croatia, was substantial, and the workers in Maček's Croatian Workers Peasant party had gradually come under our influence. This blow was aimed directly at the Communists. We believed that Maček had played a major role.

We got together immediately to draft a course of action. If I recall correctly, it was at the end of February 1941.

Tito arrived late. He was angry. Without taking his coat off, or even sitting down, he spelled out our position: in addition to writing critical articles in the illegal press and making efforts to save trade-union funds, we Communists were to infiltrate the regime's trade unions. The war prevented us from putting this policy into action. Of course, it seemed impossible to us in any case.

Shortly after, I left for Belgrade, and Ranković arrived to replace me. The immediate reason for this switchover was for Ranković to conduct trade-union activities in the name of the Central Committee, and to tackle the organizational and party problems. He was better equipped than I to deal with both. Until that time I had maintained contact with the newly formed central trade-union party commission. I also think there was another indirect, personal reason. Tito felt more related to Ranković, he felt Ranković would be more helpful and could even substitute for him in organizational matters. Tito sensed in Ranković not only a worker, and as such closer to him, but also a party man with a great ability to handle details, to spot the key facts, and to make sure they were not forgotten. I called Ranković a "genius for detail," and of course he was.

There were no other reasons. Tito, Kardelj, and I got along in every respect.

It was at the end of February, or the beginning of March, when I got on the train with Vlado Dedijer and his wife, Olga, and left for Belgrade. Vlado's semilegal publishing activities in Zagreb had come to an end. The possibilities for him there were exhausted. It was already dark when the train stopped at Mitrovica, where the Belgrade police agents replaced the Zagreb agents. For me, an illegal operator, the Belgrade agents were more dangerous. I had forged papers, and I was afraid I might run into an agent who knew me personally.

Vlado had worked as a criminal reporter for *Politika* and he knew many of the agents. He went out on the platform to see if any of them were boarding the train. Two well-dressed gentlemen passed by our carriage. There is a kind of casual elegance in the behavior of Secret Police which never escapes those who are hiding from them. I was sure those two gentlemen were agents. I saw them getting into the last carriage.

The train was already moving when Vlado came back into the compartment and told me that one of the agents was a certain Ilija, from the Criminal Police, known for his cruelties. I grabbed my case and rushed out. As the train was slowly working its way out of the station, I jumped out into the darkness, and landed on the ground, which was black with coal dust and full of puddles from melting snow.

Walking down muddy streets toward the center of town, I had time to think things over. Although I had reasonably good identification papers, I felt that staying in a hotel was not a good idea. Hotels were being carefully checked. After all, Sremska Mitrovica was an important station for the police agents. But I didn't know anyone in town.

I suddenly thought of an old, well-to-do Serbian family whose son I had known. He was a law student in Zagreb and a sympathizer. He had been a student for many years, but had just barely managed to scrape through a few exams. His parents were unhappy about it. He was an only son, which made them all the more worried. This charming, intelligent young man was wasting his time in expensive restaurants and night clubs with the "golden youth." At one time Veselin Masleša had hidden out in the family's vineyard, and I visited him there. I had met the mother, and remembered her as a sweet, pleasant woman.

But how was I to find this family? And how would I ask them to let me spend a night there?

I got into a carriage and asked the driver to take me to the family's home. "Are they the people who own the mill?" he asked. "Yes, they are," I replied. Obviously the driver knew the home of the mill owner, a source of considerable wealth in Vojvodina.

He stopped in front of a one-story house, rather typical for this part of the world. I tossed a snowball at the window, and a woman appeared. I recognized her. I told her I was passing through Mitrovica, and her son had asked me to give her a message. The poor woman ran down and opened the gate. She looked at me with fear and pent-up joy. I'd already made up my mind what to tell her.

"Your son passed an exam. . . ." "Criminal law?" she asked. "Criminal law, yes, criminal law . . ."

She took me inside and called out to her husband in great excitement. We sat down in the drawing room, and her husband walked in, knotting his tie. He was getting ready to go to his weekly card game. This powerful old man, well dressed and groomed, greeted me kindly but coldly, expressing no emotion over his boy's "success," as if he knew all too well that, even if true, this would in no way change the life style of his lost son. He excused himself and returned to the bedroom to finish dressing.

Then, looking straight into her warm eyes, I told her I was on the run from the police and that I had nowhere else to spend the night. In my experience every mother knew about the secret political sympathies of her child, and she usually shared them. I was right. She appeared confused, but she used the confusion to conceal things from her husband rather than to throw me out. She asked me to stay for coffee.

She gave me an excellent dinner, and then we played cards. Of course, I lost all the time. Just before I was about to retire into an out-of-the-way room, she asked me if I had given her the news of her son's success in order to gain access to her house. I didn't think it right to tell her the truth. Besides, her son was about to take the exams and he would never tell her if he failed anyway.

Very early in the morning the maid brought me a cup of coffee in bed. I left without having said good-bye to my wonderful hostess.

I took a bus to Zemun and went straight to Dedijer's. He was very relieved to see me.

The atmosphere of persecution and pressure grew daily, as if the country were already in a state of war. The Cvetković-Maček government was making preparations to join the Tripartite Pact and it was taking increasingly severe measures to ensure peace and order. The press was supporting the Axis Powers. We had a journalist in the Central Press Bureau, who attended the confidential press conferences of Cincar-Marković, the Minister of Foreign Affairs. This was a very important source of information for us: we now knew that, under German pressure, the government intended to capitulate.

The Central Committee, or, rather, Tito, started a magazine called *Saopštenja* (*Information*), which was a much better way of reaching the public than the traditional leaflets. *Saopštenja* was not stylistically very smooth, but it got the message across. In this maturing crisis, it was increasingly evident that it was the Communists who would take the most energetic position in the defense of the country. Daily events were proving that our charges against the government and its cowardly foreign policy were correct.

Conditions in Belgrade were far more difficult than in Zagreb. Maček and Šubašić were still in their initial stages of power. Consequently the Central Committee headquarters remained in Zagreb.

But that didn't last long. With unexpected haste, even for the Central Committee, the situation was about to undergo a radical change.

18

The Communist leadership was fully aware that the Cvetković-Maček government was making preparations to join the Tripartite Pact. Earlier developments had separated us Communists from all the other political parties, except for the Ribar-Smiljanić group and Dragoljub Jovanović's Peasant party. In fact, these two groups had become closer to us.

When Tito came to Belgrade at the beginning of March 1941, Lola Ribar arranged a meeting for him with his father, Dr. Ivan Ribar. Tito also met with people from the Serbian Cultural Club, who favored a policy of national defense. However, Ribar had very little power. We had to count on the allies we had.

Ivan Milutinović conducted negotiations with Dragoljub Jovanović before he left for Zagreb, and they went very well. Tito's negotiations didn't yield much—Ribar was on our side in any case—but his talks with members of the Serbian Cultural Club were very useful. We now had a fairly clear impression of the atmosphere prevailing among the Serbian bourgeois parties, which was in complete contrast to the submissive spirit of the government, and particularly of Prince Paul.

Now I had to conduct the negotiations myself—I was the only member of the Politburo left in Belgrade.

The Regional Committee, in agreement with the Central Committee, decided to organize demonstrations against Yugoslavia's joining the Tripartite Pact. Instructions were sent to the provincial committees to hold demonstrations whenever and wherever possible. We were also preparing one in Belgrade. We decided to publish a proclamation with the signatures of prominent cultural and political people. Gathering signatures was a tough job. People were afraid. I scheduled a meeting with Dragoljub Jovanović to discuss his participation in this action. The meeting was held in his father's country house, outside of Belgrade. Spasenija Babović, Secretary of the Regional Committee, was also present.

I had never met Dragoljub Jovanović, but I had heard a great deal about him from his former followers. I expected to see an evil, selfish man, underhanded and unstable. And so I was extra cautious.

As soon as we sat down to talk, I realized that my caution was unnecessary. Jovanović's party and we Communists were in the same boat, we were both being threatened by domestic reaction and Hitler's forces. That in itself eliminated many differences. Besides, Dragoljub Jovanović had been consistent in his co-operation with us even though we had not concluded any formal agreement, and I had no reason to doubt that he would fulfill his share of the agreement.

Jovanović didn't know my name. I was, for him, only a functionary of the Communist party. The fact that he was willing to negotiate with me meant a lot. He had previously had contacts with Masleša, but Masleša had legal status and was fairly well known. Now it was different; he was negotiating with the illegal party center, straight and to the point.

We reached our agreement on the projected leaflet and further co-operation quickly and easily. In fact, we agreed on everything.

Nevertheless there was a great difference between us.

Both he and I anticipated a period of sharp reaction and a sudden intrusion of Hitler's ideology into the life of the country, but only Jovanović was depressed about this. He told me that he anticipated a few years of darkness and violence of a kind this country had never experienced before. For him the war was a cataclysm which we couldn't resist; we had to wait for it to run its course. My own mood wasn't exactly bright, but I was not afraid of the war. Also, my feeling about the Soviet Union was different from his. We were a creation of the Soviet Union. But for him the Soviet Union was a foreign country, more or less useful, depending on the situation. Eventually we would share our destiny with the Soviet Union, but his could be different.

Jovanović was in hiding; he was also afraid he might be arrested.

He gave no indication of any foreknowledge of the *coup d'état* planned by General Simović for March 27, 1941. We Communists didn't know about it either, although we knew how alarmed some top-ranking officers were with the government's policy.

Nor did the Regional Committee know what was going on in the provinces of Serbia. We had given instructions that protests be organized against the Tripartite Pact, but we never suspected that events might take such a different turn. Military leaders, in co-operation with the nationalist organizations such as Soko and the National Defense, had also began organizing people in protest meetings. Their action joined with our own. Standing side by side were colonels, majors, and our own comrades, addressing excited groups of townspeople and peasants. Of course, our people made an effort to give these gatherings an aggressive and pro-Soviet character. Army officers and bourgeois politicians lent them the legality. The unanimity of the gatherings was tremendous. The Communists didn't indulge in any sectarianism, aware that the independence of the country was the foremost objective.

In fact, we in Belgrade knew nothing about these gatherings, held a couple of days before the events of March 27.

We held our own demonstrations at eight o'clock the evening of March 26, in several different locations, at Vračar, Njegoševa Street, and Queen Maria Street (now March 27 Street). We were to join forces and walk toward the center of the city, provided we got a lot of response. But we didn't. Only about a thousand people showed up. Fear had penetrated the ranks of our sympathizers. Contrary to expectation, the police reaction to the demonstrators was mild. They stopped them from walking toward the center of the city, thus quickly putting an end to the demonstration.

We spent the night in the apartment of Žika Vlajinić. Tito himself had stayed there a couple of times. Early the next morning Mitra went out to buy a paper and some food for breakfast. She heard about the coup and ran back. We immediately turned on the radio and heard King Peter's proclamation of the end of the Regency. It was seven o'clock in the morning. I went out to try to locate the rest of the Regional Committee. They were out looking for me. Communist groups were combing the streets, looking for contacts, and instructions.

I immediately installed myself in the apartment of a sympathizer on Molerova Street. People came by to get information. In the morning I wrote a proclamation. Vuković ran it off on our illegal presses in the afternoon, and at six o'clock it was distributed among the demonstrators.

Our position was that we should participate in the demonstrations and take over the leadership where possible. Our speakers were instructed to push our slogans: democratization of the country and support of the Soviet Union.

In the course of the day, we took over. We were among the most active and best organized. The demonstrations first began as a spontaneous outpouring of popular protest, with the active participation of Soko and other organizations. Communists spontaneously joined in. It was not till later that they contributed to the character of the demonstrations. Dozens of speakers emerged from the Communist underground. They were gaining popularity among the masses because of their firm, organized stand. Lola Ribar spoke at Slavija; Stefan Mitrović and Svetozar Vukmanović at Vuk's Monument. Rade Končar, Cana Babović, and Mitra also spoke. Communists were hoarse from speaking and screaming.

I spent the whole day in the apartment receiving reports and sending instructions. I left briefly around noon to meet with Dragoljub Jovanović. This meeting was arranged by Lola Ribar. It was held in the sanatorium on Queen Natalie Street. Mobs of people were running down the street carrying Yugoslav flags, drunk with enthusiasm.

At the meeting we agreed that the proposed proclamation against the Tripartite Pact had become obsolete. Jovanović was so happy that he was incapable of any reasonable analysis. I said that our main objective was to prevent Germany from attacking by getting Yugoslavia to sign an agreement on mutual assistance with the Soviet Union and giving democratic freedoms to the people. He agreed with me, but was unconcerned with details; the main objective had been accomplished, the honor of the nation saved. I was a lot more skeptical, fearing the instability of the government and its strong reactionary and chauvinist forces. The country's honor had indeed been saved; now it had to be defended.

We agreed to meet again. But that meeting didn't take place until three and a half years later, after the war was over in most of Yugoslavia, and in very different roles and circumstances.

In the course of the day the character of the demonstrations clarified itself. In the late afternoon, during the demonstrations in the suburbs, in which the Soko organization and the nationalists participated, the Communists took a leading role. The suburbs had separated themselves from the center of the city, the poor from the rich.

Around nine o'clock in the evening I left my apartment and walked over to Slavija, to join the largest group under our leadership. This gathering of about 15,000 people was presided over by Vladimir Popović, Rade Končar, and several members of the regional and local committees. One speaker followed another in quick succession. Slogans echoed.

The slogan of the day was *"Bolje rat nego pakt!"* ("War is better than the Pact!"). We Communists didn't favor this slogan, although we didn't oppose it either. We felt the approach was wrong. Rather, by leaning on the Soviet Union, we should try to avoid the war. There was no way of suppressing it though. Someone shouted it, and the crowd spontaneously picked it up. The strength of the slogan was in its simplicity, in its expression of national pride, and pride was something the Serbian nation has always had. The springtime had awakened new life in us. It was good to be a Serb that day.

The crowd moved slowly away from Slavija, and running into tanks and soldiers in front of the Officers' Club, it turned into Njegoševa Street. Someone shouted: "The Soviet Consulate!" which was on King Milutin Street. But a double cordon of soldiers guarded the approach to the Consulate. The crowd wavered for some time, and then a tremendous row broke out between the army officers and the ringleaders.

Rade Končar was known for his courage and determination as well as for his temper. He was almost bald, which gave his face an even more energetic expression. Intelligent, able, and above all aggressive, he emerged at the head of the Zagreb organization and was Secretary of the Croatian party and a member of the Politburo of the Yugoslav party. No one ever helped him get ahead. He did it himself. There were people cleverer and more experienced than he. Bakarić, for example, was far wiser, and Kraš far more experienced, but it never so much as occurred to either of them to seek to replace him. Like so many other idealistic revolutionaries, he was gentle and straight in his private life. He really loved his wife and his child. For him our moral rules were reality, like everything else that came from the Communist party. This splendid revolutionary was tough, of course. He had an unusually sure political instinct, and he rarely made mistakes. He was born for the revolution, and he died for it. He was executed by the Italians, in Split, during the war. His last wondrous words expressed the essence of the war: "I ask for no mercy, and would show no mercy."

This same man got into a fight with an officer, in whom he instinctively saw a "class enemy," who wouldn't allow us access to the Soviet Consulate. At first calm and friendly, the officer gradually grew exasperated and shouted that he was under orders not to let anyone through. Most of the Communists supported Končar in his readiness to attack, but their enthusiasm was under control. I finally pulled Končar aside and asked him not to provoke a conflict with the army which had brought down the old regime. Končar gave in, and the crowd started up Njegoševa Street.

Speakers continued to shout their slogans.

By the time we had reached Kalenić Market it was close to eleven o'clock. Comrades urged me to speak. I had to think of something to say to this crowd of 15,000 people, most of them workers. Something special had to be done not to let 15,000 people slip out of our hands just like that.

I turned out to be the last speaker on March 27.

I took a positive, if somewhat reserved, position: we would judge the government by its acts. We welcomed the overthrow. The country could not successfully defend itself if the government allowed no political freedom. Our demands were immediate release of all political prisoners, free trade unions, and a free press. We should look to the Soviet Union for guidance and support because the Soviet Union was the only power that could protect us from German attack. I appealed to them to elect committees in their respective institutions, to protect their rights. I asked them to join us at a meeting at Vuk's Monument at six o'clock the next day.

I felt my words were measured, although pronounced loudly and with passion. I was myself rather pleased, though the speech probably could have been more effective. I overheard someone saying: "This one speaks for the party." Silence prevailed. I had everyone's attention. A small boy climbed up on the platform. He grabbed my jacket and stared at me in fascination.

That same evening Mitra and Buha went to Zagreb to report to the Central Committee on the events in Belgrade, and to ask Tito to come to Belgrade, where the action was. Indeed, Tito arrived in Belgrade on March 29. I was waiting for him in Fingerhut's flat, although there was no longer any need for secrecy. We moved around freely and behaved as if we were a legal party. Those imprisoned in the jails were released, Moša Pijade among them, although no general amnesty had been proclaimed.

On March 28, workers and office employees had elected their own committees in a good number of institutions. But the meeting I had proposed for March 28 was not held.

The Simović government demanded that the meeting be postponed. Messengers went back and forth between government representatives and the Regional Committee, which was in session in an apartment at Kotež Neimar. Lola Ribar told us that his father, like other leftist bourgeois politicians, wanted to avoid conflict over the meeting, which in effect meant calling it off. Spasenija Babović and Blagoje Nešković had a very negative reaction to this proposition. The unstable bourgeoisie, they said, were in opposition now that the interests of the working class were at stake. The fact remained, however, that the country was facing an attack from the Axis Powers, and that if we Communists were to provoke a conflict with a government that had not as yet stated clearly its intentions, we would have to assume the political responsibility for having turned against the new regime, and also for impeding national defense. It wasn't merely a question of relations between the government and the Communists, but the fate of the whole nation. After some hesitation I decided to call off the meeting.

Unfortunately, the majority of the Regional Committee members opposed the idea. But since they were accustomed to accepting resolutions on which Ranković and I insisted, my position was reluctantly accepted.

When Tito arrived in Belgrade, I told him what had happened. We had done the right thing, he said, which didn't surprise him at all, because he knew how "sectarian" the Belgrade Communists were. Tito's comment spread fast. Everyone was pleased that we had done the right thing, and that we were called "sectarian," which meant that we were aggressive and tough, perhaps even dogmatic, Communists.

The Regional Committee consultation was anounced by a messenger whom we had dispatched on March 27 throughout Serbia. In addition to the usual organizational issues, the new political situation was thrashed out. Tito emphasized that defense of the country was our first responsibility. Co-operation with the Soviet Union and democracy appeared to be within reach, and we were to make every effort to co-operate with all groups that took the same position. At the same time he attacked "Anglophile elements" and "provocateurs" who demolished the German Tourist Bureau, the center of Hitler's propaganda in Belgrade, and burned the German flag. The consultation ended by concluding that the Communists had done very well in the period of the March 27 coup. The unity of the party was complete.

Tito returned to Zagreb after the consultation, and announced that the Central Committee would immediately shift operations to Belgrade. Conditions in Serbia had changed for the better, and we Communists had suddenly become a semilegal movement, while the situation in Croatia had taken a turn for the worse. Communists were not released from prisons and concentration camps, not even when the war started, but were left for the Ustashi regime, which killed them all.

Even so, the Central Committee didn't move immediately. The shift was obstructed by the German attack on Yugoslavia. We Communists had, of course, suspected that this would happen, but, like everybody else, we hoped against hope that we might be spared. Wasn't the Soviet Union strong enough to protect us?

19

The new Soviet Consulate had been established in Belgrade now for several months, but we Communists had had no contact with it at all. We knew that Soviet diplomats abroad were reluctant to make contacts with Communists, and that our contact had to be directly with Moscow. The public greeted the arrival of the Soviet Minister and his staff to Belgrade with curiosity and friendliness. The Soviets, for their part, played up the Slavic character of their relationship to Yugoslavia.

Even though we had no direct contact with the Consulate, we knew a great deal about the activities of its staff, and particularly the journalists. One of them was a heavy drinker and he made all kinds of statements damaging to the reputation of the Soviet Union. Ranković and I reported this to Tito, and Tito in turn sent word to Moscow. The man was recalled.

We didn't even maintain contact with the Soviet Intelligence agent who had come to Belgrade long before the diplomatic staff—in fact, some time in 1939. He was hostile to our Central Committee and said that it was composed of Trotskyites. The Regional Committee, particularly Ranković, kept an eye on him, and we suspected that the agent himself might be a Trotskyite. He drank a lot and fooled around with women, which only served to confirm our suspicions.

Considering that "Cheka" was a magic word for us Communists, representing an all-powerful organization composed of the best revolutionaries, it will be clear why the antiparty position of this man worried us a lot. It wasn't so much the influence he could have over our activities, but the possibility that he might rally some support against the new leadership and make trouble for us in Moscow.

Čile Kovačević maintained contact with him by doing him various favors, which we encouraged. Moreover, we were prepared to kill him if he indeed proved to be a Trotskyite. So we followed him carefully, and took photographs of him. Ranković showed them to Tito, who recognized the man, and ordered us to leave him alone. He was in Yugoslavia on a "special assignment," and all his talk against the Central Committee could be his way of concealing his identity.

The man's name was Mustafa Golubić. He was a nationalist revolutionary, whose work dated to pre-World War I days. He had been involved in the Salonika trials and associated with Colonel Apis Dimitrijević. He escaped immediately after the war, joined the Communist movement, and soon became an agent of the Soviet Secret Police. Among us Communists there were many tales about his great exploits in distant lands. Exactly how high he was in the hierarchy of the Soviet secret service, I don't know. But judging by Tito's reaction, he must have been fairly important.

Anyway, we stopped spying on him, and he continued to associate with people who were not particularly reliable. Shortly after the occupation, the Germans took him away.

There was one Soviet agent who was actually a member of our party. Ranković maintained contact with him, and I ran into him occasionally. He had also arrived in Yugoslavia just before the war, but he operated independently of Golubić. He had brought with him a formula for making explosives. Cut off from Moscow after the occupation, he had to rely entirely on our party. He and the two engineers who were assisting him in making the explosives were wounded by their own explosions and captured by the Gestapo.

After the occupation of Yugoslavia, Tito had several meetings with the Soviet military attaché. The Soviet government had broken relations with the Yugoslav government, thereby formally acknowledging the dismemberment of the country, and their diplomats were making arrangements to leave. We found this difficult to take, although we understood the complexity of the position: the Soviet Union was still officially on friendly terms with Germany. Tito used the meetings with the attaché as an opportunity to send reports to the Comintern and for an exchange of opinions. As far as I know, that was our sole contact.

On the other hand, Vladislav Ribnikar, director of *Politika*, continued to maintain contact with Soviet journalists in Belgrade.

The Professional

Following the Moscow trials, Ribnikar had had his doubts about the Soviet Union. His second wife, Jara, was bitter on the subject, and her comments about Stalin and the Soviet Union were quite sharp. Ribnikar was not actually a Communist; he was an eccentric drawing-room leftist. He took a trip to the Soviet Union in 1927, but more to satisfy a bourgeois intellectual curiosity than to confirm his Communist convictions.

Dedijer insisted on my meeting with Ribnikar, whom I hadn't known personally, to attempt to win him over. That was in the fall of 1940.

After a long discussion at the first dinner party at Ribnikar's villa, I forced him to waver. After the second dinner party we parted friends. After the third dinner party he was convinced that the Trotskyites were not only wrong, but connected with the fascist secret service.

Jara was harder to break. But before long she also accepted our positions. She was much younger than her husband, and to while away the time she wrote Surrealistic verse and cast longing looks at other men. She even tried to seduce me, but she was not successful. Not because she wasn't good-looking, but because I stood firm on my Communist moral standards, which I myself had helped establish, and because I couldn't imagine any other relationship with the wife of a friend. Our relationship, which she has incorrectly described in one of her books, evolved into a certain fondness, of which her husband was aware and which never exceeded the proper limits, regardless of what may have been on her mind.

Ribnikar's relationship with his wife was a very relaxed one, a marriage of mutual convenience with a young mistress, and then they grew tired of their love by virtue of having legalized it. He didn't mourn the loss of his first wife, Stana Djurić-Klajn, who had deserted him for her psychiatrist. Ribnikar had given her ample cause: he had been quite free in his relationships with other women. He was not unattractive, although there was something weak and despondent about him.

Clearly Ribnikar was a man of good progressive tendencies. But I always felt it was the danger of Hitler's Germany that in the end made him turn to Communism. It took great moral and intellectual courage for the timid man he was to decide in favor of Communism.

Ribnikar recognized, better than we Communists, the weakness and flabbiness of spirit that characterized the ruling circles.

Cynical about his own class, Ribnikar was kind and gentle with his new friends, the Communists. And like most deserters, he avoided friends from his former, "bourgeois," life, even those who had signed papers and given guarantees to get him out of concentration camps, because for him they were now "reactionaries." In spite of his own ideological slackness, he couldn't help being exclusive and intolerant, like the rest of us, by virtue of being a Communist. But in 1941 he still maintained friendly relations with his neighbors, he still had a human understanding for the reactionaries. They must have noticed the tremendous commotion in Ribnikar's house, strange people coming in and out, particularly during the occupation. But these were the top social circles, and there were no informers among them. In fact, informing was considered a low and ignoble job done by people without name or honor.

Dedijer asked me to meet him for the usual dinner at the Ribnikars' on April 4. Tasa Grigoriyev, a Soviet reporter, was expected.

Grigoriyev didn't show up till after dinner. He was young, very Russian in appearance, very controlled, even a trifle cold, and he spoke very deliberately. My own image of Soviet men was altogether different: open, talkative, friendly. Still, I was pleased to have met a Soviet man, even though my first impression was not favorable.

Early in 1944 he joined our supreme command, as a member of the first Soviet Military Mission under General Korneyev, and I got to know him very well. His assistant, Saharov, a pleasant, well-educated man, also joined General Korneyev's mission. He had been a Consulate employee, but I never met him in that capacity. Both men had been Soviet agents and used their jobs as covers. After the war they hardly bothered to conceal from us Central Committee members that they were recruiting Yugoslav citizens to work against their own government and the Central Committee.

When I first met Grigoriyev I didn't really care much whether he was a spy or not, although I can't say I was delighted by the news.

My talk with Grigoriyev wasn't particularly scintillating. He didn't know how to talk, especially with people whom he had to keep a certain distance.

We Communists were very well informed about all the moves of the Simović government. We were in close contact with people like Ribnikar who had daily contact with government ministers. We knew about Ninčić's efforts to divide Italy and Germany, and win over the former, and we interpreted this as the naïveté of a frightened "pro-Italian." We also knew that negotiations were being conducted with the Soviet government. We knew nothing, though, about the attempts of the British government to encourage Simović, or about the secret meeting between the representatives of the two governments on the Greek border, or about Eden's attempt to get in touch with Simović. We considered Churchill's greetings, in recognition of March 27, provocative in spite of their poetic beauty. We were angry at the government for being so slow in organizing the defense of the country. The proclamation of Belgrade, Zagreb, and Ljubljana seemed naïve to us, and we instinctively felt that the fascist powers would not honor it.

The meeting with Grigoriyev was by no means accidental. I never suspected Ribnikar of having worked for the Soviet secret service. His contact with Grigoriyev never exceeded the limits of political people. But of course Grigoriyev took advantage of Ribnikar's contacts with local Communist leaders. Ribnikar never worked for the Soviet service. Suspicion was cast on his wife, based on evidence presented by our own secret service about her affairs with Soviet agents and her cynical remarks about the Yugoslav Central Committee following the break in 1948. Ribnikar's son was arrested in connection with Cominform activities, and I personally intervened to have him released. But no one ever suspected Ribnikar himself, not as far as I know anyway.

Toward the end of the dinner at the Ribnikars', Grigoriyev told me that on the morning of April 6, the signing of the Soviet-Yugoslav Pact would be officially announced. He didn't tell me what the pact was, but I assumed it was a pact of mutual assistance, which we Communists had been urging for several years. He wanted us to organize pro-Soviet demonstrations in this connection, which we would have done even if Grigoriyev hadn't obliquely suggested it.

As we Communists saw it, the conclusion of such an agreement meant saving Yugoslavia from a German attack, as well as a substantial strengthening of our Communist positions and the legalization of our organization. All our goals—ideological, political, and national—combined to push us Communists to seek such a pact.

But no such agreement was ever concluded, nor did we ever manage to hold the desired pro-Soviet demonstrations.

20

As is now known, it was the Soviet-Yugoslav friendship pact—and not a pact of mutual assistance—that was announced in Moscow on the morning of April 6. But in Belgrade no one ever heard this announcement, deafened as we were by the tumult of German bombers and the roar of the Axis war machine over Yugoslavia.

We spent all of April 5 making preparations. Grigoriyev had said that the news would be announced at 7:00 A.M. The local and district committee members, and cell secretaries, were scheduled to meet in the park at Krunska Street. At 7:00 they would be dispersed to the far corners of Belgrade, to mobilize the masses, and guide them toward the center of the city, and ultimately to the Soviet Consulate. We had no reason to fear the police, but we wanted to be cautious and we recommended that the committee members keep to the side streets. At the appointed hour, people began gathering at street corners. Vukmanović, Končar, other leaders, and I were also there, waiting for the messenger with the news of the pact, before giving final instructions for action. Someone said that German radio stations were broadcasting a proclamation of the German government. Early that morning, in attempting to get Radio Moscow, I had heard wild shouting from all of the German stations. It suddenly occurred to me that it might have been a declaration of war. But wild polemics against Yugoslavia had been customary since March 27. I finally got Moscow, which turned out to be playing music, and then had to leave for the meeting.

We were in a festive mood, convinced that this would be the greatest demonstration Belgrade had ever seen, with us Communists as its leaders. "Belgrade-Moscow is our only salvation," the slogan we had pushed on March 27, had since become very popular, and we hoped that it would reach all hearts that day. In the middle of our pleasant chatting we suddenly saw two gendarmes in strange crouching positions, ordering people to move on. Someone remarked that the police simply couldn't help chasing Communists, and we were about to curse them. But then we heard a powerful explosion, the buzzing of motors, and the howling sound of a siren. People in the street were running, bent over, like rags carried by the wind. Soon the streets were deserted. I suggested we look for a more sheltered spot and moved to Kičevska Street. This move saved us. No sooner had we gone than a bomb fell, round the corner, on the exact spot where we had stood a few seconds earlier. The explosion pushed us to the ground, and we were covered by chunks of earth and asphalt. Kičevska Street was deserted, except for a peasant running after his milk cart. Someone suggested we seek shelter in the nearby cellar, but I thought that the entryway would do. From the apartments of this four-story building men, women, and children were pouring out in their nightclothes, running down to the cellar.

I looked out through the glassed opening in the door. The sky was streaked with clouds. From the Danube three bluish airplanes were approaching, releasing heavy gray weights. Bombs, I thought, flying madly toward their destination! Instinctively, and this happened to me often during the war, I felt that we were that destination. I walked back into the corridor, by the stairs, where my comrades were bunched together, at which point a powerful explosion laid us flat across the stairs. A thick cloud of smoke overcame us. "Poison gas!" someone screamed. But the smell was familiar, from many years before, when I had tried to catch fish with dynamite. I reassured them that it wasn't gas. I thought we were buried in the rubble. Then someone lit a match. The darkness was the thick dust from the crushed brick and lime. We rushed to the door, which was dangling in mid-air. A pile of bricks and beams lay high before the entrance. The four floors had been cut down clean, as if with a razor, but the ceiling of the first-floor apartment, on the street side, stood intact. The dust had penetrated our skin and clothing, and our teeth and the whites of our eyes glistened madly. No one was wounded, just a few minor cuts here and there. Vukmanović, Končar, Buha, and Vule Antić were with me. Vukmanović and Antić ran for dear life, while the rest of us found shelter in a nearby yard, deliberately deciding on a low house this time.

Fleets of planes flew overhead. The city howled with wounds.

Bombs came down attached to parachutes. Someone yelled: "Parachutists!" "Parachutists!" echoed on all sides. In the air the "parachutists" twisted and turned. They were gigantic bombs designed for special surface action. Every time one exploded—they were falling some distance away now—the earth would painfully heave under us.

This lasted for about an hour. The city lay in fire, smoke, and ruins.

We decided to walk toward our usual meeting places, and look for comrades on the way.

Where was Mitra? Had she survived? If only we had been together!

As often happens, someone had seen us entering the building that was hit by the bomb and they assumed we were dead. But Mitra refused to believe that, so she was looking for us all over the city. She couldn't find us. She finally came to a heath where party members were beginning to gather.

There, on that heath, we held a meeting of the Regional Committee and decided that comrades who were obligated to join the army do so, and that the rest leave the city to protect themselves from air raids.

We were without food, although none of us felt hunger. Those who had already experienced war, the Spanish fighters, were able to introduce a note of calm.

In the afternoon there was another raid, of about the same intensity, which we observed from the clearing. The city was being destroyed along the main streets. A house nearby, with families in the cellar, was wrenched off its foundations. Mitra was crying for the city, as if it were her child, her youth, her beauty. The poor and the rich were passing by, cursing, the poor because they hardly deserved this kind of beating, and the rich because they couldn't decide whether to save their lives or their possessions. The streets leading to the suburbs and nearby villages were packed. Now and then a car squeezed through loaded with eiderdowns and the fat wives of generals and their servants. Most of those with cars had escaped in the morning, leaving in an instant this thousand-year-old city, now turned modern in just twenty years.

That evening we decided to leave the city, and we headed south, toward Avala. The night was dark and damp. The city was bright with fires. Black smoke was rushing up into the skies. The army was on its way, somewhere: horses, oxen, and carts pushing into the black night. The officers were good-natured; soldiers cursed.

The Professional

No one believed we had the strength to defend the country. On the other hand, no one would say that he wouldn't fight.

The next day we reached Mladenovac. We walked over to Žujović's village, where I stayed overnight. The next morning, with Cana Babović, I returned to Belgrade to rescue what we could of the party machinery and the membership.

The torn city was merely beginning to suffer. There was no electricity, no water, no food. Bodies were strewn all over. There was no defense system, no first aid.

The police and the Chetniks, roaming the streets in trucks, were trying to establish "order" in a city that had been reduced from 300,000 to 30,000 inhabitants. They were shooting people, allegedly purging the city of its "fifth column" and its deserters. The city was overcome with hunger, despair, and fear. Patriotic citizens of Belgrade were actually waiting for the Germans to enter and save them from their own insane police. Every so often a shot would echo, and fresh blood would spill over the pavement, a "deserter" killed for having stolen bread from a demolished bakery. The very same policemen who had manhandled students and workers in recent years were rushing all over the city with Chetnik insignia. We Communists had to hide, even though we were the staunchest defenders of the country.

We managed to save some of our technical equipment. Much of it was lost in fires and in the panic. We located a number of our people and told them to get out of town. I stayed in Belgrade alone, with some women party members. Mitra had already left for Požega to join her mother. Then, after a discussion with Cana Babović, we decided I should no longer stay. The risk of being caught by the police was too great. How could I explain to anyone that I had no right to serve in the army? I left for Montenegro, to seek temporary shelter, and find out what was going on there.

Trains were crowded. Everyone was in a panic. The fear of spies was assuming senseless proportions. No one knew what was going on at the front lines. Fairy tales were spreading about our alleged victories. In fact, there were no front lines. There wasn't even a single radio station in operation.

Two days after my departure, the Germans entered Belgrade. Like most people, I hadn't believed this would happen so soon. I was convinced that western Serbia and Bosnia would put up a fight. At the same time, I had expected defeat.

At Gornji Milanovac neat rows of officers stood at the station waiting for the Germans. Kragujevac surrendered. It was rumored that one German tank had entered, and the town gave up. I intended to get off at Požega, but didn't. I was anxious to get to Bosnia and Montenegro as soon as possible. At Sarajevo I saw a few comrades. The Yugoslav government had just left Pale, a town near Sarajevo. Avdo Humo, whose father-in-law was a minister in the government, offered Communist help, but the offer was ignored. Also the Serbian general in charge of Zagreb's defense had refused a Communist request that the workers be armed against the Ustashi and the Germans.

There was something rotten in this government. A profound moral disintegration was seeping down from the state apparatus, from the top military ranks.

Our train was stopped near Mostar. We welled out of the cattle cars and waited for hours on the deserted fields along the Neretva River. Italian planes flew overhead, heading toward Sarajevo. Along the road, a convoy of trucks passed, loaded with soldiers from the King's Guards. They were heading south, toward Mostar and Montenegro.

Late in the afternoon the train started up again and soon we arrived in Mostar. We were not permitted to get off the train. The Italian planes continued flying overhead. The military authorities made every effort to forestall rebellious Croats from taking over. The station had been bombed, and the people on the train were terrified. But the Italians bombed the airport instead, setting a few planes afire. Mostar looked like a besieged city. Machine guns were perched at every corner in the center of the city. Croats in nearby villages, under the Ustashi influence, were in a state of rebellion, but not prepared to make an armed attack.

In the evening the passengers were squeezed into the hotel. There were constant rumors of everyone being butchered by Croatian or Turkish attackers, fortified by the continuous machine-gun fire and the roar of bombs falling through the night.

Early the following morning, a group of us, not afraid of Croats and Turks, walked to Nevesinje. People joined us along the way. At Nevesinje we were met by a committee in charge of accommodations and food for refugees. In contrast to Mostar, Nevesinje was a quiet provincial town, full of Serbian patriotic spirit. The town was peaceful, clean, and hospitable.

The following morning I was at Nikšić. The government and the King had already fled the country. The army was under orders to capitulate.

But the order had not reached Danilovgrad, whose military unit (including Blažo Jovanović and my brother) was in good condition and high spirits. This didn't last long. In the afternoon the troops from Skadar began to pull back. They had successfully defended the border, but now they were confused and bitter. The following day the Italians entered Podgorica.

The Communists had stood up very well in Montenegro, although they didn't yet feel it was their war. They believed that the "British imperialists" were using the war to their advantage. Their bitter enemies were still in power. But they also knew that the war would soon alter its character and they fought honorably.

As soon as I arrived, Blažo Jovanović gathered together a group of people in his house to discuss ways of putting aside as many weapons as they could lay their hands on. In fact, the peasants had done it instinctively, independently of anyone's orders. Soldiers on their way home had gladly given up a rifle in exchange for a piece of bread. I myself got hold of two rifles and took them with me to Bjelice, where Krsto Popivoda lived.

A unit made up of young people, strong and anxious to fight, was disbanded by its officer in the mountains near Zagarač. They were glad to have escaped capture, but they cursed the high command and the bourgeoisie that had made a deal with the Germans and the Italians. Treason and chaos were evident everywhere. There was great bitterness toward the Simović government for having fled the country without putting up an honest fight.

Through this mad chaos the German command was guiding its troops as if they were on parade.

I stayed in Montenegro, in the home of Blažo Jovanović, for another three or four days. We thrashed out the situation and decided to continue intensive activities along "military lines" with an organization of fighters.

It was striking to see how well the Italian troops behaved on entering the Montenegrin towns. In contrast to the simple Italian soldiers, who played marbles with the children in Podgorica streets, the Black Shirts stood out threateningly. Yet there was no plundering, no arrests, no use of force. Communists openly walked the streets and sat quietly in cafés. The only innovation was the compulsory greeting, a raised arm, on entering government buildings. This situation in Montenegro lasted, without basic change, until the German attack on the Soviet Union.

The Zelenaši (the Green Ones), supporters of an independent Montenegro, now began taking over from the Bjelaši (the White Ones), the supporters of the Yugoslav idea. They were organizing a new gendarmerie, composed chiefly of former Yugoslav police. The process was slow, and they received very little support. The independence of Montenegro was fine and good, but it couldn't be done in the shadow of Italian bayonets and under the Duce's banner. It was better to be conquered than shamed.

I was sorry that I had come down to Montenegro. I felt guilty, as if I had left my post. Perhaps comrades at the Central Committee would reproach me for it. They didn't, although I felt that a few of them were not happy about it.

Moša Pijade and Bora Prodanović had also fled to Montenegro. It was rumored in the Montenegrin Regional Committee that they were planning to take a boat from Boka for Africa, that is, to England. When Tito heard about this, he was angry with Pijade. Pijade always thought that it was I who had spread the rumor. I don't deny that I might have reported what I had heard at the Regional Committee, but I also believe that at one point, in the chaos that had enveloped everyone, they may have entertained the idea of escape. Prodanović was not an openly declared Communist, unconditionally tied to the party. As for Pijade, he was not only a well-known Communist, but a Jew as well, for whom the Germans represented a direct threat to life itself. I don't mean to imply that Pijade was ever an Anglophile.

Using an Italian pass, I returned to Belgrade. In Hercegovina I heard the first news about "Croatian" and "Turkish" violence. An "Independent State of Croatia" had been proclaimed, still drawing strength from established authority. Chaos was evident everywhere.

As the train approached Užice, German troops got on, with their boots and their olive uniforms. Their behavior was tough, uncommunicative, and mercilessly businesslike.

In a crowded compartment, an enormous peasant woman laboriously rose to her feet and said: "Oh, my Serbia, beautiful and rich, look what's become of you!" Everyone found her words tremendously moving, as if she had expressed the soul and the history of the Serbian people. Everyone felt shame and bitterness.

At the Belgrade station, German troops examined luggage, spreading fear by their stiff, cruel appearance. The city looked small. Corpses were strewn in the wreckage. A sour smell emanated from everything, people and food. The first posters were up announcing the shooting of one hundred Serbs for one German killed. At night shots echoed from different parts of the city. Fear, hunger, and death filled the streets. The air force was moving off toward Greece, and ground troops were on their way to Rumania.

The Croatian masses and the bulk of the Moslems had refused to fight against the Germans. But the Serbs, Montenegrins, and Slovenes had been willing to put up a fight. Among the Croats both the leaders and the masses were unwilling to fight, with the exception of the Communists, a few workers, some Dalmatians, among whom the fear of Italy and respect for the Yugoslav idea still had deep roots. Leading Serbs were entirely submissive. High-ranking officers had often surrendered their troops without resistance, although there were times when they could easily have put up a good fight.

In May Tito undertook an analysis of the war. The Central Committee had overestimated the army's willingness to resist the enemy. Indeed, under the influence of Simović's *coup d'état,* and the traditional heroism of the Serbian officers, we Communists had been convinced that the army would fight. But the leadership was demoralized, without goal or incentive. They had been trained to maintain authority and settle accounts inside the country rather than for its defense.

Another fact also emerged: the Communists hadn't performed too well. In certain situations they could have taken leadership and resisted the enemy, but they had not. Tito explained this in terms of the Communist faith in the military leadership. It was easy to say that Communists should have taken over, but how were we to do it? In spite of everything, there was a complex military mechanism to which soldiers adhered and which survived until their superiors announced that the war was over. We still had to learn how to create and direct an army.

Actually, there was nothing original in Tito's observation that we Communists had overestimated the Supreme Headquarters' desire to fight. We shared this illusion with the rest of the world, perhaps even with the Supreme Headquarters and Hitler's own high command. However, this was the first time, and so far as I know the only time, that Tito admitted his own mistake and that of the Central Committee. It wasn't that he had become more critical of himself, or that it was less important for him to maintain his authority. No! If Tito, that is we Communists, were set out to fight for power, to take over the army and the war, Tito had to speak openly. There was no hope for the old military machine. It no longer existed. Had it not been for our illusions, we would have won admiration as the only party that fought for independence to the end, even if it had been unsuccessful.

The occupation and the partition of Yugoslavia had not dealt a serious blow to the Communist organization. On the contrary, it turned the masses to Communism, and helped open new possibilities for its growth. The Communist party was the only party of general Yugoslav character. It had not compromised itself during the fall of the country. It was small, illegal, and extremely well organized. In a conversation with Molotov, in June 1944, I mentioned that, before the war, the Yugoslav Communists were few, but well organized, just like the Bolsheviks before World War I. He replied that the Bolsheviks were weak and badly organized at the beginning of World War I and that when he traveled illegally from St. Petersburg to Moscow in 1915, he could find no one to stay with except Lenin's sister, Maria Ilichina. Both parties had drawn strength from the chaos of war, but in very different ways.

We felt a need to review our experiences during the events of April 6 and to assess the state of the party. Tito scheduled a consultation in Zagreb, but the comrades from Montenegro, Bosnia, and Macedonia didn't show up. The Macedonians were not there because Šarlo, the Secretary of the Macedonian Regional Committee and a Bulgarian, believed that, with the Bulgarian occupation of Macedonia, this group should now join the Bulgarian Central Committee.

At this consultation Tito established a new thesis: the possibility of a direct Communist take-over of power, a denial of the need for the revolution to go through two stages, bourgeois-democratic and the proletarian, which had been the party position until then, following Comintern decisions. Tito also postulated a Communist take-over after the defeat of Germany, to prevent any other party or organization from doing so. Clearly the old machinery of state would be either defunct or compromised by collaboration with the enemy. Tito said that we Communists had to organize ourselves militarily so as to be able to attack our enemies at the time of their defeat, and thus be able to take power. All of this was clear to us, and yet someone had to say it. And Tito was the first one to do so. No one contradicted him. It meant that we had abandoned earlier schemes for democratic and national revolution, as well as the idea of collaboration with allies in a transitional period. In fact, there were no such parties any longer, or such power, unless we Communists, in our fear of an armed struggle for power, were to invent them. Tito spoke as a pragmatist and not as a theoretician. Practice was gaining a clear precedence over theory.

There were groups of officers hiding in the mountains of western Serbia, threatening to take over after the defeat of the Germans and "save the country" from Communists. They were promoting the idea of a Great Serbia and a purge in Bosnia and Dalmatia of all

"Turks" and "Croats." They were subjecting the peasants to military discipline, those same peasants whom they had shamefully abandoned during the enemy attack.

Our comrades in Croatia brought us the first reports of the Ustashi brutalities in Kordun and elsewhere.

A decision was made to denounce the officers, to begin an armed struggle against them, as well as against the Ustashi and their crimes. The most important thing was to collect arms and set up military committees, attached to party committees, to be in charge of collecting arms and of gathering together fighting units.

Tito informed Moscow of the Central Committee's new position. Moscow responded with some fairly sharp criticism. Dimitrov pointed out that we Yugoslavs were now faced with a national liberation struggle, and not a proletarian revolution. Tito retreated from his position. At least in words. But words later had an important effect on deeds. Some of the Comintern's terminology of national struggle entered our own "people's liberation" jargon.

At the Zagreb consultation it became clear that both the Communist party and our national history had entered a new phase. None of us could predict what course this history would take, but we were as confident as at any time in the past years.

It was decided that the Politburo of the Central Committee was to move to Belgrade. The Ustashi regime in Croatia, which had taken over the administrative apparatus almost intact, was after us. Lawlessness was growing, and this was proving to be an additional danger. In Serbia, on the other hand, state machinery had been completely demolished. There was no active political organization, such as the Ustashi in Croatia. Even Ljotić's fascist group had withdrawn, overwhelmed by the national disaster and the enemy's rule of terror.

In the meantime, a police official by the name of Tiljak was killed in Zagreb. Tiljak had been Vujković's deputy in Belgrade. Before war broke out he had been transferred to Zagreb as an expert in fighting Communism. He was then in the service of the new Ustashi regime. The comrades managed to lure him into the apartment of a woman with whom he was having an affair. This was the work of Pavle Pap and Rade Končar. Following an interrogation, they strangled him, put his body in a suitcase, and tossed it into a marsh. But the marsh dried up during the summer and the body was discovered. The Ustashi used this as an excuse to execute ten Communists, the first ten—among them Ognjen Prica and Otokar Keršovani.

Tiljak's interrogation yielded no important information. It was brief and to the point. Ranković showed me the report, written on a slip of paper. Tiljak confirmed that Voja Semleka, a former prisoner, had turned provocateur, which we in Belgrade already knew. The rest of the information was equally unimportant. But the death of a man with such rich experience in fighting Communists was obviously not without significance for the Zagreb organization.

We Communists had never before practiced such methods— murder—not even against policemen and provocateurs. But new times were coming. It was hardly an accident that it was Pavle Pap, a man with an exceptional feeling for conspiracy and technical skills, who organized and executed the job. The time had come for people like him to use their skills on a national scale. They suddenly felt awakened and ready to fight the battle to extract new power from the ruins of the old.

The old Yugoslavia had suffered defeat in the war of April 6, but it gave birth to a new Yugoslavia, strong and self-confident.

Index

Index

Bileća, 338
Bjelice, 385
Black Hills (Djilas), 155
Blagojević, 312
Bogdanović, Milan, 79, 103
Bohinj, 357
Boka, 56, 57
Bolshevism, 129, 229, 264, 283, 304, 306, 338, 345, 350, 388
Bosnia, 72, 76, 85, 94, 143, 212, 301, 383, 389; Communists in, 34, 95, 259, 286, 289, 290, 308–09
Bosnians, 37, 142, 143–46
Bourgeoisie, 33, 369, 373; under dictatorship, 9, 10; political parties of, 11, 16–17, 20, 40–45, 52, 60, 87, 254, 255, 263, 322, 330, 332; Communists and, 59, 69, 70, 86, 87, 88, 129, 247, 254, 256, 294, 296, 308, 340, 367
Bozhart (author), 10
Božić, Boris, 189, 208–10
Božinović, Neda, 325
Bracanović, Bracan, 10–11, 98
Brothers Karamazov, The (Dostoevski), 23
Broz, Herta, 351–52, 354, 357
Bubanja, Jovan, 114–16, 119
Budak, Mile, 346
Budapest, 179
Budisavljević, Srdjan, 336
Budva, 62
Buha, Vasilije, 251, 314–15, 324, 372, 381
Bujić, Branko, 197–98
Bukharin, Nikolai, 271
Bukovac, Mirko, 175, 301
Bulatović, Ilija, 244
Bulgaria, 72, 73, 140; terrorist groups of, 52; Communist party of, 342, 388
Burdžović, Rifat, 75–76, 95, 337
Butum, Slobodan Tuzlić-, 277
Byron, Lord, 56

Čačak, 311, 328
Čair, 291, 292
Čaki, Lajoš, 161, 203–05, 207, 211
Case of Dušan Vasiljev, The (Djilas), 60
Cavtović, Ivzija, 302

Cemović, Vuksan, 268
Cerović, Stojan, 59–61
Cetinje, 5–6, 54, 58–59, 61, 198, 245, 246–47, 287
Ćetković, Miloš Tujo, 10
Ćetković, Milovan, 62, 98
Chetniks, 25, 35, 60, 72, 76, 77, 86, 237, 245, 312, 316, 383
Churchill, Winston, 379
Cincar–Marković, Alexander, 365
Circuit Court prison, 106–07, 120
Čolaković, Rodoljub (Rudi), 270, 300–01
Comintern, 63, 106, 130, 131, 133, 166, 176, 179, 181, 192, 226, 259, 264, 278, 279, 280, 283, 284, 301, 302, 303, 318, 331, 332, 341, 342, 353, 355, 376, 388, 389; Open Letter of 1928 of, 11; Seventh Congress of, 132, 233; Open Letter of 1929 of, 180; and fascism, 218
Communism, 6, 29, 34, 35, 55, 83, 92, 228–29, 275; and peasants, 34, 72, 95, 103–04, 133, 204; and masses, 72, 94, 146, 182, 204, 243, 249, 250 273, 274, 282, 289, 305, 306, 307, 309, 315, 321, 370, 388; and working class, 92, 95, 96–97, 99, 103, 105, 169, 172, 204, 228, 254, 260, 261, 272, 283; nature of, 165, 313; and economics, 193, 198; condemned terrorism, 201; and unions, 243, 258, 260–61, 272, 274, 288, 305, 308, 336, 363. *See also* Communists; Soviet Union
Communist party of Yugoslavia, 68, 72, 73, 75, 83, 84, 85, 86, 89, 101, 128, 161, 192, 275, 276, 280, 281, 282, 313, 347, 351; Central Committee of (Paris), 10, 11, 20, 57, 61, 63, 68, 69, 74, 81, 83, 84, 87, 100, 129, 130, 131, 143, 168, 172, 174, 175, 177, 179, 180, 181–82, 188, 226, 230, 235, 250, 251, 252, 253, 254, 256, 258, 259, 260, 262, 264, 265, 266, 267, 270–71, 276–77, 278, 279, 280, 281, 284, 300, 301; under dictatorship, 10–11, 12, 20, 63, 93, 145, 157–58, 175, 182, 234, 294; regional committees of, 59, 61–62,

Index

Končar, Rade, 281, 282, 353–55, 361, 370, 371–72, 380, 381, 389
Koren (Italian spy), 134
Korneyev, General, 378
Kosmajac, Djordje, 111–12, 117, 120–21
Kosovo, 286
Košutić, Radovan, 18
Kotor, 52, 54, 55, 56–58, 61
Kotur, 303
Kovačević, Borislav, 18, 21, 23, 26, 44, 45, 65, 70, 94, 100, 290, 338
Kovačević, Čile, 376
Kovačević, Djoko, 262, 267–68
Kovačević, Pavle, 260
Kovačević, Veljko, 123–25
Kragujevac, 251, 252, 263, 328, 383–84
Kraljevo, 328
Kraš, Josip, 167, 172–75, 177, 281, 282–83, 371
Kritika, 360
Krleža, Miroslav, 86, 217, 342–48
Krstulović, Vicko, 304
Kun, Djordje Andrejević-, 327, 335, 351
Kurtović, Vojin, 93–94
Kusovac, Dušan, 102, 266, 278
Kusovac, Labud, 68, 74, 98, 266, 278, 300, 304

Labriola, Antonio, 226
Lapčević, Dejan, 339
Latković, Vido, 58, 59
Lazarević, Božo, 361
League of Young Communists, 100–01, 111, 262, 281, 291, 320
Lekić brothers, 247
Lenin, Nikolai, 87, 161, 200, 201, 204, 206, 207, 225, 226, 227, 275–76, 283, 295, 305, 338, 344
Lepoglava Prison, 161, 162, 186–212, 214, 215. See also Prisons, Communists in
Leskovšek, Luka, 281, 283, 354, 358, 359
L'Humanité, 331
Life for the Tsar, A (Glinka), 102–03

Life of Klim Samkin, The (Gorky), 18
Lika, 131, 134–35, 137
Literatura, 88
Literature: social, 15, 58, 66, 75, 82, 83, 86, 153, 155, 256, 343; censorship of, 78; and Communism, 70, 75, 82, 83, 87, 88 90, 93, 97, 104, 105, 155, 163, 165, 216, 227–28, 233, 278; illegal, 83, 99–100, 101, 106, 243, 247, 249, 251, 315, 323–26, 331. See also individual magazines
Ljotić, Dimitrije, 235, 389
Ljubljana, 270, 271, 279, 359
London, 67
Lopičić, Nikola, 58, 61
Luković, Niko, 58
Lunacharsky, Anatoli V., 345
Luxemburg, Rosa, 226

Macedonia, 78–79, 212, 291, 354; Communists in, 259, 286, 292, 388
Macedonians, 37, 291; nationalists, 132
Maček, Vlatko, 133, 137, 206, 217, 218, 219, 254, 306–07, 331, 332, 334, 336, 363, 366, 367
Maksimović, Desanka, 24, 81–82
Maksimović, Mara, 24
Mandžić, Pasaga, 145
Maribor, 359
Marinko, Miha, 281, 283, 355
Marinković, Venijamin, 21
Marinović, Jovan, 68, 216, 287, 288
Marković, Ivan, 144
Marković, Moma, 216, 251–52, 263, 268, 269, 308, 313, 319
Marković, Sima, 25, 69–70, 74–75, 89, 99–100, 106, 128–30, 132, 136, 166, 213, 239, 254, 304; group of, 70, 74, 75, 98–99, 100, 128, 134
Marković, Svetozar, 211
Marković, Vidak, 21, 70, 92
Marković, Vukašin, 181, 182
Martinović (secretary, Central Committee), 188
Marx, Karl, 10, 87, 163, 166, 193, 200, 225, 226, 227, 235–36
Marxism, 191, 216, 226, 227, 228, 230, 256, 275, 301, 312, 350

396